NATIONAL ACADEMIES *Sciences Engineering Medicine*

NATIONAL ACADEMIES PRESS
Washington, DC

Understanding and Addressing Misinformation About Science

K. Viswanath, Tiffany E. Taylor, and Holly G. Rhodes, *Editors*

Committee on Understanding and Addressing Misinformation About Science

Board on Science Education

Division of Behavioral and Social Sciences and Education

Consensus Study Report

NATIONAL ACADEMIES PRESS 500 Fifth Street, NW Washington, DC 20001

This activity was supported by a contract between the National Academy of Sciences and the National Science Foundation (Award No. 2153107). Any opinions, findings, conclusions, or recommendations expressed in this publication do not necessarily reflect the views of any organization or agency that provided support for the project.

International Standard Book Number-13: 978-0-309-72395-4
International Standard Book Number-10: 0-309-72395-7
Digital Object Identifier: https://doi.org/10.17226/27894
Library of Congress Control Number: 2025934029

This publication is available from the National Academies Press, 500 Fifth Street, NW, Keck 360, Washington, DC 20001; (800) 624-6242; http://www.nap.edu.

Printed in the United States of America.

Suggested citation: National Academies of Sciences, Engineering, and Medicine. 2025. *Understanding and Addressing Misinformation About Science.* Washington, DC: National Academies Press. https://doi.org/10.17226/27894.

The **National Academy of Sciences** was established in 1863 by an Act of Congress, signed by President Lincoln, as a private, nongovernmental institution to advise the nation on issues related to science and technology. Members are elected by their peers for outstanding contributions to research. Marcia McNutt is president.

The **National Academy of Engineering** was established in 1964 under the charter of the National Academy of Sciences to bring the practices of engineering to advising the nation. Members are elected by their peers for extraordinary contributions to engineering. John L. Anderson is president.

The **National Academy of Medicine** (formerly the Institute of Medicine) was established in 1970 under the charter of the National Academy of Sciences to advise the nation on medical and health issues. Members are elected by their peers for distinguished contributions to medicine and health. Victor J. Dzau is president.

The three Academies work together as the **National Academies of Sciences, Engineering, and Medicine** to provide independent, objective analysis and advice to the nation and conduct other activities to solve complex problems and inform public policy decisions. The National Academies also encourage education and research, recognize outstanding contributions to knowledge, and increase public understanding in matters of science, engineering, and medicine.

Learn more about the National Academies of Sciences, Engineering, and Medicine at **www.nationalacademies.org**.

Consensus Study Reports published by the National Academies of Sciences, Engineering, and Medicine document the evidence-based consensus on the study's statement of task by an authoring committee of experts. Reports typically include findings, conclusions, and recommendations based on information gathered by the committee and the committee's deliberations. Each report has been subjected to a rigorous and independent peer-review process and it represents the position of the National Academies on the statement of task.

Proceedings published by the National Academies of Sciences, Engineering, and Medicine chronicle the presentations and discussions at a workshop, symposium, or other event convened by the National Academies. The statements and opinions contained in proceedings are those of the participants and are not endorsed by other participants, the planning committee, or the National Academies.

Rapid Expert Consultations published by the National Academies of Sciences, Engineering, and Medicine are authored by subject-matter experts on narrowly focused topics that can be supported by a body of evidence. The discussions contained in rapid expert consultations are considered those of the authors and do not contain policy recommendations. Rapid expert consultations are reviewed by the institution before release.

For information about other products and activities of the National Academies, please visit www.nationalacademies.org/about/whatwedo.

COMMITTEE ON UNDERSTANDING AND ADDRESSING MISINFORMATION ABOUT SCIENCE

KASISOMAYAJULA "VISH" VISWANATH (*Chair*), Lee Kum Kee Professor of Health Communication, Harvard T. H. Chan School of Public Health; Dana-Farber Cancer Institute
NICK ALLUM, Professor of Research Methodology, University of Essex
NADINE J. BARRETT, Senior Associate Dean, Equity in Research and Community Engagement, Wake Forest School of Medicine
DAVID A. BRONIATOWSKI, Professor, Department of Engineering Management and Systems Engineering, The George Washington University
AFUA A. N. BRUCE, Adjunct Professor, Heinz College, Carnegie Mellon University
LISA K. FAZIO, Associate Professor of Psychology, Vanderbilt University
LAUREN FELDMAN, Professor, Department of Journalism and Media Studies, Rutgers University
DEEN FREELON, Presidential Professor, Annenberg School for Communication, University of Pennsylvania
ASHELEY R. LANDRUM, Associate Professor, Walter Cronkite School of Journalism & Mass Communication, Arizona State University
DAVID M. J. LAZER, University Distinguished Professor, Northeastern University
EZRA M. MARKOWITZ, Professor of Environmental Decision-Making, University of Massachusetts Amherst
PAMELA C. RONALD (NAS), Distinguished Professor, University of California, Davis
DAVID SCALES, Assistant Professor of Medicine, Joan & Sanford I. Weill Medical College, Cornell University
BRIAN G. SOUTHWELL, Lead Scientist for Public Understanding of Science, RTI International
JEVIN WEST, Professor, Information School, University of Washington

Study Staff

TIFFANY E. TAYLOR, Study Director
LETICIA GARCILAZO GREEN, Associate Program Officer
HOLLY G. RHODES, Senior Program Officer
LAUREN RYAN, Senior Program Assistant
HEIDI SCHWEINGRUBER, Director, Board on Science Education

National Academy of Medicine Fellow

PAULE JOSEPH, Lasker Clinical Investigator, National Institutes of Health, American Academy of Nursing Fellow (2022–2024)

BOARD ON SCIENCE EDUCATION

Reviewers

This Consensus Study Report was reviewed in draft form by individuals chosen for their diverse perspectives and technical expertise. The purpose of this independent review is to provide candid and critical comments that will assist the National Academies of Sciences, Engineering, and Medicine in making each published report as sound as possible and to ensure that it meets the institutional standards for quality, objectivity, evidence, and responsiveness to the study charge. The review comments and draft manuscript remain confidential to protect the integrity of the deliberative process.

We thank the following individuals for their review of this report:

MELISSA ARONCZYK, School of Communication & Information, Rutgers University
MAY R. BERENBAUM, Department of Entomology, University of Illinois at Urbana-Champaign
CABRAL A. BIGMAN-GALIMORE, Department of Communication, University of Illinois at Urbana-Champaign
ROBERTA S. BRAGA, Digital Democracy Institute of the Americas
THOMAS DIETZ, Center for Systems Integration and Sustainability, Michigan State University
EUGENE KONDRATOV, Digital Democracy Institute of the Americas
STEPHAN LEWANDOWSKY, Cognitive Psychology, University of Bristol
ALICE E. MARWICK, Department of Communication, The University of North Carolina at Chapel Hill

JASMINE E. McNEALY, Department of Media Production, Management, and Technology, University of Florida
KATHERINE OGNYANOVA, School of Communication and Information, Rutgers University
CLAIRE WARDLE, Department of Communication, Cornell University
RICK WEISS, SciLine, American Association for the Advancement of Science
JOHN WIHBEY, College of Arts, Media and Design, Northeastern University

Although the reviewers listed above provided many constructive comments and suggestions, they were not asked to endorse the conclusions or recommendations of this report nor did they see the final draft before its release. The review of this report was overseen by **BARBARA SCHAAL,** Washington University in St. Louis, and **BRUCE LEWENSTEIN,** Cornell University. They were responsible for making certain that an independent examination of this report was carried out in accordance with the standards of the National Academies and that all review comments were carefully considered. Responsibility for the final content rests entirely with the authoring committee and the National Academies.

Acknowledgments

This Consensus Study Report reflects the invaluable contributions of many individuals who provided their expertise, including those who served on the committee, the staff of the National Academies of Sciences, Engineering, and Medicine (National Academies), and many other experts who participated in discussions with the committee.

This report was made possible by sponsorship from the National Science Foundation and the Fred Kavli Endowment Fund. We first thank Robert O'Connor, Program Director of Decision, Risk, and Management Sciences for supporting this study and providing insight to the committee. We are also grateful to the National Academies Presidents' Committee for supporting this work.

Over the course of the study, the committee held public information gathering meetings, including a public workshop, and the members of the committee greatly benefited from presentations by, and discussions with, the many individuals who participated in these meetings: Cary Funk, Pew Research Center (until October 2023); Tina Purnat, World Health Organization (until October 2023); Claire Wardle, Cornell University (previously at Brown University until July 2024); Alice Marwick, University of North Carolina at Chapel Hill; Dietram Scheufele, University of Wisconsin–Madison; Sacha Altay, University of Zurich; Kelly Born, The David and Lucile Packard Foundation; Melissa Aronczyk, Rutgers University; Heidi Larson, London School of Hygiene and Tropical Medicine; Mark Lynas, Alliance for Science; Briony Swire-Thompson, Northeastern University; Cabral Bigman-Galimore, University of Illinois at Urbana-Champaign; Roberta Braga, Digital Democracy Institute of the Americas; Leezel Tanglao and Mark Calaguas, Filipino Young Leaders Program; Jason Young, University of Washington; Joel Breakstone, Digital Inquiry Group; Ethan Porter, George Washington University; Emily Vraga, University of Minnesota; Victor Pickard, University of Pennsylvania; Kavitha Rajagopalan, Asian Media Initiative, City University of New York; Abhishek Roy, Google; Michael Strevens, New York University; Sarah Kreps, Cornell University; and Jenn Wortman Vaughan, Microsoft Research.

The committee is also grateful for the efforts of the following authors who prepared background papers for the committee's use in drafting the report:

- Rachel Kuo, University of Illinois in Urbana-Champaign, and Sarah Nguyễn, University of Washington, on misinformation in non-English language information networks;
- Ryan Calo, University of Washington, and Nicole Buckley, K&L Gates, LLP, on opportunities for addressing misinformation through policy and legislation; and
- Joseph Polman, University of Colorado, Boulder, on science learning for navigating a complex information landscape.

Thanks are also due to the project staff. Tiffany E. Taylor of the Board on Science Education (BOSE) directed the study and played a key role in the report drafting and review process. Holly Rhodes (senior program officer, BOSE), Leticia Garcilazo Green (research associate [until 2023] and associate program officer, BOSE), and Paule Joseph (American Academy of Nursing Fellow, National Academy of Medicine) provided critical assistance in directing the project, organizing the report, and revising the writing. Heidi Schweingruber (director, BOSE) provided infinite wisdom and oversight throughout the entire study. Lauren Ryan (senior program assistant, BOSE) managed the study's logistical and administrative needs and assisted with manuscript preparation.

Finally, we thank Laura E. Yoder for providing invaluable editorial direction, Heather Kreidler (independent consultant) for fact-checking the report, and Kirsten Sampson Snyder (Division of Behavioral and Social Sciences and Education) for expertly guiding us through the National Academies review process. The committee also wishes to express its sincere appreciation to the National Academies Research Center staff for completing a literature review to support report development.

Contents

Boxes, Figures, and Table

BOXES

FIGURES

TABLE

Preface

Another hurdle in recovery from Helene:
Misinformation is getting in the way[1]
The New York Times, October 6, 2024

This headline is an outstanding example of how misinformation is perceived in the public arena. The headline makes a causal assumption that misinformation is "getting in the way" of recovery from the hurricane's devastating impact. The degree of accuracy of this assumption is a question for further study and empirical examination, but the very assumption that misinformation has a direct causal impact on relief efforts with significant negative consequences is noteworthy. And newsworthy. And is part of what motivated this report.

Information, and misinformation, is everywhere—on our phones, televisions in the gym, social media. Some of this misinformation is brain candy, simple entertainment, and inconsequential; some of it, though, has the potential to impact public health, inform policy responses, and shape people's perceptions of the world. If misinformation about science leads to beliefs that are in conflict with accepted science, the consequences can be profound. False perceptions and beliefs may lead to behaviors and support for policies that are not supported by accepted science and/or are not aligned with individual preferences and goals, with negative consequences for individuals, communities, and broader society.

[1] See https://www.nytimes.com/2024/10/06/us/hurricane-helene-north-carolina-misinformation.html

The charge to our committee—that we examine the existing evidence on misinformation about science and draw conclusions about how it spreads and its potential for harm—was a challenge on at least two fronts. One, there is no simple way to define misinformation about science; science is a process where claims are tested, accepted, and upended as knowledge accumulates. This process of revising scientific knowledge as new evidence emerges can be incremental and more like clarification, especially in domains where there are decades of confirmatory studies and the science is more settled, such as in laws of physics. But in emerging areas of science, the generation of new knowledge can be quite rapid, such as the incredible pace of growth in knowledge about COVID-19 during the first months of the pandemic. This rapid generation of new information—and its displacement of older information—can make identifying and defining misinformation at any given time complex. In addition, for individuals who are not deeply familiar with how science works, revision of scientific explanations can be confusing and raise questions about the trustworthiness of science and scientists.

A second challenge is assessing the evidence on the origins, spread, and impact of misinformation about science. Research on misinformation about science has exploded over the last decade and has been pursued in multiple disciplines. However, these different lines of research have often developed in fragmented and disconnected ways, making the synthesis work that this committee was asked to do quite difficult. Moreover, the task of reviewing the sheer volume of publications, with new studies on the topic published seemingly every day was daunting. Our interdisciplinary committee was well constituted to take on the task, but our work must be seen as a snapshot based on the available evidence at the time of this consensus study process.

The stakes in understanding the origins, spread, and the impact of misinformation about science are high. The belief that misinformation about science is a serious and a consequential problem is widely shared by many different stakeholders both inside and outside of the scientific community. In fact, some policymakers are clamoring for action to stem misinformation and arrest its spread and negative impact. Many actions in policy and legislative arenas are already under consideration.

But the committee had to engage in a delicate balancing act. One the one hand, we had to look at the evidence carefully to draw inferences and make actionable recommendations in the context of a fragmented and still-emergent evidence base. On the other hand, we do not want to downplay concerns about the potential harm that misinformation about science might cause. The evidence is clear that exposure to misinformation about science may lead to misbeliefs, which, in turn, have the potential for causing harm at the individual and collective levels. But the leap from documenting that misinformation about science is present in the information ecosystem to assumptions that individual exposure always leads to harmful behaviors with negative consequences for communities and societies is hard to justify based on current evidence. Furthermore, the evidence suggests that many widely held assumptions about the sources of misinformation about science, how it spreads, and how to combat it may need to be revised.

We still have much to learn regarding the dynamics of misinformation about science in the information ecosystem—we know little about how misinformation is shared within and affects different communities especially underserved, socially vulnerable groups; we know less about misinformation that travels through "offline" social networks and older media such as radio or television than in online contexts; and we need to better understand how particular interventions designed to combat the negative effects of misinformation can work in combination and at scale.

Our message then is that we know a lot, but in order to develop informed policy responses and help individuals and communities combat the potential negative effects of misinformation about science we need to know a lot more. We also, all of us, need to examine our assumptions about the origins of misinformation about science, how it spreads, and how we can help address it. Misinformation about science is a multi-faceted, complex phenomenon, and we all have a role in addressing it. We hope this report provides a roadmap for initial action and illuminates the areas where we need to learn more.

Tiffany E. Taylor, PhD, Study Director
K. Viswanath, PhD, Chair

Acronyms and Abbreviations

AAAS	American Association for the Advancement of Science
AI	artificial intelligence
API	application programming interface
CBO	community-based organization
CDC	Centers for Disease Control and Prevention
CEAL	U.S. National Institutes of Health Community Engagement Alliance
COVID-19	coronavirus disease 2019
DSA	Digital Services Act
DYOR	"doing your own research"
EPA	Environmental Protection Agency
EU	European Union
FDA	Food and Drug Administration
FTC	Federal Trade Commission
FYLPRO	Filipino Young Leaders Program
GDP	gross domestic product
GE	genetically engineered
GMO	genetically modified organism
GSS	The General Social Survey

HAIR	Health Advocates In-Reach and Research Campaign
ICPSR	University of Michigan's Inter-University Consortium for Political and Social Research
LLM	large language model
MI	motivational interviewing
MMR	measles, mumps, and rubella
MTBI	Mild Traumatic Brain Injuries
NASA	National Aeronautics and Space Administration
NIH	National Institute of Health
NRC	National Research Council
RCT	randomized control trial
SES	socio-economic status
STEM	science, technology, engineering, and mathematics
USPSTF	the CDC's U.S. Preventative Services Task Force
VLOP	very large online platforms
WHO	World Health Organization

Summary

The spread of misinformation about science, whether accidental or deliberate, is not new. Long before the advent of electronic media, false claims about science appeared in news publications. Following the 1906 Federal Food and Drugs Act, the current era of the U.S. Food and Drug Administration began in response to widespread misinformation about the efficacy and safety of drugs, food additives, and biological substances. Over the past decade, however, concerns about the spread of misinformation about science and the overall role of scientific expertise in civic dialogue have grown significantly. Such concerns are motivated by the belief that misinformation about science can lead to harmful outcomes for individuals, communities, and societies, such as ill-informed personal choices about disease treatment, higher rates of death from vaccine-preventable diseases, lack of appropriately responding to public health emergencies and natural disasters, and limitations on productive debate about addressing issues like climate change. The growing concerns about the potential harmful effects of misinformation about science have also led to a rapid increase in research across multiple disciplines to better understand and address this phenomenon.

With support from the National Science Foundation, the National Academies of Sciences, Engineering, and Medicine convened a study committee charged with bringing together multiple lines of research to develop a more comprehensive understanding of the sources, spread, and impacts of misinformation about science and effective strategies for mitigation. Specifically, the committee was tasked with characterizing the nature and scope of misinformation about science and its impacts on individuals, communities, and society; identifying effective solutions for mitigating its spread; providing actionable guidance toward reducing associated harms; and outlining priorities for future research.

In both public discourse and in peer-reviewed research, misinformation has been used as an umbrella term to refer to various types of false, inaccurate, incorrect, and misleading information. The broad nature of the term has made it difficult to develop a coherent understanding of the nature, scope, and impacts of misinformation, and by extension, misinformation about science. To provide clarity and focus the committee's analysis, the committee developed the following definition: ***misinformation about science is information that asserts or implies claims that are inconsistent with the weight of accepted scientific evidence at the time (reflecting both quality and quantity of evidence). Which claims are determined to be misinformation about science can evolve over time as new evidence accumulates and scientific knowledge regarding those claims advances.*** Relatedly, the committee defines disinformation about science as a sub-category of misinformation that is circulated by agents who are aware that the science information they are circulating is false (see Chapter 2).

In the course of its work, the committee identified a number of ways to advance understanding of misinformation about science and intervene, when needed, to the greatest effect. In developing recommendations, the committee prioritized actions to address misinformation about science based on relative potential for harm and also with consideration for today's complex information ecosystem, which requires concerted, multi-level action by a diversity of actors (see Chapter 9 for a deeper discussion of the report's recommendations).

SOURCES OF MISINFORMATION ABOUT SCIENCE

Through its review, the committee found that misinformation about science can originate from a diversity of sources and types of media, including but not limited to corporations, governments and politicians, alternative health and science industries, entertainment media, nongovernmental organizations, science organizations and institutions, press offices and news media organizations, individual scientists, and ordinary citizens.[1] Reasons and/or motivations for disseminating misinformation about science are diverse, but misinformation about science has greater potential for influence when it

- originates from authoritative sources,
- is amplified by powerful actors,

[1]Citations for the information presented in this summary can be found in the main text.

- reaches large audiences,
- is targeted to specific populations, or
- is produced in a deliberate, customized, and organized fashion (e.g., tobacco industry campaigns to cast doubt about the health risks of smoking).

Importantly, systematic campaigns intended to mislead the public about science-related issues like climate change, consequences of tobacco use, and heart disease, for example, are of particular concern given the associated negative outcomes for individuals and society.

Universities, research organizations, and funders of scientific research are key sources of science information. Occasionally, misinformation about science originates from reputable science organizations, institutions, universities, and individual scientists or healthcare professionals, either as a byproduct of poor science communication, distortions of scientific data, the dissemination of research findings before they are formally vetted and substantiated, or in the worst cases, scientific fraud. Misrepresentation and misreporting of scientific studies, medical developments, and health issues by press offices, journalists, and medical professionals are also ways that misinformation about science may unintentionally arise from authoritative sources. Science and medicine are among the most trusted institutions in today's society; therefore, it is important that the reliability of information on critical science issues from these sources is not compromised due to misinformation.

Recommendation 1: Some corporations, strategic communication companies, and non-profit organizations have at times embarked on systematic campaigns to mislead the public with negative consequences to individuals and society. Universities, researchers, and civil society organizations should work together to proactively counter such campaigns using evidence from science and science communication to mitigate their impact. For example, researchers, government, and advocacy organizations have come together to counter campaigns from the tobacco industry to reduce the public health impact of tobacco use. Similar efforts should be made for other scientific topics of public interest.

Recommendation 2: To ensure the promotion of accurate science information and reduce the spread of misinformation or misleading information from the scientific community:

- **Press offices of universities, research organizations, and funders of scientific research should consult with scientists to accurately report on their research findings and review draft press releases prior to dissemination. Press releases should explicitly** state that they have been reviewed by the authors of these papers, and authors should be accountable for the approved content.

- Universities, research organizations, and public and private funders of scientific research should encourage both their scientists and press offices to provide appropriate context—limitations and weight of evidence—when publicizing research from their organizations.

Recommendation 3: Scientists and medical professionals who are active in the public arena can play a critical role in communicating accurate and reliable science and health information to the public.

- **Scientists, medical professionals, and health professionals who choose to take on high profile roles as public communicators of science should understand how their communications may be misinterpreted in the absence of context or in the wrong context. They should work proactively with professional communicators and draw on evidence-based science communication strategies to include appropriate context, interpretations, and caveats of scientific findings in their public communications.**
- **Universities and research organizations who promote individual scientists to share their research with the public should provide them with training and support to take on such public communication roles.**

THE SPREAD OF MISINFORMATON ABOUT SCIENCE

Alongside the reasons and/or motivations discussed above for the dissemination of misinformation about science from various sources, the committee also identified other factors that contribute to its spread at the individual, institutional, community, and societal levels. These factors include the following:

- features of the contemporary information ecosystem that provide myriad channels through which misinformation about science can rapidly flow,
- changes within the institution of journalism that influence both the quantity and quality of science news,
- features of online platforms that make it easier for misinformation about science to spread and create new incentives, motivations, and strategies for doing so, and
- societal factors—including trust and crises.

FEATURES OF THE CONTEMPORARY INFORMATION ECOSYSTEM

Though inaccuracy in scientific claims is a long-standing issue, diffusion of such claims has become more visible within the contemporary information ecosystem, which operates across different technology platforms and in-person and virtual spaces that enhance the volume, production, speed, and spread of information. Science information can quickly travel through this ecosystem across different channels and media types (e.g., online platforms, electronic broadcasting media, internet websites), and in some cases, becomes divorced from the original context needed to appropriately evaluate the accuracy and reliability of the information.

Additionally, the rise of more participatory online environments (e.g., on social media platforms) has enabled greater information exchange across different social and professional networks but has also blurred the lines between reliable and unreliable science information. At times, this blurring can be exacerbated by generative artificial intelligence (AI). Such factors make it more challenging for consumers of information to navigate online environments, and specifically, to assess scientific expertise and the credibility of science information across sources.

> **Recommendation 4: To promote the dissemination of and broad access to evidence-based science information, funders of scientific research (e.g., federal science agencies, non-profit and philanthropic foundations) and non-partisan professional science organizations (e.g., American Association for the Advancement of Science, American Association for Cancer Research, American Psychological Association, American Society of Plant Biologists) should establish and fund an independent, non-partisan consortium that can identify and curate sources of high-quality (e.g., weight of evidence—quantity and quality) science information on topics of public interest. The consortium should also frequently review the science information from these sources for accuracy, needs, and relevance. It is particularly critical to ensure that access to such science information is openly and equitably available to all groups, especially underserved groups. Additional possible functions of the consortium could include the following:**
>
> - **identifying which sources should be included for curation,**
> - **providing ratings of accuracy for different sources,**
> - **creating short, accessible summaries of science information drawn from high-quality sources on topics determined by the consortium, and**
> - **reviewing the science information from different sources on a routine basis to update ratings of accuracy.**

Recommendation 5: Online platforms, including search engines and social media, are major disseminators of true and false science information. These platforms should prioritize and foreground evidence-based science information that is understandable to different audiences, working closely with non-profit, non-partisan professional science societies and organizations to identify such information.

CHANGES WITHIN JOURNALISM

Many adults in the United States get their science information from news media outlets, making the quality and quantity of science news production increasingly important. At the same time, decreases in funding within journalism have led to significant reductions in news coverage, especially at local levels. These cutbacks have also meant that journalists who lack specialized training in science are being assigned to cover science and health news, and insufficient expertise can make it challenging to correctly interpret scientific research and properly contextualize the findings in their reporting. Additionally, limited capacity, expertise, and resources can create science news deserts, which enable misinformation about science to spread more easily.

Journalists, editors, writers, and media organizations covering science, medical, and health issues (regardless of assigned specialty areas) serve as critical mediators between producers of scientific knowledge and consumers of science information. Local news, in particular, has broad reach and is trusted by many Americans, making it potentially valuable for mitigating misinformation about science. However, several factors may make science reporting particularly prone to the unintentional spread of misinformation about science including

- journalistic norms such as giving equal weight to both sides of a scientific debate even when the scientific evidence overwhelmingly points in one direction,
- informational and ideological biases,
- over-reliance on public relations and other information subsidies (e.g., press releases),
- exaggerations and omissions of important details from the original science articles, and
- insufficient scientific expertise among journalists.

Recommendation 6: To support and promote high-quality science, health, and medical journalism:

- **Professional science and journalism organizations, funders of news media organizations and journalism, and universities** should establish mechanisms for journalists and news media organizations to readily access high-quality science information and scientific sources, and for sharing best practices in science, health, and medical reporting. Such supports are especially important for those working in news media organizations with limited capacity or resources (e.g., local and community-centered newsrooms).

- Funders of news media organizations and journalism should make intentional investments in local and community media (newspapers, television, radio, among others) to bolster their capacity to serve the science information needs of their audiences.
- News media organizations should help to increase the visibility of high-quality science journalism and best practices in science and medical reporting through incentives, rewards, and other recognition models.
- News media organizations should increase access to high-quality science journalism by dropping paywalls around critical and timely science and health issues.

Recommendation 7: In training the next generation of professional communicators in journalism, public relations, and other media and communication industries, universities and other providers of communication training programs should design learning experiences that integrate disciplinary knowledge and practices from communication research and various sciences and support the development of competencies in scientific and data literacy and reasoning. These competencies should be reinforced through continuous learning opportunities offered by organizations that support mass communication and journalism professionals.

FEATURES OF ONLINE PLATFORMS

Characteristics of online platforms (i.e., search engines and social media) can also contribute to the spread of misinformation about science, including design and algorithmic choices that constrain the information an individual might see (e.g., those shaping individualized feeds based on prior platform activity), permissive and loosely enforced or hard-to-enforce terms of service, and limited content moderation. These conditions can also enable dedicated purveyors (both individuals and institutions) to spread misinformation about science online more easily; however, it may be difficult to convince companies to change these conditions voluntarily when doing so might conflict with other business priorities, such as maximizing number of users or attracting advertisers. Some countries have developed regulatory approaches to content moderation online, but long-standing free speech protections, while desirable, may make it challenging to readily adopt such approaches in the United States.

Further adding to the complexity of the matter, people share misinformation about science through social media platforms both intentionally and unintentionally. In general, there is strong evidence that people prefer sharing true, rather than false, information, and share information with good intentions, such as to help or warn loved ones. However, individuals may unintentionally share misinformation about science due to confusion about the credibility of the information and inattention to accuracy, among other reasons. On the other hand, individuals and institutions may knowingly share misinformation about science in order to profit financially, to accrue social rewards (e.g., followers and likes), to gain and maintain power, to erode trust, or to disrupt existing social order and create chaos (e.g., trolling). These motivations may be especially incentivized in social media environments.

SOCIETAL FACTORS

The need for high-quality science information and the potential for the spread of misinformation about science are particularly high during times of emergencies, disasters, threats, and emerging crises. Furthermore, when uncertainty and interest are both high, journalists (national and local) become critical frontline communicators of science information. Experts on emergency preparedness, disaster response, and environmental threat mitigation (e.g., government agencies and civil society organizations) could also be important sources of credible science information for the public during such times.

Recommendation 8: Government agencies at national, state, and local levels (e.g., Federal Emergency Management Agency, Centers for Disease Control and Prevention, Food and Drug Administration, state public health departments) and civil society organizations (e.g., Association of State and Territorial Health Officials or National Association of County and City Health Officials) that deliver services during times of public health emergencies, natural disasters, threats, and new crises should contribute *proactively* to building and maintaining preparedness capacity for communicating science information at national, state, and local levels by:

- **developing internal workforce capacity to produce high-quality science information for the public,**
- **bolstering capacity to engage and partner with diverse communities to understand their needs, goals, and priorities for high-quality science information,**

- **establishing and maintaining trusted channels of communication across national, state, and local levels and between crises, and**
- **working collaboratively with local news organizations to ensure that accurate, high-quality science information is disseminated to diverse publics both during emergencies as well as in preparing for emergencies.**

Social trust is another important factor that shapes people's relationship to information, influencing whether they are willing to rely on a particular source of information for personal use. In recent years, concerns have been raised about declining public trust in science as a possible facilitator in the spread of misinformation about science. The committee found that trust in science has recently declined similarly to or less than trust in other civic, cultural, and governmental institutions. However, trust in science has been relatively stable over the last five decades, though levels of trust have varied significantly by partisan identity as well as among different groups depending on the science topic, the scientist(s) or science organization(s) being considered, or respective histories and experiences with science-related institutions.

Importantly, some powerful purveyors of misinformation about science have leveraged the relatively high trust in science and the authoritative "voice" of science to facilitate spread of misinformation (see Chapter 5). Examples of some of the strategies used include the following:

- manufacturing doubt about established scientific evidence,
- creating astroturf campaigns (i.e., hiding conflicts of interest, for example, between the message and the source that sponsors it) to create the illusion of public support,
- promoting false balance in scientific debates (in part by exploiting journalistic norms requiring the coverage of "both sides"), and
- leveraging relationships with scientists or medical professionals who disagree with the prevailing weight of the scientific evidence to generate a sense of credibility.

In light of this, the committee sees a great need for more scrutiny and accountability as well as more tools/supports for consumers of information (individual and institutions). Specifically, there is a need for continuous monitoring of the current information ecosystem concerning the production, spread, and impacts of misinformation about science. Such a process, like monitoring for signals of epidemics, could better support institutions and individuals in navigating the complexities of the current information ecosystem, including proactively managing misinformation about science.

Relatedly, regulatory structures such as legislation could also improve the current information ecosystem, but the evidence on the effectiveness of such approaches in the United States context is still emerging.

> **Recommendation 9: Professional scientific organizations, philanthropic organizations engaged in supporting scientific research, and media organizations should collaborate to support an independent entity or entities to track and document the origins, spread, and impact of misinformation across different platforms and communication spheres. The data produced through this effort should be made publicly available and be widely disseminated. Various entities, including public health emergency operations centers, can serve as potential models for such collaborative efforts.**

IMPACTS OF MISINFORMATION ABOUT SCIENCE

Negative impacts of misinformation about science have been widely, but also unevenly, documented and evidenced across levels, with most research focused on individual-level impacts. The most well-documented impact of misinformation is that it can cause individuals to develop or hold misbeliefs, and these misbeliefs can potentially disrupt the ability of individuals to make informed decisions for themselves, their families, or their communities. Impacts beyond the individual-level have been more challenging to measure, given some societal harms are most consequential in the ways that they amass over time. Additionally, while a direct causal link between misinformation about science and detrimental behaviors and actions has not been definitively established, the current body of evidence indicates that misinformation plays a role in impacting behaviors that, in some cases, results in negative consequences for individuals, communities, and societies. Misinformation about science has great potential to disrupt individual agency and collective decision making, to exacerbate existing harms (e.g., health disparities, discrimination), to distort public opinion in ways that limit productive debate, and to diminish trust in institutions that are important to a healthy democracy.

Misinformation about science that involves specific communities and populations can also create and/or reinforce stereotypes, bias, and false narratives that can cause further harm to such groups (e.g., promulgation of racialized discourses that stoke violence). Relatedly, some populations have been specifically targeted by misinformation (e.g., African Americans, immigrants, low-income communities), and some of the most troubling cases are matters of public health concern, like vaccines and smoking. Given that health, educational, and wealth disparities across social groups already contribute to inequitable access to resources to support well-being (including credible science information), the impacts on communities that are typically targeted by misinformation about science may be compounded.

The committee identified many moderators of the differential impacts of misinformation about science at the individual and community levels, which may inform intervention efforts. While all people have the potential to believe misinformation, individuals are more likely to engage with misinformation and ultimately believe it when it aligns with their worldview and values, originates from a source they trust, is repeated, and/or is about a topic for which they lack strong preexisting attitudes and beliefs. The committee also found that while science literacy is an important factor in how people process and interpret science information, including misinformation, the empirical evidence suggests that science literacy alone does not ensure that an individual will be less prone to believing misinformation about science.

Within the contemporary information ecosystem, people are differentially situated with respect to science information. Social factors such as race/ethnicity, culture, socioeconomic status, geography, and access to material and social resources can influence what information people are exposed to, their information-seeking and sharing behaviors, and what actions they may take in science-related contexts. For example, an individual may believe in the safety and effectiveness of vaccines and have sufficient access to accurate vaccine information, but due to logistical challenges (e.g., time offerings are inconvenient or vaccination sites are inaccessible), they may not get vaccinated. This means that the accuracy of information is only one of a constellation of factors that result in a specific behavior.

INTERVENING TO ADDRESS MISINFORMATION ABOUT SCIENCE

In the past few decades, many efforts within the research, practice, and policy domains have been directed toward combatting the harmful effects of misinformation about science. These efforts have generally been implemented in a topically agnostic fashion and reflect attempts to mitigate the negative impacts of misinformation by disrupting the supply, demand, distribution, and/or uptake of misinformation. So far, research does not indicate that a particular point is the best place to intervene, and many of the most effective interventions target multiple points.

Supply-based interventions aim to reduce the volume of circulating misinformation and/or shift the balance in the quality of circulating information toward high-quality science content. Examples of effective approaches of this type include foregrounding credible information online, providing funding to under-sourced newsrooms, deplatforming purveyors of misinformation, and content moderation. Demand-based interventions are aimed at reducing the consumption of misinformation through approaches like increasing trust in sources of credible information, identifying and filling information voids, and increasing people's ability to detect and avoid misinformation through media literacy training. Overall, this class of approaches reflects proactive ways to support individuals as they seek out information to answer pressing questions they may have. However, it is important to note that individuals and communities facing informational challenges are not inherently more susceptible to misinformation about science. Indeed, many community-based organizations, including some locally-owned businesses, non-profit organizations, and faith-based organizations, have proactively worked to adapt and provide reliable information to fill science information voids. They are also particularly well positioned to do so because of their local ties, their awareness of local needs and concerns, and the trust that residents have in them. These assets notwithstanding, the committee found that such community-based organizations are not always sufficiently resourced.

Distribution-based interventions are designed to limit the spread of misinformation and include strategies such as algorithmic changes on platforms (e.g., demoting content in algorithmic recommendations), enforced legislation and policies (e.g., mandated disclosure laws about the use of bots), and encouragement of evaluative thinking in individuals based on insights from human psychology (e.g., nudges to consider the accuracy of content before choosing to share). The latter approach has been widely adopted with demonstrated efficacy in decreasing the sharing of misinformation by individuals. Uptake-based interventions are designed to reduce the effects of misinformation about science on people's beliefs or behaviors. Such approaches include training individuals to spot common themes, narratives, and rhetorical devices that are often associated with misinformation (prebunking[2]) or providing corrective information. Although the durability of these interventions remains a challenge, they are effective to specifically prevent belief in misinformation and reduce the sharing of misinformation by individuals.

Recommendation 10: To enhance the capacity of community-based organizations (CBOs) to provide high-quality, culturally relevant, accurately translated, and timely science information to the communities they serve, funders (e.g., government agencies, public and private, philanthropic foundations) should provide direct funding to CBOs:

[2]The committee notes that there is some conceptual ambiguity regarding the term "prebunking." Some scholars define prebunking as a sub-category of technique-based inoculation interventions, while others define it as the overarching category that encompasses all inoculation interventions (see Chapter 7).

- to identify and work with research partners to determine science information voids within the communities they serve and to develop strategies and products to fill them, and
- to develop internal capacity and capability to routinely assess science information needs and build resilience against misinformation about science, particularly among those serving non-English speaking and other underserved groups (e.g., communities of color, low-income communities, rural communities).

Recommendation 11: Organizations at national, state, and local levels that are specifically engaged in mitigating the uptake of misinformation about science at the individual level should identify and utilize effective approach(es) that are best suited to their goals and the point of intervention (e.g., before or after exposure). For example:

- When seeking to prevent uptake of misinformation about science prior to exposure, organizations should consider using prebunking techniques such as anticipating common themes and false narratives widely used in propagating misinformation, and proactively develop messages to counter them. For example, public health agencies and media organizations could counter false narratives by the tobacco industry to misinform the public about the impact of bans on mentholated cigarettes. Teaching people about common manipulation techniques used by propagators of misinformation about science is also effective.
- When seeking to prevent beliefs in misinformation about science after exposure, organizations should consider using debunking techniques such as providing detailed corrective information. Instead of merely labeling a claim as false, organizations should explain why the claim is false and, if possible, highlight why the original source might be motivated to spread misinformation (e.g., an organization spreading doubt about climate change is funded by fossil fuel companies).

CHALLENGES TO UNDERSTANDING AND ADDRESSING MISINFORMATION ABOUT SCIENCE

Considerable progress has been made to advance understanding about the causes and consequences of misinformation about science, but there are also challenges to studying this phenomenon and mitigating its impact. While misinformation interventions have become more prevalent over time, they are largely uncoordinated across actors, sectors, disciplinary domains, and intended outcomes in ways that do not inform each other. In some cases, these efforts may even push in different directions. Scalability and real-world efficacy have also been difficult to achieve for some interventions, and overall, comprehensive data are limited to investigate the nature of misinformation about science across various contexts and populations.

CHALLENGES TO SCALE AND EFFICACY

Many approaches to address misinformation about science have demonstrated efficacy in small-scale, controlled experiments, but not consistently in real-world settings or over long periods of time. Additionally, many target the individual level, despite recognition in the field that systems-level action is needed. This inadvertently places the onus of mitigating the impacts of misinformation on individuals, and also gives the perception that individual action is the most effective way to address misinformation about science. Moreover, the limited emphasis on understanding misinformation about science at higher levels and larger scales impedes progress on understanding:

- how structural and contextual factors (e.g., social class, race/ethnicity, culture, geography, social networks, and institutions) influence the origin, spread, and impact of misinformation about science,
- how other important factors (i.e., social, political, and technological) interact with misinformation about science to influence decision making and well-being,
- the larger impact that systematic disinformation campaigns can have and how to effectively intervene to counter misinformation about science from such sources, and
- the effectiveness of existing approaches to address misinformation about science, either alone or in combination.

Some systems-level approaches (e.g., filling information voids, building and maintaining trust in sources of credible information, governance) have been implemented by various types of organizations; however, their efficacy has not been rigorously tested. Importantly, the committee found that funding structures have played a key role in driving scholarly attention in the field, including which topics and interventions are most studied. Hence, the priorities of funding organizations may be especially important to establish a systems-level understanding of misinformation about science.

Recommendation 12: To strengthen the evidence base on the impacts of misinformation about science across levels and the suite of approaches to mitigate them (e.g., community-based, platform and platform design-based, policy, and regulatory approaches), funding agencies and funding organizations should direct more investments toward systems-level

research. Such investments would increase understanding of the ways that structural and individual factors may interact to influence the spread and impacts of misinformation about science.

CHALLENGES TO OBTAINING HIGH-QUALITY, COMPREHENSIVE DATA

Gaining comprehensive understandings of misinformation about science has also been limited by data scarcity across different populations and contexts. Notably, the impacts of misinformation about science and the effectiveness of mitigation have not been well-documented for underserved groups. There are many reasons for this, resulting in the exclusion of the experiences of such populations in many studies (e.g., surveys, clinical trials, observational studies). Data on these populations are especially important for understanding how inequalities may compound the impacts of misinformation.

Some progress has been made on understanding the nature of misinformation on select social media platforms; however, a comprehensive picture across all major platforms is lacking. In particular, the ability to detect and study misinformation about science on social media platforms is currently limited by inconsistent rules for data access, privacy concerns, and prohibitively expensive data costs. Such conditions may not only reduce the level of research being conducted on social media platforms, but also the quality, as scraping may become a common form of data collection. Greater accessibility and consistency in data from platforms may require the establishment of formal standards and policies.

Recommendation 13: To reduce current barriers to obtaining high-quality, comprehensive data about misinformation about science on social media platforms:

- **Social media companies should make a good faith effort to provide access to data to examine the origins, spread, and potential impacts of misinformation about science in social media environments free of charge and without any restrictions when used for non-commercial purposes, except for privacy-related data restrictions.**
- **Universities and other research institutions should facilitate the relationships between their individual researchers and social media companies to obtain more reliable data for studying misinformation about science. This should be accomplished while ensuring independence of researchers from the companies.**

1

Introduction

Science is embedded in almost all aspects of modern life, and the process of science (the investigation of phenomena through observation, measurement, and analysis) has long been used to understand the world and advance knowledge and technological innovation. From the discovery of cures for life-threatening diseases to the development of crops that can adapt to environmental threats, to the construction of vehicles and devices for exploring the ocean floor and outer space, the benefits of science to individuals, communities, and society are well documented. Additionally, information from science is often used to inform personal and policy decisions related to medical care, food supply and safety, environmental health, and national security, among others. Given there are many contexts in which this information may be leveraged to advance specific interests, the reliability of these scientific findings is critically important. Science information is typically communicated and disseminated by individuals and institutions (e.g., scientists, healthcare professionals, journalists, philanthropists, universities, science associations, non-profit organizations, governments agencies, citizens, etc.), to achieve one or more goals identified in the National Academies of Sciences, Engineering, and Medicine (National Academies) report, *Communicating Science Effectively: A Research Agenda* (2017, p. 2):

- to share the findings and excitement of science,
- to increase the appreciation for science as a useful way of understanding and navigating the world,

- to increase knowledge and understanding of the science related to a specific issue,
- to influence people's opinions, behavior, and policy preferences, and
- to engage with diverse groups so that their perspectives about science related to important social issues can be considered in seeking solutions to societal problems.

While distinct approaches may be required to accomplish each of these goals, they all reflect ways to support better integration of scientific knowledge with personal values and other considerations for decision making. Thus, misinformation related to science can greatly influence this process. For example, the spread of misinformation about science can plausibly lead to ill-informed personal choices about disease treatment, lack of planning for natural disasters, higher rates of death from vaccine-preventable diseases, and limitations on productive debate about addressing climate change and other environmental hazards (e.g., water pollution). Additionally, communities that are already experiencing risks to their well-being—due to a variety of factors including health inequities, limited access to affordable and nutritious food, environmental degradation, poverty, and structural and systemic racism—may be further harmed by the uptake of misinformation about science. For these reasons, concern about the spread of misinformation, and the overall role of scientific expertise in civic life, democracy, and policy has grown significantly in recent years (Kavanagh & Rich, 2018; Scheufele et al., 2021; Southwell et al., 2018; Watts et al., 2021). The topic of misinformation about science has garnered significant public attention not only in the news media but also from policymakers who are interested in mitigating the associated negative impacts.

Misinformation about science, however, is not a new phenomenon. For example, misinformation about vaccines dates back to the invention of the smallpox vaccine in the late 18th century, and even more recent narratives predate the era of social media and the coronavirus (COVID-19) pandemic (Colgrove & Samuel, 2022; Schwartz, 2012). Additionally, the U.S. Food and Drug Administration (FDA) was created in 1906 to enforce the Pure Food and Drug Act in response to widespread misinformation about the efficacy and safety of drugs, food additives, and biological substances (Denham, 2020; Jaafar et al., 2021). To this end, there is a long-standing body of research related to misinformation about science across diverse disciplines, including science, health, and risk communication, computational social science, history, political science, information science, journalism, law, media studies, psychology, sociology, agriculture, and engineering. Several initiatives have been launched to leverage this evidence to address misinformation about science (Cacciatore, 2021; Lazer et al., 2018). Think tanks, government agencies, non-governmental organizations, and civil society organizations, among many others, have released reports and/or have funded initiatives to do more research and make policy recommendations in this area. But to date, these efforts have not yielded a clear understanding of the state of knowledge of the problem of misinformation about science and ways to address it.

STUDY CHARGE

With support from the National Science Foundation (NSF), the Board on Science Education of the National Academies initiated this consensus study to characterize the nature and scope of misinformation about science and its differential impacts; identify solutions to limit its spread; and provide guidance on interventions, policies, and future research to reduce associated harms (see Box 1-1). A 15-member expert committee representing multidisciplinary expertise across the social, biological, and applied sciences—psychology, sociology, political science, science and health

BOX 1-1
Statement of Task

The National Academies will convene an ad hoc committee to examine the evidence base, engage stakeholders, and develop conclusions, recommendations and a research agenda. The committee's final report will:

1. Define misinformation and disinformation about science.
2. Describe the scope and nature of misinformation about science, considering the historical context and describing any ways that the problem and impacts differ across communities and social groups in the United States.
3. Develop a holistic framework for understanding the influences, mechanisms, and impacts of misinformation, applying a systems approach that considers the relationships between and impacts on individuals, groups, and societal dynamics. Case studies may be used to examine how these mechanisms and impacts differ across communities by characteristics such as race and ethnicity, social class, political affiliation, religious affiliation, or geographical region.
4. Examine existing interventions that address misinformation about science.
5. Identify the ethical considerations that should guide future interventions (including unintended consequences of those interventions) and research on misinformation about science.
6. Recommend priorities for actions to reduce harms from misinformation about science.
7. Identify priorities for future research.

communication, journalism, computational social science, information science, engineering, technology, and agricultural sciences—was appointed to examine the extant literature in science communication and misinformation and develop this consensus report (Appendix B includes brief biographies of the committee members and staff). Committee members also had expertise regarding public understanding of science, the nature of misinformation within different communities and groups in the United States and abroad, and the nature of information spread through social networks, including, but not limited to, social media platforms. Finally, the committee included community engagement experts and health practitioners, as well as those with expertise in developing and implementing responsible and ethical innovations.

STUDY APPROACH

Over the course of 15 months, the committee held several fact-finding meetings, gathering evidence from expert presentations as well as from the existing literature, which included peer-reviewed journal articles, book chapters, policy reports, editorials, white papers, and previous National Academies reports. The committee also benefited from discussions and presentations from a variety of experts who participated in four fact-finding meetings. At the first and second meetings, the committee heard presentations on the scope and composition of the science information landscape, frameworks, and considerations for defining misinformation and disinformation, different classes of interventions that have been employed to address misinformation in both the online and offline environments, and differential strategies for addressing misinformation versus disinformation.

In conjunction with the third meeting, the committee hosted a one-day public workshop that brought together researchers, practitioners, philanthropists, and policymakers, among others. The workshop featured a series of discussions on the nature, mechanisms, and differential impacts of misinformation about science and on select interventions for addressing misinformation as it relates to their respective theory of change, target audience(s), intended and unintended outcomes, and effectiveness. At the final public information-gathering session, the committee invited two discussions of topics relevant to the statement of task: understanding misinformation in the context of the history and nature of science, and implications for addressing misinformation given advancements in information technologies (e.g., artificial intelligence, machine learning, etc.).

As part of its information-gathering efforts, the committee also commissioned three papers in additional areas that were identified as important for inclusion in the report. Joseph Polman (University of Colorado Boulder) authored a paper that examined how science learning in formal and informal learning contexts can support the development of relevant competencies for navigating a complex information environment (e.g., identifying credible information, managing misinformation and disinformation, assessing, and weighing evidence, science-informed decision making, etc.). Rachel Kuo (University of Illinois Urbana-Champaign) and Sarah Nguyễn (University of Washington) authored a paper that reviewed the extant evidence on the origin(s), diffusion, and effects of misinformation about science within information networks primarily composed of non-native speakers of English and immigrant populations in the United States. Lastly, Nicole Buckley (private law firm) and Ryan Calo (University of Washington) authored a paper that described the range of possibilities for addressing misinformation through regulatory mechanisms in the United States.

STUDY SCOPE

In interpreting its charge, the committee made several decisions that shaped its review of the evidence and the conclusions and recommendations that resulted from it. These include defining key terms—science information, misinformation about science, and disinformation about science—and using these definitions as boundaries for its analysis; adopting a systems perspective in seeking to holistically understanding the spread, mechanisms, impacts, and solutions for addressing misinformation about science; and determining which documented impacts of misinformation are most consequential toward prioritizing recommended actions for intervention.

Defining Key Terms

As a mode of inquiry, science provides an important way to understand and engage with the natural and material world, and as a discipline is constituted by a set of practices, values, and concepts that scientists have established and adhere to—such as expectations of appeal to empirical evidence and acting with integrity (see Chapter 2). Science as a discipline spans the physical, biological, social, health, and applied sciences, and as a way of knowing is often leveraged by individuals, communities, and societies to make important decisions regarding human and environmental health and well-being, among other reasons. Building on this, the committee adopted a definition of "information" from Wanless & Berk (2021), defined as "anything that is processed to provide meaning of the world." Scientific knowledge at its broadest can therefore be viewed as any information that is generated through the process of science, and as such, **the committee defines *science information* as any claim about a phenomenon within any of the science disciplines.** In this consensus report, science and health misinformation is the focus, both within the institution of science and outside the institution of science—both issues of concern (West & Bergstrom, 2021). This focus includes misinformation in science (e.g., fraud, the reproducibility crisis, hype) and about science topics (e.g., climate change, genetically modified organisms, vaccines, management of pain, smoking, COVID-19) as defined by researchers themselves.

As a fundamental component of the study charge, the committee was asked to define misinformation and disinformation about science. Currently, there is general agreement among researchers who study misinformation that false and misleading information both fall into the category of misinformation (Søe, 2021). At the same time, researchers have not yet agreed on a single definition of misinformation across disciplines and methods, and there is also disagreement in the field about the importance of intentionality within the definition (Altay et al., 2023; Vraga & Bode, 2020). This lack of an explicit and consistent definition can lead to interdisciplinary misunderstandings and artificially create contradictory findings. This confusion in turn, can lead to unwarranted policy responses to misinformation that reflect either an underestimation or overestimation of the problem. Thus, a clear definition of misinformation about science is essential for advancing scientific understanding of the phenomenon and determining when and to what extent a specific intervention is needed.

In this chapter, we briefly present definitions of misinformation and disinformation about science that were developed by the committee and guided our work, and Chapter 2 of this report provides a more detailed discussion of the committee's process for developing these definitions. Importantly, the complexities in establishing widely-shared definitions are not trivial. Scientific knowledge is not static, and therefore the nature of scientific consensus is inherently contingent on current evidence. Debates arise within science as new information emerges and leads to the revision of what may have previously been understood, and at times, value judgments may largely shape scientific agreement at a given time (e.g., regarding the risks and benefits of new technologies). In addition, science can simply be poorly communicated, or it can be miscommunicated, hyped, or prone to publishing biases (Phillips et al., 2005; Southwell et al., 2019; West & Bergstrom, 2021), and currently there are no bright lines that distinguish between scientific uncertainty, science done poorly, and misinformation about science. Nevertheless, clearly defining these key terms was a fundamental aspect of the study charge, both to guide the committee's work and to function as a possible guidepost for the broader research community. The committee's definition states:

> ***Misinformation about science is information that asserts or implies claims that are inconsistent with the weight of accepted scientific evidence at the time (reflecting both quality and quantity of evidence).***

> ***Which claims are determined to be misinformation about science can evolve over time as new evidence accumulates and scientific knowledge regarding those claims advances.***

In the case of disinformation—a subset of misinformation—the notion of intent is often emphasized as a distinguishing feature of this particular information type (Freelon & Wells, 2020). However, it is difficult to measure the intent or beliefs of an agent who is sharing information, which also presents an operational challenge to research. Indeed, some agents are clearly self-interested and purely tactical in promulgating falsehoods (see Chapter 4); nonetheless, the committee determined that the intent of the sharer is immaterial to the potential harm of that information to the receiver(s) and to the way it influences and shapes their sense of what decisions or actions are possible. For these reasons, misinformation is considered to be agnostic with respect to intentionality, and in the view of this committee, misinformation is a phenomenon that encompasses disinformation. Thus, the committee also states:

> ***Disinformation about science is a sub-category of misinformation that is circulated by agents who are aware that the science information they are circulating is false.***

Here, false science information is defined as *a mischaracterization of the "weight" of evidence as found in the literature at a particular moment in time and that underpins the consensus position* (see Chapter 2).

Adopting a Systems Perspective

The committee also recognizes that people are differently situated with respect to exposure to information. The existence of the alternative press is a reflection of this reality (e.g., immigrant press, Black press, feminist press, military press, etc.). Hence, in seeking to understand the dynamics of misinformation about science (i.e., nature, scope, spread, and impact), the committee determined it was important to consider how the broader historical and contemporary contexts of people's lived experiences shape their relationships to and with information. For example, systemic factors such as social stratification, structural and systemic racism, bias, and discrimination create conditions in which access to power, resources, and opportunities are constrained on the basis of identity, and as they relate to this report, can result in disparate access to and trust in high-quality science information across groups (see Chapters 3, 5, and 6). Taking a systems perspective afforded the examination of the intersections between misinformation about science and existing risk factors and inequities, and the potential impacts these have on well-being. Globalization, including shifts in technology, labor, economy, migration patterns, and geopolitical relationships between states, also influences the relationships between people and the relationships between people and information. To that end, the committee also considered the role that history, values, culture, language, and identity play in influencing differential exposure, engagement, and impacts of misinformation about science across different communities.

Characterizing the Impacts of Misinformation About Science

Finally, the committee placed an emphasis on the misinformation about science that is most consequential. While people may be exposed to varying degrees of misinformation about science, it is possible that only a subset of this information might impair decisions that individuals or communities make with consequences for their health and well-being. Similarly, scope and scale of the misinformation provided another lens for the committee's determination about potential for greatest negative impacts. Misinformation about science that can spread to millions of people through television, radio, social media, or a statement by prominent public figures has the potential to negatively impact more people than the misinformation that a single individual might encounter in a conversation. Undoubtedly, any misinformation can pose a risk to health and well-being to some extent (Krause et al., 2020; Swire-Thompson & Lazer, 2020); however, the committee was cognizant of the importance of representing the problem as accurately as possible. Building on its review of the evidence and conclusions related to the dynamics of misinformation about science, the committee also chose to prioritize recommendations with the greatest potential for mitigating its negative impacts.

STANDARDS OF EVIDENCE

As previously mentioned, this report reflects a range of sources consulted during the course of the study process. The committee gave the most weight to empirical evidence appearing in peer-reviewed publication outlets. As with other consensus reports published by the National Academies, this committee did not focus exclusively on literature associated with any one method for information gathering. This committee similarly draws on a National Research Council (NRC) report (2002, p. 6), which has informed subsequent consensus studies, to adopt the view that "A wide variety of legitimate scientific designs are available for [...] research." This stance meant that the committee considered qualitative and quantitative evidence as well as evidence generated by experimental studies, survey research, case studies, and observational data. Across these sources of evidence, the committee prioritized information with relevant implications for understanding the production, transmission, consumption, and consequences of misinformation, and with a specific focus on science contexts. At times, the committee drew from the broader literature on misinformation, communications, mass media, learning sciences, cognitive psychology, and law and technology, and as such gave careful consideration to the strength of the evidence and degree of informativeness for reconciling existing knowledge gaps about the nature and scope of the problem of misinformation about science.

The absence of clear definitions of misinformation and related concepts, as mentioned above, complicates the assessment of published evidence. In the wake of prominent news coverage regarding the general challenges of false and inaccurate information, literature that features the keyword "misinformation" and "science" (along with other related terms) has increased considerably in recent years. For example, a search for the keywords misinformation and science on Google Scholar yields approximately 16,200 articles for the period 1990–1999; 26,800 for the period 2000–2009; 34,400 for the period 2010–2019; and 203,000 for the period 2020–2023.[1] Indeed, this body of work is rapidly advancing, and with new literature being consistently added, an exhaustive analysis of the issues addressed in this report and synthesis of the extant literature is not feasible.

It is also important to note that the extant literature includes myriad examples of manuscripts in which misinformation is not explicitly defined as a concept or in which the operationalization or measurement of misinformation is not clear. Additionally, the evidence base on the topic of misinformation also reflects studies that focus on other distinct, but related concepts to describe the various ways that information can be distorted within the contemporary information ecosystem more broadly. Such concepts include but are not limited to information disorder[2] (Wardle & Derakhshan, 2017), information integrity[3] (National Science and Technology Council, 2022), and infodemic[4] (World Health Organization [WHO], 2020). Thus, in carrying out its charge, the committee prioritized

---

[1]The committee notes that these data are not based on a systematic search of the extant literature.

[2]Wardle & Derakhshan (2017) define information disorder as the combined spectrum of misinformation, disinformation, and malinformation (truthful information used to harm).

[3]According to the National Science and Technology Council, information integrity is defined as the spectrum of information and associated patterns of creation, exchange, and consumption in society, where high-integrity information is trustworthy; distinguishes fact from fiction, opinion, and inference; acknowledges uncertainties; and is transparent about its level of vetting (National Institute of Standards and Technology, 2024, p. 9).

[4]The WHO defines infodemic as too much information, including false or misleading information in the digital and physical environments during a disease outbreak (WHO, n.d.).

publications that included clear definitions and operationalization of misinformation about science as a stimulus external to a person, and a subset of the wider universe of all publications that mention misinformation about science in some way. Because common encounters with misinformation about science involve both people as well as informational content and information environments that develop across time, the committee included not only studies of human participants but also studies in which a unit of analysis other than an individual person (e.g., a unit of media content or a community or time) constituted the primary unit of analysis. Research on misinformation about science has also largely focused on a narrow set of topics such as vaccines, COVID-19, genetically modified organisms, and climate change. Hence, throughout the report, these topics are frequently referenced as part of the committee's analysis of the evidence base and the examples used to illustrate its findings. Likewise, online platforms are a prominent source of current data about the nature of misinformation. Indeed, misinformation about science exists beyond these topics and contexts, and the committee highlights the need for more scholarly attention to a broader range of science topics and media types in the Research Agenda.

Importantly, the committee also prioritized studies of the United States in its review and analysis of the evidence, including those that consider the United States as one among multiple national cases. This focus was essential to render the committee's work feasible, as an understanding of the state of misinformation about science across the entire world lies beyond the scope of this report, and more importantly, the recommendations of this committee are most consequential for the United States. Thus, two types of studies of misinformation about science were mostly excluded from consideration: studies primarily about countries other than the United States, and studies written in languages other than English.

Finally, the committee employed a rubric to characterize the strength of the diverse research that exists on the topic of misinformation (Box 1-2). Where applicable throughout the report, the committee articulates the type of evidence being reviewed and its strength and adopted similar phrase definitions from a previous NRC report (2012) for this purpose. When reaching consensus on conclusions and developing recommendations, the committee took care not to present findings based solely on oral testimony or limited evidence as adequately supported, but instead framed them as potential areas for further investigation without recommending a specific course of action. As a result of these deliberative processes, all conclusions and recommendations outlined in this report reflect the full consensus of the Committee on Understanding and Addressing Misinformation About Science.

BOX 1-2
Characterization of Evidence

A Limited Level of Evidence:

Few peer-reviewed studies of limited scope with some convergence of findings or convergence with non-peer-reviewed literature or with practitioner wisdom.

A Moderate Level of Evidence:

A well-designed study of appropriate scope that has been replicated by at least one other similar study. Often such evidence will include both quantitative and qualitative data OR

A moderate number of smaller-scale studies (e.g., data collection at a single institution or point in time) with general convergence but possibly with contradictory results. If the results are contradictory, more weight might be given to studies that reflect recent methodological advances.

Strong Evidence:

Multiple—meaning more than one or two—well-designed qualitative and/or quantitative studies in different settings published in peer-reviewed outlets, with high convergence of findings from multiple settings and an absence of competing evidence.

SOURCE: Adapted from National Research Council. (2012). *Discipline-based education research: Understanding and improving learning in undergraduate science and engineering.* The National Academies Press. https://doi.org/10.17226/13362

REPORT ORGANIZATION

The report that follows this introduction illuminates a comprehensive view of the nature, scope, and impact of misinformation about science through broad examination of the extant literature across diverse disciplines, sources, and topics. This begins with further discussion of the committee's rationale and process for defining key terms in Chapter 2, which clarifies the phenomena that are the focus of this report, situates misinformation in the context of other distinct, but related informational phenomena, and discusses important caveats that are associated with applying definitions. In Chapter 3, the committee describes the confluence of historical and contemporary systemic factors that intersect with a rapidly changing and complex information ecosystem to influence the nature of misinformation about science and people's relationship to information, including misinformation about science. Chapter 4 examines the evidence related to the sources of misinformation about science and in Chapter 5, the committee discusses key factors and mechanisms that influence differential reach and spread.

In Chapter 6, the committee reviews the existing evidence on the impacts of misinformation about science, articulating which are most consequential and how such impacts may be similar or different across levels (i.e., individual, community, institutional, societal) and social groups (e.g., race/ethnicity, socio-economic status, geography). Chapter 7 summarizes what is currently known about the effectiveness of the range of interventions that have been employed by different sectors (i.e., government, industry, academia, civil society, and community organizations, etc.) to address misinformation about science either before or after it has been encountered. This chapter also identifies important considerations for both current and promising future interventions.

As previously noted, there is a rapidly growing body of research on misinformation about science across diverse disciplines, each bringing different theoretical and methodological lenses to study the phenomenon. To this end, Chapter 8 characterizes and discusses the state of the scholarship on misinformation about science, including some of the challenges associated with studying this topic. Finally, in Chapter 9 the committee presents its conceptual understanding of the misinformation about science landscape, which includes report conclusions and recommendations for multi-stakeholder action, as well as prioritized directions for future research.

2

Defining Misinformation About Science

Concerns about inaccurate claims related to science and scientific findings have been prominent in social discourse in the United States long before the present day, but recent concerns about an apparent rise in the prevalence of misinformation about science and its potential harms have prompted an explosion of research. This research is hampered to some extent by lack of clarity about what does and does not qualify as misinformation about science. For example, determining whether to establish information as misinformation at the level of the individual claim (e.g., accuracy of any given individual post on a social media platform) or at the level of narratives (i.e., repeated individual pieces of misinformation about science over time) (Wardle, 2023) remains an open question. Additionally, in both public discourse and in peer-reviewed research, the term misinformation has been used as an umbrella term to refer to various types of false, inaccurate, incorrect, and misleading information. The broad nature of the term has made it difficult to develop a coherent understanding of the nature, scope, and impacts of misinformation broadly, and by extension, misinformation about science.

As noted in Chapter 1, the committee developed a definition of misinformation about science to both guide its own work and as a possible guidepost for the broader research community. The committee's definition states:

> ***Misinformation about science is information that asserts or implies claims that are inconsistent with the weight of accepted scientific evidence at the time (reflecting both quality and quantity of evidence). Which claims are determined to be misinformation about science can***

evolve over time as new evidence accumulates and scientific knowledge regarding those claims advances.

The current chapter describes how the committee arrived at this definition of misinformation about science, the inherent challenges in developing a single definition, and the limitations of the definition the committee developed. The chapter begins with a broad discussion of information and misinformation, briefly summarizing different approaches to defining misinformation generally. We then turn to a discussion of misinformation about science specifically, beginning with an explanation of the processes of science and how these processes produce empirical evidence that provides robust insights about the natural, physical, and social world. The committee's definition takes into account characteristics of misinformation generally and also the unique characteristics of knowledge and evidence generated by science. Finally, the committee discusses the limitations of our definition, as well as how it can be used effectively to guide research.

CHALLENGES OF DEFINING MISINFORMATION

In the view of this committee, misinformation is a subgenre of information. Information is broadly defined as "anything that is processed to provide meaning of the world" (Wanless & Berk, 2021), a definition that incorporates both content (the concepts or ideas the information is intended to convey) and context (the identity and social position of the actors who are sharing the information, the intent of these actors, the surrounding information, the platform, etc.) as elements that would affect interpretation. Misinformation is a type of information that emerges in relation to reliable information. Reliability (or lack thereof) is determined by the system that produces the information; for misinformation about science, the contrasting system is "science" itself (i.e., a system that produces reliable science information). Definitions of misinformation, whether in general or specifically of misinformation about science, typically vary in the extent to which they incorporate different elements of context or focus primarily on the specific content of the information being conveyed.

The concept of misinformation and its variations appear in centuries-old publications such as Thomas Hobbes' *Leviathan* and Adam Smith's *The Wealth of Nations*. Samuel Johnson's 18th century dictionary of the English language defines misinformation as "false intelligence; false accounts" (Johnson, 1773). However, this long history has not led to a precise and widely-shared definition. A recent survey of experts suggests that while there is agreement on some elements of a definition of misinformation, there is disagreement on others (Altay et al., 2023). Similarly, a recent review of health-related research on misinformation identified 75 different definitions for misinformation and related terms (terms such as disinformation, fake news, malinformation, and infodemic; El Mikati et al., 2023).

Almost universally, definitions of misinformation used by researchers encompass false, inaccurate, or incorrect information. Often, definitions include "misleading" information, that is, information that is not entirely false, but that could lead to inaccurate interpretations (e.g., van der Linden et al., 2023). Concepts of falsity, deception, and harm are also common components of definitions of misinformation, but how each of these concepts is understood and the role it plays varies from definition to definition. Sometimes, definitions in the literature require that the creation or sharing of false or misleading information be unintentional in order for it to be considered misinformation (e.g., Wardle & Derakhshan, 2017). Other definitions require that the information be both false and potentially harmful (e.g., Freelon & Wells, 2020); the focus on potential harm often drives content moderation policies of social media platforms (Green et al., 2023).

The committee also considered how misinformation might be distinguished from disinformation (untrue information shared by an actor who knows it is untrue). Due to its perceived increased potential to harm, some scholars have focused attention on disinformation in particular, defined by some as information that "includes all forms of false, inaccurate, or misleading information designed, presented, and promoted to intentionally cause public harm or for profit" (de Cock Buning, 2018; Freelon & Wells, 2020). This is different from propaganda, which is "designed to link together brands, people, and nations with the goal of influencing ideas and attitudes" (Tripodi, 2022). However, due to the difficulty of determining intentionality, and the fact that it is not an intrinsic aspect of the truth claim itself, some scholars have eschewed the term disinformation (Krause et al., 2022; Swire-Thompson & Lazer, 2020).

In its deliberations around the definition of misinformation, the committee grappled with the role of an actor's awareness or intent—that is whether an actor creating or sharing a piece of information knows it is inaccurate and shares it intentionally despite or because of its inaccuracy. As noted above, intent or awareness is not an attribute of information itself; rather it is an attribute of an actor who creates or shares the information. It can be very difficult to determine intent, especially as information is shared across networks of individuals. As a result, the committee excluded intent (to mislead—or not) as an essential, definitional component of misinformation. The committee also excluded harm as a definitional requirement in part because, presumptively, misinformation is at least minimally harmful (because it undermines individual agency due to its intrinsic potential to create a false understanding of the world); and in part because whether and how much misinformation is harmful is still an open question and an area of active research (as we discuss in Chapter 6).[1]

WHAT IS UNIQUE ABOUT SCIENTIFIC KNOWLEDGE?

Any definition of misinformation about science has to account for the unique characteristics of knowledge that is generated by the scientific community through scientific inquiry. Science emphasizes the importance of empirical evidence and testable hypotheses about the world. Processes of science are intended to allow for discussion and evaluation of bodies of evidence as they evolve over time. This emphasis on empiricism and on revision of knowledge as new evidence comes to light has implications for any definition of misinformation about science. That is, the definition needs to incorporate both the notion that scientific knowledge is rooted in empirical evidence and that it can be revised over time as new evidence emerges.

In the sections below we first describe, briefly, how science works: that is how scientific evidence is gathered and tested, how conclusions are drawn, how scientists reach consensus on how to interpret existing evidence, and how and when scientific explanations might be revised when new evidence emerges. Based on this discussion, we then discuss implications for a definition of misinformation about science.

How Does Science Work?

"Science is a mode of inquiry that aims to pose questions about the world, arriving at the answers and assessing their degree of certainty through a communal effort designed to ensure that they are well grounded [in evidence]" (National Academies of Sciences, Engineering, and Medicine [National Academies], 2019, p. 27). This mode of inquiry has four key goals: first, describe the world (e.g., classifying plant species); second, explain that world (e.g., how those plant species evolved over time); third, predict what will happen in the world (e.g., how climate will affect survival of a particular plant species); and fourth, intervene in certain processes or systems to achieve a goal (e.g., consider moving threatened plant species to a more climate conducive environment; National Academies, 2019).

To achieve these goals, scientists generally employ four core practices in pursuing their inquiries. These practices include

- using ideas, theories, and hypotheses;
- relying on evidence;

[1]We do suggest that the field should (and generally does) focus on misinformation that has greater prospects for leading to harmful effects, including encouraging harmful behaviors.

- using logic and reasoning; and
- making the research open to review by their peers, often through peer-reviewed journals or conferences.

As scientists introduce ideas, build theories, or test hypotheses, they generate data, observations, and other measurements collectively known as *evidence*. The scientific process requires evidence to provide accurate descriptions of the world and to avoid false descriptions (Goldman, 1999). Generating evidence in and of itself, while necessary, is not sufficient for scientific inquiry. Using logic and reasoning to weight the quantity and quality of evidence, and associated uncertainty, according to the standards of any individual scientific field, yields expert opinions on the strength of a hypothesis or theory. That evidence, once published, provides other scientists with the details needed to find additional connections and patterns for further experimentation in the iterative testing of various hypotheses, thereby refining (or refuting) the theory. Of course, no individual research study is perfect. Assumptions, hypotheses, results, and conclusions can and should be challenged as emerging research suggests alternative conclusions and new theories. If the initial results cannot be reproduced by independent laboratories, the initial reported (but irreproducible) results are generally discarded by the scientific community. Scientific inquiry thus advances through repeated and methodical exercise of—and steadfast adherence to—this core set of scientific practices that define the craft.

In this way, science is a cumulative activity. Repeatable observations and experiments generate explanations that describe the world more accurately and comprehensively. These explanations in turn suggest new observations and experiments that can be used to test and extend the explanation. In this way, scientific explanations improve over time, as subsequent generations of scientists, often using technological innovations, work to correct, refine, and extend the work done by their predecessors.

Science is thus a social process, whose core practices (above) are based in shared principles and assumptions that shape a scientist's approach to inquiry. Five key principles of science, adapted from *Reproducibility and Replicability in Science* (National Academies, 2019a, pp. 30–33), are reproducibility, generalizability, collectivity, uncertainty, and refinement:

1. **Reproducibility** – If a scientist can repeat the methods of a specific scientific study, they should replicate the results of the original study. In other words, scientists assume the laws of nature are universal; in equivalent contexts one should observe similar results.[2]

[2]We note that in some fields, like the social sciences and biology, "equivalent context" is often difficult to specify; for example, the same experiment, a year later, with similar subjects may not constitute "equivalent" (e.g., see Munger, 2019).

2. **Generalizability** – Scientists do experiments in different contexts and under different conditions to test whether their hypothesis is generalizable to different situations. When exceptions arise, scientists go back to the drawing board to develop new theories to explain the observations.
3. **Collectivity** – Scientists build on research established by previous scientists. In a letter to Robert Hooke in 1675, Isaac Newton famously said "If I have seen further, it is by standing on the shoulders of Giants" (Chen, 2003). He meant that without the work of scientists that came before him he would not have been able to make his own scientific advances.
4. **Uncertainty** – Uncertainty is an inherent part of science. There is uncertainty in every measurement a scientist makes and in every prediction they may offer. Uncertainty can be assessed, communicated, evaluated, and, with iterative experiments and more data, reduced. But it can never reach zero. Scientists temper their expectations accordingly, setting their sights on increasing confidence in a theory or its predicted results.
5. **Refinement** – Uncertainty and the iterative nature of science are not weaknesses but strengths, for it is through exploration of uncertainties, developing theories, and testing of new hypotheses that scientists have been able to explain ever more phenomena. Scientific progress is rarely linear, and scientists are not infallible; through an iterative process of refining theories and testing hypotheses, scientists seek to provide ever greater confidence in scientific explanations and predictions.

The core practices and shared principles characterize the nature of science as a whole and the information derived from a huge variety of approaches to scientific inquiry. Of course, "science" does not speak with a single voice; likewise, there is not a single set of methods for producing knowledge that is used across all domains of science. Science is inherently heterogenous. Furthermore, as mentioned above, science is intrinsically uncertain: findings today might be rendered obsolete by tomorrow's research. The above core practices and shared principles do not counter this. Rather, they establish standards that allow for advancement through iteration, disagreement, and uncertainty.

In science it is not possible to prove with absolute certainty that a given explanation is complete and final. Some of the explanations advanced by scientists turn out to be incorrect when they are tested by further observations or experiments. Many scientific ideas that once were accepted are now known to be inaccurate or to apply only within a limited domain. However, many scientific explanations have been so thoroughly tested that they are very unlikely to change in substantial ways as new observations are made or new experiments are analyzed. These explanations are accepted by scientists as being true and factual descriptions of the natural world. The atomic structure of matter, the genetic basis of heredity, the circulation of blood, gravitation and planetary motion are just a few examples of a very large number of scientific explanations that have been overwhelmingly substantiated.

Implications for Misinformation About Science

Misinformation about science, to which we now turn, represents a distortion in the representation of information derived from the practices, principles, and approaches described above that comprise scientific inquiry and evidence-building. The definition of misinformation about science the committee adopted focuses on the (mis)match between (a) claims regarding specific scientific findings and (b) the weight of scientific evidence at the time the claim is made. Often, misinformation about science is constructed to foreground and exploit the heterogeneity and uncertainties of science. Below we highlight characteristics of scientific knowledge and scientific consensus that pose particular challenges for defining, identifying, and combatting misinformation about science.

As noted above, scientific knowledge evolves as more evidence is generated, particularly when the science itself is unsettled. The idea of "settled" science requires some explanation. It should not be implied that the knowledge on any given topic is final—all knowledge is partial—but that there is greater consensus in the case of "settled" science as opposed to on topics where scientific knowledge is still emerging. Claims may still be upended in "settled" science, albeit more slowly. An example is the screening age for mammography. There has been considerable debate over whether mammography screening to detect breast cancer should start at age 50 or much earlier. Over several decades, based on evolving science, the consensus according to the Centers for Disease Control and Prevention's (CDC) U.S. Preventive Services Task Force (USPSTF) settled on starting the screening at age 40 in the United States (USPSTF, 2024). On the other hand, consensus on emerging topics such as COVID-19 was less settled given the novelty of the virus and rapid evolution of knowledge.

Another point worth noting is the role that "at the time" plays in the committee's definition of misinformation about science. The nature of scientific inquiry, at its best, is to continually explore hypotheses that are counter to and may overturn current orthodoxy. Claims made today that are consistent with the weight of the scientific evidence may not be accepted tomorrow if new, contradictory evidence emerges. When and how long scientific claims are accepted, are questioned, and even overthrown has implications for defining misinformation.

COVID-19 serves as an interesting illustration of some of these principles, though they are not unique to COVID-19. Explanations of the origins and transmission of COVID-19 evolved continuously over several months as new knowledge and evidence accumulated. What had been a consensus about a virus that is transmitted through surfaces changed, as evidence began to accumulate, to a consensus around airborne transmission. Similarly, there was uncertainty about the potential effectiveness of hydroxychloroquine as a treatment for COVID-19 at the beginning of the pandemic. Over the next few months as more studies were published assessing the potential therapeutic benefit of hydroxychloroquine, the picture became clearer that it was not an effective treatment (Abella et al., 2021; Bull-Otterson et al., 2020; Hennekens et al., 2022; The RECOVERY Collaborative Group, 2020). The speed at which the definition of misinformation about COVID-19 began to change was extremely rapid, given the unsettled nature of the scientific knowledge regarding the virus, as opposed to the more established or long-standing evidence on such topics as the harmful effects of lead in water. That is, how settled the science is matters, but this should not imply that settled science cannot change: it can, but more slowly.

Consensus is also a reflection of power in some ways. Authorities or those in power may hold greater resources and platforms to establish consensus compared to those who may be holding dissenting views. For example, scientific consensus is generally established through peer-reviewed journal articles, scientific and medical bodies developing consensus guidelines (e.g., USPSTF), and funding agencies, among others. Such bodies and scientists working within these paradigms are not immune to bias and could potentially discount views that challenge the prevailing consensus or even promote erroneous scientific claims due to highly biased assumptions (e.g., racial superiority through genetic inheritance; Gould, 1996). Thus, given the stature of such bodies, platforms they hold, and cultural authority they have, they can influence what is considered to be reliable and legitimate science information, and by definition, what is considered to be misinformation about science, and in some cases, such determinations may be based on shared values and homophily in addition to the weight of the scientific evidence at the time (e.g., safety and benefits of new innovations and technologies; Dietz et al., 1989). As such, this may also preclude dissenting views from being aired prominently, and dissenters—whether other scientists or advocates—may or may not have comparable resources and platforms to challenge the dominant paradigm(s), thus opening themselves to criticism of spreading misinformation. Given how long it takes in the deliberative process of science to establish consensus and update it based on new knowledge, initial views on what is scientifically accepted information and misinformation about science may evolve over time with occasional dissenting views entering the mainstream. Importantly, while offering a definition of misinformation about science in keeping with its charge, the committee also recognizes the ways in which definitional decisions can drive stigma and facilitate the accumulation of economic, social, political, and cultural capital, with potential to create or exacerbate inequalities (Metzl & Hansen, 2014).

The notion of the "precautionary principle," which proposes that in the face of uncertainty, the priority should be to avoid risks even when benefits may be clear, is also relevant to the frame of reference that establishing what counts as misinformation rests on (Kriebel et al., 2001). That is, new and emerging science should undergo extensive peer-review, testing, and review by appropriate experts in the interest of protecting human safety and welfare. For instance, with respect to medical interventions, the presumption is that a new drug or procedure is not efficacious and may be risky until evidence demonstrates its value and safety. Thus, in this context, the definition of legitimate science information and misinformation about science may change as new knowledge around safety accumulates and as scientific consensus evolves as claims get tested and adjudicated. Indeed, shared values and homophily among scientists can and have often served the advancement of scientific understanding well (e.g., upholding key principles for the approach to scientific inquiry), but also underscore the complexity of applying definitions of misinformation in cases where value judgements must be deployed.

MAPPING THE BOUNDARIES OF MISINFORMATION ABOUT SCIENCE

As with many social scientific categories, the operational boundaries of misinformation are not drawn with bright lines. Furthermore, it is not a normatively neutral term—the goal of studying misinformation (unlike information more generally) is to seek to understand and control a phenomenon that may be having adverse effects on individuals or society (e.g., misunderstanding the risks of vaccines leading to decisions with adverse health effects).

In this section we discuss some classes of information that are encompassed by the committee's definition of misinformation about science. These include false science information, misleading science information, and disinformation. We also highlight two essential boundary concerns: (a) the confounding of differences in values with misinformation and (b) the line between misinformation and benign simplification. We discuss further issues in operationalizing misinformation in Chapter 8 of this report.

False Science Information

Some of the literature suggests that determining whether a claim related to scientific findings or explanations of the world should be based on a comparison to the scientific consensus on that issue (Chou et al., 2020; Swire-Thompson & Lazer, 2020) or to the "best available scientific evidence" (Southwell et al., 2022). The committee agrees that any judgment regarding the truth or falsity of a claim must be based on an assessment of the body of scientific evidence that informs the consensus position at the time. As discussed above, scientific consensus is rooted in an assessment of the relative quality and quantity of various findings—the weight of accepted scientific evidence—at that moment. While there is recognition that new evidence might call current consensus into question, for well-established theories, there are typically multiple lines of confirmatory evidence.

False science information distorts this context and exploits the notion that science is made up of sets of findings that are uncertain, evolving, and sometimes competing and conflicting. The committee defines false science information as a mischaracterization of the "weight" of evidence as found in the literature at a particular moment in time and that underpins the consensus position. Thus, for example, in 2024, the claim that "vaccines cause autism" is false, because, within a large literature carefully studying the question, the weight of evidence is decisively inconsistent with that claim (e.g., Gidengil et al., 2021). "Weight" thus reflects hierarchies of evidence; for example, a high-quality, well-designed randomized, controlled trial about hormone replacement therapy can supersede a higher quantity of observational evidence (Prasad & Cifu, 2015). However, the methodology and hierarchy of evidence must be commensurate with the empirical question at hand (Greenhalgh, 2020). Evidence from randomized controlled trials cannot be assumed to always supersede all other evidence; which evidence provides the most "weight" depends on the context.

Misleading Science Information

"Misleading information" has not been precisely defined in relevant literature. In this report, the committee interprets "misleading information" as information that is not intrinsically false, but that causes false beliefs or inaccurate understandings of science. A challenge with this construction is that "misleading" is not an attribute of the information but of the interplay of information and a given recipient (what is informative to one person may be misleading to another). "Misleading" is also potentially a challenge to operationalize, since it requires an assessment of the causal effects on cognition of a given piece of information. Put another way, for information to be misleading, we must know whether the information actually misleads people (and which people it misleads), rather than researchers' judgment about whether a piece of information is misleading.

While this committee believes that misleading science information is an important phenomenon, it is viewed to be definitionally adjacent to the concept of misinformation. The committee also argues that empirical evidence that individuals are misled by the information is a requirement in this case. Therefore, the committee adopts the construction "implies" to capture the relevant attribute of misinformation. Thus, for example, *The Washington Post* published an article titled, "Vaccinated people now make up a majority of COVID deaths" (Beard, 2022; note: the article title was subsequently changed). This headline was true and reflected the fact that the overwhelming majority of the most vulnerable individuals were vaccinated (and thus at higher risk of dying of COVID-19, even if vaccinated). The rapid recirculation of this headline within the anti-vaccine community signaled that this community understood it to imply that vaccines were not effective (Goel et al., 2023). The implication that COVID-19 vaccines are not effective would constitute misinformation.

Disinformation

Throughout this report, the committee specifically highlights disinformation alongside misinformation, both because the former is a part of the charge and also a commonly-used, related term. In the view of this committee, ***disinformation about science is defined as a sub-category of misinformation that is circulated by agents that are aware that the science information they are circulating is false.*** We deliberately distinguish between (a) the action of spreading false information without knowing that it is false and (b) the action of knowingly spreading false information, and spreading it for a variety of motivations including altruistic reasons, political, financial, and other motives (see Chapters 4 and 5 for further discussion of the reasons and motivations that institutions and individuals spread misinformation about science).

However, we note that, as a matter of scientific measurement, it is often difficult to ascertain the intent or beliefs of the actor(s) sharing misinformation, and this presents an operational challenge to researchers. The intent or beliefs of the sharer of misinformation are also immaterial to the prospective harm that misinformation about science might cause to recipients. That said, it is clear that some of the most harmful episodes of misinformation about science were knowingly driven by actors with strong material incentives to mislead people (see examples in Chapters 4 and 5). The definition we offer for misinformation is therefore agnostic with respect to the beliefs or intentions of the people or entities that share that information, and thus encompasses disinformation.

Confounding Differences in Values with Misinformation

It is important to be circumspect when using the term misinformation so that it does not simply paper over different values or salient markers of identity, such as perspectives on risk tolerance in the face of uncertainty. For instance, scientific research offers insight on morbidity, mortality, and risk, but it does not tell societies how to weigh individual versus societal risks and benefits, or the threshold at which individuals or a society should act. Those thresholds can only be reasonably and defensively set at different levels depending on the frame of reference.

For policy decisions that need to be informed by scientific evidence, it is especially important to understand when disagreements over the implications of scientific findings reflect differences in values or priorities versus misinformation about science. Science alone does not provide all of the information necessary to make sound policy decisions. Policymakers also need to consider things like relative financial costs of different policy approaches, values and goals of communities, and who benefits or does not benefit from a particular policy approach (NRC, 2012b). Careful weighing of scientific evidence in the context of this wide variety of additional factors can mean that policymakers choose courses of action that do not represent the "ideal" approach that would be chosen by scientists or other policymakers (NRC, 2012b). For example, the use of electronic cigarettes as a tool for smoking cessation is recommended by the National Health Service in the U.K. while the pros and cons are heavily debated within the U.S. scientific community (Herbst et al., 2022). Therefore, based on differences in values and goals, the U.K.'s harm reduction strategy could be viewed as inaccurate science information within other policy and government contexts that promote total cessation from the use of combustible tobacco.

Another example of this is the aforementioned ongoing debate about starting mammography screening for breast cancer at either 40 or 50 years of age. As documented by Friedman (2023), both sides of the debate have written in peer-reviewed literature about how the other side has either spread misinformation (Kopans, 2024) or recommended unethical actions (Woolf & Harris, 2012). Yet, data support either recommendation, with the former camp prioritizing case detection (accepting the risk for false positives) and the latter seeking to minimize overdiagnosis and conserve scarce resources (accepting the risk for missing cases; Friedman, 2023).

Within an academic frame of reference, a number of studies have focused on the increasing use of hype- and breakthrough-associated language in scientific publications. While emotionless styles of speaking have a long history of being favored as a way to imply objectivity (Rosenfeld, 2018), hyperbolic language has been increasing in scientific journals (Millar et al., 2019), in university press releases (Sumner et al., 2014), and in news content about science (Adams et al., 2019; see Chapter 4). Although such language may have been previously considered inappropriate for academic debate, it has become increasingly adopted, and sometimes expected, in successful funding applications (Millar et al., 2022) and in the physical and biological sciences (Hyland & Jiang, 2021).

The Importance of Context

It is also critical to acknowledge that differences in the contexts for discussions around evolving scientific knowledge also have implications for misinformation about science. Debates and dissenting views are built into the process of science where claims are constantly tested and subjected to review by other scientists. Moreover, such a process is designed for claims to be challenged and the empirical evidence supporting such claims contested. While evolving consensus is both embraced and appreciated within the science arena, new updates to consensus may not often penetrate into the public arena. In the contemporary information ecosystem marked by flattened hierarchies (see Chapter 3), conversations and debates among scientists are now taking place in the public sphere for many reasons, including those discussed in Chapter 4—publicity by institutions that produce science or scientists seeking a more public role. The challenge, however, is that changing consensus due to new evidence may inadvertently create confusion among non-scientists being perceived instead as expert disagreement and conflicting information (Nagler et al., 2023).

How inaccurate a claim can be before it must be labeled misinformation is also partly a matter of setting thresholds based on context. For example, explanations about science are often simplified in the context of education, popular culture, and journalism. In fact, research on how people process complex information makes clear that sometimes simplifications can yield more accurate beliefs than complicated and more precisely correct representations (Reyna, 2021). In some sense, information is always being simplified or presented outside of its original context, making misinformation an inevitable feature of a "sound bite" media system.

While some theories make clear recommendations on how high-quality simplifications can leave people with "gists" that are both meaningful and accurate (Reyna, 2021), the fact is that even carefully planned messages can propagate out of their original context, creating confusion or misunderstandings. As such, the boundary between simplification and misinformation must rely on both normative and objective criteria to distinguish which simplifications stray too far from the original. Simplifications of science such as metaphors are normatively accepted in education, journalism, or certain healthcare settings to facilitate understanding. In physics and chemistry, for example, we learn the first law of thermodynamics and conservation of energy: that energy can neither be created nor destroyed. Only in advanced physics does one learn exceptions revealing the oversimplification: the law can be violated, if such violations happen only for infinitesimally short periods of time, in line with Heisenberg's uncertainty principle. As another example, physicians prescribing anticoagulants routinely use the factually incorrect metaphor of "blood thinners" to explain the medicine's mechanism of action to patients.

The line where simplification stops serving goals like education and the increase of accurate understanding, and becomes misinformation is gray and interpreted through socio-cultural norms. The conservation of energy and anticoagulation examples demonstrate that a helpful simplification in one context could be considered false or misinformation in another, suggesting that any definition of misinformation focused solely on the veracity of content irrespective of context is likely insufficient. Context matters; otherwise, science educators and journalists could be credibly accused of spreading misinformation for conceptual simplifications that many would consider part of their professional responsibilities. But without a sufficient empirical basis on which to set those context-dependent thresholds (either due to lack of data, or questions that science cannot answer [Weinberg, 1972]), the basis for such decisions defaults to other values like culture, norms, or identity. This set of issues is an important area for future empirical research.

SUMMARY

Conclusion 2-1: In both public discourse and in peer-reviewed research, the term misinformation has been used as an umbrella term to refer to various types of false, inaccurate, incorrect, and misleading information. The broad nature of the term has made it difficult to develop coherent understanding of the nature, scope, and impacts of misinformation, and by extension, misinformation about science. To address the lack of a consistent definition, the committee has developed the following definition: Misinformation about science is information that asserts or implies claims that are inconsistent with the weight of accepted scientific evidence at the time (reflecting both quality and quantity of evidence). Which claims are determined to be misinformation about science can evolve over time as new evidence accumulates and scientific knowledge regarding those claims advances.

In the view of this committee, this definition affords operationalization and measurement and offers a lens for assessing the potential impacts of misinformation about science as well as the potential efficacy and plausibility of intervention efforts. Determining what constitutes legitimate science information, scientific uncertainty, and misinformation about science is nontrivial. Additionally, power lies with those who can make such definitional decisions as well as set the thresholds for when other variables besides veracity (i.e., norms, values, identity, and context) take precedence. Misinformation about science is a concern because it can yield misunderstandings of the world that, in turn, misaligns individual or collective preferences and choices (see Chapter 6). Moreover, misinformation about science might undermine trust in important societal institutions (Ognyanova et al., 2020), an issue that we discuss more in Chapter 3.

3

Misinformation About Science: Understanding the Current Context

Addressing a gathering of media professionals and researchers in the late 1940s, Hugh Beville, then director of research for NBC, spoke about the "challenge of the new media" and noted that "America is now entering a new era of electronic mass communication. These new vehicles of electronic communications will have a tremendous impact on all existing means of mass communication" (Beville, 1948, p. 3). Even earlier, Dewey (1923, p. 127) noted the impact of new technologies—the "telegraph, telephone, and now the radio, cheap and quick mails, the printing press, capable of swift reduplication of material at low cost"—to the challenge of conveying accurate information to the public for democratic participation. Those words of caution just as easily could have been written by a social science researcher in recent years. While the technical and socio-cultural dimensions of change and opportunity in the early decades of the 21st century differ from the 20th century, the collective consternation and wonder regarding changes in our information ecosystem has been relatively consistent.

The aim of the present chapter is to describe the broader contexts within which the phenomenon of misinformation about science emerges and impacts society. To more fully understand the production and spread of misinformation about science (Chapter 4 and 5), what consequences it has for individuals, communities, and for society as a whole (Chapter 6), and what can be done to counter or minimize its negative impacts (Chapter 7), it is important to understand that these phenomena do not occur in a vacuum. Rather, individuals, the communities they are a part of, and their information ecosystems are all shaped by larger societal forces. These include changing demographics in the United States (Vespa et al., 2020) as well as other larger shifts currently shaping American society, including declining trust in institutions, political polarization, racial and socio-economic divides, and other forces that shape how people are positioned relative to science and the science information environment. These forces influence, for example, to what extent and in what ways individuals and communities interact with science and scientific (mis)information, how people interpret and use (or ignore) misinformation about science, and the role that misinformation may play in shaping societal decision making.

Subsequent sections of this chapter describe two factors of contemporary American society that are particularly salient for understanding the phenomenon of misinformation about science in the view of the committee: (a) patterns of trust and confidence in institutions (including science) and their intersection with political polarization and (b) structural and systemic inequities. Next, we describe changes in the information ecosystems people inhabit, and the relevance of these changes for understanding misinformation about science. Finally, the chapter concludes with a focus on specific elements of the science information environment that inform understanding of the spread and impacts of misinformation about science, and potential solutions. One element that we leave for future chapters is regulation. Although discussed throughout the report, we pay special attention to this topic in Chapter 7, where we discuss interventions for addressing misinformation about science.

SYSTEMIC FACTORS THAT SHAPE HOW PEOPLE INTERACT WITH INFORMATION

A large constellation of societal systems and forces shape whether and how people encounter information, perceive it, make sense of it, and decide how it informs their actions in the world. This chapter elucidates the need for understanding these phenomena through a systems perspective and describes relevant factors for understanding how people and communities are differently situated with respect to information about science (National Academies of Sciences, Engineering, and Medicine [National Academies], 2016b). Communities of shared identity, geography, and affiliation can vary in how likely they are to seek out or to be exposed to information from science, accurate and otherwise; in what sources people seek, trust, and believe; and in the ability and tendencies to act on scientific information. Communities are also affected by social, legal, and political forces that shape society. Importantly, communities and society as a whole are affected by profound technological shifts shaping the information environment. These forces (both historical and contemporary, static and changing) inform this broader systemic way of understanding the phenomenon of misinformation about science. As described in some detail below, there are numerous facets or dimensions that make up the "broader context," including but not limited to: the historical and contemporary nature of the science-society relationship; structural inequalities; and declining trust and confidence in traditional institutions, including deepening political polarization. The way that individuals perceive and process information within this broader context is discussed in detail in Chapter 6 which focuses on the impacts of misinformation about science.

The Role of Science in Society

The role of science in society affects understanding of the broader context that shapes the phenomenon of misinformation about science. First, public access to accurate information from science has long been recognized as important for informing rational public deliberation and decision making in democratic societies (Bächtiger et al., 2018; Dewey, 1923; Habermas, 1970). The scientific method is generally viewed as a reliable, and thus a trustworthy, process for gaining knowledge about an increasingly complex world beset by multifaceted problems (e.g., environmental degradation, public health threats). However, decisions on matters concerning science are based not only on accurate facts but also on the values people use to make choices and to manage risks particularly under conditions of uncertainty (Dietz, 2013; NRC, 1996, 2008). Balancing between the two is challenging in the best of times (Pamuk, 2021; Rosenfeld, 2018), but misinformation can disrupt the exchange of reliable information that results uniquely from the scientific process. Healthy linkages between experts in the scientific community, the public, and decision makers—needed in democratic societies—can help ensure that these exchanges "get the science right" and "get the right science" (NRC, 1996).

Additionally, science has long held significant authority and legitimacy in society, and in the United States, this authority confers significant social power, including over consequential decisions that policymakers and other leaders make. The cultural authority of science also confers power to those who use its language, whether legitimately or not. Recognizing the cultural weight that scientists and scientific information carry is important for understanding why and how misinformation about health and science can similarly carry significant implications for individuals, communities, and societies, and why power dynamics are an important context for understanding both the problem and potential solutions. These dynamics also underscore why misinformation that arises from fraud or other misconduct within the scientific community can be more consequential than misinformation from other sources (see Chapters 4, 5, and 6 for further discussion).

Structural Inequalities

Long-standing structural inequalities within American society, including systemic racism, discrimination, and bias, intersect with and exacerbate problems of misinformation in complex and multi-faceted ways. Inequalities that stem from differences in socio-economic status or position, education level, race or ethnicity, primary language, or geography are consequential for economic, social, and physical well-being (Braveman & Gottlieb, 2014). In addition, many communities experience the effects of other areas of under-investment (e.g., Satcher, 2022) that have the potential to compound the effects of disparities in access to and ability to act upon high-quality information from science.

In the committee's view, several contexts are instructive for understanding how structural inequalities and misinformation about science intersect:

1. Structural inequalities affect access to high-quality information from science.
2. Many communities have experienced being the subjects of misinformation by the scientific community.
3. The language of science has been used to conflate disease with immigrants.
4. Experiences with past and current medical and environmental racism sow distrust and create opportunities for those who seek to exploit them to propagate misinformation.

Structural inequalities affect how individuals and communities are positioned with respect to high-quality information from science and misinformation (e.g., Viswanath et al., 2021). In particular, communities that have histories of being marginalized and under-resourced experience disparities in access to quality information about health and science, whether due to material circumstances, information vacuums, language barriers, or other factors (Viswanath et al., 2022b). For example, systemic inequalities result in people of lower socio-economic status and people in rural settings having less available, affordable, and reliable broadband internet access (Viswanath et al., 2012, 2022b; Whitacre et al., 2015), though there are other factors that shape demand for these services.

One effect of these experiences is that they shape what sources of information about science people trust, believe, and use. A recent study by the Pew Research Center (2024c) examined mistrust in institutions among Black Americans. This survey found that nearly 90% of Black Americans reported encountering inaccurate news in the media about Black people, and most of those respondents believed that those inaccuracies were intentional. Mistrust or reduced access to high-quality sources of information presents a double penalty for such communities, which may need to seek out alternative sources of information that, in turn, encourage greater distrust of scientific institutions. For example, Druckman et al. (2024b) demonstrate the enduringly higher distrust of science by women and/or by people who are Black, of lower socio-economic status, or from rural communities. Other studies have pointed out a need for a greater research focus on particular communities, including the Latino community, to understand how factors like language, values, and identity among other factors shapes how misinformation is encountered, perceived, and/or acted upon (Lewandowsky et al., 2022; Soto-Vasquez, 2023). Understanding how the lived experiences of people within these groups inform trust in scientific information and receptivity to misinformation is important for discerning which interventions may be warranted (i.e., changes in practice and policy rather than persuasion).

Second, when misinformation about particular communities conforms to existing power structures, it may be more likely to be perceived as factually accurate and accepted as true, with negative consequences for the disempowered; see, for example, Gould (1996), which provides an extensive discussion of how commentators have drawn on scientific discourse based upon misinterpreted or biased measurements to support racist theories and policies for decades. Other narratives associating immigrants with criminality are false (Ousey & Kubrin, 2018), but have persisted (Soto-Vasquez, 2023). For example, throughout U.S. history, policymakers and other authorities have employed the language of medicine (a part of the existing power structure) to conflate disease and illness with immigrants and foreigners (Markel & Stern, 2002). By contrast, a society may regard claims as misinformation, subject them to doubt, or simply ignore them, if they are not consistent with dominant power relations, while privileging claims that enforce these power relations (Kuo & Marwick, 2021).

Black Americans in particular have been subject to a long and ongoing history of medical racism dating back to slavery, including medical experimentation, disparities in access to treatment and care, and prejudice in medical decision making (Gamble, 1997; Institute of Medicine, 2003; Nuriddin et al., 2020). Experiences with medical racism, contextualized within broader histories of violence and oppression, contribute to inequality-driven mistrust in science and medical institutions among Black Americans, which can foster resistance to evidence-based communication and provide fertile ground for misinformation (Jaiswal et al., 2020). For example, misinformation narratives that resonate with the collective memory and lived experiences of trauma and discrimination—e.g., that HIV/AIDS or COVID-19 are genocidal plots against communities of color—have circulated widely in Black communities (Collins-Dexter, 2020; Heller, 2015). Fears of medical racism and other community-specific concerns are likewise exploited as the basis of contemporary disinformation campaigns targeting communities of color (Diamond et al., 2022; Lee et al., 2023). Experiences with environmental harms have also contributed to mistrust of science around topics such as water quality (Carrera et al., 2019), sanitation (Flowers, 2020), and disaster resilience and response (Bullard, 2008).

Inequities are also embedded in, and thus provide critical context for, efforts to curb misinformation about science. For example, technology companies have been slow to address misinformation on their platforms, particularly that which circulates among communities of color, and without adequate cultural knowledge about these communities and their information practices, platforms are ill-equipped to intervene effectively (Collins-Dexter, 2020). Similarly, platforms' efforts to monitor and flag misinformation in the United States tend to prioritize misinformation in English, and high-quality public health information is rarely translated; together, this creates information voids among non-English speaking communities (Bonnevie et al., 2023).

What these intersections of inequity and misinformation make clear is that the problem of misinformation about science cannot be disentangled from the legacy of racism and ongoing systemic inequalities in the United States. Approaches to understand and address misinformation (as discussed in Chapter 7) therefore require attention to these inequalities and their impacts, as well as to communities' historical and current experiences with racism and injustice.

Declining Trust in Institutions

Significant declines in Americans' trust and confidence in various institutions of civic life are also relevant to understanding the phenomenon of misinformation about science (Brady & Schlozman, 2022). Trust is defined as the willingness of an actor to depend on and make themselves vulnerable to another entity (Schilke et al., 2021). Trust matters because it affects whether citizens are willing to rely on an institution for information to make decisions.

Particularly for politicized scientific topics, such as climate change, people are more likely to make choices about who and what sources they deem credible based on perceived common interests or shared values (Lupia, 2013). The decision whether to get vaccinated, for example, depends in part on whether one believes the findings from medical science about the perceived benefits, costs, and risks of a vaccine (Jamison et al., 2019b; Larson et al., 2011). Trust in science will affect whether one believes information from the scientific establishment and will affect the quality of sources of information someone consults (e.g., Perlis et al., 2023).

It is important to note that trust in science is not the same as knowledge about scientific facts or knowledge about scientific processes, although researchers have found evidence of some relationships between various concepts, e.g., knowledge of science as a process predicts confidence in scientists to act in the best interests of the public (National Science Board, 2024). A considerable body of research on non-experts' scientific reasoning suggests that there is not a simple, consistent relationship between, for example, trust in science or science literacy, and using scientific information to inform decision making (Drummond & Fischoff, 2017a, 2020). This is in part because these factors interact with other individual-level differences (e.g., worldviews, identity, motivations, risk tolerance) to shape both how people interpret and subsequently use (if at all) such information when making consequential decisions. In addition, many researchers who investigate public perceptions of science have drawn important distinctions between one's ability to correctly identify scientific facts (e.g., Earth orbits the sun) and one's belief that the interests of scientists are aligned with one's own interests and the interests of one's community, or that scientific institutions are trustworthy (e.g., Brossard & Lewenstein, 2010). This further highlights the conditional nature of the relationships among trust in science, scientific reasoning, exposure to science-related information, and decision making (Drummond & Fischhoff, 2020).

Below, we further discuss three areas related to trust: trust in scientific institutions specifically; how political polarization impacts trust in science; and trust in other civic institutions. An additional nuance to consider around how this phenomenon is measured concerns whether surveys assess trust in the institution of science, trust in science-producing institutions like universities, or trust in scientists. It is also important to note that many surveys that assess trust and confidence trends often underrepresent some communities and populations, such as people from low-income households and people of color (Lee & Viswanath, 2020; Viswanath et al., 2022a). In Chapter 6, we discuss how exposure to misinformation within the contexts of these broader trends impacts individuals, communities, and society, and in Chapter 7, we discuss strategies for increasing trust in sources of credible science information, including institutions.

Trust in Scientific Institutions

Trust in science and confidence in scientific institutions to act in ways aligned with public interest have fared better than has trust in most institutions over the last several decades (Brady & Kent, 2022; Krause et al., 2019), though they have not been immune to the fluctuations observed across all institutions and sectors, and there are conflicting signals about whether trust and confidence have been in decline over the last decade. Figure 3-1 shows how trust in the scientific community has fared over the last 50 years (1973–2022), as measured by the General Social Survey (GSS). As the figure

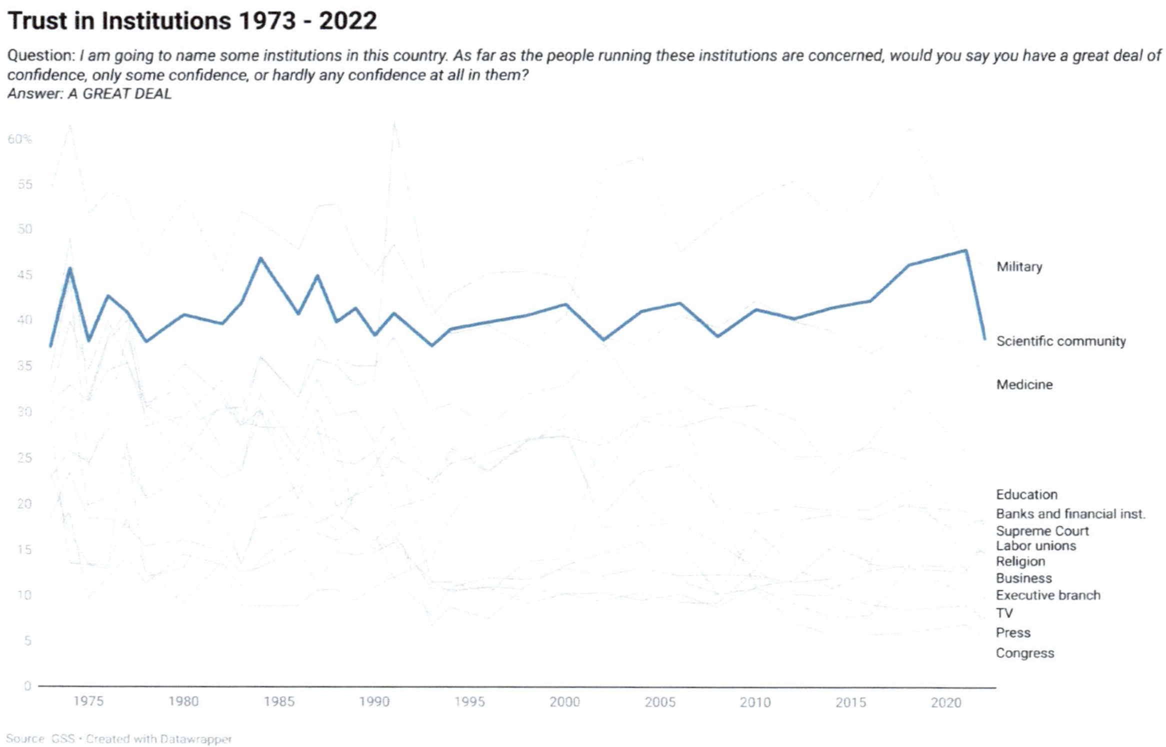

FIGURE 3-1 Trends in trust in U.S. institutions from 1973 to 2022.
SOURCE: Committee generated using data from NORC's General Social Survey Data accessed from the GSS Data Explorer website at gssdataexplorer.norc.org.

illustrates, the scientific community has been consistently one of the most trusted institutions in the United States. Further, while most institutions have suffered a major decline in trust during this period, the scientific community has enjoyed a steady level of public confidence during the past five decades, although with a notable drop from a near-high point of 48% in 2021 to a near low 38% in 2022. Other survey data suggest a significant recent decline in trust in science. The Pew Research Center (2023a) found that in 2019, 73% of U.S. adults believe that science has had a "mostly positive" effect on society; this had dropped to 57% by 2023 (with most of this drop occurring after February 2021, which roughly aligns with the drop as reported in the GSS data). Open and important questions when aligning these data sources are whether this recent drop in trust in science will be enduring; and if enduring, whether it has effects on where people get scientific information and on receptivity to misinformation about science.

Since the 1970s, there has been an unambiguous drop in levels of trust in specific institutions that are involved in the production of scientific knowledge. The percentage of people expressing a lot of confidence in medicine has plummeted from a high point of 62% in 1974, to an all-time low point of 33% in 2022; education from a high point of 49% in 1974 to just 19% in 2022; and major companies (the source of much science) from a high of 31%, last reached in 1987, to 15% in 2022. Thus, while confidence in the scientific community in the abstract has remained fairly constant, institutions that produce science-based information have seen much larger declines in confidence over the last 50 years. This variation in trust in the various institutions that produce science in turn may drive which scientific findings are trusted by whom (Pechar et al., 2018).

Public perception of science also comprises various dimensions, and not all perceptions of science move in lockstep. The notion that scientific innovation might disrupt social stability in an unwelcome way appears to have increased in the United States in recent decades, for example. Between 2014 and 2022, roughly half of respondents on the GSS agreed or strongly agreed that "science makes our way of life change too fast," an average increase of nearly 10% from levels reported from 1995 to 2012 (National Science Board, 2024). Public perceptions can also vary across various scientific fields and domains and across time. According to data reported for the 3M State of Science Index survey, for example, more people reported thinking "a lot" about the impact of science on their everyday lives in summer 2020 than was the case in fall 2019, likely because of the emergence of COVID-19 (National Science Board, 2024). Perceptions of the trustworthiness of research on different topics can vary as well. For example, perceptions of the trustworthiness of self-driving vehicles appear to change as people gain experience with these vehicles (Tenhundfeld et al., 2020). Despite general confidence in science and scientists in the United

States, it is important to note that public perceptions of novel and emergent research may differ from more established topics and that people may not consistently view all topics of scientific inquiry as equally the purview of "science" broadly considered.

Political Polarization and Trust in Science

This apparent steadiness in confidence in scientific institutions also obscures the emergence of a large partisan and ideological divide in the last generation. Polarization has been conceptualized as the clustering of opposing opinions into two groups, where shared opinions become the basis on which groups identify and interact with each other (Judge et al., 2023). Opinions from elites can further contribute to the tendency of people within polarized groups to associate only with those who share their opinions and avoid those with different views, particularly those who are more politically active or who hold more extreme views (Judge et al., 2023). Cognitive processes can also contribute to polarization. For example, as people encounter information that both supports and counters their existing opinion, they may make sense of that information in ways that serve to reinforce or strengthen their original opinion. Generally, from 1973 to 2000, substantially more Republicans indicated they had "a great deal" of confidence in science than Democrats or Independents (Figure 3-2). In the period from 2000 to 2006, confidence in science was roughly equal across all three groups (Figure 3-2). However, between 2008 and 2022, there has been a widening gap in trust in science by partisan identity, with 53% of Democrats, for example, indicating a lot of confidence in science as of 2022, and 22% of Republicans indicating this same level of confidence (Figure 3-2). Notably, the percentage of Republicans indicating a great deal of confidence in science has dropped by nearly half since 2018 (Figure 3-2). Gauchat (2012) identifies a similar but significantly earlier trend with respect to political ideology (e.g., conservative, liberal, or moderate). Additionally, a similar trend with respect to educational and medical institutions has been observed, with an overall decline in trust in both institutions across the political spectrum since 2018, and in some cases, there are notable gaps by political ideology (Davern et al., 2024; see Figure 3-3).

Affective polarization—increased animosity toward an opposing group/party versus affinity for one's own—has also shown a marked increase in recent years (Druckman et al., 2021; also see Jost et al., 2022). This increased animosity reinforces (and is reinforced by) trends toward fewer shared agreed upon facts and approaches to understanding the world (Jenke, 2023; also see Druckman et al., 2024a). For example, polarization increases the likelihood that people will accept new information that conforms with pre-existing beliefs and commitments more readily than that which challenges

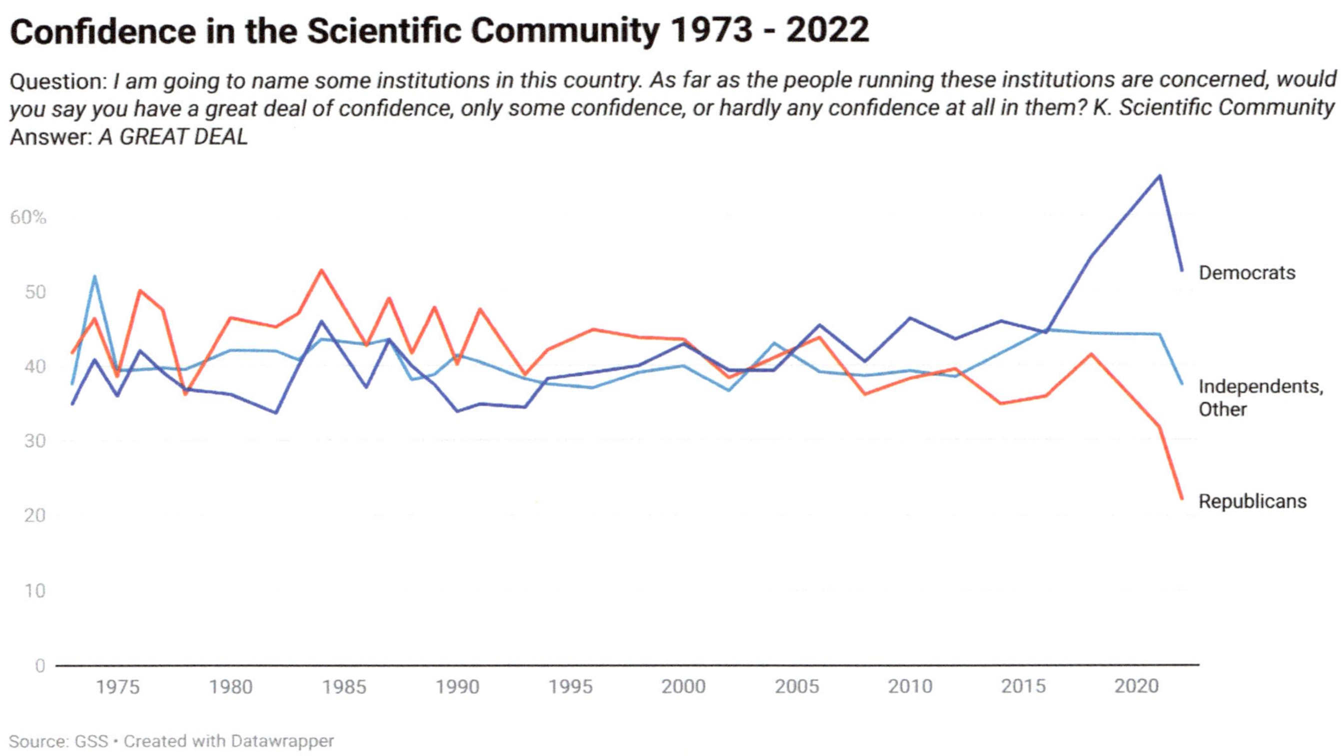

FIGURE 3-2 Trends in confidence in the scientific community based on partisan identity.
SOURCE: Committee generated using data from NORC's General Social Survey Data accessed from the GSS Data Explorer website at gssdataexplorer.norc.org.

those commitments (Jenke, 2023; Su, 2022). Political polarization may differ by topic, and a recent review suggests actual polarization around environmental issues may be less than people perceive them to be (Judge et al, 2023). Further, trust in individuals—scientists or doctors—may also differ from trust or confidence in the institution of science overall, including among the Black and Latino communities (Pew Research Center, 2022, 2024b), across a range of scientific topics.

Although partisanship and political ideology are sources of polarization, other beliefs may play a role in ideological divides. Patterns of science skepticism can vary by topic (e.g., climate change versus vaccines) and are affected by beliefs that are more nuanced than political partisanship. For example, science skepticism has been shown to be predicted by religiosity, social identity, and worldviews (e.g., individual freedom), which are not solely held by people of one political party (Rutjens et al., 2021). Other scholars have also found that focusing on partisan identity alone to explain differences in trust in science may obscure important nuances in how ideological beliefs and views about science intersect (McCright et al., 2013). Chapter 6 provides a more complete discussion about how these factors intersect to shape individual beliefs related to science information and the likelihood of holding misbeliefs associated with misinformation.

Trust in Other Civic Institutions

In contrast to trust in science and scientists, trust and confidence in other key institutions such as the press, media, and education has dropped, in some cases precipitously. Most notably, while 28% of Americans indicated a great deal of confidence in the press in the 1976 GSS, this number dropped to 7% in 2022 (see Figure 3-1), where 11% of Democrats and 3% of Republicans indicated a lot of trust in the press (see Figure 3-3). This has potentially invited or encouraged people and communities to seek out information about many issues or topics (including scientific and health-related ones) from a broader set of sources than they may have in the past. At the same time, declining societal trust in and reliance on some traditional sources of authority may be creating further openings for misinformation about science (and health) to spread more rapidly as people seek out ways to make sense of an increasingly complex world.

Societal Forces That May Warrant Further Study

As scientists seek to better understand the changing patterns in trust in institutions overall, other social and societal factors may warrant further study. The role of values is one such factor (see Sagiv & Schwartz, 2022

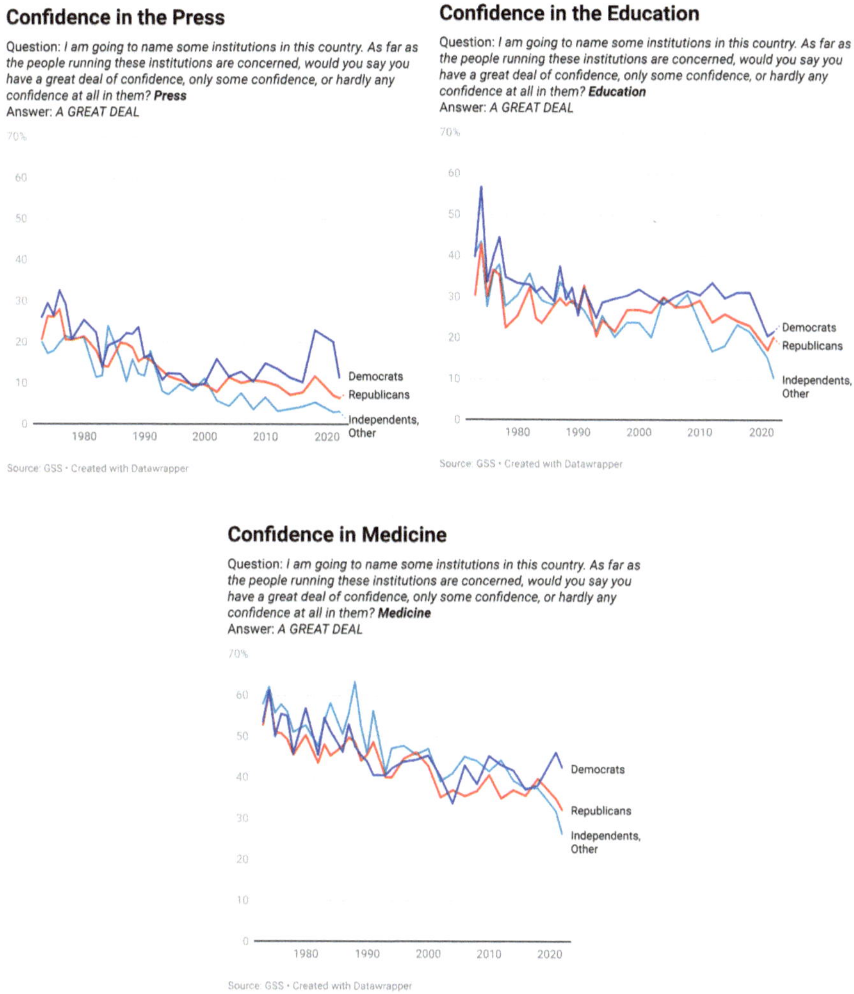

FIGURE 3-3 Trends in trust in U.S. institutions based on partisan identity.
SOURCE: Committee generated using data from NORC's General Social Survey Data accessed from the GSS Data Explorer website at gssdataexplorer.norc.org.

for a detailed review of personal values). In the United States and globally, there has been a significant increase over the past few decades in people's endorsement of individualism as a core value (Santos et al., 2017). Individualism refers to core beliefs, values, or worldviews that "promotes a view of the self as self-directed, autonomous, and separate from others" (Santos et al., 2017, p. 1228). It is possible that a growing emphasis on individualism both at the individual and societal levels plays a role in increasing interest in self-reliance to examine evidence related to issues of personal, community, or societal importance, rather than interest in relying on individuals with expertise or scientific institutions for advice. Similarly, research points to a positive relationship between prioritizing values around benevolence and concern for others and nature (as opposed to self-preservation and advancement) to pro-environmental behaviors and decision making (Sagiv & Schwartz, 2022; Steg, 2016).

An overall decline in factors associated with social capital, such as good will, empathy, trust among people, trust in civic institutions, and civic orientation, in the United States over generations is a second factor that could play a role in explaining societal trends relevant to misinformation about science (Aldrich & Meyer, 2015; Putnam, 1993, 2000). Virtual spaces created by various internet platform technologies—search, social media, encrypted messaging, etc.—offer the potential, at least, to either undermine or promote social capital through effects on networks, information, and norms (González-Bailón & Lelkes, 2022). While it is clear that virtual communities are different than from traditional communities (Memmi, 2008), the circumstances in which such communities facilitate or undermine social cohesion is less clear (Chambers, 2013; Percy & Murray, 2010; Zhou, 2020). For example, sharing of misinformation on social media may in part be driven by a desire to either maintain or build social capital within a group, although some work finds that strong social ties can also increase the effectiveness of efforts to debunk misinformation (Pasquetto et al., 2022). Others have posited that declining social capital may be linked to more extreme groups that rely more on ideology than on evidence (Lewandowsky et al., 2017).

CHARACTERIZING THE 21ST CENTURY INFORMATION ECOSYSTEM

The nexus between people, societies, and the information they are collectively producing, exposed to, and consuming comprises the information ecosystem that people experience. In fact, this interplay of individual characteristics, social forces, and technological changes means that there is not one shared experience of the information ecosystem. In this networked ecosystem, people can move between their in-person and online networks (Edgerly & Xu, 2024) and can vary dramatically in their access to accurate scientific information and exposure to misinformation. Algorithmic curation and targeting based on demographics and online activity (Brossard & Scheufele, 2022) shape how each person experiences the information ecosystem. Patterns of trust play a role in the sources for scientific information that people seek and believe on- and offline (Green et al., 2023). Moreover, economic forces are reshaping journalism, with a decline in the resources dedicated to science reporting and local news, in ways that affect all people, but may particularly affect people living outside of major cities (Kim et al., 2020a).

The range of technologies that have comprised our public information environment in the past 100 years reveals various shifts in key dimensions of those technologies that hold important implications for understanding misinformation about science. These include the level of information density or detail made possible by those technologies along with the formats (e.g., written word vs. audio-visual) and timing (e.g., delayed vs. immediate) in which information is transmitted and consumed (e.g., hierarchical vs. participatory). The past century has also witnessed moments of prominence for print media, which largely required audiences to read written content reflecting events occurring a day or a week ago, to the rise of electronic broadcast media, which delivered sounds and images to people in their homes relatively instantaneously via a limited spectrum of available frequencies on public airwaves. The latter half of the 20th century marked a shift to video content delivery via cable—for those households that could afford subscription fees—and more recent years have seen the rise of content distribution via networked computers (i.e., the internet). Structures of the contemporary information ecosystem may contribute to facilitating the dynamics of misinformation about science. Below we discuss some of the most significant structural aspects to consider: audience fragmentation and hybrid media; the emergence of new information technologies and platforms, including artificial intelligence (AI); and context collapse.

Audience Fragmentation and Hybrid Media

More recently, the information ecosystem has expanded and become substantially more complex, fragmented, and hybrid. The large audience share enjoyed by just a few broadcast television networks in the 1970s has fractured, and now many different outlets have emerged to compete for attention. For-profit media organizations continue to aggregate audience exposures over time into mass audiences for the purposes of advertising sales, but nonetheless, even when relatively large numbers of people have engaged content, individual audience members are not always interconnected with one another (Webster & Phalen, 1996). The fragmentation of audiences has not slowed the general spread of some content, per se; in fact, the availability of peer-to-peer diffusion through electronically connected social networks has sped up the pace of information (and misinformation) sharing in the 21st century relative to the 20th century.

Audience fragmentation has occurred alongside and intertwined with the rise of "hybrid media," where information and misinformation can flow among and between peer-to-peer social networks and mass media outlets.

Indeed, these communications channels are so interconnected at this point that the current information infrastructure in the United States, at least as it is available to many people, can be viewed as a hybrid array of social media platforms, broadcast channels, and media organizations that produce a range of live content and content available for asynchronous engagement by various audience members (Chadwick, 2017). The contemporary information ecosystem is a web of organizations and social networks and individual people operating simultaneously to engage, deliver, and share content with one another; as a result, in recent decades, there have been increased efforts among researchers to consider possibilities for cross-level interactions between interpersonal and mass communication channels (e.g., Altay et al., 2023; Southwell, 2005; Weeks & Southwell, 2010). There is increasing interplay and fluidity between people's online and offline communication environments (e.g., Hampton et al., 2017). An individual can interact with a friend or colleague in person in one moment and then on social media in the next. Online personal messaging platforms, such as WhatsApp and Facebook Messenger—which people often use to communicate with existing strong-tie networks of friends, family, co-workers, and community members in closed, one-on-one or small group conversations—further blur the lines between online/offline and public/private communication (Chadwick et al., 2023). Information readily flows from more public platforms like news websites or Facebook into private messaging apps, where information sharing is highly personalized, and interpersonal factors like social trust and conflict avoidance shape people's interactions with information and misinformation (Chadwick et al., 2023; Malhotra & Pearce, 2022; Masip et al., 2021).

In the contemporary ecosystem, information can more easily cross geographic, linguistic, and cultural borders than in the past, through and across global platforms like Facebook, WeChat, WhatsApp, Telegram, Signal, YouTube, and X. In addition, global migration has given rise to diasporic communities that form transnational information networks with unique communication patterns and practices (Nguyễn et al., 2022). For diasporic communities, media—especially digital media—play an important role in building and sustaining relationships in both their home and host countries (Candidatu & Ponzanesi, 2022). Some communities may rely on these sources to fill information voids when information in their native language is unavailable (Asian American Disinformation Table, 2022). Encrypted messaging applications like WhatsApp, Signal, Telegram, and WeChat are particularly popular among immigrant populations in the United States for their ability to support private communications and connect sub-populations that share identities (Trauthig & Woolley, 2023). Other data indicate that some communities rely more heavily than others on some platforms for information. For example, some surveys find that

Latino populations use Facebook, YouTube, and Whatsapp at higher percentages than other populations (Equis Institute, 2022). Finally, the openness of these systems makes them vulnerable to disinformation campaigns (Johnson & Marcellino, 2021).

Emergence of New Information Technologies and Platforms

There have been dramatic shifts in journalism and media production and dissemination over the past two decades that have important implications for the spread and potential impacts of misinformation about science. In the 21st century, the emergence of online platforms—including certain social media applications, large search engines, and websites hosted on the internet (e.g., Abbott, 2007)—has enabled the creation of a large volume of content through an increasing array of creators with limited moderation, increasing personalization of content and online social groups, and the consumption of content outside of its intended contexts (i.e., context collapse—discussed in more detail below; Kümpel, 2020). These features have enabled a qualitative shift in how people consume, interact with, and share information. Rapid advances in artificial intelligence have the potential to further transform the information ecosystem.

Increasing Volume of Content and Limited Moderation

There has been a major increase in the sheer volume of content (Gitlin, 2007), and technological changes have reduced the cost of producing and sharing information, allowing those who previously only consumed information to also become information producers and disseminators (Young & Miller, 2023c). Removing barriers to entry to the digital information space offers both tremendous opportunities to share creative expression, increase access, spread power more equitably, and promote understanding, yet may also incidentally devalue or make it more difficult to discern scientific or medical expertise. This reduction in the "barriers to entry" in the contemporary information ecosystem thus has critical implications for the (intentional and unintentional) production and dissemination of misinformation about science. At the same time, there are also "data voids" where online searches fail to provide results or only return unreliable information that can be exploited by purveyors of disinformation, such as by capitalizing on breaking news, by creating new terms or by co-opting old terms that are not typically used by other content producers (Golebiewski & boyd, 2019). In science, some of these voids may relate to conspiracy theories or rumors that scientists have not directly addressed or debunked.

This abundance of content produced by an increasing array of creators has changed the dynamics of how individuals, communities, and societies interact with information. Where high-quality information was previously scarce, the internet enables an abundance, leading some to suggest the limiting resource is increasingly people's attention (Pedersen et al., 2021). At the same time, this new ecosystem also includes large amounts of low-quality or questionable information, including about science. The World Health Organization (WHO) calls this phenomenon an infodemic, where abundant information of variable quality makes it challenging to distinguish between true and false information (Briand et al., 2021; WHO, n.d.). While the term is heavily associated with the recent COVID-19 pandemic, infodemics also manifested during other public health emergencies, including the 1918 influenza pandemic, HIV/AIDS epidemic, and SARS-CoV-1 outbreaks (Tomes & Parry, 2022). Online search is particularly important in helping people sort through the enormous amount of information available online (Brossard & Scheufele, 2013).

Online platforms currently experience limited government regulation, discussed in more detail in Chapter 7, and even broadcast television content is monitored only partially and in a post-hoc fashion for health claim accuracy (Southwell & Thorson, 2015). This lack of (government-led) regulatory oversight in turn holds critical implications for the nature of the information ecosystem that individuals and communities inhabit, as various entities in that system (e.g., privately held companies that host social media platforms) have taken on management and moderation roles to varying extents and for diverse reasons that only sometimes align with the public interest. Moreover, online platforms have shown uneven and often tardy enforcement of their own policies regarding offensive content (The Virality Project, 2022).

Personalization

The abundance of media options now available in the digital environment gives audiences the opportunity to selectively curate and personalize what kinds of information to consume (Prior, 2007). Algorithms also continue to play an important role in shaping the content people consume (Brossard & Scheufele, 2022); however, substantial evidence exists that individuals selectively expose themselves to media sources and content based on their beliefs, interests, and motivations (Feldman et al., 2014, 2018; Muise et al., 2022; Mummolo, 2016; Prior, 2007; Robertson et al., 2023; Stroud, 2008; Wojcieszak, 2021). Moreover, individuals develop different patterns of media use across combinations of media platforms, often referred to as "media repertoires" (Hasebrink & Popp, 2006). These repertoires vary according to the background characteristics of users, such as demographics, socio-economic status, and levels of political engagement (Edgerly et al., 2018; Kim, 2016). Social media platforms have additional features that provide social cues (e.g., likes, follows, and comments) that can personalize distortions of majority opinions. In other words, people receive information about the preferences of their own homophilic social networks but this can create a false impression of a more widely-held consensus (Lorenz-Spreen et al., 2020). These same features can also reinforce existing opinions or increase extremism.

The evidence related to the role of social media in creating echo chambers is more complex. With the rise of polarization within American society (Druckman & Levy, 2022; Iyengar et al., 2019), there are concerns that media consumers are increasingly siloed in ideological spaces that magnify existing beliefs and messages and provide insulation from opposing views, either accidentally or through purposeful exclusion (Arguedas et al., 2022; Nguyen, 2020). The findings are mixed for the prevalence of such spaces related to politics, with more recent studies finding more evidence of echo chambers (Cinelli et al., 2021; González-Bailón et al., 2023; Nyhan et al., 2023) than older studies (Dubois & Blank, 2018; Guess, 2021; Guess et al., 2018a). However, a recent literature review also found comparatively less evidence for how these insulated groups may form around science topics than exists for understanding how they form around political topics (Arguedas et al., 2022). Another recent review focused on the nature of the information environment related to environmental decision making similarly concluded that most people in the United States access and engage with diverse information, though this may be less true for people who hold more extreme views (Judge et al., 2023). Methodological differences may partly explain the mixed findings; some studies relying on digital trace data find more evidence of their existence than those that rely on self-reported data (Terren & Borge, 2021).

Artificial Intelligence

Technological developments in AI are evolving rapidly. Though much remains to be learned about how AI will shape the information ecosystem, it has increased the public availability of online tools that generate text, audio, images, and video that accurately mimic human activity. For example, large language models (LLMs) such as OpenAI's ChatGPT and Google's Gemini (formerly Bard) simulate the experience of chatting textually with a seemingly omniscient interlocutor. In addition, generative AI is proliferating, and many technology companies are integrating their own LLMs into their products, increasingly changing how people search and receive search results across platforms. These tools can also generate authentic-looking scientific papers (Májovský et al., 2023) and scientific visualizations (Kim et al., 2024), and there is increasing evidence of their undeclared use in published papers (Joelving, 2023) and in peer-review (Liang et al., 2024). To this end, scientific publishers have published commentaries on the topic, specifically regarding AI-generated fraud and how to mitigate its spread (Alvarez et al., 2024; Bergstrom & West, 2023; Jones, 2024).

Indeed, such technological advancements have raised concerns about the role of AI in both proliferating and curtailing misinformation, as several deepfakes—AI-generated images and videos that look real—featuring prominent individuals have gone viral on social media (Ellery, 2023; Metz, 2021). In addition, Meta, the parent company to Facebook, released a large language model (LLM) specifically designed to assist scientists with tasks such as summarizing academic papers, solving math problems, writing scientific code, and annotating molecules and proteins; but this technology only lasted three days because of its inaccuracies (Heaven, 2022; West, 2023). While empirical research on AI tools is limited given the recency of these technologies at the time of this writing, there are concerns about their capacity to generate convincing misinformation (Kreps et al., 2022; Zhou et al., 2023), including generating scientific citations that do not exist (Walters & Wilder, 2023). At the same time, these tools have also been hailed for their proficiency at detecting misinformation (Ozbay & Alatas, 2020). Indeed, automated misinformation detection has been a major research goal among more technical researchers of the topic (e.g., Joshi et al., 2023), although this is arguably a form of "solutionism" (Morozov, 2013)—the idea that all societal challenges can be solved with technological solutions—that makes unwarranted assumptions about the objectivity or universal applicability of machine-generated decisions (Byrum & Benjamin, 2022) or assumes that technology can provide the solution to more complex social challenges (Angel & boyd, 2024). Importantly, these new generative information technologies dramatically lower the production cost of information[1] and therefore increase the potential for a massive flood of information of all modalities and quality.

Decontextualization and Context Collapse

One consequence of the shifts in information production, distribution, and consumption described above is that people are now increasingly exposed to information that lacks context and nuance. One specific form of this decontextualization is "context collapse", which refers to when discrete pieces of information as well as larger narratives or stories about some issue or topic intended for one group become visible to a group other than the intended audience (Davis & Jurgenson, 2014; Marwick & boyd, 2011; Pearson, 2021). Such context collapse has implications for the spread, consumption, and potential impacts of misinformation about

[1]Although the production costs are lower for an individual, the environmental costs of generative AI are high (Chien et al., 2023).

science on individuals, communities, and society as a whole. For example, scientists may communicate with one another in a manner that presumes common assumptions (e.g., non-colloquial meanings of widely used terms) and knowledge bases in ways that can mislead non-experts (Somerville & Hassol, 2011); as a result, when communications between scientists that use such words move into the public domain, they may be interpreted by non-scientists in ways that are highly inconsistent with the original intended meanings. For example, a vaccine manufacturer drew an analogy between computer software and mRNA, describing mRNA as "the software of life" (Larson & Broniatowski, 2021); however, the software analogy was not literal. The analogy was made public on a website that did not make this clear and was seen by individuals who may have held different assumptions, including those that attributed malicious intent to vaccine manufacturers. This contributed to the conspiracy that mRNA vaccines can "change your DNA" and can "program" vaccinated individuals in a manner that would ultimately impinge upon their autonomy.

Relatedly, it is also common to consume information without the benefit of meaningful context, and in formats and time periods that differ from the original creation (Brandtzaeg & Lüders, 2018). Segments of original content, including misinformation, can continue to "live" actively online, disappearing for a time only to reappear in people's feeds long after an initial event or headline has happened. Theoretically, this content can live on indefinitely, although some evidence exists that collective attention on topics of public discussion is getting shorter and shorter (Lorenz-Spreen, et al., 2019). For example, a person's first encounter with a video clip or a print news story may not occur in the format of original broadcast but rather via peer-sharing on a social media platform or through a mobile phone text message. These variations in how people encounter the same information (or misinformation) matter because different platforms differ in the amount of explanation and context that people encounter. For example, the immediate impact that a video clip about a piece of contested or controversial science might have on an individual may be quite different for someone who sees the video embedded within the original news broadcast (which may provide much more context to inform viewers about the significance of the specific clip) versus for someone who only sees the clip shared with them by a friend on social media (which both removes the broader context and sends a socially relevant signal regarding the importance of that clip).

One set of implications of increasing decontextualization and context collapse relates to the ways in which these phenomena affect what sources of information or knowledge are viewed by various groups as legitimate, authentic, and trustworthy. Unrestricted exposure to several competing narratives, as can frequently happen in our current information ecosystem, can undermine trust in traditional sources of legitimacy, including scientific discourse (Lyotard, 1984). Lack of context appears to decrease the salience of specific information sources more than does, for example, changes in the simple volume of content. This means that the nature and format of the "encounters" that people have with information (especially via online platforms) may hold consequences for misinformation acceptance more than does the sheer torrent of misinformation available to an audience.

Complex Interactions and Consequences

It is important to note that not all changes in the broader information environment and context of contemporary life necessarily push in the direction of greater generation, dissemination, and/or uptake of misinformation about science. Under some conditions, for example, reduced barriers to entry into the digital information space may lead to better, fairer, and more just use of valid scientific information in collective or societal decision making, while decreasing the impact of misinformation. And as certain institutions lose some of their hold on power (e.g., power to define "correct" knowledge)—including ones with long histories of discrimination against certain groups and the wielding of authority and power to shape cultural and political narratives—others may gain prominence and broader acceptance, with important implications for managing the spread and/or impact of misinformation about science. For example, scientists and decision makers (e.g., natural resource managers, policymakers, and regulators) are increasingly recognizing the importance of Indigenous and traditional (ecological) knowledge, particularly around issues of sustainability and resource management (Whyte et al., 2015). These represent shifts toward valuing "the actions, strategies, resources, and knowledge that Indigenous groups mobilize to navigate environmental change" (Reo et al., 2017, p. 203).

FACTORS SHAPING THE SCIENCE INFORMATION ENVIRONMENT

The ways in which people access, engage with, share, and interpret science information is occurring increasingly online in an information environment that is rapidly transforming. Brossard & Scheufele (2022) argue:

> [...] the greatest challenge that scientists must address as a community stems from a fundamental change in how scientific information gets shared, amplified, and received in online environments. With the emergence of virtually unlimited storage space, rapidly growing computational capacity, and increasingly sophisticated artificial intelligence, the societal balance of power for scientific information has shifted away from legacy

> media, government agencies, and the scientific community. Now, social media platforms are the central gatekeeper of information and communication about science. (p. 614)

Moreover, existing social divisions in access and attention to the information circulating within the science information environment are both replicated and reinforced. For example, research shows that among U.S. adults, those with higher levels of education and higher family income express more interest in science news (Saks & Tyson, 2022), and people often consume science information based on their existing beliefs and social networks (Feldman et al., 2014; Jang, 2014; Yeo et al., 2015). As science information is increasingly shared on social media platforms, automated algorithms based on users' personal profiles govern the visibility of this content, determining whether a given user is likely to encounter credible science information or not (Brossard & Scheufele, 2022). This topic is addressed in more detail in Chapter 5.

The Quality of News Production, News Deserts, and Resource Constraints

General news outlets are a chief source of science information among Americans (Funk et al., 2017). There are an increasing number of "news deserts"[2] precipitated by two decades of newsroom cutbacks and the closing of local newspapers (Abernathy, 2018). More broadly, media deregulation, beginning in the 1980s and culminating with the passage of the Telecommunications Act of 1996, consolidated media ownership into an increasingly small number of conglomerates, thereby limiting the diversity of available information outlets and imposing commercial pressures on journalism (McChesney, 2015). These news deserts can be especially pronounced in some communities, particularly in rural areas (Abernathy, 2022).

Although science journalism as a field grew in the mid-20th century and accelerated with the space race (beginning with the launch of Sputnik in 1957), seismic shifts in the media landscape since the start of the 21st century and corresponding budgetary constraints have led many news organizations to eliminate or downsize their science reporting efforts (Guenther, 2019; Russell, 2006). The result is that science news in such outlets is of variable quality. Science reporting is often guided by journalistic values and norms that prioritize public attention over careful consideration of scientific method and evidence (Dunwoody, 2021). Many journalists lack specialized training in science (Dunwoody, 2021), which can make it

[2]"A community, either rural or urban, with limited access to the sort of credible and comprehensive news and information that feeds democracy at the grassroots level" (Abernathy, n.d.).

challenging for them to correctly interpret scientific research and present it in the appropriate context. Science news is also increasingly intersecting with politics (Russell, 2006) or is politicized (Chinn et al., 2020; Hart et al., 2020), a source of frustration for many news consumers (Saks & Tyson, 2022). Moreover, the mediated interactions between journalists, scientists, and the public, as enabled by social media platforms and other digital communication technologies, add to the complexity of the science information environment (Dunwoody, 2021). Increasingly, power resides in control over the flow of information, not its creation (Chadwick, 2017). The diversity and fragmentation of the hybrid media environment has weakened the grip of journalistic and political elites over the flow of information, and has opened the door for a diversity of communicators, including ordinary citizens, to intervene in public discourse in newly expansive ways.

Competing Interests and Public Relations

The science information environment is also increasingly competitive, particularly in the United States' diverse and decentralized information ecosystem, which has relatively low support for publicly-funded independent media (Neff & Pickard, 2021). This means that voices from the scientific community are increasingly competing with well-resourced entities and actors that vie for control to shape public discourse, including about scientific topics. To that end, organizations—ranging from powerful corporations to smaller advocacy groups—employ public relations firms to conduct "information and influence campaigns" that aim to shift public opinion and political decision making in their favor (Brulle & Werthman, 2021; Manheim, 2011). Although public relations strategies related to science issues are not new, it has become easier for professional communicators in a hybrid media system to manipulate, target, and amplify misinformation about science, especially in a largely unregulated information ecosystem where actors with the most resources have outsized influence on shaping public narratives (Pickard, 2019). In the news industry, boundaries between editorial and advertising are eroding, giving advertisers, which are a key source of financial support for many news outlets, increased influence over the quality of science information available to the public. For example, brand journalism, which includes native advertising and content marketing, is designed to make corporate promotion appear indistinguishable from objective news stories and can be finely targeted to specific audiences (Serazio, 2021). Some scholars have called for new approaches to media governance and business models to provide safeguards against undue influence over news content by advertisers (Napoli, 2019).

Changing Norms and Practices of Science Communication by Scientists

The science information environment is also shaped by the approaches used by scientists to disseminate their research, both to their peers and to the wider public. The open science movement—a broad term that refers to various efforts in recent years to make scientific research and its dissemination more broadly transparent and accessible to all of society—has brought more transparency and greater access to scientific research (Lupia, 2021), giving rise to new ways of disseminating research findings. In recent history, peer-reviewed journals have been the gatekeepers of scientific research. New publishing models are challenging that status quo. For example, preprints—posted by researchers in online open access repositories (e.g., arXiv, bioRxiv, medRxiv, SocArXiv, OSF Preprints, SSRN) before they have been peer-reviewed and accepted for publication by a journal—make new work rapidly available to any audience. Preprints allow scientists to make their research promptly and freely accessible to other scientists, accelerating the dissemination of research relative to the typical peer-review publication process, which can take months or years. Yet findings from preprints, which have not been formally vetted by the scientific community, can prove to be short-lived, flawed, or incorrect. Some preprints never end up published, and if published, the final article may be substantially revised relative to its preprint version as the result of scrutiny by peer-reviewers.

Open science initiatives often encourage (and universities and funders sometimes require) scientists to publish their peer-reviewed research in an open access format, meaning that research articles are made freely available to audiences without subscription charges. This move toward greater accessibility is important and broadly beneficial in many respects, including positive impacts on improving equitable access to scientific knowledge for communities and groups who cannot afford massive subscription fees, and potentially increasing the perception of the trustworthiness of scientists. This practice is more well-established in some disciplines than others.

An unintended byproduct of open access publishing is the growth of so-called predatory scientific journals (Swire-Thompson & Lazer, 2022). Predatory journals publish science entirely for profit and do not subject research to rigorous peer-review, essentially creating a "pay-to-play" model that can become a conduit for misinformation. Authors publish in these journals for a variety of reasons, including inexperience and professional pressures to publish frequently; predatory journals also allow bad actors to spread false scientific claims by providing a veneer of legitimacy conferred through journal publication (Swire-Thompson & Lazer, 2022; West & Bergstrom, 2021). Articles published in predatory journals are widely accessible, including through scholarly databases and search engines, with most lay audiences as well as scientists outside of their disciplines unable to discern their legitimacy (Swire-Thompson & Lazer, 2022). Furthermore, leading academic search engine algorithms, such as those used by Google Scholar, automatically index content that contains text formatted as academic references, thus facilitating the dissemination of content that has a surface similarity to credible academic sources. For example, several newsletters from the National Vaccine Information Center—a known source of vaccine misinformation (Kalichman et al., 2022)—are indexed on Google Scholar, presumably because they contain references to academic sources.

SUMMARY

Misinformation about science is a phenomenon that exists within and as a part of a broader social, political, and technological context, including the rapidly evolving information ecosystems that people inhabit in 21st century contemporary society. Table 3-1 provides an overview of the factors discussed in this chapter and their implications. This broader context holds significant implications for more fully understanding the origins, flow, spread, and impacts of misinformation about science, as well as the potential for addressing negative impacts on individuals, communities, and society as a whole. Declining trust in institutions and its intersection with partisanship and structural inequities are two salient features of this wider context that shape how people interact with information from science.

Those forces combined with a changing media landscape mean that people experience the information ecosystem quite differently. Particular features of the contemporary information ecosystem, including the fact that online platforms have greatly reduced barriers to accessing and producing information in part because they are under-moderated, are rapidly shifting the types, volume, and nature of science-related information that people encounter over the course of their daily lives. Importantly, it is increasingly difficult for people to discern accurate and credible information from and about science. It is also more possible than ever for people to exist in different, fragmented information ecosystems that online platforms, other media, and interpersonal spaces make possible and readily accessible. While the evidence about the extent to which people exist in echo chambers or filter bubbles is mixed, it is clear that the contemporary information ecosystem makes it more possible than ever for people to be exposed to content—often consumed without important, original context and nuance. Competing and vested interests as well as intentional public relations efforts are often able to capitalize on the affordances of this information ecosystem. In addition, shifts in the norms of science toward open science, news deserts and other challenges in science journalism create additional complexities. In short, understanding the challenges faced related to misinformation about science and how to address them requires understanding the broader system.

TABLE 3-1 Contextual Features and Factors That Influence Misinformation About Science

Contextual features/factors		Explanation/definition	Implications for misinformation about science
Systemic factors shaping how people interact with information	Role of science in society	A balance between the credibility and social capital of science to inform decision making and the power of people to make choices in a democratic society	Technological shifts make it more possible for people to disseminate information on an equal footing with science; misinformation can disrupt being able to make informed choices in a democracy
	Structural Inequalities	Inequalities based on education level, race or ethnicity, primary language, or geography	Societal factors shape the information ecosystems that people experience; they can limit access to high-quality information from science, increase exposure to misinformation; and increase the potential for harm
	Trust in institutions	General decline in trust in many institutions, including education, medicine, and the press; political divides in trust in science and media	People seek or encounter information about science from less reliable sources
Features of the information ecosystem	New information technologies and platforms	Social media and other internet-based large platforms emerge in late 20th/early 21st century	Massive changes to production, dissemination, and consumption of information about science, including entry of many new communicators who previously had limited/no access to large audiences
	Audience fragmentation	Different audiences distributed across different media, channels, outlets	Fewer very broadly shared trusted sources of information about science means different groups can seek out and/or be exposed to very different pieces of (mis)information about science
	Hybrid media	Information ecosystem consists of different channels and media types	Science information travels quickly across media types/ platforms, sometimes losing or shifting important context that produces misinformation

continued

TABLE 3-1 Continued

Contextual features/factors		Explanation/definition	Implications for misinformation about science
Features of the information ecosystem (continued)	Artificial Intelligence	"[T]echnology that enables computers and machines to simulate human learning, comprehension, problem solving, decision making, creativity and autonomy" (Stryker & Kavlakoglu, 2024)	Potential for negative effects include flooding of system with personalized, plausible misinformation about science, as well as for positive effects from its potential to identify and correct misinformation or make correct information from science more easily accessible
Factors shaping the science information environment	Quality and quantity of science news production	Decrease in number of dedicated science journalists; areas of the country without local news coverage; decreased funding for science journalism	Decreases in locally contextualized evidence
	Competing interests and public relations	Increasingly competitive science information environment	More points of entry for bad actors to manipulate, target, and amplify misinformation about science
	Open science movements and professional norms	Growth of preprints, availability of data	Potential for negative effects from context collapse with scientific intramural discourse and broader public discourse as well as for positive effects from increasing free access to scientific information

SOURCE: Committee generated.

Conclusion 3-1: Though inaccuracy in scientific claims has been a long-standing public concern, recent changes within the information ecosystem have accelerated widespread visibility of such claims. These changes include:

- *the emergence of new information and communication technologies that have facilitated access, production, and sharing of science information at greater volume and velocity than before,*
- *the rise of highly participatory online environments that have made it more difficult to assess scientific expertise and credibility of sources of science information, and*
- *the decline in the capacity of news media that has likely reduced both the production and quality of science news and information.*

Conclusion 3-2: Trust in science has declined in recent years, yet remains relatively high compared to trust in other civic institutions. Although confidence in the scientific community varies significantly by partisan identity, patterns of trust in science across demographic groups also vary as a function of the specific topic, the science organization or scientists being considered, or respective histories and experiences.

4

Sources of Misinformation About Science

Misinformation comes from a wide range of sources that employ a number of different strategies and tools to enhance spread, and that are driven by a variety of motivations. This chapter catalogues some of the main sources of misinformation about science, discussing how and why each source promulgates misinformation about science. Understanding the range of sources is critical to efforts to mitigate the flow and influence of misinformation. The chapter begins with a review of research on the prevalence of misinformation about science in order to develop an understanding of the scope of the problem. We then detail the institutions, communities, and individuals from which misinformation about science originates, and the reasons, both intentional and unintentional, that misinformation proliferates from these sources. The next chapter builds on this one and describes the factors that contribute to misinformation's spread.

CURRENT STATE OF MISINFORMATION ABOUT SCIENCE

In determining the prevalence of misinformation about science, the committee thought it was important to distinguish between *science (mis)-information* and *science (mis)belief* (Levy et al., 2021). Scientific information is pieces of information regarding science. Misinformation about science, then, is pieces of information that incorrectly characterize science or the state of scientific knowledge (see Chapter 2). In contrast, scientific beliefs are the beliefs that people hold regarding science. Beliefs that are misaligned with science are scientific misbeliefs. For example, a statement that adverse health effects are directly attributable to consuming genetically engineered (GE) foods is misinformation, whereas the belief that eating GE foods poses a higher risk to human health than from eating non-GE foods is a misbelief. One of the potential negative impacts of misinformation about science is that it may lead to misbeliefs, which in turn may lead to decisions that have a negative effect on individuals. The effects of misinformation about science on misbeliefs are discussed more fully in Chapter 6.

Characterizing the Prevalence of Misinformation About Science

In its review, the committee found that there is more literature on the generalizable prevalence of misbeliefs than of misinformation, arguably because the former is easier to measure. Misbeliefs are typically measured through precisely articulated false statements ("Do you think early childhood vaccines cause autism?") provided to a representative sample of individuals to evaluate their truth value. A powerful summative statistic regarding vaccine misbelief might be: 11% of the U.S. adult population believes that childhood vaccines "are more dangerous than the diseases they are designed to prevent" (Reinhart, 2020). Measuring the prevalence of misinformation content and exposure brings a wide range of distinct challenges. Measuring prevalence of misinformation first requires an evaluation of the truth value of a statement, and second, a "population of bits" of information to generalize to. Both of these requirements pose difficult challenges. First, some scientific claims (like those concerning the laws of the physical universe) are clearly true or false; however, there are many claims that include a degree of scientific uncertainty. "Vaccines are safe" is less misleading than "vaccines are dangerous"; however, neither is precisely correct, in that vaccines that are widely used are generally safe, but some vaccines can pose some dangers to some people. This characteristic of a *general* but not *universal* truth applies to many policy-related issues to which science is relevant. Thus, definitive truth assessments may be difficult to make.

Generalizing to a "population of bits" is also hard, because some forms of information that people engage with are difficult to measure. For example, one can imagine wanting to measure every bit of information someone is exposed to regarding childhood vaccines, including from doctors, friends, books, popular culture, various online sources, and so on. This, however, is a nearly impossible task. Alternatively, one might imagine an effort to measure how many statements regarding vaccines on X (formerly Twitter) are correct. This is a far more doable task (subject to the challenge of truth assessments), but much less comprehensive. This is not only because it is just one information medium, but further, the existence of content does not equal exposure. To say that a certain percentage of tweets regarding vaccines are false tells us nothing about how many people have seen those tweets, or longer-term effects on cognition for individuals who have seen them.

In determining the prevalence of misinformation about science, it is important to distinguish between two related but sometimes conflated concepts: (a) the prevalence of misinformation, scientific or otherwise, within a given media channel(s) and (b) the degree of aggregate exposure to misinformation about science in a given population. While we might expect the two to be somewhat correlated, it is possible that specific bits of misinformation about science that would appear small from a quantitative standpoint might still reach large audiences, or that large amounts thereof might only be viewed by few people or none. Here, we emphasize the former while mentioning the latter as relevant. Such measures of the amount of misinformation about science will inevitably elide vastly different types thereof, with potentially different degrees of impact. For example, one individual could be repeatedly exposed to various bits of misinformation over a given period of time, but only one or a few might measurably affect their attitudes or behavior (see Chapter 6 for more discussion of the factors that shape individual-level exposure to and engagement with information, including misinformation about science).

A recent, systematic review of 69 papers on the prevalence of health misinformation on social media before 2019 by Suarez-Lledo & Alvarez-Galvez (2021) reflects some of the key challenges to measuring prevalence. Notably, many of the included papers are not on health misinformation, as defined in this consensus report (see Chapter 2 for the committee's definition); rather they are misinformation adjacent. For example, in re-examining the set of papers ostensibly on vaccine misinformation (the most common category of misinformation examined) on Twitter/X (the most common platform studied), the committee determined that only a single paper (Love et al., 2013) of the 69 actually evaluated the scientific accuracy of vaccine claims on Twitter (coded as "unsubstantiated"). This sample of tweets, in turn, was very small (only 369 tweets were evaluated as substantiated or unsubstantiated by scientific evidence) and of limited generalizability (the sample was one week of data collection via NodeXL in 2012 using three vaccine keywords). This is not to criticize this paper—it was an early exploratory effort—but to highlight the limited evidentiary basis to make claims about the prevalence of misinformation about science. Previously, Johnson et al. (2020), which was not included in Suarez-Lledo and Alvarez-Galvez's review, examined how vaccination sentiments map across Facebook community spaces like public pages, finding that while the anti-vaccination population consists of a smaller minority of total users, twice as many anti-vaccine pages exists for user engagement compared to the pro-vaccination population. It is important to note that this study did not actually measure the content on these pages or from other parts of

Facebook such as individual profiles or private pages, which limits what inferences can be made about prevalence.

Another recent, systematic review looked at 57 studies addressing the prevalence of misinformation about COVID-19 vaccines in online platforms and survey respondents' knowledge (Zhao et al., 2023). But differences in the measures used across the studies make it difficult to draw widely applicable conclusions about the prevalence of COVID-19 vaccine misinformation. Some of the studies included in the review calculated prevalence based on samples of general social media posts about COVID-19, while others sampled only anti-vaccine posts. Some assessed respondents' awareness of various misinformation bits (exposure) through surveys, while others analyzed belief in misinformation. These limitations point to a need for researchers to reach agreement on definitions of prevalence and approaches to measurement within different communication domains to make studies more directly comparable.

Other studies have examined COVID-19-related misinformation on particular online platforms. An examination of the most viewed videos on YouTube regarding COVID-19 vaccines found a significant share (11%) had information that was in contradiction to the World Health Organization or Centers for Disease Control and Prevention (CDC; Li et al., 2022). Similarly, a study of early information being disseminated regarding COVID-19 found that more than a quarter of the top videos contained misleading information (Li et al., 2020), and Shin & Valente (2020) found that vaccine-related searches on Amazon.com mostly pointed consumers to vaccine-hesitant books. Finally, a burgeoning body of research on the popular video-sharing site TikTok has found moderate (<50%) levels of COVID-19 misinformation in their samples (Baghdadi et al., 2023; Basch et al., 2021; van Kampen et al., 2022).

There is conflicting evidence concerning the proportion of news Americans encounter online as compared to legacy media such as television, radio, and print. While consumption-based metrics such as Nielsen and Comscore indicate that TV is the dominant American news source (Allen et al., 2020), more recent survey data suggest that an increasing number of Americans engage with news via digital devices (Pew Research Center, 2024c). Nevertheless, current understanding of the prevalence of misinformation within offline channels like television, radio, film, and books is hampered by limited data about such media. Given what is known about, for example, the role of partisan media outlets (defined based on the ideological slant of their news content and/or audiences; Budak et al., 2016; Robertson et al., 2018) with large audiences in distributing misinformation about science (see later discussion on "partisan media outlets"), this represents a substantial knowledge gap.

Assessing the contribution of generally credible sources of information to the amount of circulating misinformation is also not a strong focus in the current scholarship on misinformation about science. A notable exception is Broniatowski et al. (2022), which finds that about 25% of articles from low credibility sources contain false claims, as compared to 5% of articles from higher credibility sources. Sites rated "not credible" were 3.67 times more likely to contain false claims than those rated as "more credible." Beyond that study, there is relatively little evaluation of how much news content from mainstream news media may be characterized as misinformation about science. Additionally, some studies of science-related content in mainstream news media do not use of the term "misinformation" but are essentially examining misinformation about science as defined in the context of this report. For example, a cross-national study of the quality of news coverage regarding COVID-19 (Mach et al., 2021) found that "overall scientific quality of news reporting and analysis was lowest on the populist right of the political spectrum." The committee notes that while much of the low-quality content likely meets the definition of misinformation about science presented in this report, the researchers did not label it as such. Similarly, Sumner et al. (2014) looked at the role of *misleading* academic press releases in subsequent news coverage, and what this report would define as misinformation (e.g., reporting that a study on rodents holds relevance for humans when the study did not make such a claim) is described as "exaggeration."

The scholarly focus on internet domains like websites also means that factually incorrect statements on social media platforms are generally not considered to be "misinformation". For example, while Yang et al. (2023) found that 23% of politically-related sampled images on Facebook were misinformation, these posts would have been entirely missed by judgments about misinformation only at the domain level. There is also some emergent literature on misinformation on less visible platforms like WhatsApp, Facebook Messenger, and Telegram (e.g., Almodt, 2024; Curley et al., 2022; Ng & Loke, 2021; Zhong et al., 2024); but it would be difficult to produce enough data to generalize about the prevalence of misinformation about science on such platforms given that an analysis of the unedited contents of these networks would be an unacceptable breach of privacy, and end-to-end encryption (E2EE) of some platforms makes this task extremely challenging, if not impossible. Research on health misinformation does repeatedly find substantial quantities of health misinformation in particular domains (see review by Suarez-Lledo & Alvarez-Galvez, 2021), but often does not indicate what fraction of all content is misinformation (i.e., it does not specify what the denominator for quantity of information is).

Characterizing the Exposure to Misinformation About Science

There are also multiple practical issues in making a proper estimate of the distribution of exposure to misinformation about science. The first is the challenge of measuring exposure, given the multitudinous channels of information and the lack of measures to many of those channels. A second issue is the level of effort and expertise (and therefore cost) it takes to make an attribution as to whether particular science content is misinformation. This cost is often acute in evaluating misinformation about health or science, which requires technical expertise. Many studies of science or health information used people who had obtained MDs and/or PhDs to evaluate on an item-by-item basis whether or not content was misinformation—an extremely costly approach. Third, there is a need to distinguish between and analyze the relationships between misinformation prevalence and exposure in a more systematic fashion. These are not, in principle, insurmountable challenges; however, they do point to the need for substantial investments in multiplatform measurement in this space.

SOURCES OF MISINFORMATION ABOUT SCIENCE

There are myriad sources of misinformation about science, and understanding these sources is instructive for studying its impacts and identifying leverage points of intervention. Misinformation about science can originate from ordinary citizens, as well as institutional sources including industry, media, and governments. It also comes from within science itself, via scientists and medical professionals. In some cases, production of misinformation about science may involve an organized effort, meaning that many actors and organizations work together to seed and amplify false information about a particular science topic to achieve economic and/or political goals. These organized, intentional efforts are a form of disinformation, which is a sub-category of misinformation (see Chapter 2 for the committee's discussion of these terms). In other cases, misinformation about science is an unintended byproduct of the incentives and constraints in our media, political, and scientific institutions.

Misinformation often, but not always, flows through mediated channels. As described in Chapter 3, the media system of the 21st century is best characterized as a *hybrid* of interconnected technologies and media logics (Chadwick, 2017), as opposed to the more clearly delineated media system of the 20th century. It no longer makes sense to distinguish sharply between television, radio, film, newspapers, magazines, books, and other familiar legacy media—not to mention their digital analogues, because content that appears in one medium often also appears in others. Additionally, content providers can take advantage of the internet's cheap distribution costs to produce articles, videos, podcasts, and other types of media of varying degrees of veracity. Given misinformation about science tends to be produced by a small number of repeat purveyors (Nogara et al., 2022; Pierri et al., 2023), we spend much of the next few sections examining such sources and the audiences they reach. While the following discussion is not meant to be an exhaustive accounting of the sources of misinformation, it reviews those that have emerged prominently in the literature and underscore important dynamics about the spread of misinformation. We also discuss sources that the literature suggests are systematic producers of misinformation about science; in many cases, these sources also reach large audiences.

Industry

When scientific evidence has shown a link between an industry or an industry product and environmental or public health harms, scholars report that some industries have mobilized to produce and spread misinformation that contradicts or distorts the relevant science (Björnberg et al., 2017; Dunlap & McCright, 2011; Farrell, 2015; Holder et al., 2023; Kearns et al., 2016; McCulloch & Tweedale, 2008; Oreskes & Conway, 2010b; Supran & Oreskes, 2017, 2021; Williams et al., 2022). More specifically, some industries have been reported to suppress evidence and propagate misinformation through public relations campaigns (see Chapter 5 for a discussion on industry public relations strategies) and the advertising and marketing strategies used to sell products and services (Aronczyk & Espinoza, 2021; Michaels, 2008, 2020; Oreskes & Conway, 2010b).

One of the most well-documented examples of such coordinated, systematic efforts in the literature involves the efforts of some fossil fuel companies, utility companies, public relations firms, think tanks, foundations, trade groups, politicians, partisan media, and scientists who were reported to work in concert to deny climate science and exert undue influence on policymaking around environmental issues (Björnberg et al., 2017; Dunlap & McCright, 2011; Farrell, 2015). It has also been reported that since the 1970s, some fossil fuel companies have played a role in undermining climate science and promoting misinformation about the reality, causes, and significance of climate change, in an effort to avoid financially punitive regulations on their business (Dunlap & McCright, 2011; Holder et al., 2023; Supran & Oreskes, 2017, 2021). Other work has shown that some electric utility companies have also used similar strategies to promote climate change denial (Williams et al., 2022).

Kearns et al. (2016) have also shown that in the 1960s and 1970s, the sugar industry funded influential research to challenge sugar's contributions to coronary heart disease and shift the blame to fat, and this was reported to be an effort to protect their market share. Additionally, some companies within the food and beverage industry have also been reported to use misleading marketing to sell products to consumers, often targeting children, women, and low-income communities and communities of color (Bailin et al., 2014). Researchers have also described similar campaigns to conceal the health risks of particular products or activities that have been undertaken by other industries and companies ranging from the asbestos industry (McCulloch & Tweedale, 2008) to tobacco companies (Barnes et al., 1995; Oreskes & Conway, 2010b) to the NFL (Fainaru-Wada & Fainaru, 2014; Michaels, 2020).

Many scholars also report that the supplement industry often uses health claims that are unsupported by scientific evidence to promote its products and boost sales (Ayoob et al., 2002; Rachul et al., 2020; Wagner et al., 2020; also see later section on Alternative Health and Science Media), as does the rapidly growing cannabidiol (CBD) industry (Wagoner et al., 2021; Zenone et al., 2021). Likewise, direct-to-consumer advertising for pharmaceuticals (Hollon, 1999; Wolfe, 2002), clinical genetic testing (Gollust et al., 2002), stem cell therapies (Murdoch et al., 2018), and cancer services (Hlubocky et al., 2020) can also be a potential source of misinformation about science, by overstating benefits and downplaying risks. Additionally, "greenwashing," is another form of deceptive advertising whereby some companies try to appeal to environmentally conscious stakeholders by exaggerating the positive environmental impact of their products or practices (Lyon & Montgomery, 2015). Greenwashing can involve various methods, such as using vague or meaningless claims (e.g., "all natural," "eco-friendly"), false labeling, selective disclosure, and misleading visual imagery (Aronczyk et al., 2024; Baum, 2012; Holder et al., 2023; Lyon & Montgomery, 2015).

One of the most consequential industry-led disinformation campaigns that has been documented in the literature involved the efforts by the pharmaceutical company Purdue Pharma to promote its opioid painkiller, OxyContin. Michaels (2020) reported that Purdue Pharma engaged in marketing and public relations campaigns to mislead regulators, doctors, and patients with false claims that OxyContin was not addictive and that it was a safe and effective treatment for not only acute pain but also chronic pain. Specifically, researchers report that the company relied on a selected set of small-scale studies from the medical literature to support its claims, funded new studies, paid doctors to promote the drug, and engaged in aggressive sales practices targeting primary care physicians (Armstrong, 2019; Michaels, 2020). Michaels (2020) also reported that Purdue advanced a new diagnosis, "pseudo-addiction," based on a single study with a single patient, that claimed that addictive cravings for opioids were driven by inadequate treatment for pain, thereby requiring more opioids. Additional research found that Purdue's efforts led to an exponential boom in opioid prescribing, which increased the risk for dependence and addiction (Rummans et al., 2018). It is estimated that in 2016 prescription opioids were involved in 40% of all opioid overdoses (Seth et al., 2018), and pharmaceutical industry marketing of opioids to doctors has been linked to deaths from opioid overdoses (Hadland et al., 2019).

It is important to recognize that industries can also be sources of accurate science information. For example, the pharmaceutical industry engages in valuable science communication, marketing, and education to doctors, policymakers, and the public that enables patient access to health-promoting and life-saving medicines and treatments. Likewise, corporate social responsibility has become a guiding framework for strategic corporate practice, including around the environment and climate-related issues (Latapí Agudelo et al., 2019). For example, fair trade is an example of responsible corporate practice in the environmental space. Relatedly, scholars have noted the growth of private environmental governance, whereby the corporate sector, motivated at least in part by market considerations, self-regulates to address environmental problems like climate change (Vandenbergh & Gilligan, 2017; Vandenbergh et al., 2024). The committee was not able to identify examples in the literature of industries or individual companies that have proactively and responsibly adapted to new scientific evidence that was in direct conflict with their economic interests. That said, such examples would serve as important subjects of future research and as potential models for how businesses may be able to effectively and transparently communicate and act on scientific evidence even in the face of economic risks.

Governments and Politicians

Governments and politicians can also be sources of misinformation about science. For example, research indicates that state-sponsored propaganda made by online Russian troll accounts linked to the Internet Research Agency spread vaccine misinformation on Twitter during the 2016 U.S. elections in an effort to promote political discord (Broniatowski et al., 2018). Studies also suggest that Russian state news sites were prominent sources of misinformation about genetically modified organisms (GMOs; Dorius & Lawrence-Dill, 2018). Other research shows that the Brazilian government engaged in a widespread misinformation campaign during the COVID-19 pandemic to downplay the risks of COVID-19, discredit scientifically-backed mitigation measures, and decrease trust in health decision makers (Ricard & Medeiros, 2020).

Yet, the propagation of misinformation about science by governments and politicians is not unique to social media. Both online and off, evidence suggests that some governments and politicians have been prominent sources of misinformation on science issues, ranging from COVID-19 (Blevins et al., 2021; Evanega et al., 2020) to climate change (e.g., De Pryck & Gemenne, 2017) to vaccines (Bing & Schectman, 2024; Jamison et al., 2019a). Importantly, political leaders are often highly trusted by their constituents and are afforded large media platforms, which can make misinformation from these sources especially pernicious.

Think Tanks

Think tanks, which are another potential source of misinformation about science, are typically non-profit, public policy research or advocacy organizations. Through books, reports, editorials, and experts, think tanks can influence news coverage and public discourse about science-related issues (Dunlap & Jacques, 2013; Jacques et al., 2008). Some think tanks may also be aligned with a political position, which can lead to bias in the advice that they provide (Farrell, 2016, 2019). For example, there is research showing that think tanks that are tightly connected to political actors, including philanthropic foundations and corporate funders, politicians, and like-minded media outlets, tend to amplify misinformation about science through such networks (Farrell, 2016, 2019). Ideology-based think tanks can also engage across different science domains, whereby the same think tank might disseminate misinformation about two different topics—for example, COVID-19 and climate change (Lewandowsky, 2021b). It is important to note that the extant literature on think tanks as sources of misinformation has largely focused on conservative think tanks and less so on liberal and centrist think tanks (Dunlap & Jacques, 2013; Jacques et al., 2008; McCright & Dunlap, 2000, 2003). However, given that activities of all think tanks, regardless of ideology, have the potential to be influenced by their funders, and that there is often a lack of transparency around funding and conflicts of interest, greater research attention is needed to better understand the role that think tanks as a whole play in the production of misinformation about science.

Mainstream News Media

News organizations and journalists are key mediators of science information and as such misinformation as well. As noted in Chapter 3, U.S. adults tend to rely on general news outlets to acquire science information. This is especially true during times of crisis, where public uncertainty and interest are high, and journalists become critical frontline communicators, as seen during the COVID-19 pandemic (Altay et al., 2022; Van Aelst et al., 2021). However, news from major media organizations, regardless of platform or format, can also be a source of misinformation about science due to several factors. For one, disingenuous actors often target news organizations to seed stories that contain misleading information (e.g., Armstrong, 2019; Oreskes & Conway, 2010b). In other cases, news coverage can inadvertently disseminate misinformation through unintended misrepresentations of scientific research by featuring sources or guests who make problematic claims or simply by reporting on or even trying to debunk misinformation about science.

Science is endemic to most journalistic "beats," from politics to business to lifestyle. Yet many newsrooms, especially smaller outlets, lack staff with science training (Voss, 2002), which may open the door to inaccuracies in their reporting. For example, health and medical news, (which the committee considers to be a type of science journalism) is often reported on by lifestyle or generalist reporters who may not have specialized training in science or research methods (O'Keeffe et al., 2021; Tanner, 2004; Voss, 2002). Due to time constraints and market pressures, even well-resourced outlets may over-rely on press releases and other information subsidies that can inflate or misconstrue research claims (Bratton et al., 2019; Sumner et al., 2014).

Mainstream news media organizations follow a set of professional norms and values that govern journalistic practice and shape the nature of news coverage. These norms and values, while important for legitimizing the professional practice of journalism, can also give way to misinformation about science. One chief example is the norm of objectivity, which journalists typically operationalize by giving voice to both sides of controversial issues. In the context of science, this can result in "false balance," whereby journalists cover both sides of a scientific debate, even when scientific evidence overwhelmingly points in one direction—a journalistic practice that has been exploited by actors seeking to undermine the scientific consensus (see Chapter 5). For example, the majority of news coverage of climate change in leading U.S. newspapers between 1998 and 2002, and in television news programs between 1995 and 2004 presented a balanced account regarding the existence of anthropogenic climate change and the need for climate action (Boykoff, 2008; Boykoff & Boykoff, 2004). By giving equal weight to advocates and skeptics of climate science, news media distorted the scientific consensus on global warming. Indeed, experimental evidence has shown that false balance can reduce the public's perceptions of agreement among experts on high-consensus issues (Koehler, 2016). While this practice receded in the early 2000s, it likely inflicted lasting damage on public perceptions of climate change (Boykoff, 2007; McAllister et al., 2021). There is also some evidence for false balance in media coverage of the autism-vaccine controversy. Between 1998 and 2006, about a third of U.S. and British newspaper coverage provided balanced coverage of the link between vaccines and autism, despite scientific consensus that vaccines do not cause autism (Clarke, 2008). In the British press specifically, another third of coverage *only* presented claims that supported a link between vaccines and autism (Clarke, 2008). False balance was also found to be more likely in science news stories from the 1980s to 2010s about GMOs and nuclear power, whereas stories about climate change and vaccines during that time, tended to hew toward the expert consensus (Merkley, 2020); in this case, however, this finding could very well reflect legitimate scientific debate on GMOs and nuclear power (e.g., although GMOs are not linked to human health concerns, more research is needed on their environmental impacts [National Academies, 2016a]).

Journalists also follow an "indexing" norm, whereby their reporting closely tracks the range of views expressed by government officials (Bennett, 1990), and they also rely on official sources (including elected officials and other prominent elites). In the case of COVID-19, research suggests that U.S. TV news coverage engaged in indexing practices by covering misinformed elite viewpoints, thus affording them greater prominence (Muddiman et al., 2022). Along similar lines, mainstream media also cover high-profile examples of misinformation as newsworthy events, which can contribute to their dissemination (Tsfati et al., 2020). Policies on press access at federal science agencies can further hamstring journalists' coverage of science, by restricting reporters from talking directly to government scientists and instead requiring them to speak to spokespeople and communications officers who lack subject matter expertise (Cohen, 2009; National Association of Science Writers, n.d.). At the same time, some academic scientists, who can play an important role in clarifying and contextualizing scientific research in news stories, may be unwilling to speak to reporters, due to institutional pressure to focus on publishing rather than on media and other public outreach (Woolston, 2018).

Another professional norm of journalists is valuing information that is novel, dramatic, and conflictual, as this is more likely to attract news audiences. This emphasis can give way to sensationalistic, misleading, or incomplete coverage of science. There is wide-ranging evidence of news media misrepresenting and misreporting scientific studies, medical developments, and health issues (Brechman et al., 2011; Cooper et al., 2012; Greiner et al., 2010; Houn et al., 1995; Lai & Lane, 2009; Nagler et al., 2015; Rachul & Caulfield, 2015; Selvaraj et al., 2014; Shi et al., 2022; Stefanik-Sidener, 2013; Walsh-Childers et al., 2018; Woloshin & Schwartz, 2006; Woloshin et al., 2009b; Yavchitz et al., 2012; Zuckerman, 2003). This is likely due to a confluence of factors, including journalistic norms and informational biases, over-reliance on public relations and other information subsidies, exaggerations and omissions in the original scientific articles, and lack of resources and scientific expertise on the part of journalists and news organizations (Woloshin et al., 2009b). In the digital media environment, where audience engagement is easily quantified, some newsrooms use A/B testing to determine which headlines receive the most online traffic, a practice that can sometimes result in more sensational or clickbait-y headlines (Fürst, 2020; Hagar & Diakopoulos, 2019).

Partisan Media Outlets

In contrast to mainstream news outlets, partisan media outlets present information from a specific ideological view. Unlike the partisan press of America's early democracy, where newspapers were sponsored by political parties, contemporary partisan media in the United States are typically identified based on the ideological slant of their content (Budak et al., 2016; Levendusky, 2013; Stroud, 2010) and/or the ideological composition of their audiences (Bakshy et al., 2015; Gentzkow & Shapiro, 2011; Robertson et al., 2018). Although precise measures of exposure to partisan media are difficult to obtain, current data suggest that the aggregate audience is quite large. For example, 2023 cable news ratings from Nielsen indicate that approximately two million viewers, on average, watch the most popular prime-time programs on Fox News and MSNBC each night (Johnson, 2023); yet these numbers do not reflect the total audience who tune into such news sources. A recent study that pooled data from multiple sources that unobtrusively monitor TV consumption estimates that one in seven Americans watches over eight hours per month of partisan TV news, and that many of these viewers only consume information from outlets that match their partisan orientation (Broockman & Kalla, 2024). Several other studies have reached similar conclusions regarding the size and segregation of the partisan news audience (Muise et al., 2022; Prior, 2013; Stroud, 2011).

Currently, research on misinformation about science in partisan media has mainly focused on politicized topics such as climate change and COVID-19. Studies looking at climate change, for example, have found that conservative media have been a source of climate denial and skepticism of the broader scientific enterprise, including the integrity of scientists and peer-reviewed research (Dunlap & McCright, 2011; McKnight, 2010). Further, a systematic content analysis of cable news transcripts from 2007 and 2008 revealed that coverage of climate change on Fox News cable TV network often included claims that challenged the scientific agreement on climate change, for example, by challenging the reality of climate change or that it is caused by human activities (Feldman et al., 2012). The study showed that the network also tended to feature more climate change skeptics as interview guests, relative to CNN and MSNBC, whose coverage was more consistent with the weight of scientific evidence on climate change (Feldman et al., 2012). In print media, an analysis of opinion editorials written by 80 different columnists between 2007 and 2010 revealed that nationally syndicated conservative op-ed columnists who wrote about climate change included skeptical arguments that questioned the reality, causes, and seriousness of climate change, as well as the feasibility of solutions (Elsasser & Dunlap, 2013).

In the context of COVID-19, conservative media outlets were reported as more likely to reference misinformation about COVID-19 at the beginning of the pandemic than mainstream news outlets (Motta et al., 2020). On social media, two studies found that right-wing media accounts were disproportionately responsible for spreading and amplifying COVID-19 misinformation (Yang et al., 2021; Zhang et al., 2023). Moreover, several studies have supported a causal relationship between exposure to information from Fox News and lower rates of protective behaviors in response to COVID-19, including social distancing and vaccination (Ash et al., 2024; Pinna et al., 2022; Simonov et al., 2022). But, while these studies suggest a relationship, it is important to note that a direct link between misinformation about science and adverse behaviors in response to COVID-19 has not been definitively established (see Chapter 6).

Studies on the role of partisan media outlets in the production and spread of misinformation about science, mainly climate change and COVID-19, have also largely focused on conservative media outlets and less so on more liberal-leaning media outlets. However, one study by Merkley (2020) that examined over 280,000 news stories found that liberal-leaning media outlets are more likely to engage in false balance and feature claims from polarizing viewpoints when covering issues about which Democrats are skeptical of the expert scientific community's position, including the safety of nuclear power and GMOs (Merkley, 2020, Figure H1).

Studies that have focused on the circulation of misinformation more broadly (i.e., not exclusively misinformation about science) by analyzing exposure to and engagement with online news from untrustworthy sources, as well as news from domains rated as false by third-party fact-checkers, have found that misinformation is disproportionately more likely to come from right-leaning media sources than from mainstream media or left-leaning media sources (González-Bailón et al., 2023; Grinberg et al., 2019). These patterns are important because they suggest that some individuals who are primarily engaging with more right-leaning media sources may be more likely to be exposed to misinformation, including about science, than individuals who engage with a diversity of media sources.

Ethnic and Diasporic News and Media

Although most of this report focuses on misinformation about science in the English language, misinformation among non-English speaking and multilingual communities is an important yet understudied dimension of misinformation spread. Ethnic, diasporic, and community media (e.g., media produced for and often by specific communities defined by ethnicity, language, etc.) function as trusted means for non-English speaking and multilingual communities to access in-language news and information, which can fall outside of mainstream English language media outlets (Nguyễn & Kuo, 2023). The media networks that distribute ethnic, diasporic, and community media can span local, regional, national, and transnational circulation (Nguyễn & Kuo, 2023). Media may include a range of formats, including print media, radio, cable television channels, social media sites, video streaming, etc. created by and for immigrants, groups from marginalized ethnicities and languages, and Indigenous populations (e.g., Gerson et al., 2020; Lopez, 2021; Rajagopalan, 2021). These networks may also include social media accounts and sources on YouTube, blogs, podcasts, or mobile messaging apps created by individual influencers and commentators (Nguyễn & Kuo, 2023). Media from "home countries" may also be consumed as part of this media diet and may be in English and/or in the home language (referred to as "in-language"), and may span thousands of platforms and outlets (Nguyễn & Kuo, 2023). Diasporic media considers "audience preferences, influence of viewpoints in host countries, accessibility to sources of information, and community-serving attitude" for migrants outside of the home countries (Pham, 2021, p. 512). It can act as a transnational bridging tool, transmitting information between those who identify with communities coming from a diffusion across space, cementing identity formation to one's homeland, and affording boundary maintenance within the host society (Brubaker, 2005).

While many ethnic media sources can be credible, they can also carry political biases, whether supported by local governments, or financially backed by political parties and factions—for example, *The Epoch Times,* an international, multilingual newspaper, is funded through the Falun Gong, an anti-Chinese Communist Party (CCP) spiritual movement (Owen, 2021; Roose, 2020). Some popular in-language outlets have been shown to carry different "homeland/hostland" political biases as a means of assimilation, acculturation, or survival (Shams, 2020). Popular in-language outlets that are financially backed by political parties and factions facilitate ties to opinionated and biased news for non-English readers who hold deep trust for these in-language news sources (Owen, 2021). Importantly, the distinct and specialized identities that ethnic media producers must convey in relation to mainstream media, mainstream society institutions, and the communities they serve become a strain on providing wholly accurate information in their reporting (Matsaganis et al., 2011).

Alongside ethnic media, private messaging platforms are prevalent in non-English and multilingual communities as means to connect between home and host countries, develop and maintain intimate trusted relationships, and all within the access of in-language information (Nguyễn & Kuo, 2023). These platforms include, but are not limited to, WeChat, KakaoTalk, WhatsApp, Viber, Line, Facebook Messenger, Telegram, and Zalo. In a 2020 voter survey, nearly one in six Asian Americans reported using private messaging platforms such as WeChat, WhatsApp, and KakaoTalk to discuss politics (AAPIData, APIAVote, and Asian Americans Advancing Justice, 2020). Latinx communities tend to favor WhatsApp, Line, and Facebook Messenger; South Asian communities commonly use WhatsApp and Telegram. Additionally, other non-English specific platforms such as Zalo may be popular within respective communities in Vietnam, while ephemeral media (e.g., reels) and direct messages on mainstream platforms, such as Instagram or TikTok, are widely utilized by diverse cultural groups, though not exclusive to any particular community (Nguyễn & Kuo, 2023).

It is worth noting that these preferences may vary based on language, cultural ties, and regional availability. Closed platforms are often intimate and trusted spaces for non-English speaking and multilingual communities, particularly as individuals share information across platforms and nation states, yet they are also spaces where misinformation can spread across these internal networks (Nguyễn & Kuo, 2023). Zhang's (2018) pioneering study of WeChat and how misinformation flows through Chinese diasporic communities on the platform reveals a combination of factors that amplify misinformation. These include a low barrier to entry in branded content publishing; a lack of local news coverages on issues of particular interest to Chinese immigrants; and intimate communication spaces where users are connected by common—mostly identity-based—affiliations. More recent research on misinformation about science on the WeChat platform explored the strategies users employ to evaluate information credibility in the context of COVID-19 (Zhu et al., 2022), general medical matters (Wu et al., 2024), and general science (Wang et al., 2023). Among other findings, these studies point to older relatives as common distributors of misinformation about science on WeChat (Wu et al., 2024; Zhu et al., 2022), and to fearmongering (Wang et al., 2023) as a common characteristic of the information shared. But aside from these findings, little is known about the nature of misinformation sharing within other closed platforms given limitations that researchers face to data access. Moreover, hosts and developers of closed platforms have issues identifying, moderating, and training data on problematic information posted and shared across these platforms, given how information is shared as well as tensions between commitments to privacy (e.g., end-to-end encryption) versus moderation (Nguyễn & Kuo, 2023).

Alternative Health and Science Media

Alternative health and science media provide health and medical advice that is outside of mainstream science and can contain misinformation related to various science and health topics and domains. Such sources include popular health-related TV talk shows, health blogs and websites, and social media accounts, all of which can advocate for treatments, including diets, detoxes and supplements that are not backed by scientific evidence (Stecula et al., 2022). Research also shows that alternative health and science websites can promote health- and science-related conspiracy theories and stoke fear and distrust of mainstream medicine and the regulatory processes used by the U.S. Food and Drug Administration (FDA), for example, to authorize treatments and vaccines (Marcon et al., 2017; Stecula et al., 2022).

Researchers examining health claims specifically on the health-related TV talk shows *The Dr. Oz Show* and *The Doctors* found that for a significant percentage of these recommendations either no scientific evidence to support them was found (39% and 24%, respectively) or they contradicted the best available evidence (15% and 14%, respectively; Korownyk et al., 2014). Some studies found that popular websites on complementary and alternative medicine for cancer promoted "cancer cures" that were not supported by scientific evidence and, in some cases, advised patients against conventional therapies such as chemotherapy (Delgado-López & Corrales-García, 2018; Peterson et al., 2020; Schmidt & Ernst, 2004). Likewise, many articles about stem cell therapies published on alternative science sites exaggerated claims about stem cells and stem cell science (Marcon et al., 2017). Moreover, many of the sites feature the same content and included hyperlinks to each other, creating a coordinated network of misinformation (Marcon et al., 2017). Alternative health and science sites can also promote misinformation about genetically modified foods. For example, an analysis of nearly 95,000 online articles shared on social media between 2009 and 2019 found that the most visible and persistent content related to genetically modified foods originated from alternative health sites (Ryan et al., 2020). Although this study did not determine whether these articles contained misinformation, this finding indicates that the most widely shared online content about genetically modified foods is coming from unvetted websites.

Alternative health sites are also prominent sources of vaccine misinformation (Kata, 2012). Research shows that some anti-vaccination advocates have created densely connected and highly visible online communities that include discussion forums, parenting blogs, websites, social media pages and profiles, and other social media accounts on which vaccine misinformation proliferates (Hoffman et al., 2019; Puri et al., 2020; Smith & Graham, 2019; Yuan et al., 2019). Moreover, many anti-vaccination sites can resemble official scientific sites, making it more difficult for individuals to discern their veracity (Davies et al., 2002).

Wellness culture, a version of alternative health, has flourished in the internet era, becoming a billion-dollar industry (Baker & Rojek, 2020), and may incentivize the promulgation of misinformation in order to sell products, including supplements, cleanses, and essential oils. Indeed, some popular wellness and lifestyle companies have even been implicated in making health claims about products that are not backed by scientific evidence (Garcia, 2018). Notably, scholars and journalists have also identified a connection between conspiratorial content and the treatments and supplements that are promoted on wellness sites, whereby wellness advice is sometimes presented alongside conspiratorial content in the marketing for health products (Baker, 2022).

Finally, alternative health-related media sources are significant not only in the kind of information they provide, but in that they reach large audiences. For example, at their peak in the early 2010s, *The Dr. Oz Show* attracted more than three million daily viewers and *The Doctors* nearly two million daily viewers (Block, 2013). Additionally, in 2020, the alternative health site *Naturalnews.com*, for example, reportedly attracted 3.5 million unique visitors (Collins & Zadrozny, 2020). A national U.S. survey conducted in 2018 and 2019 found that approximately 26% of Americans sometimes or regularly watch health- and medical-related TV talk shows, 22% sometimes or regularly follow social media accounts dedicated to alternative health, and 15% sometimes or regularly read alternative health blogs (Stecula et al., 2022). The survey also showed that consumers of alternative health media tend to be women, lower income, less educated, non-White, and have lower levels of trust in medical experts (Stecula et al., 2022). Thus, misinformation about science from this sector has greater potential for harm for these groups given the significant reach.

Entertainment and Popular Culture

As a source of misinformation about science, entertainment media have not been studied as widely as news and social media, but it is an area worthy of more research given that many popular scripted entertainment programs feature science topics and scientists, from medical dramas like *Grey's Anatomy* and *House* to comedies like *The Big Bang Theory*. Research has found that fictional entertainment can shape people's beliefs and attitudes, including in the domains of health and science, due to its ability to absorb audiences into a narrative world (Dahlstrom, 2014; Frank et al., 2015; Green et al., 2003; Hoffman et al., 2023). Moreover, fictional and factual narratives, even when clearly labeled as such, have been shown to be equally persuasive (Appel & Malečkar, 2012; Green & Brock, 2000;

Strange & Leung, 1999). Research also shows that people often develop misbeliefs based on factual errors contained in fictional media, even when their prior knowledge contradicts this misinformation and even when they are reminded that fiction might contain factual inaccuracies (Butler et al., 2009; Fazio et al., 2013).

Although it is expected that fictional entertainment is less concerned with empirical fact than with narrative and the verisimilitude of experience (Dahlstrom, 2021), it can still be a source of misinformation about science. Science in fictional entertainment may be over-simplified, exaggerated, or otherwise misrepresented for the sake of a compelling story or for cinematic effect. For example, producers and writers of TV crime dramas that depict forensic science like *CSI* and *Bones* judge scientific realism based on narrative plausibility rather than scientific accuracy (Kirby, 2013). In such shows, forensic evidence, including DNA tests, is widely used to solve crimes, and the unrealistic ease and certainty with which this evidence is deployed on TV has led to anecdotal concerns about a so-called "CSI effect," whereby real-life jurors demand DNA evidence from the prosecution before finding a defendant guilty—although empirical evidence indicates that this effect may be overstated (Podlas, 2005; Shelton et al., 2006).

Another source of misinformation about science in entertainment relates to the representation of scientists. Entertainment TV programs and films sometimes depict scientists in stereotypic ways (e.g., the "mad scientist") and tend to underrepresent women and people of color in scientist roles. This can skew perceptions of the scientific profession and affect trust (Kirby, 2017).

One of the few systematic content analyses concerned with the depiction of misinformation about science in entertainment examined 51 fictional entertainment TV episodes from 2018 to 2020 that featured vaccine-related plotlines (McClaran & Rhodes, 2021). The study found that 86% of episodes presented at least one anti-vaccination argument, and 60% of those episodes contained arguments based on misinformation, such as that vaccines pose a serious health risk or are part of a conspiracy. Nine episodes (40%) included the argument that vaccines cause autism, despite having been clearly debunked by the scientific community.

Movies about science, such as the 2004 blockbuster climate disaster film *The Day After Tomorrow*—which featured an unrealistically large, storm surge-driven tidal wave—may also inaccurately depict scientific phenomena and events, even as they help raise public awareness about issues like climate change (Sakellari, 2015). Although relatively rare, some fictional films feature plotlines that are entirely based on misinformation, such as the 2015 thriller *Consumed,* in which a mother discovers genetically modified food might be behind her son's mysterious illness, defying wide scientific agreement that GM food does not carry human health risks.

Outside of fictional entertainment, science and environmental documentary films—which are now finding wider audiences online and via streaming platforms—also use narrative storytelling, but in a way that is intended to be received by the audience as fact (Smith & Rock, 2014). Many science and environmental documentaries are advocacy-oriented, meaning that they are designed to be explicitly persuasive by presenting evidence to support a clear ideological viewpoint (Cooper & Nisbet, 2017). Despite the realism of the documentary genre, some documentary filmmakers have admitted to bending facts in the interest of the film's overall narrative (see Aufderheide et al., 2009). Science documentaries can sometimes make overly simplistic and misleading claims in order to advance their argument (Yeo & Silberg, 2021). Audiences' expectations that documentaries accurately reflect scientific fact make them especially concerning as a source of misinformation.

The veracity of some documentaries has also been called into question by scientists (Mellor, 2009). For example, some climate scientists have argued that the documentary *The Great Global Warming Swindle* (2007) displays "erroneous or artificially manipulated graphs, and presents incorrect, misleading, or incomplete opinions and facts on the science of global warming and the related economics" (Rive et al., 2007. p. 1). Other documentaries have been reported to perpetuate unsubstantiated claims about the measles, mumps, and rubella (MMR) vaccine (Bradshaw et al., 2022), and one study found that the release of the documentary *Vaxxed: From Cover-Up to Catastrophe (2016)* was immediately followed by a significant uptick in anti-vaccine Facebook posts that discussed vaccine refusal as a civil right (Broniatowski et al., 2020). During the first few months of the COVID-19 pandemic, the 26-minute documentary *Plandemic* was released online and shared virally on social media, achieving eight million views in the first week. Notably, Frenkel et al. (2020) reported that this documentary was part of a broader disinformation campaign that promoted multiple conspiracy theories and unsubstantiated claims, including that the pandemic was planned by global elites as a form of population control, that vaccines are harmful, and that wearing masks increase the risk of contracting COVID-19.

Celebrities, too, serve as an influential source of misinformation about science, due to their large followings and the strong emotional connections they foster with fans. For example, celebrities contributed to the amplification of misinformation about vaccines being the cause of autism (Mnookin, 2012) and are a pervasive source of health misinformation (Caulfield, 2015). Celebrities also contributed to the amplification of COVID-19 misinformation on social media (Brennen et al., 2020).

The Scientific and Medical Community

The scientific community can also be a source of misinformation about science, and this manifests in several forms. First, misinformation from within science can arise as a byproduct of hype (i.e., when media, university public relations (PR) offices, and scientists themselves exaggerate research findings in an attempt to get publicity for science; Caulfield, 2018; Caulfield & Condit, 2012; Weingart, 2017; West & Bergstrom, 2021). Scientists may artificially inflate the novelty of their research and/or the significance of their findings to increase the likelihood of getting their research published and/or funded, particularly given institutional incentives to publish and the competitive nature of the academic environment (Millar et al., 2019, 2020). Tellingly, the use of hyperbolic language in grant applications to the National Institutes of Health increased between 1985 and 2020 (Millar et al., 2022). In the worst cases, such pressures to publish may encourage scientific fraud (West & Bergstrom, 2021).

University press offices, seeking media coverage of researchers' work, also play a role in creating hype by exaggerating or over-simplifying research claims, omitting important details, or overstating causal influence in their press releases (Bratton et al., 2019; Sumner et al., 2014; Woloshin et al., 2009a). Science reporters, who often rely on these press releases, may broadcast these hyperbolic claims to wide audiences or embellish them further to gain views or readers. Studies have found a strong association between exaggeration in press releases and exaggeration in health news stories, suggesting that improving the accuracy of press releases could be a way to reduce inaccuracies in science and health news that reaches broad audiences (Bratton et al., 2019; Sumner et al., 2014).

Second, misinformation from within science also results from biases or distortions in the analysis, interpretation, presentation, and/or publishing of scientific data (West & Bergstrom, 2021). Whereas industry and political actors often inflate Type II error, or false negatives, by inappropriately emphasizing scientific uncertainty when the weight of evidence overwhelmingly supports a specific interpretation, individual scientists or teams of scientists historically engaged in "p-hacking" where scientists build theory around statistically significant findings that were discovered after examination of the data, rather than accurately reporting them as *post hoc* observations. P-hacking also includes testing out different covariates to see which yield significant findings or only reporting effects on dependent variables that turned out to be significant (Head et al., 2015). Although p-hacking was once common practice among scientists, concerns about replicability shined a light on its role in driving false-positive results, and it is now recognized as a questionable research practice that increases the likelihood of Type I error, or false positives. Steps can be taken to avoid it, for example by pre-registering an analysis plan. Publication bias is another example of Type I error inflation; it occurs when researchers are unwilling to publish papers that show null results, or when journals refuse to publish such papers (West & Bergstrom, 2021). This, too, can lead to misleading conclusions about the state of scientific evidence. Shortcomings in scientists' presentation of numeric data, such as through misleading or sloppy data visualization or unfair comparisons, can also be a source of misinformation (West & Bergstrom, 2021).

A third way that misinformation about science can emerge from within the scientific community is through preprints. This is especially true in moments of rapidly emerging, high-uncertainty socio-scientific issues or challenges. For example, preprints played an outsized role during the initial phase of the COVID-19 pandemic, when the rapid dissemination of scientific data was crucial for responding to a quickly unfolding disease outbreak (Fraser et al., 2021). News media coverage of preprints likewise surged during the pandemic; yet journalists inconsistently provided context that described preprint research as preliminary and unvetted (Fleerackers et al., 2022; van Schalkwyk & Dudek, 2022). Although preprints can provide timely access to important research findings, they also offer a breeding ground for misinformation by allowing early and unvetted scientific results to quickly spread through online platforms. For example, one of the most widely shared preprints on social media during the early pandemic was a study that erroneously claimed strong similarities between the new coronavirus and HIV (see Fraser et al., 2021), which fueled conspiracy theories that the virus had been intentionally designed (Gerts et al., 2021). The study was quickly withdrawn by the authors following criticisms from the scientific community that the results were based on a false positive (Brierley, 2021). Although some in the scientific community applauded the swift withdrawal of this paper as a win for science, particularly compared to the lengthy retraction process at many peer-reviewed journals, others lamented the fact that it circulated in the first place (Oransky & Marcus, 2020). Research articles posted on preprint archives before they have been vetted through a peer-review process, as well as the "pay-to-play" model used by predatory publishers—which allows researchers to pay to have their research published without undergoing rigorous peer-review—can both result in low quality and, at worst, deceptive and misleading scientific information circulating in the public domain (West & Bergstrom, 2021).

At times, some scientists may choose to engage in public debates about science on social media in order to correct misinformation about science that has appeared in media or political discourse. Still, in some cases, scientists' engagement on social media "can change the way they use and represent evidence," such that they prioritize persuasive goals over the careful communication of reliable, systematic research findings (Brossard

& Scheufele, 2022, p. 614). Even when intended to correct misinformation, the desire to convince skeptical audiences on social media can lead scientists and other actors to rely on anecdotes and single-study results to support their claims, or to speak outside their area of expertise which can perpetuate misleading information. Therefore, it is important for scientists to carefully consider best practices for science communication in public fora, including social media.

Previous work by Peters et al. (2008) demonstrated that media training is likely to make scientists "more confident" in communicating with the media, such as with science journalists. Additionally, a more recent study showed that scientists who received science communication training were more likely to enjoy engaging the public on science than those who did not (Parrella et al., 2022). Several organizations around the world, such as the American Association for the Advancement of Science (AAAS)[1] and the European Science Communication Network (Miller & Fahy, 2009) have developed extensive training modules to encourage scientists to engage the public and increase their confidence in their ability to communicate science to non-experts.

As previously noted in Chapter 3 of this report, scientists are generally well trusted by the public, making them important sources of information and effective engagement with the public critical. However, not all types of scientists are trusted equally. For example, Americans are more likely to trust university scientists than industry scientists (Krause et al., 2019). Trust in government science agencies, such as the Environmental Protection Agency (EPA), the National Oceanographic and Atmospheric Association (NOAA), the National Aeronautics and Space Administration (NASA) and the CDC, varies across organizations (e.g., NASA is more highly trusted than EPA; Cerda, 2024; Krause et al., 2019) and can be context dependent (e.g., trust in CDC declined during the COVID-19 pandemic; Hamilton & Safford, 2021; Latkin et al., 2020). Given a large body of research that points to the influence of source credibility—which is a function of beliefs about a source's trustworthiness and expertise—on acceptance of science information (Hocevar et al., 2017), misinformation about science from more trustworthy sources is apt to be more consequential.

Finally, medical professionals can be a source of misinformation due to inadequate knowledge or false beliefs. Doctors are also highly trusted by the public (Pew Research Center, 2019a; also see Chapter 3), and yet, healthcare professionals can be misinformed about science and subsequently

[1]AAAS Communicating Science Workshops provide scientists and engineers with training and support to more effectively engage with the public through modules based on the latest science communication research and public engagement best practices. See https://www.aaas.org/programs/communicating-science-workshops

communicate that misinformation to their patients or incorporate it into their care. For example, while some published medical research is not reliable (as discussed above), most healthcare professionals are not aware of this and may lack the skills to effectively parse the medical literature (Ioannidis et al., 2017). Doctors may also hold false beliefs due to racial and cultural biases. For example, some medical professionals falsely believe that Black and White people are biologically different and thus have different pain thresholds, which influences their treatment recommendations (Hoffman et al., 2016). Some medical textbooks have even propagated misinformation related to the racialization of pain and disease (Deyrup & Graves, 2022; Li et al., 2022a; Sheets et al., 2011), suggesting how deeply ingrained such misinformation is in the medical community. As noted earlier, doctors have also been the target and conduit for disinformation from some industries. In the 1950s, the tobacco industry disseminated literature to doctors assuring them that cigarettes were not a cause for concern (Oreskes & Conway, 2010b). In marketing opioids in the 1990s, the pharmaceutical industry convinced primary-care physicians that chronic pain was under-treated in society and that opioids were a safe, non-addictive way to treat that pain; as mentioned above, an aggressive pharmaceutical sales force recruited physicians not only to prescribe opioids themselves but also to influence their medical peers to do the same (Meier, 2018; Michaels, 2020).

Individual Sources of Misinformation About Science

Ordinary citizens can also be a source of misinformation about science. While there is some research indicating that only a small minority of internet users share content from untrustworthy sources on social media (e.g., Grinberg et al., 2019; Guess et al., 2019; Nelson & Taneja, 2018), the evidence here is limited by the difficulty with measures of misinformation and credibility as discussed earlier in this chapter. Some of the studies that have been conducted to better understand information sharing among users on social media suggest that individuals who share misinformation are more likely to be older, politically conservative, male, and less educated (Guess et al., 2019, 2021; Lazer et al., 2020; Morosoli et al., 2022a; Osmundsen et al., 2021). One specific study found that during the first three months of the COVID-19 pandemic, the majority of COVID-19-related misinformation on social media came from ordinary people; however, misinformation from elites—including politicians, celebrities, and other prominent figures—accounted for more social engagement (Brennen et al., 2020). Thus, while ordinary citizens share misinformation about science on social media, misinformation from elites is most likely to gain traction, possibly due to elites' relatively large followings. Other research likewise shows that low credibility social media content about COVID-19 is attributable to a few influential actors, or "superspreaders," who tend to be high-status, verified accounts (Yang et al., 2021). Some reasons that individuals might share misinformation about science, either intentionally or unintentionally are discussed in detail in Chapter 5.

SUMMARY

Misinformation about science is produced from a wide range of sources, including corporations, governments, the news media, partisan news outlets, a variety of "alternative" health websites and social media accounts, popular culture, the scientific and medical community, and highly motivated individuals. However, current limitations related to measurement and data access impede a comprehensive assessment of the prevalence of misinformation about science across different levels and sectors of society. In particular, more research is still needed on the prevalence of misinformation about science in traditional media contexts (e.g., TV, radio, print), closed, private messaging platforms (e.g., WhatsApp, KaKaoTalk), and across all major online platforms.

Conclusion 4-1: Misinformation about science is widely understood to originate from several different sources. These include, but are not limited to:

- *for-profit corporations and non-profit organizations that use strategic communication (e.g., public relations, advertising, promotions, and other marketing campaigns) to intentionally seed and amplify misinformation about science for financial gain, to advance ideological goals, or to mitigate potential losses,*
- *governments and politicians that either publicly discredit the weight of evidence on science issues or seed misinformation about science as part of their political agendas,*
- *alternative science and health media that advocate for treatments and therapies that are not supported by scientific evidence,*
- *entertainment media through fictional and non-fictional narratives and plotlines that oversimplify, exaggerate, or otherwise misrepresent science and scientists to be compelling or for cinematic effect,*
- *reputable science organizations, institutions, universities, and individual scientists as a byproduct of poor science communication, distortions of scientific data, the dissemination of research findings before they have been formally vetted and substantiated, and in the worst cases, scientific fraud,*

- *press offices and news media organizations due to misrepresentation and misreporting of scientific studies, medical developments, and health issues, and*
- *elite and non-elite individuals due to a variety of motivations.*

Conclusion 4-2: Not all misinformation about science is equal in its influence. Rather, misinformation about science has greater potential for influence when it originates from authoritative sources; is amplified by powerful actors; reaches large audiences; is targeted to specific populations; or is produced in a deliberate, customized, and organized fashion (e.g., tobacco industry campaigns to cast doubt about the health risks of smoking).

Conclusion 4-3: Journalists, editors, writers, and media/news organizations covering science, medical, and health issues (regardless of their assigned beat or specialty areas) serve as critical mediators between producers of scientific knowledge and consumers of science information. Yet, financial challenges in the past two decades have reduced newsroom capacity to report on science, particularly at local levels.

Conclusion 4-4: Science reporting for the general public may be particularly prone to the unintentional spread of misinformation about science. Several factors can influence this, including journalistic norms (e.g., giving equal weight to both sides of a scientific debate, even when the scientific evidence overwhelmingly points in one direction), informational and ideological biases, over-reliance on public relations and other information subsidies (e.g., university press releases), exaggerations and omissions of important details from the original science articles, and insufficient scientific expertise, among journalists, particularly at under-resourced news organizations.

5

Spread of Misinformation About Science

The spread of misinformation can be driven by a variety of factors, and some purveyors of misinformation have been shown to employ a number of different strategies and tools to enhance spread. This chapter discusses the common factors, strategies, tactics, and motivations that facilitate the spread of misinformation about science. The first section of the chapter describes key factors that contribute to its spread: digital technologies and online platforms, influence and monetization, industry public relations strategies, and information access and voids. The chapter then highlights common rhetorical tactics that are often used by actors that seek to spread misinformation about science. The last section of the chapter explores possible motivations that drive individual people to spread misinformation. Throughout the chapter, the committee discusses how spread of misinformation about science is fundamentally shaped by the broader context of the contemporary information ecosystem and systemic factors described in Chapter 3.

FACTORS THAT CONTRIBUTE TO THE SPREAD OF MISINFORMATION ABOUT SCIENCE

In addition to the various sources of misinformation—each driven by specific reasons and motivations—(see Chapter 4), the committee also identified key factors related to the contemporary information ecosystem that create conditions that facilitate the spread of misinformation about science. These factors—digital technologies and online platforms, influence and monetization, industry public relations strategies, and information access and information voids—contribute in different ways to the spread of misinformation and who is exposed to it. Moreover, as will be discussed in more detail in Chapter 7, there are currently no specific laws in the United States that directly govern or limit the spread of misinformation, which can also contribute to its proliferation. By illuminating these factors, we can better understand the pervasiveness of misinformation about science, its differential reach, and what can be done to address it.

Digital Technologies and Online Platforms

Digital communication technologies in general, and social media specifically, contribute, in part to the spread of misinformation, including in the area of science. Unlike legacy journalism with its corporate gatekeepers and institutionalized fact-checking, social media platforms offer misinformation purveyors an environment that is far more conducive to engaging amenable audiences. Multiple factors contribute to the prevalence of misinformation on social media platforms, and three of the most consequential are: incentives that are related to popular content, content prioritization algorithms that privilege emotional and controversial content, and lax content moderation policies.

Incentives

Social media entered Americans' information environments in the early 21st century, starting with Myspace as the first widely-used platform, and continuing with Facebook, X (formally Twitter), Instagram, TikTok, YouTube, Reddit, and a host of smaller players. This new medium operated based on a fundamentally different logic from mainstream media, which afforded access to only a privileged few. Social media allows age-verified users to log on and create an account, which means anyone can potentially attract large audiences if their content interests enough people. This characteristic of social media has allowed some individuals to gain grassroots fame, although it has not changed the fact that only a small proportion of users can do so (Hindman, 2010; SignalFire, 2020). From the perspective of a business that thrives on attention, viral is viral, whether the content is cute pets doing tricks or falsehoods about the causes and effects of COVID-19. In other words, there can be an economic incentive to allow popular content to flourish on social media platforms, even if it includes misinformation about science, because it attracts attention and boosts advertising revenue (Maréchal et al., 2020). However, this must also be considered against some of the disadvantages of tolerating misinformation, which include negative press, angry users, advertisers' vested interest in avoiding associations with misinformation (Interactive Advertising Bureau, 2020), and arguably even deaths (Gisondi et al., 2022). Whether social media companies are doing enough to prevent misinformation continues to be a topic of discussion with respect to opportunities for potential government regulation (Helm & Nasu, 2021).

Algorithms

As part of profit maximization strategies, social media companies can implement two types of algorithms: content shaping, and content moderation (Maréchal & Biddle, 2020b). Content shaping algorithms determine what posts users will see and are usually based on digital traces of their prior activity. Such algorithms tend to show people more of what they have already seen and expressed interest in (Kim, 2017). Content moderation algorithms automatically identify content that violates a platform's terms of service, including, in some cases, misinformation about science (also see Chapter 7 for more on moderation). Using machine learning and other adaptive and automated techniques, substantial amounts of harmful content can be flagged and taken down before it can achieve viral popularity. However, these methods are not sufficient on their own, and human content moderators are needed to screen out content that eludes automated systems (Gillespie, 2018).

In accordance with the profit motives described above, content shaping algorithms have the potential to boost the visibility of misinformation about science. This can happen in multiple ways: for example, an algorithm might inadvertently show posts containing misinformation about effective treatments for cancer to a user who views and "likes" other cancer-related content. Content shaping algorithms can also surface misinformation about science through trending topics, which achieve broad visibility through short-term bursts of attention (see Basch et al., 2021; Bonnevie et al., 2023). Because they are not based on users' past activities, trending topics can expose people to content they have not previously expressed any interest in. Whereas content shaping algorithms can amplify misinformation about science by presenting it to users, content moderation algorithms can do so by failing to flag it for removal or by incorrectly removing credible information. But misinformation is a contested category, and even humans disagree as to what qualifies (Newman & Reynolds, 2021; see also Chapter 2), so it is inevitable that algorithms designed to filter it out will fall short in some instances.

Content Moderation

Finally, some social media platforms may be slow to implement or unwilling to implement or enforce robust policies against misinformation in part because prohibitions against misinformation can be in conflict with the predominant, ad-based business model. Some social media platforms *do* forbid misinformation in certain scientific categories—including health and COVID-19—but permit it in others such as those pertaining to social issues (Waddell & Bergmann, 2020). This means that misinformation in unmoderated scientific categories may be more visible on some social media platforms. Freedom of speech is sometimes marshaled in defense of such lax policies, without much acknowledgment of their downsides (Smith-Roberts, 2018). The efficacy with which platforms enforce policies to address misinformation is a separate matter. Not all policy violations are punished equally, whereby violations committed by popular or powerful users may be exempted from enforcement (Morrison, 2021; Porterfield, 2021).

The committee found substantially less research on search engines than on social media platforms, even though 68% of website traffic comes from organic and paid search results (BrightEdge, 2019) and 88% of adults in the United States use traditional search engines (Iskiev, 2023). The literature on search engines (only some of which is specific to misinformation about science) focuses on improving the epistemic quality of search results (Granter & Papke, 2018; Mazzeo et al., 2021), understanding how information quality relates to health decisions (Abualsaud & Smucker, 2019), analyzing misinformation prevalence in search results across languages (Dabran-Zivan et al., 2023), and comparing misinformation consumption between social media and search (Motta et al., 2023). Recent work by Tripodi & Dave (2023) have employed qualitative interviewing to explore how search engines can lead users to inaccurate or misleading information, finding that optimization and advertising on search engines may create conditions that make it challenging for information seekers to find accurate information about health. But overall, the limited scope of research on search engines is likely related to the lack of availability of data from such sources.

Influence and Monetization

As suggested in the discussion of information sources in Chapters 3 and 4, there is variation in how much different actors are viewed as credible or trustworthy. Additionally, a small number of accounts may be responsible for a large amount of misinformation about science online (Yang et al., 2021). We refer to the ability to gain attention and encourage sharing of information as influence.

On social media, software agents known as bots promulgate false scientific claims on a daily basis that are read by few if any actual people (Dunn et al., 2020). Humans generally have greater power to distribute misinformation than bots (Xu & Sasahara, 2022), probably due to the bots' inability to convincingly mimic human communication patterns (Luo et al., 2022). However, bots are cheap and relatively easy to create, which may render their marginal ability to promulgate false beliefs worth the cost. Among human-controlled social media accounts, attention has long been known to follow a long-tailed distribution, wherein a small number of accounts accrue disproportionately large shares of attention (Himelboim, 2017). Accordingly, a substantial proportion of the misinformation shared on social media platforms can be attributed to a small number of prominent and highly active users (Nogara et al., 2022; Pierri et al., 2023). Many of these users are not household names, but nevertheless can reach large audiences with misinformation about science.

Aside from research studies on a few news media outlets, little quantitative research has explored how powerful actors can spread misinformation in non-social media contexts. A few studies have described how popular podcasters (Burton & Koehorst, 2020; Dowling et al., 2022) and TV channels that Goss (2023) describes as "sham journalism" misinform their respective audiences, but these are not systematic analyses. Two other relevant studies have explored talk radio. One was a survey of listeners who reported that they were relatively misinformed (Hofstetter et al., 1999). The other was a content analysis of talk radio content that found, among other results, substantial quantities of "very dramatic negative exaggeration" that "significantly misrepresents or obscures the truth" (Sobieraj & Berry, 2011, p. 40).

One reason for the lack of research on non-social media contexts may be the methodological difficulties of studying visual and audio content. Natively textual media such as newspapers, magazines, and digital text have historically been much more popular as data sources across the social sciences than non-textual media due to the greater accessibility of the former. Moreover, the state of the art in computational analysis of text has been far more advanced than for images, audio, or video: the kinds of information that can be extracted from non-textual media are much more rudimentary than what can be obtained from text. While a few studies have begun to explore misinformation beyond the textual domain (e.g., Yang et al., 2023), it is clear that the field has a way to go before its capacity to analyze images, audio, and video reaches that of text. This is an especially important area for methodological development given the massive popularity of podcasts and video platforms.

Another factor that contributes to the spread of misinformation is the ability to monetize or leverage it for profit. As discussed in the previous section, technology companies, including social media platforms, infrastructure providers (e.g., hosting companies, ad tech firms, donation platforms), and advertisers may profit financially when (mis)information circulates widely (Han et al., 2022), as is the case for social media influencers and other online content creators. Specifically, online content creators can profit from advertising revenue earned from the social media platforms and funded by advertising companies, as well as from monetization practices that circumvent social media platforms, such as affiliate marketing, selling products, or soliciting donations or subscription payments from fans (Hua et al., 2022).

Financial incentives sometimes underlie the production of intentionally fabricated news on social media platforms. For example, Silverman & Alexander (2016) reported that some producers of fabricated news in Macedonia profited from click-based advertising revenue when articles they posted on social media went viral. Additionally, other studies have shown that some political campaigns and state-level propaganda operations have employed workers to post disinformation online for extra income (Han, 2015; Ong & Cabañes, 2019).

Specific to monetization of misinformation about science, there is some limited evidence that points to financial incentives behind spreading it in venues dedicated to alternative health. Alternative health websites (discussed in more detail in Chapter 4) that spread misinformation may have commercial interests to promote alternative remedies for various health conditions (Baker et al., 2024), including alternative wellness products, and often by linking to affiliate sites (Moran et al., 2024). Another example is "The Non-GMO Project," a non-profit organization that for a fee, provides verification and labeling for non-genetically modified organism (GMO) products, including for large retailers. Studies find that consumers are willing to pay more for food with a non-GMO label (McFadden & Lusk, 2018), and as of 2019, more than 3,000 brands, representing over 50,000 products and netting more than $26 billion in annual sales, had been verified with the non-GMO label (Ryan et al., 2020). Additionally, the Non-GMO Project's websites and blogs state for example, that "the science on GMOs isn't settled" (Waddell, 2023), despite international scientific consensus about the safety of GM foods for human health, including from the National Academies of Sciences, Engineering, and Medicine (2016a), the World Health Organization (2014), and the European Commission (2015).

While these examples are suggestive, systematic analyses of the monetization of misinformation are rare. In one study, Herasimenka et al. (2023) analyzed the websites of 59 different groups demonstrated to be involved in communicating misinformation about vaccine programs and found that a large majority showed evidence of monetization. The authors noted that appeals for donations was the most common strategy used, followed by sales of information products and merchandise including health supplements and then finally third-party advertising and membership dues. Another study by Broniatowski et al. (2023a) compared the website links shared by anti-vaccine and pro-vaccine Facebook groups, finding that while monetization strategies—particularly embedded ads—were nearly universal, pro-vaccine pages were more likely to share links to monetized sources than anti-vaccine pages. This was largely due to the tendency of pro-vaccine pages to link to news websites, which are heavily monetized; when examining non-news sites separately, sites shared by anti-vaccine actors were more highly monetized. We identify the monetization motives and strategies of misinformation actors, as well as their effects, as an important area in need of additional research.

Public Relations Strategies

As briefly discussed in Chapter 4, public relations strategies are sometimes used to distort scientific evidence and spread misinformation about science in service of business and/or policy objectives. These strategies, discussed in more detail below, include questioning evidence, claiming more research is needed, conducting internal research that confirms pro-industry biases, funding academic research programs, recruiting individual scientists to speak against the weight of scientific evidence, and exploiting journalistic norms. Researchers have shown that these strategies are often part of disinformation campaigns adopted by a range of industries over the last 70 years (Michaels, 2008, 2020; Oreskes & Conway, 2010b). Importantly, public relations companies have been described as not merely carrying out strategies devised by their corporate clients, but also as the creators, developers, and enactors of these strategies (Aronczyk, 2022). Additionally, Aronczyk & Espinoza (2021) argue that science denial and obfuscation in the interest of corporate profits and power may have become institutionalized in part because of the work of public relations firms. It is also important to note that the existing evidence on the role of public relations strategies in the spread of misinformation about science largely reflects studies of the tobacco, fossil fuel, and pharmaceutical industries. In this section, the committee mainly draws upon this literature.

Science historians Oreskes & Conway (2010b), in their book *Merchants of Doubt*, have written most extensively about the "playbook" that was established by tobacco companies in the 1950s and have since been adopted by a range of industries to manufacture uncertainty surrounding available scientific evidence (see also Michaels, 2008, 2020; Michaels & Monforton, 2005). Critically, the authors describe this concept as the act of creating debate about the science by questioning the evidence and claiming that more research is needed before acting (Oreskes & Conway, 2010b). For example, Oreskes & Conway (2010b) reported that even though the science was clear that smoking increased the probability or risk of getting cancer and other diseases, the tobacco industry was able to claim that factors other than smoking could be the culprit because not everyone who smoked got cancer. Moreover, as discussed in Chapter 2 of this report, science is a dynamic, iterative process of discovery that is always evolving. To this end, Oreskes & Conway (2010b) suggest that some industries have taken advantage of the inherent tentativeness of science to create the impression that everything can be questioned and thus nothing about the existing science is certain or resolved.

Further, to cast doubt about the dangers of their products, it has also been reported that some corporations have either conducted their own research or have funded external research that is biased toward predetermined results that support the industry's position (Oreskes & Conway, 2010b). For example, Oreskes & Conway (2010b) reported that the tobacco industry, under the advisement of a public relations (PR) firm, created the Tobacco Industry Research Committee in 1954 to sponsor independent research on the health effects of smoking, which in practice was weighted toward research identifying alternative explanations for lung cancer, such as stress, infection, and genetics. Decades later, in the 1990s, the NFL was reported to use a similar strategy with the formation of the Mild Traumatic Brain Injuries (MTBI) Committee to conduct scientific research on the risks of concussions to football players and ways to reduce such injuries (Michaels, 2020). According to Michaels (2020), the committee was largely made up of football insiders, many with conflicts of interest due to financial ties to the NFL, rather than independent physicians or brain science researchers. Additionally, in the early 2000s, the MTBI Committee published a series of peer-reviewed journal articles that were reported to either minimize or deny the dangers of football-induced head injuries. Work by Reed et al. (2021) on industries that conduct their own research, shows that such efforts can similarly skew the science in favor of the companies' agenda, reporting that some pharmaceutical companies may choose to omit particular research methods that might substantiate a link between its product and serious health risks.

Another industry strategy that has been documented in the literature is the leveraging of the trustworthiness of academia and/or professional science societies by building connections through funding and partnerships. For example, Oreskes & Conway (2010b) reported that in the 1950s, the tobacco industry established a fellowship program to support research by medical degree candidates, in which 77 of 79 medical schools agreed to participate, and representatives from reputable agencies and associations were invited to its board meetings. The authors also noted that such connections with doctors, medical school faculty, and public health officials can protect an industry's reputation and, in the case of the tobacco industry, likely secured its role in national conversations related to smoking and health. Likewise, Thacker (2022) reported that since the 1990s, some fossil fuel companies have funded research programs related to energy and climate at elite American universities. Similarly, other scholars suggest that some pharmaceutical companies have funded programs at institutions of higher education in service of establishing legitimacy (Reed et al., 2021; Union of Concerned Scientists, 2019).

Relatedly, research suggests that some industry-led disinformation campaigns can often involve recruiting individual scientists who are willing to speak against the weight of scientific evidence, and as a result, such claims may be given a sense of credibility (Dunlap & McCright, 2011; Oreskes & Conway, 2010b). For example, funding in biomedical research at major universities by the tobacco industry is reported to have not only provided new data and results that challenged the link between tobacco and cancer, but also created an army of "friendly witnesses" who could provide expert testimony in lawsuits filed against tobacco companies that cast doubt on cigarettes as the primary cause of disease (Oreskes & Conway, 2010b, p. 30). Likewise, with respect to climate science, it has been reported that a cadre of credentialed scientists have been involved in challenging the scientific consensus on global warming, through appearances in the media, hearings, and press conferences, and in their writing (Dunlap & Jacques, 2013; Oreskes & Conway, 2010a). Moreover, scholars have noted that the experts who speak out against scientific consensus may appear to have field-relevant expertise but often do not (Hansson, 2017), and that many of the *same* experts who challenged the link between smoking and cancer also contested the science on climate change (Oreskes & Conway, 2010a). Legg et al. (2021) have shown that industry scientists may also participate in seemingly independent decision-making bodies and advisory groups to advocate for industry-favorable policies. Additionally, industry scientists frequently serve on science advisory boards of federal agencies and some researchers have found that industry-majority scientific boards are perceived by the public as biased toward business interests over other priorities, such as human and environmental health (Ard & Natowicz, 2001; Conley, 2007; Drummond et al., 2020).

Another public relations strategy used in industry disinformation campaigns as documented in the research literature is the creation of Astroturf or front groups that can act on behalf of corporate interests but whose corporate ties are obscured from public view (Aronczyk, 2022). Astroturf groups are designed to look like popular, grassroots efforts (e.g., to support oil and gas) but are actually a product of corporate public relations (Aronczyk, 2022; Sassan et al., 2023). Additionally, scholars report that these seemingly independent front groups allow corporations to distance themselves from disinformation campaigns (Dunlap & Brulle, 2020; Givel & Glantz, 2001; Williams et al., 2022), and such groups have been leveraged to promote climate change denial (Aronczyk & Espinoza, 2021), and disinformation about the dangers of tobacco use (Givel, 2007), and to market opioids (Ornstein & Weber, 2011).

Finally, media coverage has also been shown to play a central role in the strategies that some industries may use to manufacture debate around science issues, including efforts that exploit journalistic norms and practices to cover both sides of science debates in the interest of balance and objectivity, but in some cases may promote false balance in news reporting, as previously discussed in Chapter 4 of this report. Additionally, work by Armstrong (2019) has shown that through the efforts of their public relations firms, some industries have also been effective at distorting the broader media narrative around science issues. Moreover, research has shown that in addition to earned media, some industry disinformation campaigns have also involved paid advertising in traditional and social media to target policymakers and the public with false and misleading information. Some examples of this strategy have been documented with respect to the fossil fuel industry, whereby scholars report that paid ads have been used to downplay the risk and seriousness of climate change, promote fossil fuels as a necessity, and shift responsibility for climate change to individual consumers (Holder et al., 2023; Supran & Oreskes, 2017, 2021). Additionally, although the focus of this section is on industry strategies, activist movements have also been shown to rely on similar media strategies to challenge scientific consensus. For example, Lynas et al. (2022) reported that anti-GMO activist networks have been able to seed misinformation about GMOs in online news stories, often by relying on scientists who make statements that question the scientific consensus around the safety of GMO safety.

Information Access and Information Voids

Misinformation can also spread when people are overwhelmed by information and unsure who or what to trust, or when they are searching for answers but can't find credible information. The stakes are especially high during emergencies, when misinformation spread and uptake can have significant consequences for public health and safety. Understanding the dynamics of misinformation spread is especially important for managing infodemics that occur during fast-moving environmental and health crises. As previously mentioned, infodemics are characterized by an abundance of information (both accurate and inaccurate) as well as by information voids, which are created when public demand for high-quality information is high but supply is low (Chiou et al., 2022; Purnat et al., 2021), and both conditions can enable misinformation to spread more easily.

Relatedly, "data voids," which occur when search engine queries on a topic result in few or no results, such as in the case of breaking news, can also be exploited by bad actors to fill that void with disinformation (Golebiewski & boyd, 2019; also see Chapter 3). Tripodi (2022) has also documented what is referred to as "ideological dialects," whereby some groups may strategically use community-specific terms and phrases that when entered as keywords into a search engine will primarily return information, including misinformation, that confirms the ideological view of that community. For example, a search using the keywords "illegal aliens" will yield very different results from a search that uses "undocumented workers" as the keywords.

As discussed in Chapter 3, different social groups—especially non-White racial and ethnic groups—have access to and may experience different types and quantities of information, including misinformation, based on the differential positioning of such groups within the contemporary information ecosystem. Further, some efforts to spread misinformation to communities of color have been specifically adapted to exploit the concerns of these communities (Lee et al., 2023). For example, scholars report that Black communities who have been exposed to misinformation on social media platforms concerning vaccines have received messages that elevate concerns about medical racism and exploitation as well as ongoing structural inequalities in order to discourage this community from being vaccinated (Lee et al., 2023). For some Indigenous groups, the spread of misinformation within these communities can be largely driven by national media that then filters down to local issues (Young, 2023b). Further, some misinformation about science often intersects with long histories of extractive science within Indigenous communities, which can exacerbate existing inequalities and social divisions (Young, 2023b; see also Chapter 6). Research on Latino communities has identified "information poverty" linked to the primacy of interpersonal and social media-based information networks as a key driver of the spread and reach of misinformation within this specific community (Soto-Vásquez et al., 2020).

Lack of in-language resources is another example of how social inequalities shape the flow of misinformation about science, given this lack can create a vacuum that can be exploited and filled with unreliable information (Fang, 2021). Access to quality and reliable information often determines how non-English speakers interact with and rely upon information (Nguyễn & Kuo, 2023). Specifically, non-English speaking communities in the United States lack access to critical information regarding public health protocols or vaccines due to a lack of available and sufficient language translation and interpretation for healthcare and other social services (Yip et al., 2019). Marginalization that is created by a supply of credible science information that is predominantly in the English language can also have profound and inequitable impacts. For example, in the context of medical and health inequities, Bebinger (2021) found that in March 2020, "patients who didn't speak much, or any, English had a 35% greater chance of death" during the COVID-19 pandemic. Lack of adequate language translation and interpretation has also been described as an issue of collective access (Nguyễn & Kuo, 2023; see also Chatman, 1996 on information poverty). When information is only made available in one dominant language, there are information voids created for both in-language and culturally-relevant translations (Nguyễn & Kuo, 2023). Ryan-Mosley (2021), in looking at Asian American communities, argues that the lack of accurate language translations on websites have created exclusionary, careless, and discriminatory online environments. To this end, many community-based groups and organizations, though often under-resourced, have stepped in to fill in this gap by making their own in-language guides and materials (Nguyễn & Kuo, 2023; also see Chapter 7 for more discussion).

It is imperative to note that translation work is not a direct one-to-one process due to cultural, contextual, dialectical, and technological characteristics of information, and as such, the process of translation may inadvertently change the context and meaning of the original information. For example, in the Spanish language, when discussing "healthcare" there are specific phrases in reference to the general system, coverage, insurance, and literal care; similarly, translating the word "advocacy" may create debates, given existing words in the Spanish language do not adequately capture the concept (Equis Research, 2022). English dominance in the keywording processes of knowledge production also creates limits on what is searchable, since bits of misinformation and disinformation translate differently or may be described differently across other languages (Nguyễn & Kuo, 2023). This in turn creates a bottleneck in the accessibility of language translation of misinformation and disinformation, let alone in the accessibility of empirical research about misinformation that is associated with mistranslation and out-of-context interpretation. Additionally, there are high costs associated with translation work and major hurdles to ensure the translator (whether human or artificial intelligence) has the expertise that requires in-depth knowledge and analysis of regional and temporal dialects. Consequently, there is also a variety of unaddressed misinformation in non-English languages, given the lack of investment in robust content moderation on the part of social media companies, labor-intensive work for human translators, and the unreliability of machine language translations (Nasser, 2017; Nicholas & Bhatia, 2023). Misinformation in the Spanish language that targets Latinos in the United States has been noted as a particular problem that is, in part, due to limited fact-checking of non-English language content on social media platforms (Sanchez & Bennett, 2022).

RHETORICAL TACTICS

While the nature of misinformation about science varies across issues, there are some common rhetorical themes that recur regardless of the issue and source, and that are used strategically by purveyors of disinformation, including within some industries, governments, and activist campaigns. Diethelm & McKee (2009) identify five elements that are commonly used in arguments to challenge a scientific consensus; these include claiming of conspiracies, use of fake experts, selective use of evidence (cherry picking), imposing impossible standards for research, and using logical fallacies. These five characteristics are also known by the acronym FLICC: Fake experts, Logical fallacies, Impossible standards, Cherry-picking of evidence, and Conspiracy theories (Cook, 2020).

The first, claiming of conspiracies, occurs when any agreement among scientists is attributed to a conspiracy among elites to suppress the truth. The second characteristic is the use of fake experts (i.e., scientists who appear to have relevant qualifications but whose views are completely contradictory to established knowledge [as discussed above]) that can result in the denigration of scientists whose research findings support the established consensus. For example, such scientists can be subject to harassment and intimidation, through verbal attacks on their credibility, as well as through lawsuits and Freedom of Information Act requests (Levinson-Waldman, 2011; Quinn, 2023; also see Chapter 8 for more discussion). The third characteristic is selectivity, or cherry-picking evidence to support an anti-consensus position or reject well-conducted research that reaches undesirable conclusions. The fourth characteristic involves imposing impossible standards for what research can deliver. One example described by Diethelm & McKee (2009) is when arguments denying the reality of climate change point to the absence of accurate temperature records prior to the invention of the thermometer. Similarly, some activist campaigns commonly include calls for more research to establish the safety of vaccines, particularly randomized controlled trials. However, withholding life-saving vaccines from a control group would be considered unethical. Thus, such research may be impractical if not impossible (Kata, 2012). The fifth characteristic is science denialism, which, according to Diethelm & McKee (2009), is the use of misrepresentation and logical fallacies, such as red herrings, straw men, and false analogies.

Research also reveals additional tactics and tropes (e.g., appeals to personal values, using de-contextualized scientific claims to support inaccurate beliefs) that are commonly used within specific communities or as part of a similar approach to spread misinformation. Importantly, these additional strategies have been most documented for the topic of vaccination. Furthermore, these tactics reflect and often exploit key features of the contemporary information ecosystem (discussed in Chapter 3), such as audience fragmentation and context collapse, both of which facilitate exposure to competing narratives about science and can lead to differences in who people see as trustworthy sources of science information. One example of a common trope are arguments against vaccination that frequently center on values like individual freedom and choice, and highlight concerns about government intervention (Broniatowski et al., 2020; Hoffman et al., 2019; Hughes et al., 2021; Kata, 2012; Moran et al., 2016). Such concerns are reported to often be associated with an expressed mistrust of the scientific community (Hoffman et al., 2019). Appeals to civil liberties with respect to the topic of vaccination have also developed alongside increasing social media activity promoting state-level mobilization against vaccine mandates (Broniatowski et al., 2020).

Another common trope associated with the spread of misinformation about science is to encourage "doing your own research" (DYOR), which urges people to seek out additional or alternative information to verify facts and evidence before making decisions (Carrion, 2018; Hughes et al., 2021; Kata, 2012; Tripodi et al., 2024). While it is reasonable and even desired to seek out more information and verify facts and evidence, the DYOR tactic is not actually in support of a reasonable quest for more information. Rather, the call to DYOR can reflect and cause doubts in substantiated or more settled science, and is consistent with reduced trust in public institutions (i.e., the absence of trust necessitates independent verification; Luhmann, 1979) and post-modernist thinking, whereby truth is seen as contestable and reflective of one's own lived experiences; and the implication is that doctors, scientists, and other officials may not have all the answers (Carrion, 2018; Kata, 2012). Those who embrace the DYOR perspective may adopt epistemologies that are not bound by expectations of internal consistency or burden of proof (Birchall & Knight, 2022; Carrion, 2018), and may also exhibit an overreliance on people who are not scientific experts as key sources for science- and health-related information (Baker et al., 2024; Hughes et al., 2021; Kata, 2012; Nichols, 2017). Additionally, survey research conducted by Chinn & Hasell (2023) suggests that when people endorse the idea of "doing your own research," they are more likely to hold misbeliefs about COVID-19 and are less trusting of scientific institutions.

In some cases, purveyors of misinformation may promote "inaccurate narratives" by extracting accurate information from its original context and aggregating it in specific ways (e.g., clipping livestreams, selectively sharing scientific preprints; Wardle, 2023). Examples of this strategy may even be found in the scientific literature: a study that re-analyzed published research rejecting the consensus on anthropogenic climate change revealed that "[a] common denominator [in such research] seems to be missing contextual information or ignoring information that does not fit the conclusions" (Benestad et al., 2016, p. 699). Other scholars have also noted how particular talking points and "patterns of information" allow for subtle segmentation of populations whereby through the use of precise keywords people can selectively search for material supporting particular (accurate and inaccurate) narratives (Tripodi, 2022, p. xiii). Moreover, this can also give the impression that a person is "doing their own research" (Tripodi, 2022).

Strategies to spread misinformation about science is also not limited to verbal rhetoric. Visuals, including memetic images that circulate widely online, also are used strategically to misrepresent science. For example, some anti-GMO campaigns have used images of needles inserted into fruit and of surreal depictions of plant hybrids (i.e., "Frankenfood") to convey the unnaturalness and questionable safety of GM crops (Clancy & Clancy, 2016). Specific examples of misleading imagery relating to the topic of climate change have also been reported (see Lewandowsky & Whitmarsh, 2018).

INDIVIDUAL MOTIVATIONS

As discussed above, political, ideological, and/or economic motivations may drive some institutions and groups to spread misinformation about science. However, the motivations that might drive individuals to spread misinformation are less well understood. A relatively understudied area, most of the research on individual motivations focuses on misinformation about politics or "fake news" in social media contexts. But within the extant research, multiple motivators that drive the spread of misinformation among individuals have been described; one being monetization as discussed above. Others described in the sections that follow include confusion and inattention, social motivations, partisan motivations, persuasion and activism, emotion, and disruption (i.e., a desire to generate chaos).

Confusion and Inattention

Most people want to share accurate information (Pennycook et al., 2021), and reputational concerns typically discourage people from sharing false content (Altay et al., 2020; Waruwu et al., 2021). Thus, in some cases, people may share misinformation because they are unable to discern that it is false, due to either a lack of digital literacy skills (Guess et al., 2020) or because of motivated reasoning that leads some individuals to uncritically accept information that comports with their existing beliefs (Pereira et al., 2023; Peterson & Iyengar, 2021; Taber & Lodge, 2006; Vegetti & Mancosu, 2020). Some misinformation sharing has also been shown to be confusion-based (Pennycook et al., 2021). Yet, even when people can correctly discern the accuracy of information, they may still share misinformation, in part, because their attention is focused on factors other than accuracy. Priming people to attend more closely to the accuracy of social media content can reduce misinformation sharing, lending support to this inattention explanation (Pennycook & Rand, 2022a; Pennycook et al., 2021).

Social Motivations

While confusion and inattention account for some misinformation sharing, people also often knowingly and intentionally share misinformation. In the United States, in 2016, 14% of adults reported sharing a political news story online that they knew at the time was made up (Barthel et al., 2016). Similarly, a 2018 survey of British social media users found that 17.3% of those who share news on social media admitted to sharing news in the past month that they thought was made up when they shared it (Chadwick & Vaccari, 2019). Individuals who intentionally share misinformation may be motivated by a complex constellation of social and psychological factors. Sharing information is an inherently social process, for example, people share information to improve their social status and to build and maintain relationships (Bobkowski, 2015; Bright, 2016). Specific motivations for sharing information on social media that have been reported include for self-expression, to inform, influence, provoke, entertain, or connect with others (Chadwick & Vaccari, 2019). Thus, many of the same reasons that people share accurate information extend to misinformation—they want to pass along interesting and useful content, express themselves, spark conversation and affiliate with others, and show that they are "in the know" (Apuke & Omar, 2021; Chen et al., 2015, 2023; Yu et al., 2022).

People may also share false information, even if they suspect it may be false or are unsure of its veracity, if they think it could benefit or protect someone from harm (Duffy et al., 2020). This altruistic motive to help or warn others has been found to be a strong predictor of sharing misinformation about COVID-19 on social media in Nigeria, where altruism is a strong cultural trait (Apuke & Omar, 2021), as well as a strong predictor of the willingness to share food-safety rumors among Chinese WeChat users (Seah & Weimann, 2020). Focus groups conducted in Africa similarly revealed that sharing misinformation, including health misinformation, is motivated by a "civic duty" to create awareness and warn others about issues of public concern (Chakrabarti et al., 2018; Madrid-Morales et al., 2021). This is often coupled with a "just in case" attitude, whereby people feel that the utility of the information, if it ends up being true, makes it worth passing along despite its questionable credibility (Madrid-Morales et al., 2021). In addition, community norms can play a powerful role in the spread of misinformation (DiRusso & Stansberry, 2022; Kata, 2010). That is, if misinformation is widely accepted within a particular community, community members will be more likely to share it. Moreover, if information that is shared violates community norms or comes from sources deemed untrustworthy by the group, that information and its source may be disparaged (DiRusso & Stansberry, 2022).

People also share misinformation to generate social engagement online, and this has been shown to be motivated by the positive social feedback that is built into the structure of social media platforms, such as likes and comments, which can overwhelm the motivation to share accurate information (Ren et al., 2023). Additionally, it has been reported that people expect that conspiracy theories will generate more engagement than factual content; this may be due to the strong emotional valence of conspiracy theories (Albertson & Guiler, 2020; van Prooijen et al., 2022a). Moreover, social media environments facilitate social feedback, which may habituate social media users to share dubious information in anticipation of social rewards (Ceylan et al., 2023; Ren et al., 2023). Habitual social media sharers are conditioned to share information that attracts others' attention and as such may do so without concern for accuracy, even when they are primed to consider accuracy and even when the information contradicts their personal views (Ceylan et al., 2023). Other recent evidence suggests that when people simply think about whether to share content on social media, this can actually distract from their ability to discern the accuracy of that content due to a shift in their attention to non-accuracy-related motivations and factors that drive sharing choice (Epstein et al., 2023). In other words, users may develop a social media mindset as described in Epstein et al. (2023), that is characterized by prioritizing content sharing and personal motivations for sharing content over assessing the accuracy of content.

Some people may also share misinformation in order to expose it as false (Metzger et al., 2021). For example, findings from focus groups conducted in Spain revealed that people sometimes share misinformation with the intent to correct or critique it (Ardèvol-Abreu et al., 2020). In Denmark, tweets containing misinformation about the COVID-19 mask debate were often shared to reject the misinformation; yet many of these tweets were also reported to have used humor to stigmatize or mock the misinformation spreader rather than to engage using substantive arguments (Johansen et al., 2022). This type of sharing behavior can inadvertently contribute to confusion in the information environment, especially when no effort is made to correct the false or misleading claims (Johansen et al., 2022).

Partisan Motivations

Individuals who intentionally share misinformation may also be driven by partisan motivations (i.e., individuals may share misinformation that supports their political in-group to express their partisan identity and associate with like-minded others [Marwick, 2018]). This is likely tied to the anticipated social rewards derived from sharing misinformation (as described above), and in such cases, the identity that is signaled by information is more important than its accuracy. Misinformation that supports one's in-group does not pose the same reputational costs as other types of misinformation (Waruwu et al., 2021). One of the few studies that has systematically analyzed various individual-level motivations for misinformation sharing found that partisan motivations are central (Osmundsen et al., 2021). The study found that on Twitter in 2018–2019, individuals who strongly identified with a political party were more likely to share content from politically congenial "fake news" sites, and this was reported to be potentially driven by their hostile feelings toward political opponents (Osmundsen et al., 2021). On the other hand, Osmundsen et al. (2021) did not find that poor reasoning skills (in contrast to Pennycook & Rand, 2019) or apolitical trolling drove "fake news" sharing; however, political cynicism was positively related to sharing "fake news" sources affiliated with both political parties. Following from these results, the sharing of misinformation about science topics that are subjects of political debate, like climate change or masks, might be motivated by political animus. Partisan motivations can also facilitate the spread of misinformation about science, in part because of the loss of trust in some scientific institutions (see Chapter 3).

Persuasion and Activism

Individuals also share misinformation with the intent to persuade or influence others. For example, a study based on representative surveys in six Western democracies, including the United States, found that a primary reason that individuals are willing to share social media posts containing conspiracy theories about immigration and COVID-19 is because they are convinced by or agree with the misinformation and feel the message needs to be told to others (Morosoli, 2022b). In other cases, individuals who share misinformation about science may be motivated by activism or the desire to create social change (Perach et al., 2023). Scholars also argue that misinformation can serve as a catalyst of social movements (Earl et al., 2021), whereby some activists may use it to raise awareness, amass support for their cause, build community, and promote collective action (Moran & Prochaska, 2023), including around science issues (Kata, 2012; Lynas et al., 2022; Seymour et al., 2015). In the digital era, scholars also note a rise in "participatory propaganda," whereby persuasive online messages that originate with political, corporate, or other strategic actors are then passed on by receptive target audiences to their broader social networks, thus increasing the reach and potential influence of the original message (Lewandowsky, 2022; Wanless & Berk, 2019). Target audiences can also play a more active role by finding evidence and creating content that fits existing misinformation narratives and frames, which can then be amplified by elites and those with large followings in a cycle of participatory disinformation (Starbird et al., 2023)

Emotions

Emotions, and particularly negative emotions, are also associated with misinformation sharing. Passing along negatively charged misinformation—i.e., "bad news"—may be a way for some people to manage their own uncertainty and anxiety (Wang et al., 2020). For example, anxiety is a predictor of willingness to share misinformation (as well as accurate information) about COVID-19 (Freiling et al., 2023). In China, exposure to food-safety related misinformation has been shown to trigger negative emotions that leads to more frequent sharing of that misinformation through both online and face-to-face communication channels (Wang et al., 2020). Fear and anger have also been reported as motivators for sharing misinformation about science (Ali et al., 2022). However, negative emotions are not the only emotions that are associated with online sharing. Paletz et al. (2023) found that several different discrete emotions are associated with online sharing, including both positive (happiness) and negative emotions (anger, sadness, fear), as well as emotions that differ in their levels of arousal or emotional activation (amusement and pride).

Disruption

Finally, some people may also share misinformation to disrupt the social order and inflict chaos. Individuals who engage in online trolling have been described as "agents of chaos on the Internet" (Buckels et al., 2014, p. 97), due to deceptive, destructive, and/or disruptive online behaviors—including sharing misinformation. Such individuals may seek to offend and engender negative emotional responses from their targets, often purely for the "lulz," i.e., because they find it funny (Marwick & Lewis, 2017). Buckels et al. (2014) also reported that those who engage in online trolling may derive enjoyment from victimizing others as signaled by high levels of sadism.

In some cases, however, individuals want to create chaos for more instrumental purposes. "Need for chaos" is a dispositional mindset that reflects a desire to gain status by disrupting the established order (Petersen et al., 2023). It has been reported that people who have a high need for chaos may feel socially and economically marginalized and, in turn, may direct animosity toward elites and people of all political allegiances (Petersen et al., 2023). Such individuals may also be motivated to spread hostile rumors targeting political elites in order to destroy the existing social order

(Petersen et al., 2023). Thus, unlike those who are motivated to share misinformation due to a particular partisan identity (Osmundsen et al., 2021), those with a high need for chaos may share misinformation regardless of which party it helps or hurts, as they want to stoke social conflict and damage the entire system (Petersen et al., 2023). Furthermore, sometimes state-sponsored actors use similar techniques, presumably in an attempt to erode trust in their adversaries' institutions, such as when messages both promoting and opposing vaccination were reported to be shared from troll accounts operated by the Russian Internet Research Agency (Broniatowski et al., 2018).

Summary of Individuals' Motivations

In sum, existing research reveals an array of sometimes competing and often overlapping individual-level motivations for misinformation sharing. Inconsistent findings across studies are likely attributable, at least in part, to differences in research methodologies. For example, Pennycook et al. (2021), who found inattention to be a leading explanation for misinformation sharing, studied *intentions* to share false headlines in an experimentally contrived social media context. On the other hand, Osmundsen et al. (2021), whose results pointed to partisan motivations as a key driver for misinformation sharing, combined actual behavioral sharing data with survey responses, but tracked the sharing of misinformation at the source level rather than at the story or headline level. To date, research highlighting altruistic motives largely reflects self-reported data. More research is needed to examine the robustness of these findings and to better understand how motivations may vary based on contextual factors and individual differences, as well as whether motivations for sharing misinformation specifically about science may vary from those driving the spread of political misinformation and unreliable news, for example.

Motivations are important to understand because they could inform potential interventions. Inattention to accuracy could be overcome with accuracy reminders or nudges (Pennycook et al., 2021). If people share misinformation due to altruistic motives, fact-checking may be helpful. However, if people share misinformation to signal their political affiliation, hurt political opponents, create chaos, or to earn money, accuracy or fact-checking based interventions will not be effective. To reduce misinformation sharing motivated by partisan or ideological bias, interventions may need to target polarization and/or mistrust in the political system (Van Bavel et al., 2021). Likewise, if people are motivated by the social reward structure on social media to post misinformation due to its engagement potential, a solution may be to change the incentive structure to reward the sharing of accurate information (Ceylan et al., 2023; Ren et al., 2023).

Finally, we note that motivations may be linked to the specific type of misinformation in question. Many of the instances of misinformation about science discussed result from a substantial profit motive. The target audiences of such misinformation may be more likely to believe it due to mistrust of the medical establishment and the imperative to find working treatments when conventional medicine has failed. The long-term efforts of industry, government, and other actors to obscure risks to public health and/or the environment also may lead audiences to be skeptical of consensus claims of safety (Goldenberg, 2016). Other types of misinformation about science with less obvious commercial origins (e.g., astrology) may connect with target audiences' shared identities grounded in interest in spirituality (Smith, 2023).

SUMMARY

The spread of misinformation about science is facilitated by key factors in the contemporary information ecosystem as well as by, common strategies used to undermine credible science information. Digital communication technologies can facilitate the spread of misinformation; however online platform companies may face mixed incentives on the issue of addressing the problem since the sharing of any information on platforms, including misinformation, can be lucrative. Furthermore, there are widely-adopted strategies to spread misinformation about science, including "manufacturing" doubt, promoting false balance in scientific debates (in part by exploiting journalistic norms requiring coverage of "both sides"), cultivating relationships with scientists who disagree with the prevailing consensus, and creating Astroturf campaigns to generate the illusion of public support and credibility. Additionally, some of the recurring themes in misinformation about science that have been identified include: claims of conspiracies among scientific, government, and corporate elites; the use of fake experts with questionable or nonexistent credentials; cherry-picking evidence; calling for impossible evidentiary standards to support scientific agreement; and denial of the weight of the scientific evidence using logical fallacies.

Purveyors of misinformation about science also commonly appeal to individual liberties and encourage followers to "do their own research," (i.e., seeking out sources that contradict the weight of the evidence on science issues). For individuals, major motivations for spreading misinformation can include financial gain, confusion or inattention, maintenance of social ties, signaling of partisan affiliation, persuasion of the unconvinced, management of negative emotions, and disruption of the social order. Finally, race, ethnicity, language, and social class (as well as other demographic characteristics of individuals and communities) constitute important determinants of the spread and reach of misinformation, with under-resourced communities and communities of color having disproportionately less access to reliable information and other resources that could reconcile information voids and more effectively build resilience against misinformation that is specifically tailored to these groups.

> *Conclusion 5-1: Individuals share information for a variety of reasons—for example, to improve their social status, to express a particular partisan identity, or to persuade others to adopt a certain viewpoint. Individuals may inadvertently share misinformation in the process of sharing information, and this may be due to their confusion about the credibility of the information, their inattention to accuracy, or altruistic efforts to help or warn loved ones, among other reasons.*

> *Conclusion 5-2: In some cases, individuals and organizations may knowingly share misinformation to profit financially, to accrue social rewards (e.g., followers and likes), to accrue and maintain power, to erode trust, or to disrupt existing social order and create chaos (e.g., trolling). These motivations may be especially incentivized in social media environments.*

> *Conclusion 5-3: The spread of misinformation about science through social networks on social media and through online search platforms is affected by design and algorithmic choices (e.g., those shaping individualized feeds based on prior platform activity), permissive and loosely enforced or hard-to-enforce terms of service, and limited content moderation. Moreover, platform companies may not voluntarily implement approaches to specifically address such issues when they are in conflict with other business priorities.*

> *Conclusion 5-4: Science has traditionally been recognized as an authoritative civic institution that produces many benefits for individuals, communities, and societies. Yet, at times, scientific authority has been co-opted by individuals and organizations feigning scientific expertise, and by science and medical professionals acting unethically in ways that contribute to the spread of misinformation about science (e.g., speaking authoritatively on scientific topics outside of one's area of expertise).*

6

Impacts of Misinformation About Science

In this chapter, we examine the impacts of misinformation about science with the aim of understanding those that most warrant intervention to prevent harm to individuals, communities, and society. Misinformation has the potential to disrupt the ability of individuals to make informed decisions for themselves, their families, or their communities; to further existing harms and negative stereotypes about groups that exacerbate discrimination and stoke violence; to distort public opinion in ways that limit productive debate; and to diminish trust in institutions, which is important to a healthy democracy. However, not all misinformation is equally consequential, and the relationship between misinformation and its impacts are neither simple nor linear.

As described in Chapter 3, the phenomenon of misinformation about science does not exist in a vacuum. Changes in the contemporary information ecosystem and a range of social, technical, historical, and societal forces affect the information individuals seek and encounter by virtue of both their individual characteristics and choices, and in how they and their communities may be differently situated with respect to the information ecosystem. As a result, the effects of misinformation about science are also differential (Samudzi, 2017; Singh et al., 2022; Southwell et al., 2023). Effects on individuals are influenced and shaped by their own individual characteristics and views (van der Linden et al., 2023), as well as by the structural and cultural contexts of their lived experiences, access to material and social resources, and community embeddedness of their social lives (Crenshaw, 2017; Goulbourne & Yanovitzky, 2021; McCall, 2005; Smedley, 2012). Moreover, in addition to differences among individuals and communities, not all misinformation is equal in terms of reach, scale, attention, and likelihood to be believed and acted upon, as discussed in Chapters 4 and 5.

The inherent difficulty of demonstrating causal links within a complex and interrelated system of factors poses a challenge for decision making about whether and how to intervene to address misinformation about science. On the one hand, focusing only on the limited evidence that clearly implicates misinformation as the direct cause of harm could suggest less intervention than might be warranted to prevent harm (Ecker et al., 2022; Lewandowsky et al., 2017). Conversely, making decisions based primarily on concerns about exposure to misinformation without examining the factors and nuances that shape whether and when that exposure leads to harm could lead to interventions that are excessive, antidemocratic, or counterproductive (Krause et al., 2022; Nyhan, 2020).

Despite the limited evidence for simple, linear connections between misinformation and individual behavior, there are certain situations where misinformation has greater potential for harm. We argue that the potential for harm is greater when the effects happen at scale in ways that disrupt individual agency or collective decision making, as well as when information is amplified by elites or part of a well-resourced campaign; when the effects are potentially severe, as with life and death decisions and those that provoke violence; and when the misinformation has the greatest potential to exacerbate existing harms, as when communities experiencing racism or health disparities are targeted.

In this chapter, we first discuss the nature of evidence about the impacts of misinformation. Subsequent sections describe the evidence for the impacts of misinformation for individuals, communities, and society, and the implications for informing decisions about intervention.

THE NATURE OF THE EVIDENCE ABOUT THE IMPACTS OF MISINFORMATION

We consider multiple types of evidence, including randomized control trials (RCTs)/experiments, longitudinal studies, correlational studies, and case studies that elucidate (a) the mechanisms by which misinformation *can potentially* cause harm at the individual, group, and societal levels and (b) the evidence that exists about the harms that can be attributed to or are associated with misinformation about science. Although experiments and longitudinal studies provide stronger causal evidence than do correlational and case studies, the latter provide useful information about how misinformation affects individuals and society at large.

Accurately measuring and documenting the precise causal effects of misinformation is difficult. Human beliefs and behaviors are influenced by many interacting factors, challenging researchers' abilities to directly measure the effects of misinformation in isolation. Although from an experimental design perspective RCTs provide strong evidence of these types of direct effects, there are very few RCTs on the effects of misinformation for both ethical and practical reasons. Ethically, decisions to purposefully expose people to false information should be made with great care, balancing the benefits of the knowledge learned to the potential harms to participants. Practically, RCTs are not always well suited to addressing some of the most important questions about the effects of multiple and prolonged exposures to misinformation about science, which has been likened to the effect of drops of water on a rock. The impact of each individual drop is difficult (if not impossible) to measure, but over time the water can completely change the shape of the rock (Wardle, 2023). Further, RCTs are designed to measure the average effect of an intervention on a sample (e.g., the effect of exposure to misinformation on U.S. adults). However, a focus on average effects misses potentially large changes at the ends of the distribution or on specific subsamples of the population. Misinformation that has no effect on most of the population but leads to large behavioral changes in a small minority can still, in theory, have harmful effects. Other methodologies may be more apt for making causal inferences for phenomena that occur in complex systems (Sugihara et al., 2012), and where random assignment is not possible, including matching on potential confounding variables and using panel designs that combine cross-sectional and time-series data (see Lorenz-Spreen et al., 2023 for a more complete discussion).

There are other limitations that make studying consequential impacts challenging. The effects of misinformation on different populations and communities remain understudied (Collins-Dexter, 2020; Soto-Vásquez, 2023). The gray literature from organizations whose research focuses on these populations have provided an important source of information for this report. In addition, few studies measure the effects of misinformation at the group and societal levels, though this is an important area for further study (Broda & Strömbäck, 2024).

IMPACTS OF MISINFORMATION FOR INDIVIDUALS

Much of the popular interest and research on the effects of misinformation has focused on the individual (Phillips & Elledge, 2022), and how it affects their beliefs, knowledge, attitudes, and/or behaviors. The following sections describe the relationship of misinformation about science to misbeliefs, the factors that make some individuals more receptive to misinformation when they encounter it, and the relationship of misinformation about science to detrimental behaviors at the individual level.

Holding Misbeliefs

For individuals, the most direct consequence of misinformation is that it alters people's beliefs and causes misbeliefs (i.e., false beliefs; Adams et al., 2023; van der Linden et al., 2023). In the view of this committee, holding misbeliefs about science can be harmful because it can disrupt individual agency. When people hold misbeliefs caused by misinformation, they lose the ability to use the best information from science to make informed choices and, as a result of this loss, face an increased likelihood of acting against their best interests and those of their families and communities. The potential harms from this disruption are further compounded when it occurs at scale. To more fully understand where potential harms from misinformation may be greatest, it is useful to examine the forces that increase the likelihood that an individual will be more receptive to believing misinformation when they encounter it.

Forces That Shape People's Beliefs

People encounter information (or misinformation) with their own sets of pre-existing beliefs, personal and social commitments, values, and goals. These, along with the natural human cognitive biases and heuristics that all people have and use (Tversky & Kahneman, 1974), shape how and the extent to which people search, uptake, and ultimately use information when making decisions. Decades of work have demonstrated people's tendencies to selectively seek, attend to, evaluate, and recall information that confirms one's prior beliefs or values, while ignoring or dismissing information that contradicts them (Kunda, 1990). These processes, including motivated reasoning (Kunda, 1990) and confirmation bias (Nickerson, 1998), can lead to biased assimilation of evidence, where information that is perceived to be in line with what we have encountered previously is generally treated with less skepticism and is more readily accepted as true or accurate (e.g., Pennycook et al., 2018). The evidence suggests that there is a recursive relationship that involves holding misbeliefs; seeking (mis)information about those misbeliefs; encountering similar, but new, misinformation; and adopting new misbeliefs (e.g., Slater, 2007).

This tendency to seek out or believe information that confirms pre-existing views can be especially robust for scientific topics that are the subject of political debate or when a topic becomes associated with a political figure or party, or for other topics about which people already have strong opinions (National Academies of Sciences, Engineering, and Medicine [National Academies], 2017; Stroud, 2008). When these beliefs comport with important identities and worldviews, people can also develop increasingly strong and polarized attitudes and resistance to attitude change (Lord et al., 1979; Nickerson, 1998; Taber & Lodge, 2006). These processes can also affect how people perceive the credibility and trustworthiness of scientific sources and experts, and the likelihood that people will selectively trust or distrust scientific authorities depending on their alignment with their ideological preferences or group identities (Lewandowsky & Oberauer, 2016). Moreover, encountering information repeatedly over time likely increases perceptions that such information is accurate and can be relied upon to inform decision making, and this applies to encountering misinformation about science as well (Pillai & Fazio, 2021; Unkelbach et al., 2019).

Well-established models of decision making (e.g., Theory of Planned Behavior; Value-Belief-Norm Model; e.g., Dietz, 2023; Steg, 2023) also highlight how values shape what people believe to be true and highlight too the role of norms and identity in how people make sense of information. On issues that may be associated with an important identity (e.g., environmentalist), people consider what they believe people "like them" do or should do (Dietz, 2023). Other dimensions, including concern for others (empathy) and reliance on others (trust) or perceptions of self- and collective-efficacy also impact decisions and behaviors, particularly around assessments of risk. Perhaps one of the most important contributions from these literatures is the consistent finding that people generally do want to act in accordance with the best available evidence but also in ways that are consistent with their pre-existing beliefs, values, and goals. These dual commitments can provide an opening for misinformation to warp decision making. For example, misinformation about the potential downsides of transitioning one's home heating and cooling system from a fossil fuel-burning furnace to an electric heat pump may stop an individual from choosing to do so because of pre-existing (mis)beliefs about a related but distinct issue (e.g., whether climate change is driven primarily by human actions).

Finally, decades of research in social psychology and allied fields have repeatedly revealed how foundational social interaction is to an individual's interpretation of the information they encounter throughout the course of their daily life. For example, network homophily is a well-known phenomenon in which people with similar beliefs tend to cluster together, meaning that they are less likely to be exposed to new information (Henry et al., 2021). In addition, foundational work on social conformity, interpersonal influence, and social norms (e.g., Asch, 1951; Cialdini & Goldstein, 2004) helps to explain how misinformation can continue to propagate through social networks, influence individuals' and groups' understanding of the world, and (in some cases) shape individual and collective decision making, even when that information is seemingly easy or obvious to identify as false or misleading. As a result, learning about new ideas can be inhibited (see Henry, 2017 for a review on the relationship between networks and learning in public policy contexts).

This foundational work helps to explain the cognitive biases and heuristics that all people have and use to navigate the world. They also help to demonstrate the importance of understanding how individuals may be situated in the broader context discussed in Chapter 3 and differentially exposed to the sources of misinformation about science discussed in Chapter 4. Patterns of declining trust in institutions, including shifts in increasing political and ideological divides, and experiences with structural inequities are forces that can intersect with pre-existing beliefs, values, and attitudes. They may also play a role in shaping the groups that an individual associates with in person and online, the norms and identities associated with these groups, and the sources that people believe and trust for information. Such patterns and experiences also highlight the potential for existing views and attitudes to be reinforced and strengthened through features of online information environments. However, as discussed in Chapter 3, the evidence on the extent to which people interact in echo chambers is mixed. In the next sections, we turn to discussions of the factors associated with the nature of exposure to misinformation and characteristics of an individual that can play a role in increasing receptivity to misinformation, potentially causing consequential misbeliefs about science.

Increased Receptivity to Misinformation About Science

Research shows that most people believe some misinformation (Berinsky, 2023), but it is useful to examine what factors may lead some people to be more receptive to it when they are exposed to it. Receptivity encompasses both active and passive consumption and acceptance of misinformation about science. In the view of the committee, receptivity is a more apt term than the more passive term, "susceptibility."

Exposure to misinformation leads to misbeliefs just as exposure to accurate science can teach people correct information (van der Linden et al., 2023). This has been demonstrated in meta-analyses of experimental studies in lab settings (Chan & Albarracín, 2023; Chan et al., 2017) as well as in real-world settings (e.g., Feldman et al., 2012). Specifically, Feldman et al. (2012) found that exposure to misinformation about climate change from news media was associated with misbeliefs about global warming, despite controlling for a range of potential demographic, media use, and other predispositions. Further evidence for the effects of exposure to misinformation on beliefs also exists for topics outside of science (see Butler et al., 1995; Kim & Kim, 2019).

As Figure 6-1 depicts, characteristics of the misinformation and characteristics of the individual (and the confluence of these two sets of characteristics) can impact how people evaluate misinformation and to what extent they are receptive to it. In the sections that follow, we outline

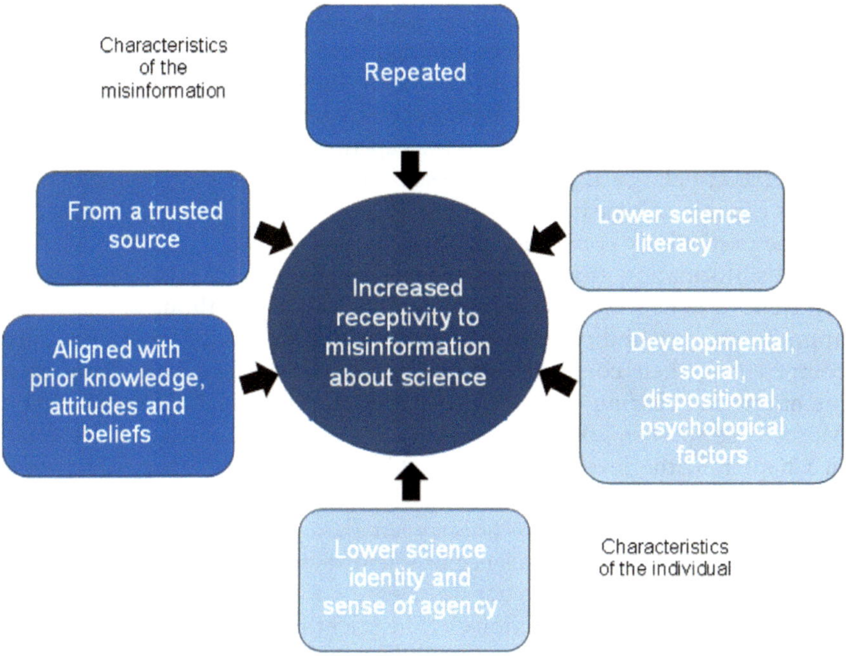

FIGURE 6-1 Key drivers of receptivity to misinformation about science.
SOURCE: Committee generated.

the evidence for each set of characteristics and conclude with a brief discussion of the implications.

Repetition and Trusted Sources Exposure to misinformation is more likely to lead to misbeliefs when it is repeated and when it is from a trusted source. Characteristics of information and the persuasive tactics employed in designing and sharing (mis)information can undoubtedly influence the extent to which audiences are receptive to that information. Repetition, for example, plays a large role in people's beliefs. Over 40 years of research finds that repeated information is more likely to be judged as true than novel information (see Dechêne et al., 2010 for a meta-analysis and Unkelbach et al., 2019 for a recent review). Repetition can increase belief in simple trivia statements (e.g., Fazio, 2020b), true and false political news headlines (Pennycook et al., 2018), advertising claims (Hawkins & Hoch, 1992), conspiracy theories (Béna et al., 2023), and health-related headlines (Pillai & Fazio, 2024). What's more, repetition can influence belief even when people have prior knowledge that contradicts the misinformation (Fazio, 2020b; Fazio et al., 2015). For example, repetition has been shown to increase belief in the false statement, "The Minotaur is the legendary one-eyed giant in Greek mythology," even among people who were able to correctly indicate that a one-eyed giant is called a Cyclops (Fazio et al., 2019). These effects of repetition can occur both in lab-based settings (see Henderson et al., 2022, for a review) and when the repetitions occur in daily life (Fazio et al., 2022; Pillai et al., 2023). These findings suggest that well-resourced efforts capable of repeatedly reaching large audiences with misinformation may be particularly consequential.

Misinformation that comes from a trusted source also impacts receptiveness. When individuals encounter information about science, they appraise the credibility of the communicator (knowledge or perceived competence), their confidence in the communicator or source, and their intentions for sharing the information (Fiske et al., 2007; Lupia, 2013; Mascaro & Sperber, 2009; Shafto et al., 2012). As described in more detail in Chapter 3, the levels of trust, credibility, and confidence that people have in science, scientists, knowledge-producing institutions, and sources of information about science affect what they believe and will act upon. For example, confidence in science or scientists may play an important role in how willing people are to act on scientific information or advice based on it (Lupia et al., 2024). Actions by the scientific community that demonstrate trustworthiness and accountability, including demonstrating commitments to scientific best practice, transparency, and open access, may play important roles in the public's confidence in science (Lupia et al., 2024). In addition, as described in Chapter 3, communities who have experienced current or historical harms from science may have lower levels of trust in authoritative sources of scientific information. These relationships may help to explain why misinformation from sources that are more likely to be believed and trusted (e.g., misinformation due to misuses of the cultural authority of science or misinformation amplified by trusted "elites") can be especially consequential (O'Brien et al., 2021). However, some have noted that rather than being more receptive to misinformation, many people are increasingly skeptical of all new information and unsure of what to believe (Equis Institute, 2022).

Aligned with Prior Knowledge, Attitudes, and Beliefs As described in the earlier section of this chapter, individuals may consciously or subconsciously compare new information they encounter to their existing understanding. Individual differences in literacies (i.e., media, informational) and existing knowledge may directly predict holding misbeliefs (see Ecker et al., 2022), but this is, itself, not evidence for effects of misinformation about science. However, these individual differences may predict greater receptivity and different types of reactions to misinformation about science, including the extent to which individuals engage with misinformation, adopt new misbeliefs or engage in problematic behaviors following exposure.

Holding strong attitudes or firmly-held prior beliefs about a topic has been associated with having lower objective knowledge about that topic, but in general there appears to be weaker effects of misinformation on attitudes than on beliefs (van der Linden et al., 2023). Fernbach et al. (2019) found that people in the United States holding extremely negative attitudes toward genetically modified (GM) food (i.e., extreme GM opponents) had both low levels of objective knowledge about the science behind GM food and high levels of self-assessed knowledge (see Chapter 5's discussion of "do your own research" as a recurring theme associated with misinformation about science). They also found that this pattern applied to opponents of gene therapy, another application of genetic engineering technology. Similarly, Motta et al. (2018) found that anti-vaccine policy attitudes in the United States were associated with low levels of objective knowledge about vaccines and immunology, but high levels of perceived understanding. In both cases, the authors suggested that providing factual information or correcting misconceptions may not be enough to change people's attitudes, as they may be resistant to new evidence or alternative perspectives.

Not all studies have found a negative relationship between knowledge and extreme attitudes, at least when those extreme attitudes are positive. For example, Fonseca et al. (2023) conducted a survey of U.K. adults and found that people with strong attitudes toward genetics (whether positive or negative) had higher levels of self-confidence in their understanding of science than those with more ambivalent attitudes. However, compared to those who are more ambivalent, those with strongly positive attitudes had higher levels of objective knowledge. Those with strongly negative attitudes had lower levels of objective knowledge than those who were more ambivalent. The authors proposed a model to explain this finding: the more someone believes they understand the science, the more confident they will be in their acceptance or rejection of it (Fonseca et al., 2023).

The "Dunning-Kruger" effect, described as when "people suffering the most among their peers from ignorance or incompetence fail to recognize just how much they suffer from it" (Dunning, 2011, p. 251) sheds further light on the complex relationship between knowledge and beliefs. For instance, Light et al. (2022) showed how groups with the least knowledge about controversial science issues have the most confidence in their knowledge. Examples include "whether genetically modified (GM) foods are safe to eat, climate change is due to human activity, humans have evolved over time, more nuclear power is necessary, and childhood vaccines should be mandatory" (p. 1). The converse to the problems of overconfidence are the benefits of well-earned confidence: people who are both knowledgeable and confident are better able to make sense of controversial science topics than those who are knowledgeable but lacking in confidence. For instance, Peters et al. (2019) showed that people who have high "numeracy," or numerical literacy, and high confidence levels are better able to cope with making sense of health situations imbued with data than those who are knowledgeable but lack confidence.

One explanation for the relationships between knowledge and confidence is motivated reasoning. For example, Radrizzani et al. (2023) found that trust in relevant sciences increased during the COVID-19 pandemic among adults in the U.K., but also became more polarized; those who reported lower trust in scientists prior to the pandemic reported that their trust in scientists had decreased over time, while those reporting higher pre-pandemic trust tended to report becoming more trusting over time, indicating that respondents pre-existing views were strengthened.

Developmental, Social, Dispositional, Psychological Factors Theory borrowed from the study of media effects suggests that individual differences can influence effects of misinformation about science in two ways (see Valkenburg & Peter, 2013). First, individual dispositional, developmental, and social characteristics can predict exposure to and/or engagement with misinformation about science. Dispositional dimensions of receptivity[1] to media effects are those individual characteristics that shape how people select and respond to media including gender, values, attitudes, beliefs, and motivations, among other elements (Valkenburg & Peter, 2013). We expand on some of these dispositional dimensions (e.g., prior attitudes and beliefs) below. Developmental factors can include those that shape media consumption in childhood as well as those in adulthood affected by life stage, such as childrearing. Though some studies have examined age or cohort as a possible individual difference variable in receptivity to science and/or health misinformation (e.g., Nan et al., 2022), the findings are somewhat mixed and limited across different contexts. This presents an opportunity for future research. Lastly, social characteristics include the interpersonal, institutional, and societal contexts that shape one's receptiveness to misinformation about science. Individuals do not form attitudes or beliefs in a vacuum; social networks are crucial in understanding how beliefs are formed and spread and how they influence decisions (e.g., Frank et al., 2023; Henry, 2021). Furthermore, group identity and descriptive and injunctive norms have been shown to be influences on individuals' "planned behavior" (e.g., Ajzen, 2020). Individual differences can moderate the possible response states triggered by exposure to and engagement with misinformation about science (Valkenburg & Peter, 2013; see Figure 6-2).

---

[1]Valkenburg & Peter (2013) use the term "susceptibility."

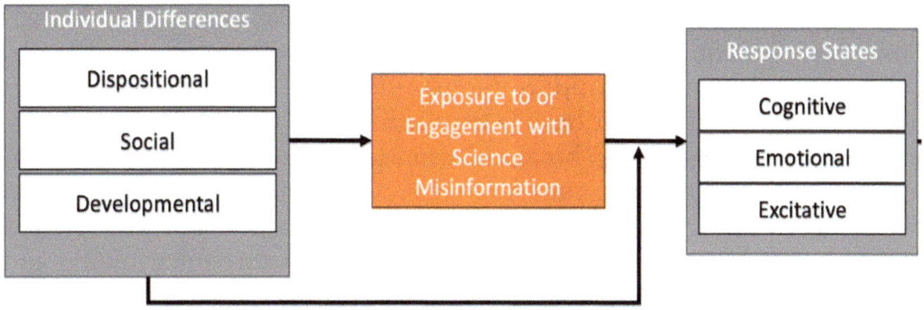

FIGURE 6-2 Individual differences influence receptivity to misinformation about science.
SOURCE: Based on Valkenburg & Peter, 2013.

People may believe misinformation because it fulfills their psychological needs to understand the world, to feel in control, or to feel connected to their community (Young, 2023a). Most of the existing research on such factors has focused on belief in conspiracy theories; however, in the committee's view, these findings would be expected for other types of misinformation, though this should be explored in future research. For example, people who felt more uncertain about themselves, their place in the world, and their future were more likely to believe COVID-19 conspiracy theories (Miller, 2020), and belief in conspiracy theories is linked with greater need for uniqueness (Imhoff & Lamberty, 2017; Lantian et al., 2017). Conversely, reminding people about times when they have felt in control reduces belief in conspiracy theories (van Prooijen & Acker, 2015). As such, one might expect exposure to false narratives and belief in misinformation to correlate with improved psychological functioning as people are able to fulfill their psychological needs. However, current research suggests that those needs actually remain unfulfilled (Douglas et al., 2017).

Anxiety, such as the chronic anxiety that many experienced during the COVID-19 pandemic (Brown et al., 2023) is also associated with increased belief in conspiracy theories (Grzesiak-Feldman, 2013), and neuroticism is correlated with false rumors (Lai et al., 2020). In another study, people with higher scores on depression screening questionnaires were more likely to endorse misinformation (Perlis et al., 2022). And while it is unknown whether belief in conspiracy theories is a cause or consequence, it is associated with negative mental health symptoms (Bowes et al., 2021).

Science and Health Literacy Science knowledge and science literacy are often used interchangeably in the literature, although science literacy tends to encompass broader features than knowledge about science, such as cultural appreciation, recognition of expertise and personal dispositions, such as inquisitiveness and openness (National Academies, 2016b). Despite its commonsense appeal, the weight of the current evidence does not support a simple relationship between having higher science literacy and being more discerning between accurate and inaccurate information, more critical of dubious claims and sources, and more open to updating beliefs based on new evidence (see Box 6-1). Indeed, science literacy and cognitive competencies are often regarded as key factors for avoiding and resisting misinformation about science. But such an assumption mirrors the public deficit model, or the knowledge deficit hypothesis, which posits that public skepticism and negative attitudes toward science (or in this case openness to misinformation about science) are the result of a lack of public scientific literacy (Besley & Tanner, 2011; see Suldovsky, 2016). However, a large body of literature investigating the effects of knowing scientific facts, or of science literacy and literacy-adjacent cognitive competencies (e.g., critical reasoning ability, cognitive reflection, deliberation, knowledge calibration) on receptiveness to misinformation about science calls for a more nuanced understanding. For example, in some cases, there is a positive relationship between the tendency to use analytical reasoning and belief accuracy (Landrum et al., 2021; Pennycook & Rand, 2019). In others, there is no clear relationship: Attari et al. (2010) find that most people make the

BOX 6-1
Consensus on Consequences of Science Literacy

The National Academies (2016b) report *Science Literacy: Concepts, Contexts, and Consequences* found that the evidence on the extent to which science literacy is causally related to various outcomes—such as the use of scientific knowledge, perception of U.S. international standing in science, health literacy, and health behaviors—is mixed and inconclusive. The report also noted that, while there is overall a small positive relationship between literacy and attitudes toward science, there are many confounding factors that influence these outcomes, such as prior beliefs, values, motivations, emotions, social networks, media exposure, or trust in sources.

The National Academies committee concluded that science literacy is not a simple antidote for misinformation or a guarantee for informed decision making. Rather, it is a multifaceted construct that requires different types of knowledge and skills for different contexts and domains. Moreover, it is not only influenced by cognitive factors, but also by motivational, emotional, social, and cultural factors that shape how people encounter and process science information. Therefore, interventions to enhance science literacy need to be tailored and targeted to specific audiences and situations.

same errors in estimating energy use from household appliances despite varying literacy levels. Moreover, some studies have found that individuals with greater science literacy and education have even more polarized beliefs than the less well-informed when it comes to controversial science topics, such as climate change, evolution, and stem cell research (Drummond & Fischhoff, 2017a).

Although a particular level of science knowledge or literacy does not solely explain receptivity to misinformation, when combined with other factors, the likelihood of individual receptivity to misinformation about science increases. Science literacy is an important competency that enables informed decision making; however, it also interacts with other factors, such as worldview, political orientation, religious affiliation, identity, values, emotions, and motivations, and this constellation of factors influence how people process and interpret science information (e.g., Kahan et al., 2012).

Other cognitive dimensions related to science knowledge and attitudes have also been suggested and tested empirically. Science curiosity (Kahan et al., 2012) and scientific reasoning (Drummond & Fischoff, 2015), for example, tap elements of literacy that are less factual and more process based. These have been found to be less predictive of polarized beliefs than fact-based measures of literacy.

In a related vein, health literacy is assumed to "enable individuals to obtain, understand, appraise, and use information to make decisions and take actions that will have an impact on health status" (Nutbeam & Lloyd, 2021, p. 161). While the definition does not explicitly address misinformation about health, the idea of an ability to obtain correct information and appraise information proposes a mechanism through which health literacy may play a role in how individuals are exposed to and influenced by misinformation. Some studies have also focused on understanding the role of so-called functional, interactional, and critical health literacy skills, which allow people to *discriminate* between sources of information and critically extract meaning and relevance for their situation and conditions (Nutbeam, 2000).

Sense of Agency and Identity as a Science Learner

Evidence is growing that a sense of agency and identity as a science learner, in both childhood and adulthood, increases individual capability, motivation, and likelihood to use science in a variety of settings (Avraamidou, 2022; Hinojosa et al., 2021; Polman & Miller, 2010; Shirk et al., 2012). Developing epistemic agency in science—shaping the knowledge and practice of science in their communities—is important for all learners (Stroupe, 2014), and especially for learners who need to combat structural barriers to their inclusion when they encounter it (Polman,

2023). Furthermore, such identification with science, technology, engineering, and mathematics (STEM) intersects with other identifications such as gender (Carlone et al., 2015; Steinke et al., 2024), race (Nasir & Vakil, 2017), or political views (Walsh & Tsurusaki, 2018). Positioning someone as capable in science, regardless of gender, race, or marginalized status, can help increase inclusion in STEM. Alternatively, positioning someone as incapable in science can lessen motivation and use (Brown et al., 2005; Sengupta-Irving, 2021). Research on conspiracy thinking also indicates that some communities seek to assert their epistemic agency by "doing their own research" (a common rhetorical tactic discussed in Chapter 5; Olshansky et al., 2020).

Detrimental Behaviors and Actions

Overall, researchers tend to find large consistent effects of misinformation on beliefs and much smaller effects on behavior (Adams et al., 2023; van der Linden et al., 2023). Partially, this is because behaviors (like getting vaccinated) are determined by multiple factors, which may or may not be related to beliefs (Hornik et al., 2020). For example, there are many people who are open to getting vaccines but cannot do so because of transportation or other logistical difficulties (Peña et al., 2023). Currently, most research to explore the link between misinformation, misbeliefs, and behavior has measured behavioral *intentions* (self-reported survey responses about what participants would likely do; Adams et al., 2023; Schmid et al., 2023). This is often due to resource constraints, but direct measures of behavior are particularly valuable and should be examined in future research.

Despite these limitations, misinformation can affect individual behavior in consequential ways. For example, belief in misinformation about cancer treatments may lead patients to make choices that increase their risk of death through delayed or lack of treatment, toxic effects, harmful interactions with other therapies, or economic harms (Johnson et al., 2022). Research in the United States from early 2021 (just after the first COVID-19 vaccines were approved) found that the amount of vaccine-related misinformation shared on Twitter by users in a region forecasted changes in vaccine hesitancy in that region 2–6 days later (Pierri et al., 2022). In addition, initial belief in COVID-19 conspiracy theories predicted people's actual vaccination behavior over the subsequent weeks or months in both the Netherlands and United States (van Prooijen & Böhm, 2023). Another study found that although online content flagged as misinformation on Facebook causally produced lower intention to vaccinate, few were exposed to this content; of more concern was the misleading content that was found to be more prevalent on mainstream media outlets and appeared to have an impact on behavioral intentions (Allen et al., 2024).

A recent meta-analysis of 64 laboratory-based RCTs examining the impact of health misinformation across the world found that none of these studies directly measured impacts on health or environmental behaviors. Approximately half of these studies indicated evidence for impacts on the psychological antecedents of behavior, including knowledge, attitudes, or behavioral intentions, as discussed above (Schmid, 2023). Several studies examined impact on trust, norms, and feelings, and the authors posited that the role of these factors in mediating the impact of misinformation warrants further study. They also noted a lack of diversity across different demographic groups in the samples of the studies they examined.

One example that illustrates this type of experimental work on the impacts of misinformation on behavioral intentions involved exposure to an anti-vaccine conspiracy theory. Exposure to such misinformation was found to decrease participants' stated likelihood to immunize a fictitious child against a novel disease (Jolley & Douglas, 2014). Similarly, exposure to COVID-19 vaccine misinformation in September of 2020 reduced participants' intentions to receive the vaccine (Loomba et al., 2021). However, when other participants were exposed to misinformation about the COVID-19 vaccine in June of 2021 (after the vaccines had been in use for 6 months), the false headlines did not decrease vaccination intentions (de Saint Laurent et al., 2022). In addition, exposure to conspiracy theories about the human papillomavirus vaccine (HPV) led to decreases in intentions to get immunized, but only among participants with low prior knowledge about the vaccine (Chen et al., 2021). Thus, current research suggests that the effects of misinformation on behavior are likely to be greatest when people are first forming an opinion about a topic or issue. More research is needed to establish who is most likely to act on their misbeliefs associated with misinformation in harmful ways.

UNDERSTANDING HARMS AT THE COMMUNITY LEVEL

As Chapter 3 described, the phenomenon of misinformation about science is best understood through a systems perspective, where individuals are affected by the contexts in which they live and encounter (mis)information. Understanding the psychology of misinformation and how it effects individuals is important, but understanding potential for harm at the community level is important for understanding differential impacts on a larger scale and for informing solutions that do not place the onus solely on individuals. Below, we describe the structural factors that influence receptivity to misinformation and potentially lead to compounding harms. Of particular concern is misinformation that could lead to violent or threatening behavior.

Structural Factors Influencing Receptivity to Misinformation About Science

Individuals belong to various communities that are differentially situated with respect to health and science information in the information ecosystem, as described in Chapter 3. Additionally, there are broader cultural and societal factors that shape experiences, perceptions, and behaviors related to science and health information, and by extension, misinformation. The sections below describe in more detail the role of community- and societal-level factors such as socio-economic status, information access, marginalization, and racism in the effects of misinformation about science including how these factors contribute to differential receptiveness. Moreover, when communities are receptive to misinformation and it disrupts informed decision making, it can compound existing harms, such as the health disparities that many communities face due to poverty, racism, environmental degradation, and/or communication inequalities (Viswanath et al., 2020). Finally, it is important to understand when misinformation might be especially consequential and intervention warranted to prevent (further) harm, such as when communities are targeted with disinformation campaigns (Collins-Dexter, 2020).

Socio-economic Status

Stratification, whether measured in terms of income, education, occupation, or other measures of socio-economic status (SES), is central to any conversation about the study of effects of misinformation about science. Science and health literacy are not equally distributed throughout society. A review of several papers on health literacy concluded that downstream social determinants such as education, occupation, and income are associated with access to and acting on health information (Keen Woods et al., 2023; Stormacq et al., 2019). In fact, SES is strongly associated with holding accurate knowledge in areas such as science, health, environment and politics, and these SES-based knowledge gaps grow as information spreads more widely (Tichenor et al., 1980; Viswanath & Finnegan, 1996). These findings are particularly relevant to understanding misinformation's effects in times of scientific uncertainty and fast-paced generation of scientific information.

By extension, several studies have shown associations between SES and exposure to and prevalence of misinformation. At the macro level, a study of survey responses from 35 countries noted that the lower a country's gross domestic product (GDP; i.e., GDP per capita, a measure used to gauge a country's total economic output) is, the greater the prevalence of COVID-19 misinformation (Cha et al., 2021). Similarly, a study with over

18,000 respondents across 40 countries also found an association between lower GDP and a high prevalence of COVID-19 misinformation (Singh et al., 2022). They also found that poorer countries were more likely to be exposed to and believe misinformation, and they showed higher rates of vaccine hesitancy than countries with higher GDP (Singh et al., 2022). Other national and global studies have shown associations between SES and health, and that low literacy is strongly correlated with low socio-economic and social standing (Buckingham et al., 2023; Sørensen et al., 2015). In one study, the authors examined eight European countries and found that, among these countries, SES is positively associated with health literacy skills (Sørensen et al., 2015). Several studies illustrate an association between health literacy and health disparities and risk perceptions (Berkman et al., 2011; Stormacq et al., 2019). Lower levels of health literacy are associated with structural barriers, such as lower levels of education and limited educational opportunities, policies and practices that are either discriminatory or not culturally tailored, and lower levels of trust in the healthcare system. These factors have been shown to limit access to resources and skills important to health literacy in some communities (Muvuka et al., 2020).

Information Access

As discussed in Chapters 3 and 5, communities vary in their access to reliable information about science. Some communities experience an overabundance of information (e.g., infodemics during public health emergencies), and others experience information voids (see Chapter 5). Further, there are relevant differences in the media preferences across communities (see Chapter 4), which may influence the type of information particular communities are more likely to encounter or consume (Soto-Vásquez, 2023). Importantly, some social media platforms have attempted to combat misinformation, such as by restricting vaccine-related content to only reputable sources, which, while reducing misinformation about vaccines, inadvertently created information vacuums (Guidry et al., 2020).

The issue of "digital inequalities" also affects different communities variably (Barnidge & Xenos, 2021). For example, rural areas face unique challenges (Perera et al., 2023; Vassilakopoulou & Hustad, 2021) with respect to equal access to reliable broadband internet, while urban areas experience "digital redlining," the creation or furthering of inequity in marginalized geographical areas through inequitable access to technology (Popiel & Pickard, 2022). Such inequalities can limit the ability for some communities to participate in and understand a new and rapidly changing information society (Vassilakopoulou & Hustad, 2021), including the ability to discern and act upon reliable science information.

Marginalization and Racism

Misinformation's impact on communities that have been marginalized because of race, ethnicity, nationality, or language must be understood within their broader socio-cultural and political context. Many of these communities are often treated as monoliths, but in fact are quite diverse in history, cultural contexts, language, socio-economic conditions, and patterns of trust—elements that matter for understanding the impacts of misinformation. Such homogenous labeling can also obscure specific disparities between these communities, which has implications for their relationship to information and also the impacts of misinformation about science. For example, the Latino community is composed of many distinct communities that shape how they interpret and experience harms. Cuban American communities differ in important ways from Mexican American communities, and there are variations even within those communities. The Asian American community includes people who speak over 50 languages (Asian American Disinformation Table, 2022). Likewise, African Americans belong to a broad and diverse population of Black people and people of African ancestry, who also have unique histories and cultures. This rich diversity can also provide sources of strength and resilience in the face of misinformation about science, not simply sources of vulnerability (Cabrera et al., 2022). Community-led strategies that demonstrate the resilience of these communities are discussed in Chapter 7.

Despite this resilience, long-standing educational, occupational, housing, wealth, and health disparities are well-documented across these communities. Health disparities, including the unequal prevalence of risk conditions, morbidity, and mortality, are deeply rooted in historical and current-day societal structures, and in the organization of institutions and practices. Structural racism, or the myriad ways in which social institutions and processes perpetuate discrimination, is an important factor in these unequal and harmful outcomes (Bailey et al., 2017). Its impact is evident in various health indicators, including kidney disease, HIV, cancer, and COVID-19. The historical legacy of structural racism fosters inequalities and fuels distrust among marginalized communities, who may justifiably question systems that have been exploitative and not designed for their benefit (Bonilla-Silva, 1997; Gee & Ford, 2011). Overall, few studies have paid sufficient attention to such communities, and more research is needed that explores the impacts of misinformation and the strategies that the communities themselves are developing to combat it (Soto-Vasquez, 2023). Therefore, analyzing the impact of misinformation about science necessitates a comprehensive understanding of these effects on individual, group, and population levels, considering various social institutions and the context of both historical and current inequities.

Some communities have had experiences in which misinformation about science was used to justify violence or disenfranchisement. This includes painful histories, such as the eugenics movement, where what was once considered the scientific consensus was determined over time to be misinformation that was based on racist, biased, and discriminatory research.[2] Evidence suggests that these types of experiences among non-English communities may affect how they may perceive and believe science misinformation and disinformation. For example, misinformation and disinformation about Native and Pacific communities historically being used to justify land theft and occupation as well as ongoing displacement (e.g., the science of blood quantum logics to dispossess Native people from their homes [Arvin, 2019; Kauanui, 2008]); myths about Indigenous communities as "backwards" and "anti-science" (Smith, 1999); and erasures of violence such as nuclear testing in the Marshall Islands (Teaiwa, 1994).

Research shows that racialized discourses of disease have also been used to stoke anti-immigrant sentiments (Shah, 2001) and as justification for state-sanctioned measures of control, such as during the AIDS epidemic in the early 1990s (Paik, 2013). Racism against various groups has also been observed as a recurring theme in online misinformation about COVID-19 (Brennen et al., 2021; Criss et al., 2021). In particular, individuals of Chinese descent have been inaccurately scapegoated as carriers or creators of the disease (Holt et al., 2022; Kim & Kesari, 2021). This phenomenon may not be a coincidence—existing research suggests that conspiracy theories and prejudice may share the same underlying psychological characteristics, but this possibility has not yet been studied directly (Freelon, 2023). Box 6-2 illustrates how the phenomenon of misinformation about science can be differentially experienced in immigrant and diaspora communities.

Targeting

Some communities have also been the targets of misinformation and disinformation. For example, scholars report that the tobacco industry engaged in efforts to direct misleading information, such as through advertising, with devastating impact on Black, Latino, poor, homeless, and other marginalized and minoritized populations (Apollonio & Malone, 2005; U.S. National Cancer Institute, 2017). Menthol cigarettes were also reported to be heavily marketed toward defined audience segments, particularly African Americans (Anderson, 2011; Wailoo, 2021). Inaccurate information about vaccines and autism that targets Black people has also been deployed in the United States (see for example, Stone, 2021). Similarly, in the Democratic Republic of Congo (Vinck et al., 2019), the spread of

[2]See https://www.genome.gov/about-genomics/fact-sheets/Eugenics-and-Scientific-Racism

BOX 6-2
Vaccine Hesitancy and Conspiracy Theories in Immigrant and Diaspora Communities

Much of the existing and accessible scholarship about non-English misinformation focuses on COVID-19 vaccination, given heightened scholarly attention and interest in misinformation and disinformation during the COVID-19 pandemic. In the Vietnamese diaspora, the spread of misinformation during the beginning of the COVID-19 pandemic could be categorized into three main types of narrative: false information and conspiracy theories about virus origins, general development of the global pandemic, and prevention and treatment for the virus (Nguyen & Nguyen, 2020). This study also found that the Vietnamese population was willing to "turn to any source they trust in daily life," even those without traditional credibility, leading to misinformed actions and beliefs (Nguyen & Nguyen, 2020, p. 445). Some misinformation that circulated among immigrants and communities of color also reaffirmed lingering institutional distrust, as in, for example, statements that wrongly asserted that the vaccines would be ineffective for anyone who was not a Caucasian male because only cells from male fetuses were used for testing (Johnston, 2021). These erroneous statements about vaccine efficacy represented a conflation turned into misinformation about real issues regarding disparities in demographic representation in clinical trials (Giusti et al., 2021).

For others, vaccine hesitation has also connected to lived diasporic experiences of militarized and state violence, which may lead to fears that vaccine enrollment or institutional encounters might result in government policing, data collection, and surveillance. In Pakistan, conspiracies emerged about vaccines having microchips with the power to control and surveil, or that COVID-19 was a fake disease (Khan et al., 2020). These conspiracies have also been tied to the U.S. CIA's fake Hepatitis B vaccination drive in 2011 that tried to collect DNA samples in search of Osama Bin Laden (Iqbal, 2021; Martinez-Bravo & Stegmann, 2022). In Mexican and Central American migrant communities, vaccine hesitancy has been tied to conspiracies that the vaccine will be used by the U.S. government to track and deport individuals (Sesin, 2020). This research points to the importance of taking into account of these histories and intersecting systems of violence wrought by institutions and states in uneven ways in different communities.

SOURCE: Nguyễn, S., & Kuo, R. (2023, unpublished). [Misinformation in non-English information networks]. Commissioned paper for the Committee on Understanding and Addressing Misinformation about Science.

misinformation asserting that the outbreak of the Ebola virus was not real has been reported.

There is evidence that specific communities that have been targeted by anti-vaccine disinformation campaigns have higher rates of vaccine hesitancy, strengthening the link between misinformation and misbeliefs about vaccines. One prominent example is the Somali immigrant community in

Minnesota and the resulting outbreak of measles in 2017. The community was concerned that their children were being diagnosed with autism, a diagnosis that was rare in Somalia. Scholars report that anti-vaccine activist groups then targeted the community, spreading misinformation about the safety of childhood immunizations and promoting the false claim that the MMR vaccine causes autism (DiResta, 2018; Molteni, 2017). Immunization rates for young children of Somali descent in Hennepin County were later reported to have dropped from over 90% in 2008 to 36% in 2014 (Hall et al., 2017). The resulting measles outbreak infected 75 people before being contained (Minnesota Department of Health, 2017). A similarly sized measles outbreak in Washington state was estimated to cost ~3.4 million dollars in terms of the public health response, productivity losses, and direct medical costs (Pike et al., 2021), with others suggesting that even that cost is likely an underestimation (Cataldi, 2021).

Discrimination and Violence

Misinformation can also foster discrimination or violence. Some evidence exists that misinformation has led to violent destruction of infrastructure (Jolley & Paterson, 2020). Additionally, discrimination and violence against specific groups based on race or ethnicity warrant important consideration. Establishing a direct causal link between exposure to misinformation and subsequent increases in discrimination or violence is challenging, which likely contributes to the existing gap in the literature. Yet, the consequences of this potential connection are severe (Irfan, 2021). This is particularly true when that misinformation is propagated by elite individuals, and some recent studies have explored this issue within the context of COVID-19. For instance, Chong et al. (2021) identified an association between the spread of misinformation, disinformation, and historical stereotypes with an increase in racist attacks against Asian and Black individuals during the pandemic. Tessler et al. (2020) reviewed patterns of violence and discrimination against Asians and Asian Americans during the pandemic and suggest that the rise in such incidents against Asian individuals and businesses during the pandemic was linked to beliefs about the origins of and potential carriers of COVID-19. The authors also draw parallels between the anti-Asian sentiment during the pandemic and the anti-Arab and anti-Muslim sentiment following the 9/11 attacks, which extended beyond Arabs and Muslims to also affect Sikhs, Indian Americans, Lebanese, and Greeks (see Perry, 2003). Kim & Kesari (2021) argue that both the spread of misinformation and increasing patterns of violence toward Asians and Asian-Americans can be traced back to rhetoric by elite individuals that more closely resembles hate speech misinformation. However, they suggest further research is needed to explore the intersections between hate speech, violence, and misinformation (Kim & Kesari, 2021).

CONSEQUENCES OF MISINFORMATION AT THE SOCIETAL LEVEL

The consequences of misinformation about science at the societal level are challenging to measure, given the multiple factors involved and the interrelated nature of those factors. Furthermore, some societal harms are most consequential in the ways that they amass over time, as with misinformation associated with the addictiveness of opioids. Many studies of societal-level impacts of misinformation have focused on political contexts, such as effects on elections. Some of this literature with particular relevance to misinformation about science includes research on the effects of misinformation on: trust in institutions; collective decision making; public health; and the scientific enterprise.

Effects on Trust in Institutions

Scholars have argued that misinformation can erode trust in institutions, including science and the media, especially when that misinformation takes the form of conspiracy narratives related to authorities and institutions (e.g., see Hofstadter, 1964; Rutjens & Većkalov, 2022; van der Linden, 2015). For instance, exposure to untrustworthy news sources has been linked to a decrease in trust in mainstream media over time (Ognyanova et al., 2020). Similarly, reading about COVID-19 conspiracy theories has been shown to reduce participants' trust in institutions and diminish support for government regulations (Pummerer et al., 2022).

The causal direction of the relationship between exposure to conspiratorial misinformation and low trust in institutions remains unclear. Belief in conspiracy theories is strongly predicted by pre-existing mistrust in authorities and institutions (e.g., Abalakina-Paap et al., 1999; Einstein & Glick, 2015; van Prooijen et al., 2022b), suggesting that the connection between exposure to such kinds of misinformation and low institutional trust may be more complex or iterative. Further research is needed to explore the relationship between misinformation and trust in institutions, particularly to clarify the directionality and potential feedback mechanisms involved.

Many individuals rely on mainstream media sources for their information about science (Funk et al., 2017; National Science Board, 2024). Given the reach and potential impact of mass media, it is important to examine how misinformation about science might have consequences for the media. As discussed in earlier sections of this chapter, exposure does not equate to attention to or belief in that information. However, some evidence does exist that misinformation affects trust in journalism. Media coverage of misinformation may inadvertently increase the repetition of the misinformation, or lead to second order effects, such as increased feelings of cynicism, apathy, disengagement, or unhealthy levels of skepticism of all information, both accurate and inaccurate (Guess & Lyons, 2020). Further, in one experiment, participants who read tweets about fake news were more distrustful of news media and less likely to correctly label accurate news stories as real as compared to participants who read tweets about the federal budget (Van Duyn & Collier, 2019). Scholars also find some evidence that "fake news" websites influence the issue agendas of partisan media online (Vargo et al., 2018).

Collective Decision Making

Some misinformation, whether intentional or unintentionally produced, can stymie having a shared set of facts around which to debate policy options. Public debates about policy-relevant science topics that are also primed for misinformation have been affected by disputes over evidence, as well as by well-organized campaigns to spread false claims, increase doubt, and mischaracterize the state of science (see Chapters 4 and 5). Some scholars have expressed particular concern that political polarization around scientific topics is increasing, such that there are fewer shared epistemologies for what constitutes reliable evidence for claims (Lewandowsky et al., 2017, 2023). Others have argued that disputes over agreed upon facts and policy options have long existed (Nyhan, 2020), and that such facts can still be productively debated (Judge et al., 2023).

Misinformation that disrupts the ability for scientific evidence to inform productive decision making at different levels of government (local, state, national) is potentially harmful simply by virtue of the scale of potential influence. As described in Chapter 3, science plays a unique role in society because it provides a reliable way to describe the current status of an issue, determine potential causes and influences, and estimate risks and predict the likely outcomes of different choices. However, it is important to underscore that scientific evidence alone is not sufficient for making individual and policy choices, particularly in cases where scientific uncertainty may be high (e.g., new technologies). Decades of work in the social sciences dispute simple models of people as rational actors who dispassionately weigh facts to make choices (Dietz, 2023). Similarly, evidence from the science of science communication clearly demonstrates that simply providing facts, regardless of how accurate, accessible, and understandable the information is, will not automatically lead to courses of action that are in accordance with what scientists believe they should be (National Academies, 2017). But despite these limitations, misinformation about science that disrupts the ability to discern reliable information from science for use in decision making has great potential for harm.

Public Health and Medicine

Some of the most consequential societal effects of misinformation about science have been documented within public health. Disinformation campaigns have been linked to decreased vaccination rates and delayed rollouts of beneficial public health campaigns. The link between misinformation and vaccine hesitancy has been demonstrated in both observational longitudinal studies and case studies of specific communities. For example, Wilson & Wiysonge (2020) examined the link between disinformation campaigns about vaccines and actual vaccination rates across 166 countries. They found that a one-point increase in the five-point disinformation scale was associated with a two-percentage point drop in average global vaccination rates year on year. Such a lack of vaccine demand during the pandemic likely had tragic consequences. Some have estimated that between 178,000 to over 300,000 American lives could have been saved with higher COVID-19 vaccination rates (Zhong et al., 2022).

Misinformation can also harm public health when it delays the implementation of beneficial interventions. For example, the delayed rollout of antiretrovirals in South Africa as a treatment for AIDS was reported to, at least in part, be due to government officials' promulgation of medical misinformation (Baleta, 1999; MacGregor, 2000), and is estimated to have cost more than 330,000 lives (Chigwedere et al., 2008). Similarly, Golden Rice, a genetically-modified crop designed to reduce vitamin A deficiency, was first developed in the 1990s and has yet to be widely adopted due to concerns over genetically-modified organisms (GMOs) and prominent misinformation campaigns (Wu et al., 2021). Meanwhile, vitamin A deficiency is reported to be a major health problem affecting 29% of children between six months and five years of age in low- and middle-income countries (as of 2013) and contributes to preventable blindness and increased mortality from measles and diarrhea (Stevens et al., 2015).

Misinformation about science may also have direct and indirect impacts on clinical care. Prior to the pandemic, burnout among healthcare practitioners was high and rising. Additional qualitative research suggests that clinicians may feel ill equipped, untrained, and lacking sufficient time to adequately address medical misinformation either at the point of care or online (Amanullah & Ramesh Shankar, 2020; Leo et al., 2021; Sharifi et al., 2020). Some clinicians were also reported to have experienced moral distress treating critically ill patients who had chosen not to receive a COVID-19 vaccine (Klitzman, 2022). While it is not clear what impact medical misinformation is having on healthcare workers, levels of burnout, and, therefore, patients, this intersection will continue to be an important area of study.

The Process of Science

The presence of misinformation may also alter scientific priorities, funding for science, and the ways that scientists communicate. In areas where misinformation is rampant (e.g., climate change), researchers are forced to spend time and energy combating false beliefs rather than producing new knowledge. As one example, Lewandowsky et al. (2015) argue that claims that opposed scientific agreement around climate change, such as that global warming had paused, led to a large number of research papers and reports rebutting or providing further context on that claim (including two special issues in *Nature* journals and a large section of the Intergovernmental Panel on Climate Change's AR5 report) despite the "pause" only existing when trends are calculated starting in one specific abnormally warm year. Similarly, Wakefield et al.'s discredited study (1998) that asserted a link between autism and the MMR vaccine was reported to have changed scientific priorities and led to multiple new studies, meta-analyses, and expert panel summaries all finding no link between vaccines and autism (e.g., Institute of Medicine, 2004; Jain et al., 2015; Madsen et al., 2002; Pietrantonj et al., 2021; Taylor et al., 2014).

In addition, science knowledge, science interest, and trust in science are correlated with public support for government funding for science (Besley, 2018; Motta, 2019). Thus, if exposure to misinformation reduces science knowledge, interest, or trust, public support for science and science funding may decrease. As mentioned above, there is some evidence that misinformation can decrease accurate knowledge and trust in institutions, but there is a lack of research examining the direct costs of misinformation on public support of science.

SUMMARY

Understanding the consequences of misinformation about science requires a systems perspective. Misinformation has the potential to directly and/or indirectly harm individuals, families, communities, and society. The strongest evidence of harm supports the argument that misinformation can cause misbeliefs, which is an important potential harm in the committee's view because it disrupts individual agency. While most research to date has focused on how misinformation affects individual beliefs, knowledge, and attitudes, less evidence exists for how misinformation leads to detrimental behaviors, and most of this research has measured behavioral intent. Nevertheless, some effects on behavior are consequential for well-being, particularly when the consequences are severe, when they affect people who are already experiencing harm, or when they happen at scale through targeted campaigns and elite amplification. Of particular concern, there is also evidence showing that the consequences of misinformation about science are differential across class, language, race/ethnicity, and place, as well as where these intersect, and that the effects on individuals are influenced and shaped by structural and cultural contexts of their lived experiences, access to material and social resources, and community embeddedness of their social lives. These connections warrant further study. Some evidence suggests that there may be important consequences of misinformation at the societal level by contributing to declining levels of healthy trust in institutions, affecting public health at scale, impeding productive discussion and collective decision making, and shaping the process of science itself. These societal-level consequences have been more difficult to establish empirically but remain an important area of study.

Conclusion 6-1: Many historically marginalized and under-resourced communities (e.g., communities of color, low-income communities, rural communities) experience disproportionately low access to accurate information, including science-related information. Such long-standing inequities in access to accurate, culturally relevant, and sufficiently translated science-related information can create information voids that may be exploited and filled by misinformation about science.

Conclusion 6-2: Most research to date on misinformation, including misinformation about science, has focused on its relationship to individuals' knowledge, attitudes, beliefs, and behavioral intentions. Some research has examined the impact of misinformation on behavior. From this work, it is known that:

- *Misinformation about science can cause individuals to develop or hold misbeliefs, and these misbeliefs can potentially lead to detrimental behaviors and actions. Although a direct causal link between misinformation about science and detrimental behaviors and actions has not been definitively established, the current body of existing evidence does indicate that misinformation plays a role in impacting behaviors, that in some cases, results in negative consequences for individuals, communities, and societies.*
- *Individuals are more receptive to misinformation about science, and, consequently, most affected by it, when it aligns with their worldviews and values, originates from a source they trust, is repeated, and/or is about a topic for which they lack strong pre-existing attitudes and beliefs.*

- *Science literacy is an important competency that enables informed decision making but is not sufficient for individual resilience to misinformation about science.*

Conclusion 6-3: Many individual-level factors such as personal values, prior beliefs, interests, identity, preferences, and biases influence how individuals seek, process, interpret, engage with, and share science information, including misinformation. Social factors, including race, ethnicity, socio-economic status, culture, social networks, and geography also play a critical role in affecting information access. This constellation of factors shapes an individual's information diet, media repertoires, and social networks, and therefore may also determine how much misinformation about science they encounter, the extent to which they engage with it, and whether it alters their beliefs.

Conclusion 6-4: The accuracy of the science information people consume is only one factor among many that influences an individual's use of such information for decision making. Even when people have accurate information, additional influences can lead them to make decisions and engage in behaviors that are not aligned to the best available evidence. At the individual level, these include their interests, values, worldviews, religious beliefs, social identity, and political predispositions. At the structural level, access to material and social resources such as healthcare coverage, affordable nutritious food, internet connectivity, and reliable transportation among others may play a particularly important role.

Conclusion 6-5: Misinformation about science about and/or targeted to historically marginalized communities and populations may create and/or reinforce stereotypes, bias, and negative, untrue narratives that have the potential to cause further harm to such groups.

Conclusion 6-6: Overall, there is a critical need for continuous monitoring of the current information environment to track and document the origins, spread, and impact of misinformation about science across different platforms and communication spheres. Such a process, like monitoring for signals of epidemics, could better support institutions and individuals in navigating the complexities of the current information ecosystem, including proactively managing misinformation about science.

7

Intervening to Address Misinformation About Science

As described in earlier chapters of this report, misinformation about science can be consequential for society in many ways, including potentially distorting public perceptions of personal, ecological, and societal risks; disrupting agency for individual and collective decision making across a wide array of critical issues; and disrupting societal stability. Intentional, strategic, and evidence-based efforts to address these and other negative impacts on individuals, communities, and humanity (as well as other species on the planet) offer potential solutions for effectively mitigating such impacts. Over the course of this chapter, the committee presents an overview of such efforts to date—efforts that have been undertaken by a wide range of actors across myriad issues. Alongside this, the chapter includes a framework for organizing this diverse, multidisciplinary, multi-sector domain of scholarship, practice, and policymaking. Throughout, we refer to intentional efforts with the explicit goal of addressing one or more (perceived) consequences of misinformation about science as interventions. This chapter begins with a brief history of interventions aimed at addressing misinformation about science followed by a discussion of interventions that are currently in use and the evidence for their effectiveness.

A BRIEF HISTORY OF INTERVENING TO ADDRESS MISINFORMATION ABOUT SCIENCE

Historical efforts to address misinformation about science in the United States can be clearly seen within the country's broader history of mass media. Since the advent of various mass media in the United States, the occasional publication of misleading information about science has raised concern from scientists, public officials, and observers. For example, during the American Revolutionary War, General George Washington's smallpox inoculation orders faced headwinds of opposition in the form of pamphlets and erroneous claims (Wehrman, 2022). In the 19th century, long before the advent of electronic media, demonstrably false claims about science also appeared in print news publications. In 1869, for example, newspapers in the northeastern United States such as the *Syracuse Standard* featured stories warning about a supposedly deadly caterpillar, the tomato hornworm, despite a body of entomology research that discounted any fatal threat to human beings (O'Connor & Weatherall, 2019).

Sometimes concern over such false claims has led to policy initiatives and interventions to mitigate the impacts of such content, and over time, some institutions and professional organizations in the United States have developed efforts to address inaccuracies in media content. Examples of this include the Food and Drug Administration's (FDA's) Bad Ad program regarding pharmaceutical advertising (O'Donoghue et al., 2015) and fact-checking initiatives run by the Annenberg Public Policy Center of the University of Pennsylvania (Amazeen, 2020; Young et al., 2018). However, the appearance of false claims in media outlets has not always been met with immediate institutional response, and the story of formal organizational efforts to mitigate misinformation through intervention has been a complex and iterative one that only in recent years has included peer-reviewed evaluation of such efforts, for example, Aikin et al. (2015), Ecker et al. (2022), and Kozyreva et al. (2024).

Despite individual complaints about the publication of falsehoods in newspapers and other print publications, formal calls among professional journalism associations to avoid spreading falsehoods did not emerge prominently until the late 19th century and early 20th century (Ward, 2010). Moreover, these initial efforts to address misinformation in journalism took multiple forms. An exhaustive journalism textbook intended to educate professional journalists about the missteps of false claims, *Steps into Journalism*, by *Chicago Tribune* literary editor Edwin Shuman (1894), emphasized the obligation of the reporter to "reproduce facts" (Ward, 2010, p. 141). In 1923, the American Society of News Editors, and in 1926, the professional journalists' association Sigma Delta Chi (which later would become the Society of Professional Journalists), formally proposed codes of ethics that emphasized objectivity and truthfulness, which led to a widely adopted professional code of U.S. journalists that explicitly emphasized the need to seek truth and report it (Ward, 2010). In 1934, nearly a dozen journalists founded the National Association of Science Writers "to foster the dissemination of accurate scientific knowledge" (Barton, 1934, p. 386). The association's emphasis on publishing science content intended for public audiences, in part, reflected decades of advocacy by some leaders in the American educational system to develop science curricula in U.S. schools to help promote public understanding and acceptance of innovations in science, technology, engineering, and mathematics. While these formal attempts to establish a code of ethics among professional journalism organizations are imperative for the field when addressing misinformation, it should be noted that there is still some difficulty in the journalism field contending with inaccuracies in modern news coverage (see Chapter 4 for more details).

Alongside professional codes from associations, federal government actors in the early 20th century also acted to thwart the potential effects of misinformation in service of product promotion, namely claims about the efficacy and safety of medicines and foods that were not supported by scientific research. Consider the case of so-called patent medicines like snake oil liniment and other elixirs that were prominently marketed to consumers in the United States from the mid-19th century through the early 20th century (Jaafar et al., 2021). Despite the phrase "patent medicine" that was sometimes used to describe such products, typically these products had not been formally patented under U.S. law and did not include accurate and exhaustive labeling of ingredients. *Rattlesnake Bill's Oil*, for example, was manufactured in Belleville, New Jersey; however, rattlesnakes were not typical in New Jersey at the time (Jaafar et al., 2021). Popular concern about such products encouraged the enactment of the Pure Food and Drug Act of 1906 (Denham, 2020; Jaafar et al., 2021). That act set the stage for the development of what would later become the FDA, which gained authority to oversee the safety of food, drugs, medical devices, and cosmetics in 1938.

Public concern over false or misleading labeling of products led to support for the Pure Food and Drug Act of 1906, but this policy primarily focused on claims about the ingredients in products rather than claims about the benefits of said products (Denham, 2020). Since then, regulatory oversight of misinformation about medicines and food has evolved through a series of iterations and policy debates. But not all health-related products are treated equally in the United States. Whereas medicines must be approved by the FDA before they can be sold or marketed, dietary supplements currently do not require such approval (see U.S. Food and Drug Administration, 2022). The regulation of claims has also been nuanced in terms of the exact message content in question.

The iteration of regulatory considerations for food and drug claims (e.g., eventual consideration of claims about product benefits and not just claims about the ingredients in a bottle) suggests increased acknowledgement over time by regulators that misinformation can include different components or elements of claims as well as various formats of accompanying material. In other words, policymakers have come to acknowledge that misinformation is not a monolithic entity present in uniform doses in the information ecosystem, but rather a collection of different possibilities for error and deception (only some of which have sparked sufficient public concern to inspire attention). Moreover, the U.S. experience of regulating the advertising of medicines and food highlights a tension that interventions to address misinformation have continued to face in the 21st century: characterizing claims as false or misleading depends on the existence of a formally recognized, scientific evidence base against which these inaccurate claims contrast. This presents a challenge that extends to many different claims involving science: if the respective scientific research does not exist yet, claim accuracy is difficult to define and therefore poses challenges for mitigation.

In the latter half of the 20th century, U.S. governmental regulation of false claims about certain food and drugs evolved to include corrective efforts to address misinformation in instances where clear contrasts between product claims and existing scientific evidence existed. This emphasis on corrective advertising acknowledged the possibility of intervening with audience members directly to address misbeliefs due to exposure to misinformation, reflecting a different type of intervention than restricting actors from publishing false claims in the first place. Beginning in the 1970s and extending through recent decades, U.S. federal agencies have considered possibilities for corrective advertising as a remedy for false claims in product advertising (Aikin et al., 2015; Armstrong et al., 1983; Wilkie et al., 1984). First, corrective advertising in the United States has been a policy lever that highlights the extent to which advertising regulation has primarily been a matter of post-hoc detection of misinformation rather than prevention of (or censorship against) the initial appearance of misinformation. Second, corrective advertising, at least as demonstrated by the FDA, has primarily focused on providing accurate factual knowledge to consumers as a specific goal for mitigating misinformation (e.g., U.S. Food and Drug Administration, 2022), a goal which does not necessarily address irreversible behavioral effects that may have stemmed from earlier exposure to misinformation. Additionally, such interventions can potentially return audiences to a state of knowledge that existed before misinformation exposure, but that goal is not the same as the elimination of behavioral consequences that may have occurred in the immediate wake of exposure to misinformation (e.g., product purchase or intake which cannot be undone), suggesting an important limit to this policy intervention.

Finally, during the first decades of the 21st century, researchers and practitioners began to explore and document approaches outside of regulatory policy to counteract individual misbeliefs resulting from exposure to misinformation as well as to consider further steps that might eliminate some types of false claims from popular circulation. In the next sections, we discuss the state of the science on such approaches, which now reflects insights from many academic disciplines (e.g., psychology, education, communication, computer science) and multiple sectors (including academia, for-profit corporations, non-profit organizations, policymaking). Indeed, efforts to mitigate potential negative effects from misinformation are now more prevalent, although interventions to specifically address misinformation about science are less prevalent than for other topical domains (e.g., political misinformation). Moreover, the committee found that current efforts are largely uncoordinated across actors, domains, scientific theories, and intended outcomes.

RECENT INTERVENTIONS TO ADDRESS MISINFORMATION ABOUT SCIENCE

After reviewing the existing landscape of recently documented interventions intended to reduce the negative effects of misinformation about science, the committee has discerned a wide range of intervention objectives, suggesting that there are many different points at which organizations have attempted to act. Some efforts involve systems-level intervention to affect the physical prevalence of misinformation in information environments, whereas many efforts—the bulk of those reported in peer-reviewed social science literature—have addressed individual beliefs and decisions (see Kozyreva et al., 2024 for an expert review of individual-level interventions). Interventions can be designed to target different parts of the broader information ecosystem and to utilize different approaches to achieve varied goals. To organize our discussion of existing interventions, the committee has identified four places to intervene to disrupt the effects of misinformation about science: supply, demand, distribution, and uptake (see Figure 7-1).

It is important to note that these four categories are non-exclusive. For example, an intervention may aim to reduce both belief in and sharing of misinformation, thus targeting both uptake and distribution. In fact, many of the most effective misinformation interventions target multiple intervention points. Below we summarize the evidence behind some of the most popular interventions in each category. Given that many interventions target multiple intervention points we describe each intervention in the section where it best fits, but also acknowledge the interventions' other goals.

Supply-Based Interventions

Supply-based interventions are designed to reduce the amount of misinformation circulating in society and/or change the balance between

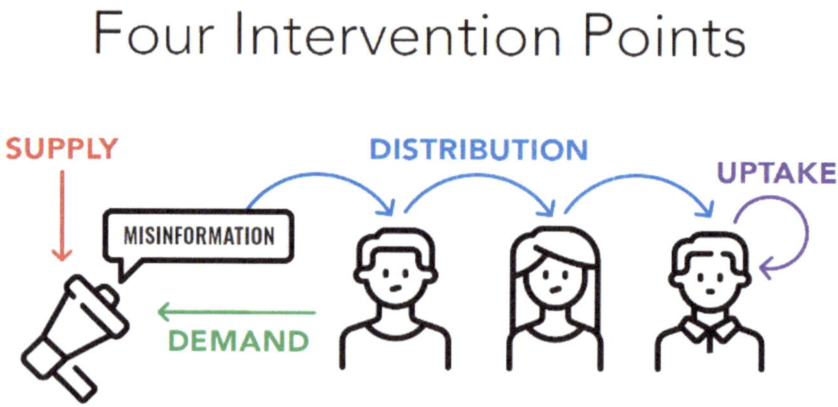

FIGURE 7-1 The four points where misinformation interventions may aim to intervene.
SOURCE: Committee generated.

low-quality and high-quality information. Consequently, these interventions include approaches that might increase the prevalence of high-quality content (e.g., attempts to improve science journalism by funding non-profit newsrooms or training journalists) or reduce the prevalence of low-quality content (e.g., by penalizing low-quality content producers using tools such as boycotts, litigation, or legislation and regulation).

There is some evidence to suggest the efficacy of supply-based interventions, for example, Dunna et al. (2022); however, since these interventions typically require buy-in from social media platforms they tend to be difficult to implement, may be resource intensive, and are difficult to replicate in a scientific setting. For some of the supply-based interventions that have been proposed, such as engaging in litigation against content producers, the information that is available on them is also difficult to evaluate, and whether there is sufficient appetite for implementation remains in question (Tay et al., 2023). Although some of these interventions may be amenable to formal policy analysis and evaluation procedures, to date, this committee is unaware of formal attempts to conduct these analyses.

Some supply-based interventions that have been implemented include the imposition of a "strikes" or penalty-based system, whereby purveyors of misinformation are warned by social media platforms that they could face penalties (e.g., account suspension) for continuing to post misinformation.[1] To the committee's knowledge, the efficacy of such interventions

[1]Meta: https://transparency.meta.com/enforcement/taking-action/penalties-for-sharing-fact-checked-content/

has not been systematically evaluated. Other supply-based approaches, especially those that increase the prevalence of high-quality information have also, to our knowledge, not been systematically evaluated for their impact on addressing misinformation.

Demonetization

The premise of demonetization strategies is that misinformation transmission can be a profitable endeavor (also see discussion on monetization in Chapter 5). In particular, economic incentives afforded by the "attention economy" enable individuals or organizations to make money by disseminating misinformation (Davenport & Beck, 2001; Global Disinformation Index, 2019; Ryan et al., 2020). Misinformation has also spread through targeted advertisements (Jamison et al., 2019a) and has been used for marketing purposes (Ballard et al., 2022; Mejova & Kalimeri, 2020). Purveyors of misinformation may profit from their activities through several mechanisms, including earning revenue from platforms by garnering engagement (Hughes & Waismel-Manor, 2021) or by soliciting direct donations (Ballard et al., 2022; Mejova & Kalimeri, 2020). This raises the possibility that news organizations and social media platforms might be able to reduce the dissemination of misinformation by taking actions designed to reduce its economic value (Bozarth & Budak, 2021; Han et al., 2022; Papadogiannakis et al., 2023; Zeng et al., 2020).

Consistent with these findings, some social media platforms have attempted to place restrictions on advertising revenue. For example, Facebook no longer allows advertisements that promote vaccine misinformation, whereas YouTube has "demonetized" channels that promote some types of misinformation—that is, disallowing them from obtaining revenue from ads (Gruzd et al., 2023; Li et al., 2022b). Despite these efforts, there are relatively few systematic evaluations of the efficacy of such demonetization strategies (although see Dunna et al., 2022; Kim et al., 2020b), in part due to lack of access to data for researchers. Another challenge to measuring the efficacy of these is how to operationalize monetization itself with only a small number of studies (Broniatowski et al., 2023a; Herasimenka et al., 2023) providing measures of this construct. Of these, some measures have not yet demonstrated generalizability or scalability.

Deplatforming

Deplatforming refers to the removal of objectionable accounts from social media platforms (e.g., for violating those platforms' terms of service). As a strategy for reducing exposure to misinformation, deplatforming is controversial, in part because it has often been equated with censorship and raises concerns regarding potential infringements on freedom of speech (although one study suggests that most individuals prefer the removal of harmful online content; see Kozyreva et al., 2024). On one hand, some studies found that deplatforming purveyors of hate speech can reduce the amount of future hate speech on the platform, especially when combined with efforts to degrade the networks that they have formed (Chandrasekharan, 2017; Jhaver et al., 2021; Klinenberg, 2024; Saleem & Ruths, 2018; Thomas & Wahedi, 2023). On the other hand, some studies suggest that deplatforming objectionable accounts on one platform may simply shift their content to other, often more fringe, platforms (e.g., Ali et al., 2021; Bryanov et al., 2022; Buntain et al., 2023b; Mitts et al., 2022; Newell et al., 2021; Ribeiro et al., 2024; Velásquez et al., 2021). Notably, these fringe platforms tend to have smaller audiences, likely leading to a net reduction in hate speech online. However, reducing the volume of objectionable accounts through deplatforming may not necessarily translate to reducing exposure to misinformation (Broniatowski et al., 2023b).

Moderation

Rather than removing objectionable accounts, some social media platforms have engaged in content moderation—for example, removing or banning objectionable content or communities where that content is shared. Current content moderation methods allow for the removal of specific pieces of misinformation that meet pre-defined criteria. Such moderation has long been a part of the social media landscape, especially in the case of content that is subject to legal liability (see later discussion on governance approaches). By some measures, content removals may be deemed successful. For example, compared to prior trends, Facebook successfully removed roughly half of all posts in anti-vaccine pages and groups during the COVID-19 pandemic (Broniatowski et al., 2023b). However, no change in overall engagement with vaccine misinformation was observed, suggesting that, as with removing objectionable accounts, removing content alone may not reduce exposure to misinformation.

Typically, content moderation decisions are made by a combination of algorithms that identify potentially objectionable content (see Chapter 5 for more on the role algorithms play in shaping and moderating content), and by human content moderators with a large variance in training, linguistic competence, cultural competence, and compensation, with the latter covering the range from volunteer work, through online crowdsourced workers, to professional roles (Cook et al., 2021). However, content moderation efforts are not able to be done at the scale and speed of the mass spread of (mis)information. Additionally, only the most common misinformation is most likely to be removed, while less common or novel misinformation may still go viral before it is detected. Furthermore, algorithmic approaches to content moderation are often brittle, easily circumvented, and subject to false positives (Gillett, 2023; Hassan et al., 2021), even when augmented with human supervision. This means that motivated purveyors of misinformation may still be able to spread it, although casual platform users may not be as likely to come across it in passing.

In addition, content moderation is challenging due to prominent definitional issues. For example, defining "misinformation" or "hate speech" in a manner that can be uniformly enforced by content moderators is difficult, and can lead moderators to focus on obsolete misinformation while ignoring new misinformation that has not yet been fact-checked (Broniatowski et al., 2023b). Even when definitions are clear, such as illegal content, determining when a specific item matches the legal definition may be difficult and is rarely scalable (Castets-Renard, 2020). See Box 7-1 for a short discussion of how the European Union (EU) is attempting to improve content moderation practices to address misinformation about science.

Finally, in general, assessing the efficacy of content moderation is challenging due, in part, to the difficulty in establishing consistent standards for defining objectionable content, and applying these standards. Thus, it is difficult to say to what extent content moderation efforts are successful, and more evidence is still needed to make that determination. Importantly, content moderation also carries with it the risk of trauma to moderators themselves (Steiger et al., 2021).

Decredentialing

The COVID-19 pandemic motivated a number of professional societies to take actions to address misinformation about science and medicine. Professional coalitions, including a broader coalition of medical specialties, set and enforce professional and ethical standards among their ranks (Jurecic, 2023). A joint effort by the American Board of Internal Medicine, the American Board of Family Medicine, and the American Board of Pediatrics supported the Federation of State Medical Boards' position of taking disciplinary action against physicians who spread medical misinformation (Baron, 2022; Baron & Ejnes, 2022; Federation of State Medical Boards, 2021). Others, such as the American Board of Obstetrics and Gynecology, have also released statements informing physicians that spreading misinformation/disinformation about reproductive health, contraception, abortion, or COVID-19 could lead to loss of certification (American Board of Obstetrics & Gynecology, 2021, 2022). In addition, nursing organizations such as the National Council of State Boards of Nursing have released statements addressing COVID-19 misinformation being spread by nurses and threatening discipline for nurses who disseminate misleading or incorrect information on COVID-19 and vaccines (National

BOX 7-1
European Union's (EU's) Digital Services Act

In August of 2023, a dynamic, paradigm-shifting law, the Digital Services Act (DSA), targeting illegal content, transparent advertising, and disinformation went into effect in the EU. The law seeks to improve internet platforms' moderation practices to address growing concerns about abusive, illegal, and misleading content (European Digital Rights, 2018). Prior to passing the DSA, the EU did not specifically regulate internet companies' approaches to content moderation. Thus, similarly to the United States, misinformation and disinformation were moderated primarily at the discretion of the individual companies that host users' speech. Content moderation under the DSA is chiefly horizontal: the DSA "attempts to address illegal content and govern the content moderation practices of [all] social media platforms" (European Digital Rights, 2018). To do so, the DSA establishes a framework of "layered responsibilities targeted at different types of services (i.e., intermediary services, hosting services, online platform services, and very large online platforms services)" and compiles "E.U.-wide asymmetric obligations to ensure transparency, accountability, and regulatory oversight of the E.U. online space" (Madiega, 2024). For example, the DSA operationalizes a "notice and action" mechanism: internet service providers that fail to act on receipt of notice of illegal content could lose the benefit of the limitation of liability under the Act.

Going further, the DSA contends that very large online platforms (VLOPs) will be subject to "specific obligations due to the particular risks they pose regarding the dissemination of both illegal and harmful content" (European Parliament, 2022). The European Commission expects that VLOP regulations would assist EU institutions in addressing harmful (not just illegal) content. VLOP rules additionally intend to curb the spread of disinformation by "including provisions on mandatory risk assessments, risk mitigation measures, independent audits and the transparency of [...] 'recommender systems' (algorithms that determine what users see)" (European Parliament, 2022).

Overall, the DSA represents a shift in the EU's technology law canon. Chief among its positive aspects include its "harmonization" function. At present, EU member states have slightly varied rules surrounding notice and takedown procedures geared toward internet companies, similar to the way that states' laws vary in the United States. The DSA standardizes process so internet platforms will face the same level of regulation across the EU (once content is identified as "illegal"). Another strength lies in the DSA's differentiation between "ordinary" and "very large platforms." Transparency obligations differ as between ordinary platforms and VLOPs. Logically, the Commission hoped to place additional responsibility on VLOPs (platforms with more than 45 million monthly active users) because of the degree to which it felt they influence public debate (Madiega, 2024). On the flip side, the Commission sought to curtail the extent to which the cost of moderation could shutter smaller intermediaries (Hendrix, 2022). It is still early days for the DSA, and more remains to be known about the effectiveness of this legislation.

SOURCE: Buckley & Calo (2023).

Council of State Boards of Nursing, 2021). Decredentialing initiatives have been controversial, and there is currently no data on either the number of people who have lost their certifications or the impact of such revocations on the person affected, on those who follow them, or on the supply, distribution, or uptake of misinformation.

Additionally, some laws have been created to penalize individuals thought to be spreading misinformation about science not in furtherance of fraud or another crime (Buckley & Calo, 2023). For example, the California Assembly Bill 2098[2] defined the promotion of COVID-19 misinformation as "unprofessional conduct" for purposes of licensure standards and authorized the California Medical Board to revoke the licenses of doctors who diverged from "contemporary scientific consensus." This bill was subsequently approved by the governor and made into law in 2022.

Foregrounding Credible Information in Algorithms

A variant of content moderation or content classification is adjusting the algorithms that shape search engine and social media content feeds to favor content produced by sources deemed to be scientifically credible. The Council of Medical Specialty Societies, the World Health Organization, and the National Academy of Medicine, for example, have recommended the coding of platform accounts to specifically label some scientific organizations to be considered for elevation in search results (see Burstin et al., 2023; Kington et al., 2021). Such work poses challenges in instances in which formal organizational accreditation is not readily available (e.g., for-profit organizations as opposed to non-profit and government entities with established vetting or accrediting procedures). Nonetheless, the establishment of clear and transparent labeling systems to identify media platform accounts as generally credible sources that rely on peer-reviewed scientific evidence could be assessed, and at least one organization—YouTube (and its parent company, Google)—has implemented some account credibility labeling. To date, there is limited empirical evidence on the effects for users of search engines or social media platforms that have adopted extensive labeling systems, and additional research that evaluates this approach is needed.

Demand-Based Interventions

Demand-based interventions are designed to reduce the consumption of misinformation. Additionally, people are not simply passive consumers of information; they often seek it out either to confirm their pre-existing

[2]AB-2098 Physicians and surgeons: unprofessional conduct (2021–2022): https://leginfo.legislature.ca.gov/faces/billTextClient.xhtml?bill_id=202120220AB2098

beliefs or to answer pressing questions. Thus, demand-based interventions aim to prevent people from turning to misinformation and instead provide accurate information either by filling information voids (e.g., by providing credible information to answer people's questions), increasing trust in sources of accurate information, or by increasing people's ability to notice and avoid misinformation (e.g., by enhancing people's ability to spot accurate information through literacy programs).

Addressing Information Needs

People often seek out science- and health-related information in order to answer questions they may have. Many U.S. adults value scientific research's ability to address those questions, and their confidence in scientists to act in the best interests of society has remained steady for decades (see Chapter 3). As recently as 2018, the majority of Americans reported having sought information about science in the past 30 days (National Science Board, 2022). For example, a person might ask when is it okay to leave COVID-19 isolation or even what is so special about the new space telescope? Interventions that are aimed at addressing information needs seek to ensure that people can easily find accurate, up-to-date information answering their questions (reducing the likelihood that they will be exposed to and engage with misinformation). From this perspective, what might otherwise appear to be demand for misinformation is actually the result of credible information voids.

One potential opportunity for addressing these information needs lies in interactions between health professionals and patients. Public health and healthcare organization staff can respond to patient questions and offer assistance to patients in navigating their information environments (Southwell et al., 2019). Organizations can also create specific job roles similar to what the U.S. Centers for Disease Control and Prevention did with its CARE ambassador program for travelers during the Ebola outbreak of 2014–2016 to address patient concerns about specific topics (Prue et al., 2019). However, strategies that rely on expanded capacity for audience engagement or new job roles require organizational capacity dedicated to misinformation mitigation and evaluation of that approach. For example, during the initial years of the COVID-19 pandemic, the U.S. National Institutes of Health Community Engagement Alliance (CEAL) in Florida partnered with the Osceola County Department of Health and local food drive organizations to answer people's questions, share health resources, and provide information about vaccination sites (Otero, 2021). In addition, CEAL also partnered with community barber shops to provide accurate information about COVID-19 to barbers who could then listen to their patrons' questions and concerns and provide accurate health information

(National Institutes of Health Community Engagement Alliance, 2023). This type of community interaction is likely critical for preventing or correcting misbeliefs; however, because of resource constraints, such initiatives are often thinly documented and rarely formally evaluated for their effectiveness. Nevertheless, multiple community and civil society organizations have emerged to track and combat misinformation in specific ethnic communities such as the Asian American Disinformation Table, Disinfo Defense League, Xīn Shēng Project, Co-Designing for Trust, Conecta Arizona,[3] and Digital Democracy Institute of the Americas (Nguyễn & Kuo, 2023). Box 7-2 highlights a community-based organization (CBO), the Tayo Project, and how it worked to combat misinformation about science within its community. Moreover, these efforts underscore the importance of being deliberative about audience values as part of any communications effort to address their science information needs (Dietz, 2013).

Local newspapers and television stations could also help to address laypeople's information needs, and as a result, reduce demand for misinformation (Green et al., 2023a). In general, Americans report relatively low confidence in news media compared to past decades (Pew Research Center, 2019b), but local news is one information source that is still trusted by many Americans with relatively few partisan differences. In 2022, 71% of American adults reported having some or a lot of trust in their local news organizations (Liedke & Gottfried, 2022). Additionally, local television news has broad reach: in 2022, on average, 3.1 million televisions tuned into local evening news, 3 million televisions tuned into local late news, and 2 million televisions tuned into morning news each day (Pew Research Center, 2023b). These numbers are similar to or higher than those for the most watched national news shows: in 2022, *The Five*, the most-watched Fox News show, averaged 3.4 million viewers, and MSNBC's 9pm show slot, reflecting the most-watched non-Fox News shows, averaged 1.8 million viewers (Katz, 2023). It is known that trusted messengers play an important role in counteracting misinformation about science (e.g., Knudsen et al., 2023; see also later discussion on increasing trust in sources of credible science information). Thus, local news organizations may be an untapped resource for mitigating misinformation about scientific research. At least one recent study has noted that local television news stories featuring parenting and child development science can have a positive effect on parents' perceptions of the value of such research (Torres et al., 2023). However, as discussed in Chapter 3 of this report, long-standing decreases in financial resources and the number of reliable local news sources may limit this potential (Abernathy, 2018; Hayes & Lawless, 2021).

[3]See https://conectaarizona.com/

BOX 7-2
The Filipino Young Leaders Program's (FYLPRO) Tayo Project

Efforts to provide accurate information for specific communities offer promise as a way of mitigating potential misinformation effects. The Tayo project originally started by members of the FYLPRO as a virtual help desk in fall 2020 to address COVID-19 misinformation by providing a reliable information source for community members within the Filipino diaspora. To create a strategy, the founding team conducted extensive interviews with individuals, including elders and parents of young children, COVID-19 survivors, and workers' rights activists, on local community needs and concerns. As Tayo expanded, they also incorporated media monitoring techniques to inform their work, including the use of social listening tools like Sprout Social and Junkipedia, and also created a community tipline submission form.

Beyond fact checking false information, Tayo uses the practice of *kwentuhan* (traditional Filipino oral storytelling/talk story) through a multiplatform and multidisciplinary lens to connect communities with information and culturally tailor content to meet their audiences where they are. They have used a mix of community education webinars and workshops, local health clinics, and bilingual public service campaigns. For example, when discussing the novel mRNA vaccines with their community, Tayo created a new analogy using longsilog (a type of traditional Filipino breakfast plate) and its ingredients to explain how the vaccine was effective without altering the recipient's DNA. While such an analogy might be ineffective for many Americans, it resonated with their audience and helped debunk misinformation about the vaccine. Tayo's work to counteract vaccine misinformation and hesitancy in Filipino communities also has included documenting and publishing first-person accounts of immunization processes. Their model offers one case of community-led and informed public health communication. While originally created as an ad hoc response to COVID-19, Tayo has evolved into a long-term program for cultivating community care and resilience in the face of ongoing structural inequity and disinvestment.

SOURCE: Nguyễn & Kuo (2023).

Finally, one way to identify science information voids and circulating misinformation about science is through "social listening tools." These tools include those developed to assist journalists and researchers with gaining transparency into social media platforms (e.g., CrowdTangle—which Meta shut down in August 2024, Pushshift, etc.), along with tools focused on specific topics (e.g., Project VCTR,[4] which tracks vaccine-related media conversations) or regions (e.g., iHeard St. Louis,[5] which identifies health-related

[4]See https://projectvctr.com/
[5]See https://stl.iheard.org/

misinformation spreading in the city). Some tools focus on what people are posting or searching for online (e.g., CrowdTangle) while others directly ask community members about what they are hearing (e.g., iHeard St. Louis). These tools are designed to raise public awareness about misinformation, enabling those working to oppose misinformation (e.g., public health officials) to quickly track and adapt to misinformation narratives as they emerge (also see Chapter 8, Box 8-1). Unfortunately, these tools are not available to all researchers, and data access is often at the discretion of social media companies (Ledford, 2023; Pequeño IV, 2013; Tromble, 2021).

Increasing Trust in Sources of Credible Science Information

Reported trust in representatives of scientific institutions predicts intended adherence to information shared by that institution (see Prue et al., 2019). Trust in science as a process or trust in scientists may also discourage acceptance of misinformation attributable to other sources, and at least one intervention study has attempted to increase trust in science directly as a way of attempting to reduce acceptance of misinformation about science. Agley et al. (2021) conducted a randomized controlled trial in which participants either learned about the scientific process or did not. Perceived trust in science was slightly improved in participants who learned about the scientific process and those with greater trust in science were also less likely to believe misinformation about COVID-19. Regarding the latter finding, the authors noted that this was an indirect effect (Agley et al., 2021).

To date, research on trust in information sources has been inconsistent with respect to conceptualizing and measuring trust. In some cases, trust has been described in terms of beliefs that other people or institutions are credible or reliable (see Siegrist et al., 2005), but the concept of trust in science has not been consistently operationalized (Funk, 2017; Siegrist et al., 2005; Taddeo, 2009). In one study, residents in rural North Carolina were asked to define trust in the context of information sources about wildfires. In response, most noted the importance of perceived credibility and reliability, but at least some also noted the importance of sharing interests with the source and the specific importance of local information outlets that are economically or socially aligned with them (Southwell et al., 2021). Further, Lupia et al. (2024) noted that "confidence in science," "confidence in the scientific community," and "trust" are all commonly used in survey research as measures for public views of or trust in a particular information source. The term "confidence" was said to most accurately reflect the survey questions asked, and while over time, public confidence has declined in many institutions, confidence in science is higher than confidence in nearly all other civic, cultural, and governmental institutions for which data are collected (Lupia et al., 2024; also see Chapter 3). Importantly, although respondents expressed relatively high confidence in science, they also raised concerns about the degree to which the values of scientists align with their own and scientists' ability to overcome biases and distortive incentives in their work (Lupia et al., 2024). This is consistent with at least one case study that suggests that the values expressed by a scientist may influence audience trust in presented information (Elliott, 2017). Therefore, greater transparency in science around values and adherence to scientific norms and incentives could be an important way to improve public perceptions of science, and, as a result, increase public trust in science as a source for reliable information.

Professionals working at state and local agencies, such as departments and associations of public works and health, are trusted experts in specific areas such as emergency preparedness, disaster response, and environmental threat mitigation (Bergner & Vasconez, 2012). As such, these agencies and associations are also well positioned to engage in science communication efforts that could supplant the influence of misinformation about science. As previously noted, perceptions of economic or social similarity with an information source (in addition to intellectual credibility or reliability) influences the extent to which people perceive a source to be trustworthy. To date, the potential effectiveness of communications strategies that emphasize shared interests between audiences and institutions on enhancing trust perceptions and subsequent resistance to misinformation about science has not been adequately studied in peer-reviewed research and warrants further exploration. But in light of existing divides in trust, including more recent ideological and partisan divides that were amplified during the COVID-19 pandemic (Green et al., 2023a), such professionals may play an especially important role in communications and messaging efforts that seek to resonate with the entire population.

Opportunities for effective mitigation through trusted channels of communication may also lie directly within communities, whereby information, including about health and science, is often disseminated through intermediary institutions, such as faith-based organizations, grassroots CBOs, or community health centers (Seale et al., 2022). A recent study also showed that since the COVID-19 pandemic, organizations like museums, zoos, and science centers have also become prominent sources for trustworthy information (Dilenschneider, 2023). Serving as cultural and linguistic brokers, these institutions work to reduce barriers and promote access to a myriad of resources and information in traditionally underserved and under-resourced communities (Seale et al., 2022). More importantly, given the trust that community residents typically have in them, such intermediaries may serve as critical partners to address misinformation about science (Korin et al., 2022), particularly around filling information voids with accurate information. Indeed, various communities have established a number of initiatives, including peer-peer education, fact-checking, and community-led media literacy programs, to resist, counter, and develop resilience against the negative impacts of misinformation about science (Nguyễn & Kuo, 2023).

Literacy Related to Science, Health, and Digital Media

People can vary in their ability to discern the accuracy and value of information they encounter based on available cues, and skills that scholars often have labeled in terms of literacy appear to play important roles in that discernment. Definitions of various types of literacy have evolved over time, although key threads have been adopted by many researchers. In the 2016 National Academies' report *Science Literacy: Concepts, Contexts, and Consequences,* science literacy is defined as a multifaceted construct that requires different types of knowledge and skills for different contexts and domains (National Academies, 2016b). Furthermore, science literacy is not only influenced by cognitive factors, but also by motivational, emotional, social, and cultural factors that shape how people encounter and process science information (National Academies, 2016b). More recently, the National Science Board (2024) describes science literacy as the extent to which people understand the nature of science as an iterative process of empirical observation and testing. Additionally, it reports that such skills are linked to confidence in science. In a widely cited piece, Berkman et al. (2010, p. 16) describe health literacy as "the degree to which individuals can obtain, process, understand, and communicate about health-related information needed to make informed health decisions." Similarly, in a recent study, Nutbeam & Lloyd (2021) indicated that health literacy is assumed to "enable individuals to obtain, understand, appraise, and use information to make decisions and take actions that will have an impact on health status" (p. 161). In the case of digital media literacy, researchers have cited the focus of Kemp et al. (2021, p. 104) on "capabilities and resources" needed to benefit from information, as a useful working definition. Literacy skills, in part, help people discern the likely accuracy of information by affording consideration of how information is generated and presented by sources.

When encountering misinformation in online contexts, people who are not familiar with the digital information environment may be less able to distinguish between signals of credible and non-credible content. Interventions to build digital media literacy skills include providing individuals with *digital media literacy tips* (Guess et al., 2020) that may help them to distinguish between credible and non-credible sources. An important caveat to raise regarding digital media tips involves the limited utility of some heuristic strategies. A simple recommendation to avoid websites that end in .com or to trust .org or .gov sites, for example, ignores variation within each of these domain levels on web sources. A dot-com source of a car manufacturer or trade group can provide credible information on how electric versus gasoline-powered engines work and some .org sites are created by for-profit interest groups. Websites within each category can also have differential utility for different purposes (Polman et al., 2014; Radinsky & Tabak, 2022). Another heuristic with limitations involves a recommendation to consider the professional appearance or layout of a website; however, sophisticated purveyors of misinformation can incorporate good user design (Wineburg et al., 2022). As the digital information environment continues to change due to technological advancements, so will the useful signals of credible information. For example, the emergence of tools based on large language models (LLMs; e.g., chatbots and AI-mediated search engine results) has altered the ways that people find information and has also removed some of the credibility signals that people commonly rely on, such as proper citations and signs of uncertainty (Augenstein et al., 2024). These changes may pose additional challenges for individual navigation of the contemporary information ecosystem, and it remains to be determined what new digital media literacy skills may be needed.

A related technique, *lateral reading,* encourages individuals to seek out more information about a source as they are reading information from that source (Wineburg et al., 2022). The lateral reading strategy was originally developed as part of the Civic Online Reasoning initiative at Stanford University (McGrew, 2020; McGrew et al., 2018; Wineburg & McGrew, 2019; Wineburg et al., 2022) for social studies instruction. Lateral reading of websites is based on the practices of expert fact checkers, who rather than spending large amounts of time reading "vertically" within a website (i.e., from the top to the bottom of any one page), read "laterally" across multiple websites to compare and contrast information from multiple sources, as when jumping across a large set of tabs in a web browser. Fact checkers also seek to analyze evidence, and exercise "click restraint" while looking at the overview information on a search engine results page. Rather than clicking on one of the first three results as novices do, they scan through several pages of results, and open tabs to read laterally across a selected set. Although the empirical research on lateral reading strategies specifically applied to science education contexts is limited in scope (e.g., Breakstone et al., 2021; Pimentel, 2024), this approach has promise for supporting individuals (students and adults alike) in discerning the accuracy of science information, given its demonstrated efficacy in other subject areas (Breakstone et al., 2021; McGrew, 2024; Osborne & Pimentel, 2022; Wineburg et al., 2022).

A key for *science* educators incorporating digital media literacy into their instruction is focusing on how an understanding of science practices, concepts, and scientific expertise can inform the evaluation of science information (Osborne & Pimentel, 2022; Polman, 2023). Knowledge of the scientific process, methods, and social norms, and aspects of the nature of science are helpful, including how replication across vetted, empirical studies builds scientific consensus and how this consensus can evolve as sometimes contradictory evidence accumulates—but this is not a reason to dismiss science evidence (see Chapter 2). Without such explicit instruction, students may know very little about the science information environment (Polman et al., 2014), and so science educators can also help them understand, for instance, that in the science enterprise, documents like press releases should not be given equal weight as consensus reports or peer-reviewed original research articles (Osborne & Pimentel, 2022; Polman, 2023). Such an approach can even be effective for adults, as demonstrated in one study conducted by Smith et al. (2022) that involved a 2.5-day boot camp training for journalists during the lead-up to the 2020 elections. As part of the training, participants learned about how science works and how to include scientific evidence in their reporting, and six months after the training, the stories written by these journalists contained more peer-reviewed scientific material and less tentative language about scientific facts compared to before the training (Smith et al., 2022).

Other media literacy interventions include *technique-based inoculation*, which is intended to educate individuals on how to detect signals of misinformation (Lewandowsky & van der Linden, 2021; Traberg et al., 2022). These inoculation interventions warn people about persuasive attempts and then expose people to a weakened form of the manipulation strategy to increase their resilience. For example, an inoculation intervention may teach people about the "fake experts" strategy used in many disinformation campaigns in order to increase people's ability to recognize the technique, and as a result, their resilience against misinformation. Technique-based inoculation interventions targeting a variety of manipulative techniques (e.g., emotional language, ad hominem attacks, conspiratorial thinking) have been successfully implemented as online games (e.g., Basol et al., 2020; Maertens et al., 2021), videos (e.g., Roozenbeek et al., 2022), and articles (e.g., Cook et al., 2017), and are effective at increasing people's ability to spot the manipulative techniques and decreasing their belief in false information. Like other educational interventions, the positive effects of technique-based inoculation wear off as people forget the intervention (typically after a few weeks); however, the benefits are longer-lasting if people are given a booster test every few weeks (Lu et al., 2023; Maertens et al., 2021). One criticism of technique-based inoculation is that it may make people skeptical of all new information rather than specifically incorrect information, in part because some of the manipulative techniques (e.g., emotional language) are also present in accurate news stories. Thus, technique-based inoculation can sometimes lead people to be more distrustful of both accurate and inaccurate information rather than improving their ability to distinguish between the two (Altay, 2022; Hameleers, 2023; Modirrousta-Galian & Higham, 2023). Despite these limitations, initial evidence suggests that providing feedback on the ways people can be manipulated by misinformation can lead to better accuracy in distinguishing between true and false headlines (Leder et al., 2023).

Importantly, although literacy skills may affect misinformation interpretation, literacy skills alone do not appear to fully account for the sharing and spread of misinformation in a network. That means that interventions to improve literacy alone may improve understanding among some people but may not necessarily eliminate the spread of misinformation, per se. Literacy may decrease users' demand for and uptake of misinformation while not affecting the distribution of misinformation about science. Using experimental evidence, Sirlin et al. (2021) have demonstrated that although study participants' digital literacy was related to their ability to discern falsehood, digital literacy was not predictive of an individuals' intention to share misinformation. As Southwell et al. (2023, p. 122) have noted, "confusion about the credibility of information or misinformation is not necessarily the same as the likelihood of sharing misinformation with peers," but there are times when individuals may share information because they are confused.

Beyond digital media literacy, an array of efforts to teach people about how scientific institutions operate can also be considered. Although much of formal science education in the United States focuses on preparing individuals to pursue careers in science, there is evidence that learning about what scholars have labeled socio-scientific issues supports the development of science literacy, particularly for learners who do not pursue careers directly involved with science (Aikenhead, 2006; Feinstein, 2011; Feinstein et al., 2013; Polman et al., 2014; Roberts, 2007, 2011). Feinstein (2011, p. 168) has referred to this as "science literacy [for] competent outsiders." Being a competent outsider to science involves knowing how to apply and use scientific thinking, concepts, and practices in everyday situations, one of which is discerning misinformation about science. Such a science literacy embeds epistemic understanding of how science is practiced, disciplinary core ideas, and cross-cutting concepts (NRC, 2012a, 2013). It also incorporates strategic and mindful reliance on credible sources, and application into civic and political life (National Academies, 2016b). Educating "competent outsiders" is more likely to be successful if it involves purposeful, collective sensemaking instead of solely asking people to make "individual truth judgments" (Feinstein & Waddington, 2020). This suggests possibilities for interventions that involve engaging people and local communities in learning about how scientific research is conducted and can be interpreted in the context of specific issues affecting those local communities, such as water quality monitoring. Such an approach is consistent with calls for science communication professionals to better attend to values alongside scientific facts when seeking to inform public participation in science decision making (Dietz, 2013). However, the impact of such science education interventions on uptake of misinformation about science has not been studied.

Literacy-focused approaches have been criticized for framing the misinformation problem as one of individual vigilance and avoidance (boyd, 2017), and yet, outside of formal education contexts, such education is rarely required (Livingstone, 2011). Additionally, those who voluntarily engage in media literacy education may be motivated by pre-existing concerns with misinformation's harmful effects, while those most likely to believe and share misinformation (e.g., older adults) may lack access to or interest in media literacy education (Moore & Hancock, 2022; Vaportizis et al., 2017). Consequently, such approaches may widen the social gaps between those who possess the knowledge and motivation to resist misinformation and those who lack it (Livingstone, 2011). These observations also suggest that while effective in some instances, media literacy alone will likely not be sufficient to counteract the problem of misinformation.

Distribution-Based Interventions

Distribution-based interventions are designed to limit the spread of misinformation. These interventions include actions taken by online platforms, such as content moderation; approaches to encourage online platforms to take action, such as through legislative means (e.g., amending Section 230 of the Communications Act of 1934, which was enacted through the Communications Decency Act of 1996); and actions aimed at reducing misinformation sharing by individuals.

Whereas supply- and demand-based interventions seek to reduce the prevalence and intake of misinformation, respectively, some distribution-based interventions seek to reduce the exposure of individuals to misinformation by targeting the online platforms on which such information may be hosted or the actions of individual users on the platforms. Like supply-based interventions, the evidence base for the efficacy of platform-level distribution interventions is limited. Nevertheless, some quasi-experimental studies have been carried out to evaluate the efficacy of specific policies including those that ban hate speech or individual accounts intentionally spreading misinformation on social media platforms (Broniatowski et al., 2023b; Chandrasekharan et al., 2017; Gu et al., 2022; Jhaver et al., 2021).

Architectural Remedies

A small number of distribution-based interventions targeting platforms' architectures—that is, their structural design features such as groups, pages, and interaction options—have been proposed. For example, Broniatowski et al. (2023b) observed that vaccine misinformation on Facebook during the COVID-19 pandemic was facilitated by complex interactions between Facebook's page, group, and newsfeed structure. Furthermore, while not currently the case, Forestal (2021) proposed a framework for how social media platforms could be explicitly designed to promote deliberative democracy and build communities that are not as receptive to misinformation. Key design elements proposed included the establishment of a community with a durable presence, clear community boundaries, and flexible incorporation of new members, thereby enabling users to engage in fundamental civic practices (Forestal, 2021). Preliminary evidence also suggests that some interventions involving the use of community structures may effectively lessen the likelihood of misinformation being created and spread (Abroms et al., 2023). Though not specific to science, there is moderate evidence demonstrating that the fact-checking skills of groups of lay users on social media are comparable to professional fact-checkers, and therefore can be effectively harnessed to reduce the spread of misinformation in news content on social media platforms (Allen et al., 2021, 2022; Banas et al., 2022; Godel et al., 2021; Martel et al., 2024; Pennycook & Rand, 2019). Specifically, lay users assign ratings to news content based on accuracy, quality, or trustworthiness. These crowdsourced ratings can then be incorporated into social media ranking algorithms, leading to a reduction in the visibility of inaccurate, low-quality, or untrustworthy content.

"Soft" Content Classification Remedies

Several approaches to reducing the distribution of misinformation implement "soft" content remedies (Goldman, 2021; Grimmelmann, 2015). Most of these remedies are premised on the idea that content distribution is driven by algorithmic amplification. For example, this content might be highly ranked within a given social media platform's content recommender system. Consequently, information that has been classified as misinformation may be *demoted* or completely *removed* from algorithmic recommendations, meaning that the content is still present, but that it would rarely, if ever, appear at the top of a social media user's feed since other content would displace it. This approach is limited by the fact that a platform representative is needed to classify particular content as misinformation, which may not be noticed until it has already gone viral. Therefore, a related approach seeks to downrank such content using *correlates of viral misinformation* (e.g., angry reaction emoji; Broniatowski et al., 2023b). A third approach seeks to identify content that is likely to go viral before it has done so, by introducing *friction* into the content recommendation system, and thus enabling content moderators a chance to review and, if necessary, downrank content before it has caused harm (Kozyreva et al., 2024). One such approach, known as a *viral circuit breaker*, briefly pauses, and then flags, classes of certain viral content for review before it is allowed to widely spread (Simpson & Conner, 2020). To date, the efficacy of these approaches has not been tested by researchers outside of social media companies.

Content Labeling

Rather than removing or demoting individual posts or users, platforms can also choose to label content with additional information (see Morrow et al., 2022, for a review) in order to reduce the spread of misinformation. For example, a post may be labeled as "False information reviewed by independent fact-checkers," or posts may include a banner label, e.g., "Visit the COVID-19 Information Center for vaccine resources," along with a link. Both of these content-labeling approaches have been or are currently used by social media companies (Polny & Wihbey, 2021). However, aside from source labels and warning labels (see later discussion on these uptake-based interventions), very little research has examined the effects of other types of labeling, such as indicating that content has been manipulated or created by artificial intelligence; providing information about who else has shared the content; or providing additional context around when an article was first written, or a photo was first posted (to prevent, for example, a photo from a 2015 conflict being presented as if it happened yesterday). More research is needed to understand the effectiveness of the different types of content labels currently used by platforms and to create novel labels that may be even more effective. Moreover, insights from the behavioral sciences, library sciences, and food sciences could also contribute to an understanding of the effects of content labels in specifically addressing misinformation about science (Lorenz-Spreen et al., 2020; Wolkoff, 1996; Yeh et al., 2019).

Mathematical Simulation Models

In the absence of comprehensive data, another distribution-based approach involves the use of mathematical simulation models to forecast the efficacy of different types of interventions (e.g., Bak-Coleman et al., 2022; Johnson et al., 2019). The units of analysis of these models differ between studies, with some investigators focusing on individuals and others focusing on clusters of users (e.g., pages on social media platforms, in which a small number of administrators may broadcast content to a large number of potential followers). These models are used to generate simulated outcomes and suggest potential remedies such as content removal, viral circuit breakers, and deplatforming. While each method alone is predicted to have some benefit, the largest reductions in the spread of misinformation is predicted to be when multiple approaches are combined (Bak-Coleman et al., 2022).

Psychology-Based Interventions

A separate class of interventions seeks to use insights from individual human psychology to reduce misinformation receptivity and distribution. These interventions are motivated by different theoretical frameworks. For example, *accuracy nudges* grow out of dual-process theories (e.g., Stanovich & West, 2000), which presume that humans believe and share misinformation because they are not paying attention to signals of misinformation (Pennycook & Rand, 2022a). Consequently, accuracy nudges seek to encourage individuals to consider the accuracy of content that they encounter, typically by asking people to rate the accuracy of one or more social media headlines. Overall, accuracy nudges reliably decrease people's intentions to share misinformation (Pennycook & Rand, 2022a) and their actual sharing behaviors (Pennycook et al., 2021). The approach is also very easy to implement and scale. However, the reported positive effect is very small and likely declines quickly (Pennycook & Rand, 2022b). In addition, the accuracy nudge approach is only effective when people have the knowledge required to determine if the information is correct or incorrect (Pennycook & Rand, 2021).

Similarly, friction-based approaches aim to slow down decision making and provide people with an opportunity to rethink their initial choices. For example, asking people to explain how they know that a headline is true or false has been shown to decrease intentions to share, in the case of false headlines (Fazio, 2020a; Pillai & Fazio, 2023). Friction-based interventions have also been employed on some social media platforms to encourage reading an article before sharing (Hern, 2020), to promote civil discussions (Lee, 2019), or to reduce sharing of unverified information (Fischer, 2021). The efficacy of such approaches used by social media platforms needs further research and some of the information that could be helpful for researchers to better understand these approaches may not be readily accessible.

Finally, *fuzzy-trace theory* posits that people make decisions based on meaningful *gist mental representations*, which are moments where a person recalls the overall general meaning of something but not the verbatim context (Reyna, 2021). According to this theory, people may be encouraged to share or resist information if they are presented with messages explaining the essential bottom-line meaning of the decision to share this information in terms that cue motivationally-relevant values. For example, a person may be more prone to remember that there is a huge increase in the likelihood that their child could get sick if un-vaccinated than to remember an actual number that their doctor provides; this difference plays into their decision making on whether to vaccinate their child (Reyna, 2021). Thus, unlike other dual-process approaches (which aim to promote reliance on effortful deliberation) and social-psychological approaches (which aim to take advantage of social cues in lieu of deliberation), gist-based approaches seek an intermediate approach, which provides a person with a rationale for making a decision (e.g., sharing or not sharing content) that is motivationally relevant (see Reyna et al., 2021, for a review).

Governance Approaches

Legislative, regulatory, or voluntary actions taken by governments, private citizens, and/or corporations as oversight for the informational environment have also been deployed to govern the spread of misinformation about science. For example, fines, penalties, or litigation targeting purveyors of false content fall within this category, as well as regulations and laws that might make content distributors liable for the spread of misinformation.

With respect to advertising content, the Federal Trade Commission (FTC) enforces truth-in-advertising laws whereby all advertisements "must be truthful, not misleading, and, when appropriate, backed by scientific evidence" (FTC, n.d.). The enforcement of these laws applies to any medium where advertisements appear including magazines, television, billboards, or online. Further, the FTC pays special attention to advertisements with claims that can directly impact consumers' health or finances (e.g., food, over-the-counter medicines, vitamins and dietary supplements, alcohol, and tobacco). Specifically, in cases of deceptive advertising in health and fitness, the FTC works in coordination with the FDA and also the National Institutes of Health (NIH) regarding the substantiation of health-related claims. Direct actions taken by the FTC when an organization is in violation of any truth-in-advertising law include sending a warning letter to the company about the unlawful conduct and the possibility of facing a federal lawsuit if the company continues such conduct (FTC, n.d.). The FTC reports that this is one of the most effective ways that the agency eliminates false and misleading information from the marketplace, given an overwhelming majority of companies quickly take steps to come into compliance upon receiving FTC warning letters (FTC, n.d.).

Similarly, the FDA works to provide numerous avenues to address concerns around misinformation. For example, its website contains multiple resources for the general public in different languages on how to identify misinformation online and how to file a report about misinformation to the appropriate channels (FDA, n.d.a). The FDA also routinely hosts workshops and podcasts episodes focused on misinformation about specific public health concerns including cancer, COVID-19, and mpox (FDA, n.d.b). In July 2024, the FDA announced new revisions to its draft guidance on addressing misinformation about medical devices and prescription drugs. Specifically, this guidance seeks to provide organizations with approaches to address misinformation about medical products created by an independent third party, and to ensure that the general public is receiving the "accurate, up-to-date, science-based information they need to inform their decisions about medical products to maintain and improve their health" (FDA, 2024, p.2). At the time of this consensus report, the draft guidance was still pending approval.

In recent years, the Communications Decency Act under the regulatory authority of the Federal Communications Commission (FCC) has received a great deal of attention in the context of governance approaches to addressing misinformation online, and namely Section 230 of the Act (National Academies, 2021), which was enacted by Congress in 1996 to foster the growth of the internet by providing certain liability immunities to internet-based technology companies (see Box 7-3 for a brief history of this legislation). Since this time, the internet has evolved in unanticipated ways, and concerns about issues like concentration of power, misinformation and disinformation, algorithmic-mediated content and advertising, and online abuse have motivated the exploration of potential solutions that include revisions to Section 230 (National Academies, 2021). Indeed, multiple proposals have been made to amend Section 230 as a way to govern misinformation; these efforts fall into three categories, as described below (Buckley & Calo, 2023).

The first category includes efforts that seek to increase platform transparency and regulate certain categories of problematic speech as a response to the concern that certain types of misinformation are being spread unchecked. Some efforts in this category also seek to address Section 230's disproportionate impacts on women, people of color, and LGBTQIA+-identifying people. The second category includes actions by legislators that are directed toward a specific subcategory within a platform that can be subject to liability. In this way, legislators have the opportunity to limit a given platform's immunity or to make platforms "earn" immunity by changing how they monitor and manage inappropriate content. Finally, the third category involves concerted efforts to reduce or completely remove a platform's immunity protections provided under Section 230 by revealing biased moderation and content removal practices (e.g., only sanctioning certain groups of people). In contrast to such proposals for reform, some have argued that changes to Section 230 could result in the over-policing

BOX 7-3
Section 230

Broadly, Section 230 of the U.S. Communications Decency Act is a federal law from 1996 that shields internet platforms that host users' speech from an assembly of laws that might otherwise find them legally responsible for what their users post. Specifically, Section 230 asserts that "[n]o internet provider or user of an interactive computer service shall be treated as the publisher or speaker of any information provided by another information content provider" (47 U.S.C. § 230(c)(1)). At the same time, the law's "Good Samaritan" provision protects platforms from liability if they elect to remove or moderate offensive user content: providers will not be held liable for "any action voluntarily taken in good faith" to restrict access to certain objectionable material "whether or not such material is constitutionally protected." In other words, even speech the government could not censor is subject to liability-free moderation if the platform acts in good faith (47 U.S.C. § 230(c)(2)).

Although Congress enacted Section 230 to encourage good faith efforts by platforms to remove or moderate specific types of objectionable content (e.g., obscene, excessively violent, harassing), given their freedom from liability, the courts, with one or two exceptions, have interpreted the law to grant platforms broad immunity from liability. This expanded interpretation of Section 230 immunity enabled the growth of the internet and the emergence of a variety of platforms, but also made it very difficult for plaintiffs to address online abuse and other forms of harassment, many of whom have been women or members of minoritized groups (Brannon & Holmes, 2024; Geary, 2021). Thus, in spite of the intent that Section 230 would push internet platforms toward moderation, subsequent judicial interpretation limits recourse for addressing the spread of false information online, including misinformation about science.

SOURCE: Buckley & Calo (2023).

of speech, the shutting down of internet services, and other unintended consequences (Buckley & Calo, 2023; National Academies, 2021). In 2023, two cases[6] involving Section 230 were argued before the Supreme Court as part of an effort to determine whether algorithmic recommendation of user-generated content could subject platforms to liability for that content; however, the Court relied on other statutes without fully addressing the scope of Section 230 (Holmes, 2023).

Attempts that seek to address misinformation about science through regulation may also be limited by the First Amendment, namely the

[6]See *Twitter, Inc. v. Taamneh*, https://www.supremecourt.gov/opinions/22pdf/21-1496_d18f.pdf, and *Gonzalez v. Google LLC*, https://www.supremecourt.gov/opinions/22pdf/21-1333_6j7a.pdf

commitment to free speech in the United States, which overall is desirable, but may leave allowances for some online misinformation to go unchecked. For instance, the fact that misinformation is misleading or even untrue does not necessarily remove it from the ambit of free speech protections (Buckley & Calo, 2023). Specifically, the First Amendment states:

> Congress shall make no law respecting an establishment of religion, or prohibiting the free exercise thereof; or abridging the freedom of speech, or of the press; or the right of the people peaceably to assemble, and to petition the Government for a redress of grievances.[7]

Notwithstanding the reference to "Congress," the First Amendment has been interpreted to apply to any state actor, meaning anyone representing the federal or local government; however, individuals and institutions operating in a private capacity are not subject to the First Amendment. That is, a private company does not necessarily implicate the First Amendment when it decides to take down certain content (Buckley & Calo, 2023). Some legal scholars[8] observe that courts interpreting the First Amendment must answer at least two questions. The first is "coverage," that is, whether the content or activity at hand is protected by the Constitution at all. Assuming First Amendment coverage, the court then has to decide what level of scrutiny to apply. Prior restraints on speech, as well as government actions that discriminate based on viewpoint or content, are subject to strict scrutiny. However, the regulation of commercial speech, that is, advertising or economic solicitation, receives a higher level of review by the courts, and statutes and regulations routinely require disclosure of truthful information, such as when the FDA requires warnings on cigarettes. But while there are narrow cases wherein misinformation may be subject to regulation and liability, how free speech doctrine may or may not hinder the extent to which misinformation about science can be regulated remains a thorny issue. For now, opportunities to dampen or penalize claims of misinformation about science are still possible when they are associated with commercial activity (e.g., false claims that a vitamin is effective in treating a medical condition), involve fraud, or are specifically intended to cause certain kinds of harm such as a financial panic (Buckley & Calo, 2023).

Finally, a more promising route for governing misinformation may involve required reporting or labeling of content, given laws or regulations that mandate disclosure tend to fare better than limits on speech. For example, recent amendments to Washington State election law require political

[7]U.S. Constitution, First Amendment.

[8]Frederick Schauer, Speech and "Speech"—Obscenity and "Obscenity": An Exercise in the Interpretation of Constitutional Language, 67 GEO. L.J. 899 (1979).

actors to label the use of deepfakes in election-related media (Senate Bill 5152, 2023), and California's law requires that political or commercial automated accounts or "bots" come with warning labels (California Code, Business and Professions Code - BPC § 17940 *et seq* (SB 1001); also, see Buckley & Calo (2023).

Uptake-Based Interventions

Uptake-based interventions are designed to reduce the effects of misinformation on people's beliefs or behaviors. These interventions assume that misinformation is already present online and seek to limit its effects using techniques such as fact-checking, educational and literacy campaigns, and psychological interventions. Such interventions can either come prior to exposure (e.g., prebunking), during exposure (e.g., source credibility labels), or after exposure (e.g., debunking and motivational interviewing), but all share the goal of preventing misbeliefs.

Prebunking

In contrast to debunking interventions that occur after exposure to misinformation, prebunking occurs before people are exposed to misinformation. Such interventions can include the technique-based inoculations summarized above (e.g., Traberg et al., 2022) along with warnings presented immediately before viewing online misinformation (e.g., Brashier et al., 2021; Grady et al., 2021). Quasi-experimental evidence suggests that such warnings might have reduced the number of "likes" of anti-vaccine content on some social media platforms (Gu et al., 2022). In addition, prebunking can include warnings about certain topics, narratives, or arguments that are often used in misinformation (e.g., Jolley & Douglas, 2017; Maertens et al., 2020). The latter type of prebunking is sometimes called issue-based inoculation (van der Linden et al., 2023). For example, in one study, some British parents read a short article refuting common anti-vaccine conspiracy theories prior to reading an article containing vaccine misinformation, while others were exposed only to the misinformation (Jolley & Douglas, 2017). Participants in the first condition were less likely to believe that vaccines are dangerous and had higher vaccination intentions in a hypothetical scenario. Misinformation about science often repeats common themes and narratives, making it an ideal topic area for such content-based prebunking interventions. However, to date, there is significantly more research on the effectiveness of warning people about manipulative techniques than warnings about common misinformation themes and narratives.

Source Labels

Source labels provide information about the credibility of a source based either on the outlet's adherence to common journalistic standards or a reputation for spreading misinformation. In laboratory studies, the inclusion of this source information improved participants' discrimination between true and false claims and decreased liking and sharing of false posts (Celadin et al., 2023; Prike et al., 2023). However, a large field study found that providing source labels on social media posts, visited URLs, and search engine results did not reduce people's intake of information from low-quality sources (Aslett et al., 2022). The benefits of source labels are likely modified by how noticeable they are and whether people pay attention to the label; for example, Fazio et al. (2023) show evidence that people do not regularly attend to many credibility signals. In addition, there is some evidence that when judging the accuracy of a headline, people are more swayed by the plausibility of the headline rather than the reliability of the source (Dias et al., 2020). Finally, as discussed in Chapter 4, misinformation about science can originate even from generally trustworthy new sources or other sources of credible science information; therefore, source labels may not be sufficient as a standalone approach to help consumers avoid misinformation. While overall, source labels show some promise as a misinformation intervention, the details of implementation are important, and more field studies are necessary to examine their effects on misinformation intake, sharing, and belief.

Debunking

Any correction that comes after exposure can be considered a debunking intervention. Sometimes also described as fact-checking, debunking approaches can be implemented at multiple levels of detail, ranging from simple statements that a given statement is false to a very detailed article-length refutation. Debunking is one of the most well-studied misinformation interventions (see Lewandowsky et al., 2020 and Prike & Ecker, 2023 for a guidebook for practitioners), and correction of misbeliefs stemming from false claims about science has been implemented by a wide range of groups, including federal government agencies (e.g., Aikin et al., 2017) and university research groups (e.g., Lewandowsky et al., 2020).

Researchers have examined the corrective effect of misinformation debunks in controlled laboratory studies (e.g., Ecker et al., 2017, 2020; Swire-Thompson et al., 2021) and in field tests in real-world situations (e.g., Bhagarva et al., 2023; Bowles et al., 2023; Pasquetto et al., 2022; Porter & Wood, 2021; Porter et al., 2022). In general, debunking is more effective when an alternative factual explanation is provided (Kendeou et al., 2013; Lewandowsky et al., 2012; Seifert, 2002). For example, to correct the misbelief that meteors are hot when they reach Earth, a more effective debunk will explain why meteors are cool (the outermost layer gets vaporized when entering the atmosphere and the inside does not have time to heat up again), as compared to just stating that the claim is false (Kendeou et al., 2019). In addition, debunks that provide more detailed information (particularly more than a simple true/false label) tend to be more effective and have a longer lasting effect (Chan & Albarracín, 2023; Ecker et al., 2020). Debunks are also more effective when they come from trusted sources, again emphasizing an important role for trust in addressing misinformation (Ecker & Antonio, 2021; Pasquetto et al., 2022; Zhang et al., 2021).

Additionally, there have been reported concerns that misinformation debunks could backfire and actually increase belief in misinformation for some recipients (e.g., Nyhan & Reifler, 2010, 2015); however, large-scale replications have found no evidence of widespread backfire effects (Haglin, 2017; Nyhan et al., 2019; Wood & Porter, 2019). In their summary of the literature on backfire effects, Swire-Thompson et al. note that "it is *extremely unlikely* that, at the broader group level, [...] fact-checks will lead to increased belief in the misinformation" (Swire-Thompson et al., 2020, p. 292). People do vary in their acceptance of corrections (e.g., Susmann & Wegener, 2023); however, their beliefs tend to remain stable after reading a correction rather than increasing.

There are, however, valid criticisms to the debunking approach. First, debunking is inherently a reactionary process. Only after a falsehood is circulating in the information environment can it be corrected and debunked. What's more, creating accurate and effective debunks is time-consuming, and corrections are often posted only after widespread exposure. Second, like most interventions, the effectiveness of misinformation debunks fades over time with the positive effects lasting everywhere from only a few weeks to multiple years (Carey et al., 2022; Kowalski & Taylor, 2017; Swire-Thompson et al., 2023) and minimally affect subsequent behaviors and attitudes (Porter et al., 2023). Finally, in the current media environment, fact-checks may rarely reach the people who saw, or are most likely to believe, the original misinformation (Hameleers & van der Meer, 2020; Zollo et al., 2017).

Motivational Interviewing

Motivational interviewing (MI) is another form of a debunking intervention, and is traditionally a smaller scale approach (i.e., one-on-one) in comparison with other uptake-based interventions. Rather than passive intake of text or video, MI consists of a dialogue between practitioners (e.g., doctors, nurses) and clients. This approach was inductively established through treating patients with substance use disorder by clinical psychologists in the 1980s (Miller & Rollnick, 2023). MI practitioners are trained to combine empathy, curiosity, and compassion with technical skills like open questions, affirmations, reflections, and summary statements, to partner with individuals, evoke motivation for change, and, if appropriate, create plans for accomplishing patients' identified goals.

A wealth of evidence has established the efficacy of MI in facilitating behavior change across numerous health behaviors (Lundahl et al., 2013; Palacio et al., 2016; Schwenker et al., 2023). For example, MI-based interventions have been shown to increase the likelihood that parents harboring questions or concerns about vaccination would consent to vaccinate their children (Brewer et al., 2020; Gagneur et al., 2018a,b; Lemaitre et al., 2019). It has also shown promise in promoting uptake of vaccines against human papillomavirus (Reno et al., 2018, 2019). This success led to MI being widely recommended by nurses, doctors, and the Centers for Disease Control and Prevention (CDC) for use in promoting COVID-19 vaccination (Boness et al., 2022; Breckenridge et al., 2022; CDC, 2021a; Gabarda & Butterworth, 2021), and studies are beginning to confirm its efficacy in that context as well (Cogordan et al., 2023; Pyne et al., 2023). These studies usually do not directly assess whether participants hold misbeliefs about vaccines due to misinformation; however, the increase in vaccination following this intervention suggests that MI could have played a role in their decision to vaccinate their child or themselves.

Adaptations of MI to community settings have also shown promise in vaccine promotion but require more research on their effectiveness. For example, one NIH CEAL regional team incorporated MI into its peer-delivered communication program for primarily Black and Latinx communities in Washington, District of Columbia, and Baltimore, Maryland (Douglas et al., 2023). Lay community members who were trained to facilitate motivational interviews used the technique amongst their families, friends, and co-workers; half of the trained facilitators later reported the MI techniques were very effective and led some of their personal associates to consider getting a COVID-19 vaccination (Douglas et al., 2023).

An adaptation of MI to online communities, *community-oriented MI* (Scales et al., 2022), in which peers leverage evidence-informed communication techniques within an over-arching MI-based approach (Scales et al., 2023), has also shown promise. In a quasi-experimental observational study on Facebook, researchers found that threads discussing misinformation about COVID-19 vaccines whereby the intervention was employed were associated with lower engagement compared to matched control threads, and notably, there were also fewer replies containing negative emotions on these threads (Scales et al., 2023). Thus, when used in online spaces, MI techniques may also decrease the distribution of misinformation. While more work remains to be done, this initial research suggests that MI can be successfully adapted to online and in-person communities to enhance motivation for health protective behaviors, in part by attenuating the influence of misinformation.

CONSIDERATIONS FOR INTERVENING TO ADDRESS MISINFORMATION ABOUT SCIENCE

The wide diversity of approaches to addressing misinformation about science described above reflects at least an implicit (and often explicit) recognition that the challenge is, at its root, a systems-level problem rather than a problem that primarily resides within individuals (even though many of the interventions that have been proposed and tested are designed and aimed at individual (mis)information "consumers"). There is a parallel here to how modern medicine recognizes that much of health (and ill health) stems from systems-level factors (e.g., social determinants), and yet the vast majority of diagnosis and treatment is at the individual patient level (and oftentimes with only limited recognition of or attempts to address the interactions between systems-level and individual-level factors).

The strong focus on both individual-level consequences of misinformation about science as well as individual-focused approaches to intervening is not "wrong," per se, but it does focus attention away from the important insight that misinformation about science (its causes, consequences, and potential solutions), as described throughout this report, is in fact just a small part of a much bigger, complex system (or set of interlocking systems) that encompasses the ways humans come to understand their world as well as make consequential decisions in that world, both individually and collectively. That is, misinformation about science can be treated as merely one component among many in the complex systems that shape how people make decisions and how those decisions affect their lives and well-being. Other aspects of those complex systems may be just as important—or in many cases, perhaps more important—in affecting human decision making and well-being (among other outcomes). This is not to say that addressing misinformation about science is unimportant, but rather to highlight that choices around intervention in a complex information system warrant consideration of other components beyond "misinformation" per se.

For example, community-specific (including intentionally targeted) misinformation about certain health-related behaviors does not exist in a vacuum, and thus, interventions to address negative impacts of that misinformation similarly cannot be effective in a vacuum. Widespread distrust in the medical profession may be a key feature of the broader health decision-making environment for some communities that allows for more downstream effects of targeted misinformation to emerge. In some cases, then, the most effective interventions to address those proximal effects of misinformation may in fact be well upstream of the misinformation itself—e.g., (re)building trust between historically underserved or mis-served communities. This relationship between health professionals and a community could be much more important than trying to refute particular pieces or narratives of misinformation (though such downstream interventions may also be important as part of a holistic, systems-oriented approach to improving health decision making and autonomy in those communities).

Again, the important insight here is that while interventions that specifically target misinformation are potentially effective in addressing certain consequences, they cannot stand alone. A systems-level analysis of the broader challenges facing individuals, communities, and societies is critical and should be brought to bear when decisions are being made about which interventions are chosen, how they are designed, and in what ways they are implemented on the ground. It is in the view of this committee that interventions to address misinformation about science cannot happen in a vacuum.

The Importance of Culture and Community

A misinformation intervention may also be more or less effective in different communities due to differences in pre-existing knowledge, cultural references, and communication norms. For example, in the context of an intervention that would involve Indian young adults correcting misinformation about COVID-19, Malhotra & Pearce (2022, p. 2303) found that local politeness norms were important for conversations that addressed misinformation and that this decreased the sense of direct confrontation, disrespect, or "questioning the competency of higher status elders." For communities that hold age and class hierarchies to specific cultural and social traditions/norms, the requirement to break those norms can interfere with the effectiveness of such an intervention.

Similarly, for the Filipino diasporic communities, multiple intersecting factors were reported to impact the circulation of information and access when trying to discuss COVID-19 (Nguyễn & Kuo, 2023). These factors included the economic context of Filipino workers within U.S. healthcare infrastructure (Nasol & Francisco-Menchavez, 2021); the historical context of U.S. colonization of the Philippines in the aftermath of the Spanish American War in 1898, which created a conditional and limited pathway of migration (see Ngai, 2004); the cultural context of contemporary multigenerational households; the religious context of participation in the Catholic church as tied to histories of Spanish and U.S. colonization; the political context of martial law previously under Ferdinand Marcos, and populist control under Rodrigo Duterte followed by the presidency of Ferdinand

Marcos Jr; the technological context whereby Facebook users in the Philippines represented the second largest source of data harvested by Cambridge Analytica in major data breach (Deinla et al., 2021; Occeñola, 2019); and the socio-scientific context of the Dengvaxia immunization controversy in 2016 that eroded public trust in the public health sector and significantly decreased overall vaccination rates (Mendoza et al., 2021). Collectively, these contexts inform Filipino communities' relationship to information, technologies, and institutions, and as such may all need to be considered when seeking to address misinformation within these communities.

As previously mentioned, faith-based institutions are important trusted intermediaries within communities, and particularly around health communications and messaging (Seale et al., 2022). Additionally, culturally and linguistically diverse communities tend to prioritize their social networks and interpersonal communication when seeking out information, and also prefer to receive information from people they know or share similar attributes with (Seale et al., 2022), and this is more likely the case in times of crisis and disaster (Steelman et al., 2015). Although a 2019 study by the Pew Research Center noted that people have less confidence in their clergy's guidance on personal matters and social issues (e.g., finances, mental health, immigration, global climate change) compared to guidance on religious issues, 50% or more of the respondents had either some or a lot confidence in their clergy's guidance on all areas assessed (Pew Research Center, 2019c, p. 33). Thus, for some people, their faith could be intimately tied to their decisions related to health, suggesting the need for interventions to also account for this relationship. Moreover, the effectiveness of interventions that involve collaboration with community brokers, for example, to reduce demand for misinformation, could also be limited if the nature of the intervention does not align with the broker's own beliefs (Seale et al., 2022), and so this factor should be considered as well.

Ethics

The possibility of intervening to address misinformation about science also raises important ethical considerations, and in considering the effects that interventions to address misinformation could have on an individual's perceptions and behaviors, the committee notes the relevance of normative ethics in determining what ought to be implemented (Varkey, 2021). An intervention's ability to effectively counteract or prevent consequences from occurring does not alone offer sufficient justification for its implementation. Freiling et al. (2023) have specifically called for caution in implementing misinformation interventions that focus on behavior change outcomes if such behavior change involves policy questions, which should weigh population values and input and not simply empirical scientific evidence.

Additionally, an empirical review of the prevalence of misinformation may not provide all the evidence needed for an organization to ethically determine whether and how to counteract that misinformation.

In the case of corrective efforts to address individuals' misbeliefs resulting from misinformation exposure, a key question involves what the expected default state of belief should be about the topic in question. People can hold beliefs that thematically align with misinformation without those beliefs being influenced by exposure to misinformation, and this can complicate efforts to measure an individual's ability to detect and subsequently reject misinformation (Paquin et al., 2022). For example, a person could form an inaccurate impression of the efficacy of an advertised medical product based on its appearance or brand name and not necessarily after seeing an explicitly inaccurate claim. It is also not the case that corrective efforts should necessarily wipe a person's mental slate clean of a certain topic, and such an assumption could not only undermine the evaluation of corrective efforts but also encourage unduly far-reaching corrective messages that involve more than the specific false claim(s). Additionally, Baker & Martinson (2001) have argued that organized communication efforts intended to promote, for example, the availability of accurate scientific information, and especially persuasive efforts to correct misinformation, should account for five ethical principles. Specifically, these principles, collectively known as the "TARES test," include *truthfulness* (of the claims), *authenticity* (of the source of information), *respect* (for the audiences), *equity* (in the application of strategies), and acknowledgement of *social responsibility* (for the common good). In the context of misinformation interventions, these principles could help to guide discussions about the empirical evidence on certain robust, but potentially condescending corrective efforts to address inaccuracies in people's understandings of science and what the costs of such efforts might be.

At the community and societal levels, the prospect of restricting any content currently available online or via various media can also raise ethical concerns. One ethical dilemma involves discrepancies between the information preferences of different communities. Some groups may believe content moderation will unfairly restrict access to information that is not inaccurate for that group. Other groups may see some information as valuable for a community even when it may be an example of misinformation.

To the committee's knowledge, explicit ethical guidance in the context of misinformation interventions has not been established, and such guidance could also be informed by the well-known *Belmont Report* regarding the participation of human subjects in research. Specifically, the committee believes that the Report's articulation of three principles: (a) respect for persons, (b) beneficence, and (c) justice can at least provide an ethical framework for current and future interventions (National Commission for the Protection of Human Subjects of Biomedical and Behavioral Research, 1979). Some of these principles are similar to the "TARES test" discussed above.

The principle of *respect for persons* acknowledges individual autonomy and respect for people's judgments with minimal restraints on their actions unless they are causing harm to others. Given that some interventions on misinformation are related to freedom of expression and speech, the principle of respect for person is a useful reminder. A pithy way to characterize the second principle, *beneficence*, is "do no harm." Beneficence essentially draws attention to the notion of intervening in ways that prioritize maximizing benefits and minimizing harms. Third, the underlying theme behind the principle of *justice* is equality in benefits and treatment accruing broadly despite people's backgrounds, social status, and other characteristics. This set of principles may be especially important to guide empirical investigations of the efficacy of misinformation interventions that involve intentional exposure to known false content. An experimental design in which some people are exposed to accurate information and some people are exposed to inaccurate information has implications for adherence to the principles of *beneficence* and *justice*. Recent work from Murphy & Greene (2023) discusses ethical considerations around conducting misinformation research that exposes people to false information. Institutional review boards can also offer important oversight regarding when such exceptions can be made (in weighing risks and benefits of inquiry) and what the debriefing processes for participants in such studies should entail.

Habituation

Interventions that involve repeated exposure over time and across contexts (e.g., warning labels, accuracy prompts) carry the risk of habituation on the part of individuals who encounter them. People may become so accustomed to seeing such interventions that they simply come to ignore them, reducing their efficacy (Lloyd et al., 2014). In some cases, repeated exposure to interventions that involve extra effort on the part of individuals may even cause some negative reactions as people become annoyed by them (e.g., having to make extra clicks or choices to see information that has been tagged as misinformation).

False Sense of Security

There may also be a risk that as individuals encounter more and more misinformation warnings and other related interventions that they come to over-rely on these warnings to tell them when they have encountered a piece of misinformation. As a result, individuals may develop a false sense of security regarding information they encounter that is *not* tagged as potentially misleading or false, engendering greater uptake and downstream effects of that misinformation. In laboratory studies, explicitly labeling some claims in a body of content as being false can lead people to believe that other claims in that same body of work are true because that information is not labeled (Pennycook et al., 2020).

Overgeneralized Skepticism

Some researchers have suggested a different potential consequence of repeated exposure to psychological interventions in this space, namely, that individuals come to treat *all* (or much) information they encounter throughout their daily lives as suspicious and thus untrustworthy (Altay, 2022; Hameleers, 2023; Hoes et al., 2024; Modirrousta-Galian & Higham, 2023). As concern about misinformation has grown and received significant media coverage in recent years, it is possible that people have become overly skeptical of much of the information they encounter, even when it comes from reliable and trustworthy sources (e.g., mainstream newspapers). In one study, exposure to tweets from politicians, journalists, and activists about "fake news" led to lower trust in media generally and less accurate identification of true news as real (Van Duyn & Collier, 2019).

In a related vein, interventions to combat misinformation about science may in fact lead to greater levels of distrust in reputable institutions, including science itself. This may happen through multiple pathways. For example, the role that social media platforms can play in moderating the content their users see (whether through direct content moderation or through the use of opaque algorithms that select tailored content for users) has the potential to generally decrease trust, particularly in the context of highly politicized and polarized issues. In line with concerns regarding the potential for overgeneralized skepticism, exposure to and general knowledge of interventions in this space may lead people to be overly skeptical not only of the information they encounter (especially online) but also of the individuals, institutions, or organizations that produce that information (e.g., science and scientists).

SUMMARY

Misinformation about science has a long history in the United States, as do approaches to combat it. However, only in the past few decades has there been large-scale scientific research on the efficacy of misinformation interventions. Such interventions can occur at many levels targeting individuals, communities, organizations, media, online platforms, or the broader information environment. In addition, interventions differ in their priorities, targeting one or more of four intervention points: supply, demand, distribution, and uptake. The most well-understood interventions are individual-level solutions to misinformation, such as improving media literacy, encouraging evaluative mindsets, and correcting misbeliefs through debunking techniques. However, systems-level interventions, such as filling information voids, foregrounding accurate information, and increasing trust, are also needed and are currently understudied. Potential legal remedies also face implementation challenges given American jurisprudence and precedent, although mandated disclosure laws often have survived once adopted. At this point, researchers have identified a number of potentially useful tools and interventions to mitigate misinformation about science that organizations could opt to try. More research is needed to further assess the effectiveness of these interventions in real-world contexts and how they can best be combined to decrease the influence of misinformation about science in the United States.

Conclusion 7-1: Many initiatives are currently exploring ways to address misinformation through various interventions. Such interventions have been generally implemented in a topically agnostic fashion and target one or more of four intervention points to combat the negative impacts of misinformation: supply, demand, distribution, and uptake. So far, there is no indication that a particular point is the best place to intervene, and many of the most effective interventions target multiple points.

Conclusion 7-2: Community-based organizations (CBOs) have attempted to mitigate misinformation in their communities and are particularly well positioned to do so because of their ties to the local residents, their awareness of local needs and concerns, and the trust that residents have in them. However, whether and when CBOs' efforts to mitigate misinformation are effective, and whether they have sufficient capacity to do so, are not well understood.

Conclusion 7-3: The role of legal and regulatory efforts to address misinformation about science remains to be explored more fully. Current approaches include several efforts to amend Section 230 of the U.S. Communications Decency Act of 1996 and mandated disclosure laws at the state level (e.g., laws that require warning labels about "deep fakes" or online "bots"). Other countries have deployed regulatory approaches to bolster content moderation practices on online platforms (e.g., Europe), which are being considered for useful adaptation into the United States context.

Conclusion 7-4: Providing warnings about common manipulative techniques and false narratives, providing corrective information (especially when accompanied by explanatory content), and encouraging evaluative thinking (e.g., lateral reading, accuracy nudges, friction) are effective individual-level solutions to specifically prevent belief in misinformation about science and reduce the sharing of misinformation about science by individuals, although the durability of these interventions is a common challenge.

Conclusion 7-5: Efforts to mitigate misinformation have become more prevalent over time, although interventions to specifically address misinformation about science are less prevalent than for other topical domains (e.g., political misinformation). Additionally, efforts to intervene have been largely uncoordinated across actors, sectors, disciplinary domains, and intended outcomes.

8

The Study of Misinformation About Science

In this report so far, we have offered a definition of misinformation about science, examined the contextual factors that shape its dynamics, including various sources and mechanisms of production, spread, and reach; and have discussed what is known from the evidence base about its impacts and the effectiveness of existing interventions. This chapter examines misinformation about science as the subject of a field of study—that is, research about this topic also coheres as a distinct discipline.

An important context here is that the study of misinformation in and of itself extends well beyond science-related topics, and while science is the emphasis of this report, other subjects can often be incorporated in research studies on misinformation about science. For example, the COVID-19 pandemic laid bare the intersections between misinformation about science, crisis, politics, and the media (Ferreira Caceres et al., 2022). Thus, studying misinformation about science often necessitates the study of misinformation more broadly. Throughout this chapter, discussions oscillate between the study of misinformation, generally, and misinformation about topics that relate specifically to science. This is not a mistake but rather is a characteristic of this field of study. To this end, we begin by situating misinformation about science within the multidisciplinary field of misinformation in general. We then review the approaches that are being employed across various disciplines to both understand and address the phenomenon. Finally, we discuss some of the current challenges to research including data limitations, methodological needs, and increased politicization of the topic.

MISINFORMATION: AN EVOLVING, MULTIDISCIPLINARY FIELD OF STUDY

Misinformation as a field of study has been challenged by some who have argued that such a field cannot exist, largely on the grounds that it is too early to investigate misinformation (Avital et al., 2020; Habgood-Coote, 2019), or that "there can't be a science of misleading content" (Williams, 2024). Concerns regarding the measurement and operationalization of the concept of misinformation are valid; these are ongoing challenges that the field is and will continue to grapple with going forward. However, criticisms of the field based on its origins, primary methods of study, and key findings about impacts hold less merit. Misinformation as an area of inquiry did not begin in response to Brexit or the 2016 U.S. election (Kharazian et al., 2024). The study of misinformation, and particularly misinformation about science, existed before these major events (Lim & Donovan, 2020) and concerns about informational challenges were present during previous pandemics, including the 1918 influenza pandemic, HIV/AIDS, severe acute respiratory syndrome (SARS), and many others (Tomes & Parry, 2022).

The field also rests on decades of research on rumors (e.g., Allport & Postman, 1946), propaganda (e.g., Bernays, 1928), and conspiracy theories (e.g., Hofstadter, 1964). Gordon Allport and Leo Postman wrote about rumors, as an object of study, more than half a century ago (Allport & Postman, 1946), and subsequently, Tamotsu Shibutani examined rumors from a sociological perspective, within news environments and crisis events (Shibutani, 1966). Research on propaganda has a long, rich history (Anderson, 2021). Historians have long examined the role that scientific expertise and credentials can play in the inducement of doubt about the connection, for example, between smoking and lung cancer, human activity and global warming, and dichlorodiphenyltrichloroethane (DDT) and environmental health (e.g., Michaels, 2006; Michaels & Monforton, 2005; Oreskes & Conway, 2010b). Proctor & Schiebinger (2008) have written about the making and unmaking of ignorance. The field of psychology includes a vast literature addressing the context-relevant elements of belief and attitude formation in the evaluation of information (e.g., Johnson et al., 1993; Petty & Cacioppo, 1986); and philosophers such as Harry Frankfurt have previously addressed "bullshit"—a type of misinformation characterized by complete disregard for truth—head on (Frankfurt, 2005). What may seem contemporary regarding the study of misinformation are actually research questions that have been actively investigated for decades. In other words, the study of misinformation is not new, and misinformation as a multidisciplinary field of study encompasses this rich history of scholarship.

As a multidisciplinary field—one in which multiple disciplines contribute without the blending of methods (van den Besselaar & Heimeriks,

2001)—the evidence base on misinformation reflects the results and methods from a number of long-standing disciplines, including anthropology, communication studies, computer science, engineering, history, law, political science, psychology, science and technology studies, and sociology. Furthermore, an argument could be made that a new interdisciplinary field is emerging, where there is a blending of methods, new frameworks, new syntheses, and new research collaborations that can be exceptionally useful across topics and disciplines.

In the last decade, the field has seen new and increased scholarly attention toward misinformation on social media platforms in particular. Between 2006 and 2023, there have been nearly 30,000 published articles that have used the old Twitter application programming interface (API) to collect and analyze social media user data (Murtfeldt, 2024). The broad access to data on Twitter during this period also means that an outsized number of studies reflect research conducted using Twitter data. Many of the topics from the top most-cited articles of this pool reflect issues that are germane to misinformation, such as understanding the factors that influence the spread of true and false information, assessing the credibility of information across news sources, understanding scientific misunderstandings from commercial advertising, and assessing AI capabilities for detecting false news (Murtfeldt, 2024). However, with the recent changes around data access at X (formerly Twitter), the number of research projects engaging with social media data has dropped dramatically (Murtfeldt, 2024), and as a result, some groups have moved to conducting studies on other social media platforms. That said, continual changes in data access will likely also shape what can be known about misinformation in the context of social media environments (see the section later in this chapter on "Challenges of obtaining high-quality data from social media contexts"). Importantly, there is a critical need to distribute the field's attention across other forms of media, including radio, television, and podcasts (see Chapter 4).

Overall, there has been an increase in the number of publications related to misinformation. For example, as of August 8, 2024, a search on Web of Science (Core Collection)[1] yields nearly 9,000 articles that have been published since 2020 with the term "misinformation" in either the title, abstract, or as part of the keywords. We note that this is likely an underestimate of the total number of articles published about the topic, given our understanding that "misinformation" is only one term that captures this field of research. Nevertheless, it is clear that scholarly attention on the subject has grown dramatically in recent years, and is perhaps linked

[1]Web of Science (Core Collection) is an online, paid-access platform that provides reference and citation data from academic journals, conference proceedings, and other documents in various academic disciplines.

to increases in funding support for proposed projects on misinformation (Figure 8-1).

For understanding misinformation about science specifically, it is important to distinguish between studying misinformation *in* science (or, research that in some way does not adhere to the shared principles and assumptions of scientific inquiry: reproducibility, generalizability, collectivity, uncertainty, and refinement; see Chapter 2) and *about* science (or, information on science- and health-related topics that in some way diverges from the interpretation based on accepted scientific evidence). Most researchers focus on the latter, while a smaller group of researchers are focused on topics related to misinformation *in* science, such as the rise in predatory journals (Bartholomew, 2014), agnotology (i.e., the study of how doubt or ignorance are created around a topic as a result of the publication of inaccurate or misleading results; Bedford, 2010; Proctor & Schiebinger,

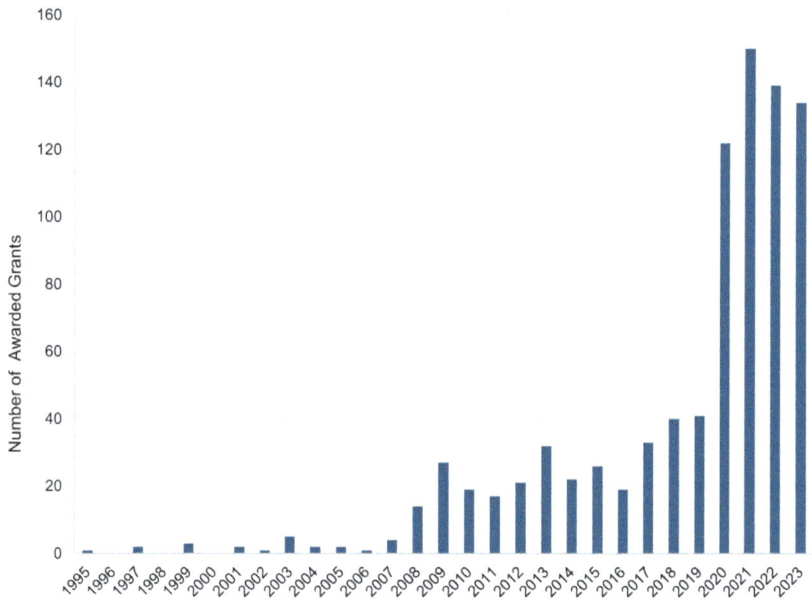

FIGURE 8-1 The number of grants awarded by funding agencies to support projects with the word "misinformation" in either the title, abstract, or key words.
SOURCE: Committee generated using all awarded grant data provided by Clarivate's Web of Science Grant Index[1] (retrieved on August 8, 2024).

[1]Clarivate's Grant Index is an online resource as part of the Web of Science platform that provides paid access to standardized data for awarded grants from 400+ funding agencies around the globe.

2008), reputation laundering (Bergstrom & West, 2023), and scientific fraud (Crocker, 2011). In the view of this committee, both aspects are important for obtaining a comprehensive understanding of the problem of misinformation as it relates to science and establishing approaches to strengthen the institution of science and public trust in science.

METHODOLOGICAL APPROACHES FOR STUDYING MISINFORMATION ABOUT SCIENCE

The many disciplines incorporated in the study of misinformation about science, bring a diversity of qualitative and quantitative research methods including experiments (Pennycook et al., 2021), surveys (Roozenbeek et al., 2020), interviews (Malhotra et al., 2023), digital ethnography (Haughey et al., 2022), computational approaches (Ferrara et al., 2020; Shao et al., 2016) and design science research (Hevner, 2004; Krafft & Donovan, 2020; Simon, 1988; Young et al., 2021). These various research methods have been employed to measure the spread of misinformation on social media (Del Vicario et al., 2016), test receptivity to misinformation and theories of motivated reasoning and confirmation bias (Zhou & Shen, 2022), evaluate the impact of misinformation on trust and political attitudes (Tucker et al., 2018; van der Linden et al., 2020), develop automated methods to detecting and interrupting the flow of misinformation (Shu et al., 2017), design new interfaces that promote healthy democratic discourse (Young et al., 2021), and inspire new policies of intervention (Calo et al., 2021).

More recent data collection efforts have largely been focused on vaccine misinformation, COVID-19 misinformation, and misinformation about climate change (Murphy et al., 2023). The data sets are typically large-scale social media data from either X or Facebook, with researchers using X more frequently because of its past policy that provided more access to its data.

Additionally, the research methods employed to study misinformation about science are almost identical to the methods employed to study other topics. In fact, many researchers studying the spread of misinformation and disinformation during U.S. elections also study misinformation about vaccines. Methods likewise are cross-disciplinary and nominally topic-agnostic, and this crossover is due, in part, to the significant overlap between the skillsets required to develop tools for studying misinformation of all types. For example, surveys can be designed to incorporate a question about hydroxychloroquine or one about voting intention. Cognitive assessments can be included in experiments about measles vaccines or about trust in the media. Computational sociologists can collect and analyze a collection of tweets about COVID-19 or a collection about the Boston Marathon bombing. Historians of science can study the role of corporate actors around climate change or corporate actors around smoking. That said, while social science methods are common and can be deployed to study misinformation in a variety of realms, there are also differences when they are applied to the study of misinformation about science. For example, studying misinformation about science requires some degree of scientific expertise in the subject matter being studied in order to make a determination regarding the weight of the accepted scientific evidence. In this case, the appropriation of methods from another domain to the study of misinformation about science might require that additional nuances be considered (see Chapter 2).

The application of qualitative methods, in particular, to the study of misinformation about science facilitate understanding of the role of context and nuance that complement quantitative research findings (Polleri, 2022; Teplinsky et al., 2022). This suite of methods (e.g., ethnography, interviews, focus groups, content analysis, discourse analysis) can also shed light on otherwise invisible aspects of misinformation about science (Roller, 2022), and become essential in the face of limited access to data from technology platforms that makes quantification a challenge (Bandy, 2021; Schellewald 2021). Qualitative research may also be particularly useful for understanding the different ways that information can be distorted as it traverses the 21st century information ecosystem, thus facilitating later quantification of information that appears in each category. Moreover, qualitative methodologies also played an important role in guiding public health response to questions and concerns about COVID-19 vaccines that emerged due to misinformation (see Box 8-1).

By nature, qualitative work does not always easily fit into the same discussions and dominant paradigms that quantitative work speaks to more directly. For example, debates about the amount (i.e., prevalence) of misinformation or how to categorize various types of it, which are common in quantitative studies, are less of the focus of qualitative research. Robust qualitative research and quantitative research are complementary to each other, and the intertwining of observational and experimental evidence is crucial for understanding causal inference on human behavior (Bailey et al., 2024; Greenhalgh, 2020; Greenhalgh et al., 2022). However, while qualitative research contributes significant insights to the understanding of misinformation about science, relatively little of this work is routinely brought into conversation with quantitative research on misinformation.

METHODOLOGICAL APPROACHES FOR ADDRESSING MISINFORMATION ABOUT SCIENCE

The potential negative impacts associated with misinformation about science are complex (see Chapter 6) and necessitate responses that can address this complexity. Several uptake-based interventions show promise for

BOX 8-1
The Application of Qualitative Methods During the COVID-19 Pandemic

Misinformation about COVID-19 has become a major focus of scholarly attention, and qualitative methods have played a central role in shaping public health responses to the surge in information produced about COVID-19. Some examples cases are discussed below and are also emblematic of how interventions for addressing misinformation about science can effectively merge insights from both qualitative and quantitative methodologies.

Seeking to increase COVID-19 vaccine uptake and demand, the Centers for Disease Control and Prevention (CDC) released a guide, "How to conduct a rapid community assessment: A guide to help you understand your community's needs around vaccination" (CDC, 2024). One example assessment commissioned by the CDC involved teens in participatory, qualitative research to understand information needs around adolescent COVID-19 vaccination, identify strategies to increase vaccine uptake, and understand the vaccination intentions of parents/guardians of younger children. This ground-up, demand-based approach allowed researchers to better understand vaccination attitudes, opinions, and behaviors while also providing nuanced recommendations for further intervention (Senft, 2021).

During the COVID-19 pandemic, the CDC also offered additional guidance on establishing "social listening" mechanisms of online conversations, questions, and rumors about vaccines (CDC, 2021b; Kolis et al., 2024). Given this approach was mostly quantitative in nature, guidance was provided on merging streams of quantitative and qualitative data in the form of international recommendations jointly made by the World Health Organization (WHO) and the United Nations Children's Fund (UNICEF; WHO & UNICEF, 2023). Over 1,000 researchers and public health professionals worldwide were trained in such mixed-method approaches, which helped to shape responses to the infodemic in a number of countries. Since then, additional resources continue to be developed to better understand a community's overall information needs through leveraging qualitative methods, for example, through stories (Wilhelm, 2023), as well as extending similar methodologies to understanding circulating misinformation about other science topics like cancer (Teplinsky et al., 2022).

SOURCE: Committee generated.

immediate implementation: there is moderate-to-strong evidence supporting the efficacy of remedies such as prebunking, debunking, lateral reading, and digital media literacy tips in helping individuals recognize and/or reduce the sharing of misinformation about science online (see Chapter 7). These techniques have therefore earned a place in the suite of tools to address the spread of misinformation about science in online contexts.

The most widely tested interventions to address misinformation are rooted in methodological individualism and are amenable to experimental research given existing tools. Individuals can be recruited to participate in randomized controlled trials (RCTs) in a laboratory or online setting where they are exposed to carefully selected stimuli that are intended to be representative of misinformation about science that individuals might actually encounter online. These individuals' behaviors, intentions, attitudes, and beliefs can be indexed using well-designed psychometric instruments. While this research on interventions is robust and dynamic and has established the existence of several effective remedies, it is also true that effects are small and durability of the effects are questionable. Methodologies that focus on individuals also raises questions about how best to study interventions and effects at the group or institution level (Chater & Loewenstein, 2023).

OVERARCHING CHALLENGES TO STUDYING AND ADDRESSING MISINFORMATION ABOUT SCIENCE

Despite the advancements made in the study of misinformation about science, challenges remain. This section discusses some of these challenges within three broad categories: (a) defining, conceptualizing, and theorizing about misinformation about science and its mitigation; (b) methodological and data limitations across different contexts, populations, and groups; and (c) occupational health and safety of researchers.

Challenges of Conceptualization and Definition

One of the more fundamental challenges to studying misinformation is how to define and operationalize it, including how inaccurate a claim must be before it is labeled as misinformation. Moreover, as previously mentioned in this report (see Chapter 2), there is some disagreement in the field regarding whether certain informational phenomena constitute misinformation and the importance of intentionality within the definition (Altay et al., 2023). This lack of conceptual clarity may be a byproduct of the rapid expansion of the field of misinformation research since 2016, as well as the nature of the scholarship in this arena, in which studies are designed, planned, and conducted within different disciplinary silos with little cross-fertilization (Broda & Strömbäck, 2024). Nevertheless, clear, widely shared, and context-specific definitions of misinformation are critical for studying this phenomenon in ways that yield effective results and underpin disciplinary coherence. Additionally, such agreement helps to establish a legitimate basis for intervention. In the absence of such shared definitions and operationalizations across channels and media types, choosing the most appropriate and efficacious set of tools for measurement or for intervening becomes highly challenging.

Another challenge for studying misinformation is establishing the appropriate unit of analysis. Misinformation, as addressed in research literature, appears as a phenomenon that exists at a range of units of analysis (i.e., aggregations), from the individual to the massively cumulative (Southwell et al., 2022). While studies have often focused on the wide-ranging effects of single, specific instances of false information, the contemporary concern about misinformation among scholars, policymakers and interested groups is not primarily about disconnected, errant claims about science, or these "atoms of content" (Wardle, 2023). Rather, current concern in both the academic and public arenas tends to center on the effects of larger streams of information, whether through viral, emergent spread among true believers, or coordinated efforts by knowing actors (disinformation). There has been a recent push to move away from the single, specific instance as the focal point of research to broader units that allow for wider perspectives. For example, to evaluate the effects of a single claim questioning the harm of cigarette smoking by the tobacco industry, circa 1975, is to miss the potentially multiplicative effects of decades of multichannel and multitarget efforts by the industry (see Chapter 4). The impact of considering units of analysis for understanding the nature of misinformation is also illuminated in a more contemporary example. A blog post may contain false statements about a treatment for a disease. While individual statements in the post may be classified as misinformation, could an entire post be classified as such? If the blog habitually disseminates such false assertions, how should it be described? Similarly, what term should be used to describe how this one blog may be part of a network of similar blogs with similar claims?

Some broader units of analysis appearing in contemporary research include *source-based classifications of misinformation*, which involves categorizing information coming from particular sources and web domains based on the reliability of the source (Cordonier & Brest, 2021; Grinberg et al., 2019), and *narrative-based classifications of misinformation*, where, by taking true information out of context and aggregating it in specific ways (e.g., clipping livestreams, selectively sharing scientific preprints), actors can promote "inaccurate narratives" (Wardle, 2023). The factually correct, but potentially misleading aforementioned *Washington Post* headline, "Vaccinated people now make up a majority of COVID deaths," is an example of the latter, in a case where a news article from reputable sources was used to amplify misinformation narratives (see Chapter 2; Beard, 2022; Goel et al., 2023). Thus, the fact that misinformation exists as various units—some of which are difficult to measure—presents a challenge to establishing an accurate understanding of the phenomenon, including, as discussed above, the lines around what is and is not misinformation in any given context, and the wide range of impacts it has. Agreement in the field on this component is also important for the purposes of measurement and guiding interventions.

Challenges in Theorizing About Intervention Effects

Another major challenge of studying misinformation about science lies in showing why interventions are effective. Despite the rapid, explosive growth in both academic and industry research on interventions to address misinformation in recent years, there remain large gaps in the collective understanding of the real-world efficacy of many of the approaches that have been proposed, developed, and implemented. Many tools that appear to be efficacious in small-scale, controlled experiments do not appear to fare well in real-world settings (Nordon et al., 2016). Researchers has struggled to identify why this is the case; however, one aspect of this *efficacy gap* is that many interventions may be relatively effective at addressing certain aspects of the broader problem (e.g., reducing spread of viral misinformation) but ineffective with respect to the most consequential outcomes of interest (e.g., the formation of misbeliefs with the potential to negatively affect real-world decision making). Despite extensive replication of a small number of effects, the implications of the underlying theoretical mechanism(s) have not been tested as rigorously. In other words, although a specific effect may replicate several times in a laboratory setting, rote replication alone is insufficient to predict generalizability outside the experimental context. To achieve such generalizability, a clear theoretical mechanism is needed to explain *why* a particular intervention is effective, and to make predictions about the specific contexts under which replication can be expected.

Some of the most generalizable interventions that *do* exist are rooted in such mechanisms. For example, prebunking is rooted in inoculation theory (Cook et al., 2017), and accuracy nudge interventions are rooted in dual-process theories of human cognition (Pennycook & Rand, 2021). However, in practice, experiments differ in the degree to which they test the underlying theoretical mechanisms, for example, the uptake of misinformation about science. Even more limited are critical tests that enable scientists to determine which of several possible theoretical explanations are most scientifically parsimonious by facilitating the explanation of several different effects with as few theoretical assumptions as possible (e.g., Pennycook & Rand, 2019, who designed an experiment to adjudicate between dual-process and motivated reasoning explanations for misinformation sharing). Such critical tests of theoretical mechanisms contribute to a cohesive research program, resulting in a contribution to generalizable scientific knowledge.

An emerging body of scholarship has begun to review existing empirical evidence and link that evidence to promising theories (e.g., expectancy value theory, dual-process theory, and fuzzy-trace theory). For example, the target article of a *Journal of Applied Research in Memory and Cognition* (JARMAC) special issue reviewed the evidence on different theoretical explanations for why misinformation about COVID-19 might be compelling and implications for risky decision making (Reyna et al., 2021). But despite significant evidence in analogous fields (e.g., medical decision making), approaches to testing interventions for addressing misinformation about science still remain largely focused on testing specific experimental effects, with comparatively little theoretical justification. Thus, it remains to be determined why specific interventions work, what might be driving effect sizes, and in what contexts they will be ineffective. Moreover, research to advance understanding of misinformation about science would also benefit from deeper engagement with a broad set of theoretical perspectives from other disciplines such as the behavioral and decision sciences.

Challenges of Scaling Up Interventions

Closely tied to the issue of efficacy is the challenge of scaling up and broadly disseminating many of the proposed interventions aimed at addressing misinformation that are coming out of academic and industry research. It is unknown whether interventions that have positive impacts at the individual level are useful for countering community- and societal-level consequences of widespread misinformation about science in the information ecosystem. This is in large part because they simply are too onerous to deploy at the massive scale needed. In addition, interventions are often more effective when targeted for a given context and require collaboration and refinement with the target population. There is moderate evidence that some platform-level interventions (e.g., deplatforming) are effective for reducing volumes of harmful content (Chandrasekharan, 2017; Jhaver et al., 2021; Saleem & Ruths, 2018; Thomas & Wahedi, 2023); however, even these effects may simply be "drops in the bucket" given the rapid proliferation of tools (e.g., large language models) for spreading information, including misinformation. Here again, a theoretical understanding of *why* misinformation spreads could lead to significant resource savings, and absent such a mechanism, the expense required to test the efficacy of interventions at scale may be prohibitive.

The pace of scientific publishing is also too slow to conduct experimental tests each time a new type of misinformation appears. For example, if we assume that misinformation about the COVID-19 pandemic is fundamentally different from misinformation about future pandemics, then requiring extensive experimental testing prior to deploying interventions could result in that misinformation causing irreversible damage and harm in the interim. Encouragingly, the evidence base in science is cumulative; therefore, theoretically-motivated approaches can inform preliminary responses while empirical work is being conducted. Indeed, the very purpose of scientific theory is to make predictions based upon empirical regularities that can extend to novel settings. Thus, a clear understanding of theoretical mechanisms can support proactive responses to new sources of misinformation about science.

The very nature of the research conducted also poses challenges to scaling up interventions. As stated above, a majority of studies surrounding interventions to address misinformation are rooted in methodological individualism. In other words, the unit of analysis is the individual decision maker, and interventions are designed to target individuals at the time decisions are made. These studies, by design, randomize across cultural, social, and community-based contexts, and therefore a single study may not take all of these important social factors into account. Similarly, questions about the influences of different technological affordances are typically outside the scope of these studies. Thus, there is a dearth of scholarship on evidence-based strategies for addressing misinformation that explicitly take into account relevant social, cultural, and technological factors, especially at the level of specific communities.

Finally, it is worth briefly mentioning that current funding models have also played a role in shaping the existing scholarship on interventions for addressing misinformation. For example, the scope of work reflected in requests for proposals (RFPs) have dictated where attention and resources in the field are directed. This means that if funding priorities consistently emphasize research needs around individual-level solutions (Chater & Loewenstein, 2023), then gaps will remain in understanding the nature of the problem and potential solutions at higher levels and larger scales (e.g., community-based, platform and platform design-based, policy, and regulatory approaches).

Challenges of Obtaining High-Quality Data from Social Media Contexts

Another issue hampering research in this area is lack of access to certain kinds of quantitative data that would greatly elucidate how misinformation about science originates and spreads on social media, one of the major spaces within which misinformation now propagates. Historically, many social media companies made at least some public data available through APIs, which provided machine-readable data in bulk for researchers and corporate partners alike, and in some cases, free of charge. However, in recent years, some of the most useful APIs for researchers have been eliminated or made prohibitively expensive by their parent companies (Ledford, 2023; Pequeño IV, 2023; van der Vlist et al., 2022). These decisions have had several downstream effects, most notably a reduction in research on the platforms in question but have also created conditions in which researchers have had to develop unsanctioned methods of collecting data automatically, a process known as scraping (Trezza, 2023). While it may be the only option for collecting certain kinds of data, scraping is not ideal because of the inconsistency of the data it provides as well as the potential legal risks to which it may expose its practitioners (Luscombe et al., 2022).

Obtaining access to social media data may be especially challenging for researchers at lesser-resourced institutions or those without sufficient external funding. The decision by the platforms to charge for access to data also shifts the power in determining what topics can be studied using social media data from researchers to funders of research (both internal and external). Other data access models, such as TikTok's, still do not require payment for its data, but are limited to researchers in the United States and Europe. Additionally, qualifying researchers are required to submit project proposals when applying for access, and TikTok reserves the right to reject proposals at will.

After adopting multiple data access systems over the years, including APIs and invite-only research projects, in 2023 Meta introduced a novel system that could serve as an industry model. It now provides access to data through remotely-managed "clean rooms" in which all analyses must be conducted—thus, no raw data can be downloaded locally, only aggregate statistics and models. Similar to TikTok, researchers must apply to access the data, but applications are processed and evaluated by the University of Michigan's Inter-University Consortium for Political and Social Research (ICPSR),[2] meaning that Meta has no prerogative to veto projects that may cast them in a negative light. At the time of this consensus report, this initiative is in its infancy, but attempts to strike a balance between maximizing both user privacy and researchers' access to data at scale.

Even when APIs were more plentiful than they are now, the data they provided were limited in both scale and scope, and substantial inconsistencies in the kinds of data provided by different platforms impeded multi-platform research. Some APIs, such as Twitter's, Facebook's, and Reddit's, included data about sharing and reactions ("likes," "favorites," and similar affordances), but not other types of information such as how many times a post was viewed, clicked on, or otherwise interacted with. Another point worth noting is that while these data provided information on what is being posted, they did not necessarily reflect real-world exposure and attention to this information (Lazer, 2020). At the same time, both the user interfaces and APIs of video-sharing sites including YouTube and TikTok featured view (but not engagement) counts.

Thus, the ability to answer as simple a question as how many times a given piece of misinformation about science has been viewed online depends on arbitrary decisions by the parent company. This issue is exacerbated by the fact that many of these metrics, in turn, might be gamed (whereby many of the actors that are circulating misinformation, in

---

[2]Social Media Archive @ICPSR. Available at https://socialmediaarchive.org

turn, might seek to manipulate indicators of how widely circulated a piece of information was). Therefore, researchers studying multiple platforms—a long-recommended best practice for social media research—contend with incommensurate data from companies that have made different decisions, and consequently are not adequately able to understand, for example, how misinformation travels between platforms. Without industry standards and/or governmental policies to impose consistency with respect to the provision of data, multi-platform research on misinformation will likely continue to be rare and limited.

Finally, even at its best, social media contexts are not sufficient for studying misinformation about science or even other topics. The substantial amount of research on misinformation based on social media data makes this point worth reiterating. Moreover, even though social media contexts are currently the dominant focus of most misinformation research, the field is still unable to approximate what fraction of exposure to misinformation is from social media. Not everyone is an active social media user, and even for those who are, social media does not necessarily account for the full scope of their exposure to misinformation. Within specific platforms, some users may be more visible than others: for example, those who participate in hashtag campaigns or who use certain keywords may be better represented in study samples than those who do not. Studies based on platforms used by most of a given population, such as Facebook with U.S. adults, still cannot effectively generalize to offline target populations because behavior may be platform-specific. In other words, research on misinformation about science that is based on Facebook data can reveal how people engage with such misinformation on Facebook, but these findings may not be generalizable to other platforms like X and Reddit, or even to non-social media contexts (e.g., TV, radio, podcast, private messaging apps, face to face). Importantly, studies on social media that require users to opt in, such as experiments, may also suffer from selection bias: people who are least trusting of conventional authorities such as mainstream news are more likely to believe misinformation (Zimmermann & Kohring, 2020), but they may also be less likely to participate in such research. Moreover, even those who choose to opt in may change their behavior to appear more socially acceptable, given that people know that consuming certain kinds of misinformation may reflect poorly on them (Yang & Horning, 2020).

Challenges of Obtaining Comprehensive Data Across Populations: Data Absenteeism

The study of misinformation about science is also beset by data absenteeism, which is defined as the "absence of data [...] from groups experiencing social vulnerability" (Viswanath et al., 2022c, p. 209). Historically, this has included, among others, non-White racial groups, sexual and gender minorities, lower-income immigrants, people with disabilities, and those who live in geographically remote locations. Data absenteeism manifests differently across methods. In surveys and experiments that rely on participant recruitment (e.g., clinical trials), it can arise due to issues such as the amount of compensation offered; the quality, locations, and numbers of study advertisements; the requirement to take time from work to participate; and historical distrust between the scientific community and minoritized community groups. Additionally, standard survey research design practices such as probability sampling, limited callbacks, and recruitment costs could limit data collection from a more representative population. Social factors—including stigma, racism, legal status, competing demands, lack of reliable transportation, and challenges with childcare, among others—may also make it difficult for some individuals (e.g., those from low socio-economic positions) to participate in misinformation research (George et al., 2014; Nagler et al., 2013; Viswanath et al., 2022c).

For observational studies, like those based on social media trace data, data absenteeism manifests as differences between the general population and the user base of the platform in question. In other words, participation on certain social media platforms, especially those that are usually relied on for research such as X or Facebook may not be representative of the general population, thus denying a voice to certain groups (Viswanath et al., 2024). The user base on X, for example, has historically had an overrepresentation of young people (Auxier & Anderson, 2021; Cox, 2024). Furthermore, globally as well as domestically, what is known about misinformation about science is likely biased toward western, educated, industrial, rich, democratic populations (Henrich et al., 2010), while little is known about how the levels of exposure and impacts of misinformation about science might differ among non-Western populations.

For any science communication research that assesses the audiences, the lack of participation by some groups can be compounded by standard approaches often used to gather data (Lee & Viswanath, 2020; Viswanath et al., 2022c), and while the reasons for this are varied, all of them are addressable. Cyberinfrastructure, which is often relied upon for data collection may be poor in underserved areas, making it difficult to collect data. For example, poor communication infrastructure remains a persistent problem in rural areas, poorer neighborhoods in cities, and in lower-income countries (Viswanath et al., 2022a; Whitacre et al., 2015). Additionally, frequent interruptions in telecommunication services, such as cellphone disconnections, could preclude data collection from some groups. Likewise, digital devices are often major tools for data collection, yet the continuing digital divide among different groups could preclude participation in misinformation research.

Clearly, data absenteeism is a significant challenge, and confidence in results and ensuing inferences from studies that suffer from it leads to data chauvinism (i.e., faith in the size of data without considerations for quality and contexts) and misleading generalizations (Lee & Viswanath, 2020). The refrain that underserved groups are "hard to reach" is also misleading given they are "hardly reached," thereby straining the reliability of misinformation research (Viswanath et al., 2022c). These phenomena require even more critical attention in the era of "big data" when the effects of science infodemics and the ways to address them grow more urgent. While it may require more work to incorporate historically excluded people into misinformation research studies, an incomplete understanding of this topic will persist without doing so.

Challenges of Study Design

Research design is particularly germane when evaluating the effects or the lack of effects of misinformation beyond the individual level and in understanding the impact of misinformation on underserved groups such as those from lower socio-economic status and minoritized communities. Causal relationships between exposure and effects are most studied using RCTs or lab or field experiments where there is greater control between exposure to stimulus (bits of misinformation about science) and effects such as the development or reinforcement of inaccurate science knowledge and misbeliefs, that in turn, can influence attitudes and behaviors (e.g., denial of climate change or vaccine hesitance). RCTs are not without limitations and caveats (Bailey et al., 2024; Greenhalgh et al., 2022):

- Real-world conditions can hardly be replicated in experimental contexts given there is a multiplicity of influences that interact with exposure to misinformation leading to certain effects.
- The act of exposing people to misinformation, on purpose, could be viewed as unethical though it is often acceptable practice in deception studies in the context of psychological research when followed by debrief (Boynton et al., 2013).
- More critically, few RCTs and experiments include members from historically underserved groups (e.g., communities of color, low-income communities, rural communities; Kwon et al., 2024).

On the latter point, medical mistrust among Black communities has certainly been shaped by past atrocities at the hand of science and medical institutions (e.g., unethical gynecological surgeries performed by J. Marion Sims on three Black women slaves, the Tuskegee Study of Untreated Syphilis on Black men, and the unethical collection of human cells from

Henrietta Lacks, a Black woman, for medical research; Bajaj & Stanford, 2021; Beskow, 2016; Wall, 2006). Yet, historical patterns of mistrust only partially explain the absence of Black Americans from research studies. Contemporary realities, particularly structural racism, continue to plague these communities (Bailey, 2024), and other factors have been identified as explanations for the lack of participation of Black Americans in clinical trials: lack of awareness about trials, economic factors, and communication issues (Harris et al., 1996). The extent to which these same factors may similarly influence the participation of Black Americans in science communication (including misinformation) studies requires deeper exploration.

Challenges of Researcher's Health and Safety

As discussed previously in this report, some scientific issues have become politicized over time (Druckman, 2022), and this reality can make studying misinformation about such topics challenging in ways that go beyond the standard challenges of gathering data, running analyses, and interpreting results. For many researchers studying misinformation, the challenges could also include Freedom of Information Act requests, lawsuits, subpoenas, online abuse, and other forms of intimidation and harassment (Quinn, 2023). Such incidents have led some researchers and universities to either discontinue or at least reduce research focused on tracking online misinformation—commonly characterized as a "chilling effect" on scholarship (Quinn, 2023). Researchers have just begun to talk about this publicly (Starbird, 2023), but many have spoken anonymously for fear of reprisal. To this end, additional safeguards may be needed at research institutions and universities to specifically support researchers at all levels (including graduate and postdoctoral levels) who study misinformation. In the past, climate change researchers have faced similar challenges (Levinson-Waldman, 2011), so there may be lessons to be learned from this arena for those studying misinformation of all types. But the potential to quell inquiry goes beyond the individual researchers in the spotlight. In light of the additional foreseen challenges, graduate students may choose different research directions, and universities may be less likely to make long-term investments in this research area, given it may result in increased legal fees.

Researchers studying misinformation about science are also exposed to potentially violent and graphic content on the internet, including hate speech and imagery and videos during violent conflicts, which can negatively impact their psychological well-being (Holman et al., 2024; Pluta, 2023; Steiger et al., 2021). Additionally, some systematic disinformation campaigns do not exist in a vacuum (Kuo & Marwick, 2021) and are linked in ways that may, for example, connect a researcher studying vaccine misinformation to the latest QAnon conspiracy theory. The impact on mental health of researchers studying misinformation on a daily basis is unknown and worth more empirical scrutiny. One might be able to draw lessons from other professions such as healthcare and clinical medicine where burnout and other threats to mental well-being are not uncommon (National Academies, 2019b; Office of the Surgeon General, 2022).

SUMMARY

It is clear that there has been long-standing scholarly attention dedicated to understanding the nature of different types of false information (e.g., rumors, misinformation, propaganda). Such efforts reflect the interest of multiple disciplines, including communication studies, computer science, engineering, history, law, political science, psychology, science and technology studies, sociology, among others, and has resulted in the development of a suite of methods and tools to both study these phenomena and intervene to mitigate negative impacts. In recent years, discourse on misinformation has become widespread in the public arena. At the same time, building a robust evidence base that documents the prevalence, spread, exposure, and effects has been challenging. The challenges in studying misinformation about science are manifold and include inconsistent and evolving definitions of what constitutes as misinformation; lack of access to data on social media platforms and connecting them to the larger information ecosystem; study designs that can provide confidence in causal inference between exposure and outcomes; and data absenteeism. As it relates to misinformation about science specifically, there has also been uneven scholarly attention toward understanding the nature of the phenomenon across science topics (e.g., vaccines vs. women's health issues) as well as the challenges associated with studying highly politicized topics. These challenges are not insurmountable, and responding to these challenges has the potential to lead to new and informative research directions for the field.

> *Conclusion 8-1: There has been considerable emphasis on studying misinformation about science and potential solutions at the individual level. In contrast, there has been limited emphasis on understanding the phenomenon of misinformation at higher levels and larger scales, which may inadvertently place the onus on the individual to mitigate the problem. There has been limited progress on:*
>
> - *Understanding how structural and contextual factors such as social class, race/ethnicity, culture, and geography, and social networks and institutions influence the origin, spread, and impact of misinformation about science.*
> - *Understanding how other important factors (i.e., social, political, and technological forces) that shape the information*

environment interact with misinformation about science to influence decision making and well-being.

- *Understanding the larger impact that systematic disinformation campaigns can have and how to effectively intervene to counter misinformation about science from such sources.*
- *Understanding the effectiveness of existing approaches to address misinformation about science, either alone or in combination, with an eye toward better design, selection, and implementation.*

Conclusion 8-2: Some progress has been made on understanding the nature of misinformation on select social media platforms; however, a comprehensive picture across all major platforms is lacking. The ability to detect and study misinformation about science on social media platforms is currently limited by inconsistent rules for data access, cost-prohibitive data restrictions, and privacy concerns.

9

Conclusions, Recommendations, and Research Agenda

The committee was tasked with characterizing the nature and scope of misinformation about science and its differential impacts; identifying solutions to limit its spread; and providing guidance on interventions, policies, and research toward reducing harms from it. To this end, the committee examined the existing body of evidence from diverse disciplines investigating misinformation about science (e.g., agricultural science, communication, computational social science, engineering, history, information science, journalism, law, media studies, political science, psychology, and sociology) to yield this consensus report.

This chapter summarizes the committee's conclusions and outlines 13 recommended actions toward prioritizing capacities, resources, and policies to better understand misinformation about science and intervene, when needed, to the greatest effect. The committee's recommendations reflect prioritized actions to mitigate misinformation about science based on relative potential for harm. They also reflect today's complex information ecosystem where action is needed at multiple levels (i.e., individual, community, organizational/institutional, societal) and involve a diversity of actors who are well positioned to employ specific mitigation strategies (e.g., community and civil society organizations, funders, media companies, policymakers, regulators, science communicators, scientists, medical professionals, and scientific institutions/organizations). Given the complex and multi-layered nature of the spread and impact of misinformation about science, the committee's recommendations have the greatest potential to effectively mitigate the negative consequences of misinformation about science when implemented in concert, rather than independently.

In presenting the committee's conclusions and recommendations, we begin by defining misinformation about science and describing the contemporary information ecosystem in which the science information environment is embedded. We then describe key sources of (mis)information about science and the possible paths of influence by which it originates and spreads. Third, we discuss the impacts of misinformation about science at different levels (individual, community, and societal) and describe which specific impacts are documented empirically. Finally, we review the range of interventions that are being employed to address misinformation about science and discuss their documented effectiveness.

DEFINING MISINFORMATION ABOUT SCIENCE

Establishing a clear definition of misinformation about science was an essential part of the committee's charge. Currently, there are many terms used in social science research to describe information that deviates from accuracy (e.g., conspiracy theories, disinformation, fabricated news, malinformation, misinformation, propaganda, rumor), but across different disciplines and methods, there is some disagreement about key concepts within their meaning (Altay et al., 2023; Søe, 2021; Vraga & Bode, 2020). Misinformation specifically, is often used as a broad term to describe falsehoods, and there is some debate about which phenomena are distinct from this broader concept (Altay et al., 2023; Vraga & Bode, 2020). Defining what constitutes misinformation about science is also nontrivial, in part because of the contingent nature of scientific consensus. Moreover, science can be poorly communicated or misrepresented, and there are currently no bright lines between scientific uncertainty, science done poorly, and misinformation about science. Thus, to provide clarity and focus for its analysis and to offer a guidepost for the broader research community, the committee developed a definition of misinformation about science (see Chapter 2 for further discussion of considerations for defining misinformation about science).

Conclusion 2-1: In both public discourse and in peer-reviewed research, the term misinformation has been used as an umbrella term to refer to various types of false, inaccurate, incorrect, and misleading information. The broad nature of the term has made it difficult to develop a coherent understanding of the nature, scope, and impacts of misinformation, and by extension, misinformation about science. To address the lack of a consistent definition, the committee has developed the following definition: Misinformation about science is information that asserts or implies claims that are inconsistent with the weight of accepted scientific evidence at the time (reflecting both quality and quantity of evidence). Which claims are determined to be misinformation about science can evolve over time as new evidence accumulates and scientific knowledge regarding those claims advances.

Given that scientific knowledge is not static, we reiterate that "at the time" is a significant component of the definition. That is, a scientific claim that is considered to be inconsistent with accepted scientific evidence at one point in time could, through the generation of new empirical evidence, become a reasonable alternative view on the topic at a later point. We also note that while the contingent nature of scientific agreement may be seen as a given from the perspective of scientists, updates to scientific understanding due to new evidence can inadvertently create confusion for non-scientists.

Much attention has also been paid to disinformation and its conceptual relationship to misinformation. In the literature, the concept of intent is often included as a distinguishing feature of this informational phenomenon (Freelon & Wells, 2020); however, intent is difficult to evaluate and operationalize. In defining misinformation, the committee determined that the motive or intent of the agent promulgating the information is immaterial to the potential impacts of that information on the recipient of the information. ***Therefore, the committee considers disinformation about science to be a sub-category of misinformation that is circulated by agents that are aware that the science information they are circulating is false.***

THE CONTEMPORARY INFORMATION ECOSYSTEM

The science information environment is primarily composed of scientific research findings and science news in both print and broadcast forms. Importantly, science news has been significantly impacted by decades of newsroom cutbacks and the closing of local newspapers (Abernathy, 2018). As discussed in Chapter 3, the science information environment is nested within and shaped by the broader 21st century information ecosystem. This broader information ecosystem is characterized by advanced information and communication technologies that have greatly enhanced the volume and speed of the production, and dissemination of both accurate and inaccurate science information. Moreover, the media system of the 21st century information ecosystem is a hybrid of interconnected digital technologies and media types (e.g., search engines, social media, internet websites, electronic broadcast media) as opposed to the predominantly analog media system of the 20th century. This means that science information can quickly travel across different channels and media types, and in some cases, can become divorced from the original context needed to appropriately evaluate the accuracy and reliability of the information (e.g., a screenshot of a news article headline and photo circulating through online platforms apart from the associated content of the article). Additionally, online platforms have enabled a flattening of hierarchies across professional and social networks (a phenomenon that has been characterized as "context collapse" [Davis & Jurgenson, 2014]) in ways that enhance information exchange but may also blur the lines between reliable and unreliable sources of science information. Additionally, the rise in the production and dissemination of information via generative artificial intelligence (AI) along with the more recent integration of AI into search engine results may make it even more challenging to discern reliable science information (Memon & West, 2024). All of these advancements, though beneficial in many ways, add to the complexity that consumers of science information have to navigate within contemporary online environments.

Conclusion 3-1: Though inaccuracy in scientific claims has been a long-standing public concern, recent changes within the information ecosystem have accelerated widespread visibility of such claims. These changes include:

- *the emergence of new information and communication technologies that have facilitated access, production, and sharing of science information at greater volume and velocity than before,*
- *the rise of highly participatory online environments that have made it more difficult to assess scientific expertise and credibility of sources of science information, and*
- *the decline in the capacity of news media that has likely reduced both the production and quality of science news and information.*

In recent years, there has also been increased attention to public trust in science as a reliable source of information, including concerns that declines in trust may contribute to the spread and uptake of misinformation about science (Lupia et al., 2024). Current data suggest that trust in science and confidence in scientific institutions has actually fared better than a number of other institutions over the last five decades (Brady & Kent, 2022; Krause et al., 2019). But a notable decline was observed in 2022, and levels of confidence in the scientific community vary significantly by partisan identity (Davern et al., 2024). Additionally, patterns of trust and mistrust in science and other civic institutions also varies across demographic groups and, in some cases, have been shaped by negative historical experiences with such institutions (Bui, 2021; Peña, 1997; Visperas, 2022). See Chapter 3 for a detailed discussion about trends in trust in different U.S. institutions over time.

Conclusion 3-2: Trust in science has declined in recent years, yet remains relatively high compared to trust in other civic institutions. Although confidence in the scientific community varies significantly by partisan identity, patterns of trust in science across demographic groups also vary as a function of the specific topic, the science organization or scientists being considered, or respective histories and experiences.

SOURCES AND SPREAD OF MISINFORMATION ABOUT SCIENCE

Misinformation about science is produced from a range of institutional and individual sources, and spreads through the same channels and many of the same mechanisms as accurate information about science (see Chapters 4 and 5 for detailed discussions of the various sources of misinformation about science and how it spreads). It can also be difficult to draw a clear line between sources of misinformation about science and the mechanisms for its spread. For example, a single source might create original content, produce it in various formats, and distribute it to others. This content might be picked up and shared by others, but it might also be "re-created" and packaged differently, making an individual both a "spreader" and a "producer."

Historically, misinformation about science has emerged from news stories (e.g., news reports in the mid-1800s that misrepresented the tomato hornworm as a deadly caterpillar; O'Connor & Weatherall, 2019), from advertising (e.g., the marketing of oil made from rattlesnakes—so called "snake oil"—as an effective cure for various illnesses in the late 1800s; Jaafar et al., 2021), and even from research propagated by prominent scientific institutions (e.g., eugenics research in the 19th and early 20th century—based on the false premise of racial superiority through genetic inheritance; Grant & Mislán, 2020). Over time, it has become clear that misinformation about science is not limited to one type of medium or to a particular source, and there are differences across sources in terms of their relative influence on the spread of misinformation about science, and consequently, the potential impacts on individuals, groups, and society.

As discussed in Chapter 4, strategic campaigns are especially effective in spreading disinformation about science for profit or other personal interests, and in some cases, specific populations have been intentionally targeted by such efforts (e.g., the sugar industry targeting low-income and communities of color [Bailin et al., 2014], and the tobacco industry's marketing to Black communities [Wailoo, 2021]). Misinformation about science can also unintentionally originate from the scientific and medical community, including universities press offices, research organizations, and individual scientists and healthcare professionals. This can occur as a result of exaggerations or oversimplifications of research claims in press releases, distortions in the interpretations of scientific data, omissions of details about the preliminary nature of research published in the form of preprints, deviations from evidence-based science communication strategies when engaging in debates about science in the public arena, dissemination of misinformation to patients as a result of inadequate knowledge of the latest consensus on the part of the medical provider, and the propagation of false information based on racial and cultural biases (e.g., in medical textbooks). Other key sources of misinformation about science with great potential for influence include elite individuals, government actors, and news media outlets.

Conclusion 4-1: Misinformation about science is widely understood to originate from several different sources. These include, but are not limited to:

- *for-profit corporations and non-profit organizations that use strategic communication (e.g., public relations, advertising, promotions, and other marketing campaigns) to intentionally seed and amplify misinformation about science for financial gain, to advance ideological goals, or to mitigate potential losses,*
- *governments and politicians that either publicly discredit the weight of evidence on science issues or seed misinformation about science as part of their political agendas,*
- *alternative science and health media that advocate for treatments and therapies that are not supported by scientific evidence,*
- *entertainment media through fictional and non-fictional narratives and plotlines that oversimplify, exaggerate, or otherwise misrepresent science and scientists to be compelling or for cinematic effect,*
- *reputable science organizations, institutions, universities, and individual scientists as a byproduct of poor science communication, distortions of scientific data, the dissemination of research findings before they have been formally vetted and substantiated, and in the worst cases, scientific fraud,*
- *press offices and news media organizations due to misrepresentation and misreporting of scientific studies, medical developments, and health issues, and*
- *elite and non-elite individuals due to a variety of motivations.*

CONCLUSION 4-2: *Not all misinformation about science is equal in its influence. Rather, misinformation about science has greater potential for influence when it originates from authoritative sources; is amplified by powerful actors; reaches large audiences; is targeted to specific populations, or is produced in a deliberate, customized, and organized fashion (e.g., tobacco industry campaigns to cast doubt about the health risks of smoking).*

Changes Within Journalism

Many adults in the United States get their science information from news outlets, making the quality and quantity of science news production especially important (Funk et al., 2017). In the past few decades, however, the institution of journalism has experienced decreases in funding which has led to significant reductions in local news coverage and a major downsizing in reporting across many news organizations (Minow, 2021). At the same time, public trust and confidence in the media and journalists has steadily dropped—while 23% of Americans indicated high levels of confidence in the press in the 1973 General Social Survey (GSS), only 7% did in 2022 (Davern et al., 2024). This constellation of factors create conditions in which misinformation about science can more easily spread.

Science reporting is often guided by journalistic values and norms that prioritize capturing public attention over careful consideration of the process of science and the nature of scientific evidence (Dunwoody, 2021). Layoffs in journalism have meant that journalists who lack specialized training in science are being assigned to cover science news (Dunwoody, 2021). Insufficient expertise in science and scientific research methods may make it challenging for journalists to correctly interpret scientific research and properly contextualize the findings in their reporting. Moreover, issues related to health and wellness, which in the context of this report is considered to be a category of science, are often reported on by journalists who specialize in lifestyle, trends, or general news (O'Keeffe et al., 2021, Tanner, 2004; Voss, 2002). This kind of topic-based segmentation within journalism also creates conditions that can lead to the unintentional spread of misinformation about science from news media organizations.

Conclusion 4-3: Journalists, editors, writers, and media/news organizations covering science, medical and health issues (regardless of their assigned beat or specialty areas) serve as critical mediators between producers of scientific knowledge and consumers of science information. Yet, financial challenges in the past two decades have reduced newsroom capacity to report on science, particularly at local levels.

Conclusion 4-4: Science reporting for the general public may be particularly prone to the unintentional spread of misinformation about science. Several factors can influence this, including journalistic norms (e.g., giving equal weight to both sides of a scientific debate, even when the scientific evidence overwhelmingly points in one direction), informational and ideological biases, over-reliance on public relations and other information subsidies (e.g., university press releases), exaggerations and omissions of important details from the original science articles, and insufficient scientific expertise, among journalists, particularly at under-resourced news organizations.

Features of Online Platforms

Specific features of online platforms contribute to the spread of misinformation about science. For example, online platforms often have content prioritization algorithms that privilege emotional and controversial content over credibility along with lax content moderation policies and practices (see Chapter 5). Such conditions also make it easier for dedicated purveyors (individual and institutions) to spread misinformation about science. Additionally, while social media platforms are designed to make information easily accessible and shareable across social networks and groups, they may also create environments that distract from the truthfulness of material shared (Epstein et al., 2023). In general, there is strong evidence that people prefer sharing true, rather than false information (Pennycook & Rand, 2021) and share information with good intentions. Furthermore, individuals who share information about a science topic that is inconsistent with the weight of accepted scientific evidence at that time, may actually believe that what they are sharing is a true interpretation of the scientific evidence. Nevertheless, a variety of factors can lead to either the intentional or unintentional spread of misinformation about science online.

Conclusion 5-1: Individuals share information for a variety of reasons—for example, to improve their social status, to express a particular partisan identity, or to persuade others to adopt a certain viewpoint. Individuals may inadvertently share misinformation in the process of sharing information, and this may be due to their confusion about the credibility of the information, their inattention to accuracy, or their desire to help or warn loved ones, among other reasons.

Conclusion 5-2: In some cases, individuals and organizations may knowingly share misinformation to profit financially, to accrue social rewards (e.g., followers and likes), to accrue and maintain power, to erode trust, or to disrupt existing social order and create chaos (e.g., trolling). These motivations may be especially incentivized in social media environments.

Conclusion 5-3: The spread of misinformation about science through social networks on social media and through online search platforms is affected by design and algorithmic choices (e.g., those shaping individualized feeds based on prior platform activity), permissive and loosely enforced or hard-to-enforce terms of service, and limited content moderation. Moreover, platform companies may not voluntarily implement approaches to specifically address such issues when they are in conflict with other business priorities.

Exploiting Trust in Science

Some purveyors of misinformation about science have leveraged the relatively high trust in science and the authoritative "voice" of science to facilitate spread of misinformation. In some cases these efforts take the form of intentional campaigns that employ key strategies to spread misinformation about science, such as manufacturing doubt about established scientific evidence, creating Astroturf campaigns (i.e., hiding conflicts of interest, for example, between the message and the source that sponsors it) to create the illusion of public support, promoting false balance in scientific debates (in part by exploiting journalistic norms requiring the coverage of "both sides"), and leveraging relationships with scientists or medical professionals who disagree with the prevailing weight of the scientific evidence to generate an illusion of credibility (see Chapter 5).

Conclusion 5-4: Science has traditionally been recognized as an authoritative civic institution that produces many benefits for individuals, communities, and societies. Yet, at times, scientific authority has been co-opted by individuals and organizations feigning scientific expertise, and by science and medical professionals acting unethically in ways that contribute to the spread of misinformation about science (e.g., speaking authoritatively on scientific topics outside of one's area of expertise).

Recommendations to Promote the Spread of Accurate Information About Science

Considering the complexities of the current information ecosystem and what is known about sources and mechanisms of the spread of misinformation about science, the committee recommends the following prioritized actions to enhance the visibility and prevalence of accurate science information while minimizing the spread of misinformation about science.

Recommendation 1: Some corporations, strategic communication companies, and non-profit organizations have at times embarked on systematic campaigns to mislead the public, with negative consequences to individuals and society. Universities, researchers, and civil society organizations should work together to proactively counter such campaigns using evidence from science and science communication to mitigate their impact. For example, researchers, government, and advocacy organizations have come together to counter campaigns from the tobacco industry to reduce the public health impact of tobacco use. Similar efforts should be made for other scientific topics of public interest.

Recommendation 2: To ensure the promotion of accurate science information and reduce the spread of misinformation or misleading information from the scientific community:

- Press offices of universities, research organizations, and funders of scientific research should consult with scientists to accurately report on their research findings and review draft press releases prior to dissemination. Press releases should explicitly state that they have been reviewed by the authors of these papers, and the authors should be accountable for the approved content.
- Universities, research organizations, and public and private funders of scientific research should encourage both their scientists and press offices to provide appropriate context—limitations and weight of evidence—when publicizing research from their organizations.

Recommendation 3: Scientists and medical professionals who are active in the public arena can play a critical role in communicating accurate and reliable science and health information to the public.

- Scientists, medical professionals, and health professionals who choose to take on high profile roles as public communicators of science should understand how their communications may be misinterpreted in the absence of context or in the wrong context. They should work proactively with professional communicators and draw on evidence-based science communication strategies to include appropriate context, interpretations, and caveats of scientific findings in their public communication.
- Universities and research organizations who promote individual scientists to share their research with the public should provide them with training and support to take on such public communication roles.

For some topics (e.g., genetics, epidemiology), it is likely that legitimate scientific evidence can be misused to support inaccurate beliefs (Lee et al., 2021; Nam & Sawyer, 2024), so it is especially important for researchers in such areas to be mindful about how their findings are communicated and disseminated. As such, the committee acknowledges that even if the actions in the above recommendation are taken, it may not prevent others from sharing the information in ways that distort the original or intended meaning. Therefore, it is also important for these stakeholders (i.e., scientists, medical professionals, health professionals, universities, and research organizations) to evaluate when the benefits of sharing this information publicly outweigh the risks of the information being distorted. Notwithstanding these considerations, the committee sees a critical need for more supports for scientists to effectively engage with the public in order to minimize the spread of misinformation about science (see Chapter 4).

Recommendation 4: To promote the dissemination of and broad access to evidence-based science information, funders of scientific research (e.g., federal science agencies, non-profit and philanthropic foundations) and non-partisan professional science organizations (e.g., American Association for the Advancement of Science, American Association for Cancer Research, American Psychological Association, American Society of Plant Biologists) should establish and fund an independent, non-partisan consortium that can identify and curate sources of high-quality (e.g., weight of evidence—quantity and quality) science information on topics of public interest. The consortium should also frequently review the science information from these sources for accuracy, needs, and relevance. It is particularly critical to ensure that access to such science information is openly and equitably available to all groups, especially underserved groups. Additional possible functions of the consortium could include:

- **identifying which sources should be included for curation,**
- **providing ratings of accuracy for different sources,**
- **creating short, accessible summaries of science information drawn from high-quality sources on topics determined by the consortium, and**
- **reviewing the science information from different sources on a routine basis to update ratings of accuracy.**

Recommendation 5: Online platforms, including search engines and social media, are major disseminators of true and false science information. These platforms should prioritize and foreground evidence-based science information that is understandable to different audiences, working closely with non-profit, non-partisan professional science societies and organizations to identify such information.

The approach of privileging accounts or information from organizations deemed credible has been suggested and implemented by some organizations such as the Council of Medical Specialty Societies, the World Health Organization, and the National Academy of Medicine (Kington et al., 2021). Through elevating information from such sources of credible science information, it is implied that misinformation from other sources is expected to recede in the background. Moreover, in contrast to post-hoc approaches to moderating inaccurate science information online, this recommendation reflects a more proactive approach that platforms can take to increase the supply of high-quality science information.

Recommendation 6: To support and promote high-quality science, health, and medical journalism:

- **Professional science and journalism organizations, funders of news media organizations and journalism, and universities should establish mechanisms for journalists and news media organizations to readily access high-quality science information and scientific sources, and for sharing best practices in science, health, and medical reporting. Such supports are especially important for those working in news media organizations with limited capacity or resources (e.g., local and community-centered newsrooms).**
- **Funders of news media organizations and journalism should make intentional investments in local and community media (newspapers, television, radio, among others) to bolster their capacity to serve the science information needs of their audiences.**
- **News media organizations should help to increase the visibility of high-quality science journalism and best practices in science and medical reporting through incentives, rewards, and other recognition models.**
- **News media organizations should increase access to high-quality science journalism by dropping paywalls around critical and timely science and health issues.**

Recommendation 7: In training the next generation of professional communicators in journalism, public relations, and other media and communication industries, universities and other providers of communication training programs should design learning experiences that integrate disciplinary knowledge and practices from communication research and various sciences and support the development of competencies in scientific and data literacy and reasoning. These competencies should be reinforced through continuous learning opportunities offered by organizations that support mass communication and journalism professionals.

The committee recognizes the limitations in adopting some of the recommended actions above, given the current financial challenges faced by the news media. Nonetheless, there is a critical need to support news media to maintain the capacity for high-quality science reporting, especially given its essential role in communicating science information to the general public.

Importantly, during times of crisis and emergencies, and when uncertainty and interest are high, journalists (national and local) become critical frontline communicators of science information (Altay et al., 2022; Van Aelst et al., 2021). Moreover, during times of emergencies, disasters, threats, and new crises, the need for high-quality science information and the potential for the spread of misinformation about science are particularly high. Additionally, researchers have demonstrated the negative impact that bad actors can have, specifically during a crisis event (Bennett & Livingston, 2018). Therefore, experts on emergency preparedness, disaster response, and environmental threat mitigation could also be important sources of credible science information for the public during such times.

Recommendation 8: Government agencies at national, state, and local levels (e.g., Federal Emergency Management Agency, Centers for Disease Control and Prevention, Food and Drug Administration, state public health departments) and civil society organizations (e.g., Association of State and Territorial Health Officials or National Association of County and City Health Officials) that deliver services during times of public health emergencies, natural disasters, threats, and new crises should contribute *proactively* to building and maintaining preparedness capacity for communicating science information at national, state, and local levels by:

- **developing internal workforce capacity to produce high-quality science information for the public,**
- **bolstering capacity to engage and partner with diverse communities to understand their needs, goals, and priorities for high-quality science information,**
- **establishing and maintaining trusted channels of communication across national, state, and local levels and between crises, and**
- **working collaboratively with local news organizations to ensure that accurate, high-quality science information is disseminated to diverse publics both during emergencies as well as in preparing for emergencies.**

UNDERSTANDING THE IMPACTS OF MISINFORMATION ABOUT SCIENCE

Misinformation about science has the potential to directly and/or indirectly impact individuals, communities, and societies (see Chapter 6 for an in-depth discussion of the evidence on the impacts of misinformation about science). For example, misinformation about science can undermine evidence-based personal and policy decisions. It can also reinforce negative stereotypes about specific groups, exacerbating discrimination and marginalization, and in some cases, stoking violence. However, current evidence substantiating a direct causal relationship between misinformation and harmful behaviors is weak. Importantly, most studies exploring the link between misinformation, misbeliefs, and behaviors measure behavioral intentions (what an individual will likely do), rather than measuring behavior directly. Furthermore, the majority of studies investigating the impacts of misinformation focus on the individual level (e.g., Phillips & Elledge, 2022), with relatively limited evidence about societal-level impacts. The committee notes that impacts at the societal level can be challenging to measure, given some societal harms are most consequential in the ways that they amass over time.

Social Inequality

Drivers of social inequality, such as education, race/ethnicity, class, and geography, shape how different communities and groups are situated with respect to access to high-quality science information and also exposure to misinformation about science (Viswanath, 2006; Viswanath et al., 2022a). For example, many low-income communities and communities of color have disproportionately less access to high-quality science and health information, and science information is rarely translated to other languages besides English. In addition, in the United States, platforms' efforts to monitor and flag misinformation tend to prioritize content in the dominant English language (Bonnevie et al., 2023), leaving misinformation in other languages largely unchecked. All of these factors (i.e., disproportionate access to high-quality information, lack of in-language information, and unequal regulation of misinformation in non-English languages) create information voids within these communities.

Conclusion 6-1: Many historically marginalized and under-resourced communities (e.g., communities of color, low-income communities, rural communities) experience disproportionately low access to accurate information, including science-related information. Such long-standing inequities in access to accurate, culturally relevant, and sufficiently translated science-related information can create information voids that may be exploited and filled by misinformation about science.

Individual-Level Impacts

In the view of the committee, a primary reason that misinformation is important to understand is because it can lead to the formation of misbeliefs in individuals (Adams et al., 2023; van der Linden et al., 2023). These misbeliefs can, in turn, lead individuals to make ill-informed decisions for themselves and/or their communities. It is important to note that people can certainly hold misbeliefs independent of exposure to misinformation. Nevertheless, current evidence suggests that exposure to misinformation about science as well as psychological and social factors that increase individual receptivity to it, all play a role in causing potentially consequential misbeliefs about science.

Additionally, while all people have the potential to believe misinformation (Berinsky, 2023), there are a number of factors that, either alone or in combination, influence whether an individual will be more or less receptive to it (i.e., demonstrate more or less openness to engaging with misinformation, and ultimately believe it). These include characteristics of the information itself (e.g., repeated information), how people appraise the sources of information (e.g., credibility, trustworthiness, confidence), and their prior knowledge, attitudes, and beliefs (e.g., science literacy, strong attitudes or firmly held beliefs about a topic, worldviews, values) (see Chapter 6). Importantly, the current empirical evidence does not support a simple and linear relationship between science literacy and resistance to misinformation (i.e., being more discerning about accurate and inaccurate information, more critical of dubious claims or sources, or more open to updating beliefs based on new evidence). In fact, while it is clear that science literacy is an important factor in how people process and interpret science information, including misinformation, other factors are also involved in these processes, such as religious beliefs, values, social identity, media repertoire, social networks, and values (Kahan et al., 2012; National Academies of Sciences, Engineering, and Medicine, 2017).

Conclusion 6-2: Most research to date on misinformation, including misinformation about science, has focused on its relationship to individuals' knowledge, attitudes, beliefs, and behavioral intentions. Some research has examined the impact of misinformation on behavior. From this work, it is known that:

- *Misinformation about science can cause individuals to develop or hold misbeliefs, and these misbeliefs can potentially lead to detrimental behaviors and actions. Although, a direct causal link between misinformation about science and detrimental behaviors and actions has not been definitively established, the current body of existence evidence does indicate that misinformation plays a role in impacting behaviors, that in some cases results in negative consequences for individuals, communities, and societies.*

- *Individuals are more receptive to misinformation about science, and, consequently, most affected by it, when it aligns with their worldviews and values, originates from a source they trust, is repeated, and/or is about a topic for which they lack strong preexisting attitudes and beliefs.*
- *Science literacy is an important competency that enables informed decision making but is not sufficient for individual resilience to misinformation about science.*

As noted above, the impacts of misinformation about science on individuals are also shaped by social factors, including race/ethnicity, culture, socio-economic status, geography, community embeddedness (i.e., the closeness of interpersonal relationships and social ties within their community), and access to material and social resources (Crenshaw, 2017; Goulbourne & Yanovitzky, 2021; McCall, 2005; Smedley, 2012; Viswanath et al., 2000). Specifically, these factors influence what information individuals are exposed to, their information-seeking and -sharing behaviors, and what actions they may take in science-related contexts. For example, an individual who is a regular consumer of alternative health media (e.g., popular health-related TV talk shows, health blogs, websites that advocate for treatments not supported by scientific evidence) may hold misbeliefs about the efficacy of natural home remedies for serious illnesses, leading them to refuse conventional medicinal treatments—a decision that is linked to greater risk of death (Johnson et al., 2018). On the other hand, an individual may believe in the safety and effectiveness of vaccines and have access to sufficient vaccination information, but due to logistical (e.g., time offerings are inconvenient or inaccessible) or transportation difficulties, they may not get vaccinated.

Conclusion 6-3: Many individual-level factors such as personal values, prior beliefs, interests, identity, preferences, and biases influence how individuals seek, process, interpret, engage with, and share science information, including misinformation. Social factors, including race, ethnicity, socio-economic status, culture, social networks, and geography also play a critical role in affecting information access. This constellation of factors shapes an individual's information diet, media repertoires, and social networks, and therefore may also determine how much misinformation about science they encounter, the extent to which they engage with it, and whether it alters their beliefs.

Conclusion 6-4: The accuracy of the science information people consume is only one factor among many that influences an individual's use of such information for decision making. Even when people have accurate information, additional influences can lead them to make decisions and engage in behaviors that are not aligned to the best available evidence. At the individual level, these include their interests, values, worldviews, religious beliefs, social identity, and political predispositions. At the structural level, access to material and social resources such as healthcare coverage, affordable nutritious food, internet connectivity, and reliable transportation, among others, may play a particularly important role.

Community- and Societal-Level Impacts

While most research on misinformation focuses on the individual level, some findings at the community and societal levels are emerging. Misinformation about science can disrupt the ability to discern reliable information from science for use in collective decision making, distort public opinion in ways that limit productive debate, and diminish trust in institutions that are important to a healthy democracy (see Chapter 6). Additionally, when misinformation about science reflects popular discourses in society about specific groups, it may be more likely to be perceived as factually accurate and accepted as true, with negative consequences for those groups (e.g., racialized discourses equating disease and illness with immigrants and foreigners, which then stoke anti-immigrant sentiments and violence; Paik, 2013). Misinformation about science can also perpetuate long-standing racism, discrimination, and marginalization, which in some cases, negatively impacts the extent to which some communities of color have access to, trust, and use information from the scientific community (Arvin, 2019; Gee & Ford, 2011; Kauanui, 2008; Teaiwa, 1994).

Relatedly, some populations have been direct targets of misinformation about science. For example, misinformation campaigns about menthol cigarettes have been heavily marketed toward African Americans for decades with severe impacts (Anderson, 2011; U.S. National Cancer Institute, 2017; Wailoo, 2021), and more recently, misinformation about Ebola and vaccines have also been targeted to African countries and Black neighborhoods, respectively (Campeau, 2023; Vinck et al., 2019). Indeed, some of the most troubling impacts of misinformation about science occur within public health when it delays the implementation of beneficial interventions, and the relationship between misinformation and vaccine hesitancy is the most notable (Pierri et al., 2022; Viswanath et al., 2022b; Wilson & Wiysonge, 2020). For example, the 2017 measles outbreak among the Somali immigrant community in Minnesota was found to be associated with a significant drop in immunization rates among young children of Somali descent (from 90% in 2008 to 36% in 2014), following the targeted spread of misinformation about vaccines (that vaccines cause autism) within this community (Hall et al., 2017).

Given that significant health, educational, and wealth disparities across social groups already contribute to inequitable access to resources to support well-being (including credible science information), the impacts on communities that are typically targeted by misinformation about science may be compounded. These realities highlight the importance of a better understanding of the problem at the scale of the broader information ecosystem in order to delineate which structural factors may exacerbate the impacts of misinformation about science. Additionally, they suggest the critical need for more scrutiny and accountability within the current information ecosystem with respect to sources of information as well as more supports for consumers of information (individual and institutions) to navigate the current complexities.

Conclusion 6-5: Misinformation about science about and/or targeted to historically marginalized communities and populations may create and/or reinforce stereotypes, bias, and negative, untrue narratives that have the potential to cause further harm to such groups.

Conclusion 6-6: Overall, there is a critical need for continuous monitoring of the current information ecosystem to track and document the origins, spread, and impact of misinformation about science across different platforms and communication spheres. Such a process, like monitoring for signals of epidemics, could better support institutions and individuals in navigating the complexities of the current information ecosystem, including proactively managing misinformation about science.

Recommendation 9: Professional scientific organizations, philanthropic organizations engaged in supporting scientific research, and media organizations should collaborate to support an independent entity or entities to track and document the origins, spread, and impact of misinformation across different platforms and communication spheres. The data produced through this effort should be made publicly available and be widely disseminated. Various entities, including public health emergency operations centers, can serve as potential models for such collaborative efforts.

In thinking about more expansive ways to leverage the data collected through monitoring and documentation, these entities could also explore the possibility of establishing thresholds of concerns toward informing if and when various stakeholders should intervene. Such intervention thresholds would also need to be commensurate with the values, needs, and priorities of the different communities. To a large extent, such monitoring also depends on the ability to access data from social media to track and identify misinformation about science and allow appropriate actions for interventions. Yet this has become increasingly difficult to do as most social media platforms' application programming interfaces (APIs) are either disallowing access to such data or making it difficult to access and analyze the data (see Chapter 8).

INTERVENING TO ADDRESS MISINFORMATION ABOUT SCIENCE

Efforts to address misinformation about science operate across many levels—for example, individual, community, platform, and the broader information environment—and have generally been implemented in a topically agnostic fashion, although some have been intentionally employed to address climate misinformation (Farrell et al., 2019; Lewandowsky, 2021a; Spampatti et al., 2024). Efforts to address misinformation about science typically target one or more of the four intervention points: supply, demand, distribution, and uptake (see Chapter 7 for a more detailed discussion of the range of existing approaches to address misinformation).

Supply-based interventions seek to reduce the volume of circulating misinformation and/or shift the balance in the quality of circulating information by either increasing the production of high-quality science content (e.g., by foregrounding credible information online or by providing funding to under-resourced newsrooms) or reducing the production of low-quality science content (e.g., through punitive measures, such as deplatforming, decredentialing, or content moderation). Demand-based interventions are aimed at reducing the consumption of misinformation with the premise that people seek out information to answer pressing questions they may have. These approaches are proactive and may include increasing trust in sources of credible information, increasing people's ability to notice and avoid misinformation, and/or filling information voids to reduce the likelihood of people turning to misinformation.

Indeed, efforts to develop and promote ongoing trusted channels hold promise for addressing science information voids. Community-based organizations (CBOs), including some locally-owned businesses, non-profit organizations, and faith-based organizations, are trusted sources of information to community residents on many topics, including science and health. To this end, there is moderate evidence to suggest that cultivating relationships with, and relying upon, such trusted intermediaries can be an effective way to overcome informational challenges, as in the case of the Health Advocates In-Reach and Research Campaign (HAIR), which is a community-based network of barbers and stylists who engage in community health promotion around issues such as colorectal cancer, COVID-19, and vaccines (University of Maryland School of Public Health, n.d.). Yet, further research needs to be conducted to determine how to evaluate these interventions and replicate their successes across different communities.

Distribution-based interventions are designed to limit the spread of misinformation about science, and include psychology-based strategies to encourage evaluative thinking in individuals, voluntary actions taken by platforms to reduce the presence of misinformation through algorithmic changes (e.g., demote or remove content from algorithmic recommendations), and governance approaches that involve law and policy mechanisms for regulating misinformation (e.g., mandated disclosure laws about the use of bots, amendments to Section 230 of the Communications Decency Act of 1996). Governance approaches using law or policy is currently an area of ongoing exploration for feasibility and effectiveness in addressing online misinformation about science in the United States and globally. However, long-standing free speech protections within the U.S. context, particularly protections afforded under Section 230 of the Communications Decency Act of 1996, have made it challenging to address misinformation at the distribution or platform level. Given these challenges, several efforts to reform Section 230 have been proposed, and existing laws such as those dealing with libel or state-level mandatory disclosure laws are being used to stem misinformation at the platform level. Promising approaches to content moderation are being tried in other countries such as Europe, and their suitability and feasibility for adoption into the United States remains to be fully explored.

Psychology-based interventions related to demand have been more widely adopted. These approaches include "accuracy nudges" to encourage individuals to consider the accuracy of the content they encounter before choosing to share (Pennycook & Rand, 2022a), introducing friction to slow-down the speed at which individuals make decisions to share content (Fazio, 2020a), and presenting individuals with the gist or bottom-line meanings of their decision to share content (e.g., sharing or not sharing this content signals alignment with democratic values). Accuracy nudges have been successful in decreasing people's actual sharing behaviors (Pennycook et al., 2021) and are relatively easy to implement; but similar to some demand-based interventions, the effect sizes are small and non-durable (Pennycook & Rand, 2022b). Moreover, the efficacy of accuracy nudges is also dependent on an individual's ability to determine if information is accurate or not (Pennycook & Rand, 2022a).

Uptake-based interventions are designed to reduce the effects of misinformation about science on people's beliefs or behaviors. These interventions assume that misinformation is already in circulation and seek to limit its negative effects on individuals before, during, or after exposure to it. This class of interventions include prebunking, debunking, motivational interviewing (to enhance motivation in individuals to engage in health protective behaviors), and providing warning labels about source credibility. Uptake-based interventions are the most well-studied, particularly prebunking and debunking techniques. It is important to note that debunking efforts can be time-consuming, and in isolation, cannot sufficiently manage the pace and scale of widespread misinformation due to being inherently reactionary. Additionally, the effectiveness fades over time (lasting anywhere from a few weeks to a few years), and it is often difficult to ensure that fact-checks actually reach the individuals who were exposed to the original misinformation.

Conclusion 7-1: Many initiatives are currently exploring ways to address misinformation through various interventions. Such interventions have been generally implemented in a topically agnostic fashion and target one or more of four intervention points to combat the negative impacts of misinformation: supply, demand, distribution, and uptake. So far, there is no indication that a particular point is the best place to intervene, and many of the most effective interventions target multiple points.

Conclusion 7-2: Community-based organizations (CBOs) have attempted to mitigate misinformation in their communities and are particularly well positioned to do so because of their ties to the local residents, their awareness of local needs and concerns, and the trust that residents have in them. However, whether and when CBOs' efforts to mitigate misinformation are effective, and whether they have sufficient capacity to do so, are not well-understood.

Conclusion 7-3: The role of legal and regulatory efforts to address misinformation about science remains to be explored more fully. Current approaches include several efforts to amend Section 230 of the U.S. Communications Decency Act of 1996 and mandated disclosure laws at the state level (e.g., laws that require warning labels about "deep fakes" or online "bots"). Other countries have deployed regulatory approaches to bolster content moderation practices on online platforms (e.g., Europe), which are being considered for useful adaptation into the United States context.

Conclusion 7-4: Providing warnings about common manipulative techniques and false narratives, providing corrective information (especially when accompanied by explanatory content), and encouraging evaluative thinking (e.g., lateral reading, accuracy nudges, friction) are effective individual-level solutions to specifically prevent belief in misinformation about science and reduce the sharing of misinformation about science by individuals, although the durability of these interventions is a common challenge.

Recommendation 10: To enhance the capacity of community-based organizations (CBOs) to provide high-quality, culturally relevant, accurately translated, and timely science information to the communities they serve, funders (e.g., government agencies, public and private, philanthropic foundations) should provide direct funding to CBOs:

- to identify and work with research partners to determine science information voids within the communities they serve and to develop strategies and products to fill them, and
- to develop internal capacity and capability to routinely assess science information needs and build resilience against misinformation about science, particularly among those serving non-English speaking and other underserved groups (e.g., communities of color, low-income communities, rural communities).

Recommendation 11: Organizations at national, state, and local levels that are specifically engaged in mitigating the uptake of misinformation about science at the individual level should identify and utilize effective approach(es) that are best suited to their goals and the point of intervention (e.g., before or after exposure). For example:

- When seeking to prevent uptake of misinformation about science prior to exposure, organizations should consider using prebunking techniques such as anticipating common themes and false narratives widely used in propagating misinformation, and proactively develop messages to counter them. For example, public health agencies and media organizations could counter false narratives by the tobacco industry to misinform the public about the impact of bans on mentholated cigarettes. Teaching people about common manipulation techniques used by propagators of misinformation about science is also effective.
- When seeking to prevent beliefs in misinformation about science after exposure, organizations should consider using debunking techniques such as providing detailed corrective information. Instead of merely labeling a claim as false, organizations should explain why the claim is false and, if possible,

highlight why the original source might be motivated to spread misinformation (e.g., an organization spreading doubt about climate change is funded by fossil fuel companies).

CHALLENGES TO UNDERSTANDING AND ADDRESSING MISINFORMATION ABOUT SCIENCE

While considerable progress has been made to better understand the causes, consequences, and potential solutions to misinformation about science, there are also challenges to studying this phenomenon and mitigating its impact. Some of the challenges include scalability of interventions (e.g., the mismatch between single-shot and/or individual-level interventions, on the one hand, and, on the other, the dynamic, complex nature of misinformation about science at larger scales), testing efficacy versus effectiveness (e.g., the common use of artificial laboratory-based tasks for testing efficacy over real-world conditions), and obtaining high-quality data (e.g., inadequate data including data absenteeism and data collection methods across various contexts and populations).

Challenges of Scale and Efficacy

As noted above, approaches (designed or proposed) for addressing misinformation about science are primarily aimed at the individual level. This emphasis has inadvertently placed the onus of mitigating the problem of misinformation on individuals, despite recognition in the field that systems-level action is needed (Altay et al., 2023; Bak-Coleman et al., 2022; van der Linden et al., 2023). Indeed, literacy-focused approaches have been criticized for framing the problem of misinformation as one of individual vigilance and avoidance (boyd, 2017). Some systems-level approaches (e.g., filling information voids, building and maintaining trust in sources of credible information, governance) are already being employed by various types of organizations; however, such approaches have not been rigorously tested for efficacy and durability. More importantly, addressing misinformation through interventions has been pursued in parallel tracks across sectors and academic disciplines in ways that do not inform one other and, in some cases, may even push in different directions.

Conclusion 7-5: Efforts to mitigate misinformation have become more prevalent over time, although interventions to specifically address misinformation about science are less prevalent than for other topical domains (e.g., political misinformation). Additionally, efforts to intervene have been largely uncoordinated across actors, sectors, disciplinary domains, and intended outcomes.

While many approaches to addressing misinformation about science have demonstrated efficacy in small-scale, controlled experiments, current understanding of their effectiveness in real-world settings is limited. Additionally, many experiments to understand the efficacy of interventions are rooted in methodological individualism. Therefore, it is challenging for a single study to take into account all of the relevant social and cultural factors that also shape how misinformation about science affects individuals and communities.

Current funding mechanisms (e.g., requests for proposals) also play an important role in shaping misinformation studies. Funding support has yielded a better understanding of impacts and interventions at the individual level to an extent, but not levels beyond the individual (i.e. networks of individuals, communities or society as a whole). Importantly, the abundance of evidence at the individual level risks giving the perception that this approach is the most effective way to address misinformation about science (Chater & Loewenstein, 2023; Maani et al., 2022). It is also still unknown whether interventions that are effective at the individual level are useful for countering community- and societal-level impacts of misinformation about science.

Conclusion 8-1: There has been considerable emphasis on studying misinformation about science and potential solutions at the individual level. In contrast, there has been limited emphasis on understanding the phenomenon of misinformation at higher levels and larger scales, which may inadvertently place the onus on the individual to mitigate the problem. There has been limited progress on:

- *Understanding how structural and contextual factors such as social class, race/ethnicity, culture, and geography, and social networks and institutions influence the origin, spread, and impact of misinformation about science.*
- *Understanding how other important factors (i.e., social, political, and technological forces) that shape the information ecosystem interact with misinformation about science to influence decision making and well-being.*
- *Understanding the larger impact that systematic disinformation campaigns can have and how to effectively intervene to counter misinformation about science from such sources.*
- *Understanding the effectiveness of existing approaches to address misinformation about science, either alone or in combination, with an eye toward better design, selection, and implementation.*

Recommendation 12: To strengthen the evidence base on the impacts of misinformation about science across levels and the suite of approaches

to mitigate them (e.g., community-based, platform- and platform design-based, policy, and regulatory approaches), funding agencies and funding organizations should direct more investments toward systems-level research. Such investments would increase understanding of the ways that structural and individual factors may interact to influence the spread and impacts of misinformation about science.

Challenges of Obtaining High-Quality, Comprehensive Data

Two main challenges exist for obtaining the optimal data to study misinformation about science, as discussed in Chapter 8. The first is availability of data about online platforms; data are either impossible to obtain or are prohibitively expensive to obtain. This creates particular challenges for researchers at lesser-resourced institutions, who may lack sufficient funding to conduct research on platforms. As a potential solution to some of these data challenges, some countries have established mechanisms to facilitate adequate data sharing between online platforms and researchers, (e.g., Article 40 of the European Union's Digital Services Act).[1] Overall, data on a wider range of platforms are still needed.

Conclusion 8-2: Some progress has been made on understanding the nature of misinformation on select social media platforms; however, a comprehensive picture across all major platforms is lacking. The ability to detect and study misinformation about science on social media platforms is currently limited by inconsistent rules for data access, cost-prohibitive data restrictions, and privacy concerns.

Recommendation 13: To reduce current barriers to obtaining high-quality, comprehensive data about misinformation about science on social media platforms:

- **Social media companies should make a good faith effort to provide access to data to examine the origins, spread, and potential impacts of misinformation about science free of charge and without any restrictions when used for non-commercial purposes, except for privacy-related data restrictions.**
- **Universities and other research institutions should facilitate the relationships between their individual researchers and social media companies to obtain more reliable data for studying misinformation about science. This should be accomplished while ensuring independence of researchers from the companies.**

---

[1]For more information, see https://www.eu-digital-services-act.com/Digital_Services_Act_Article_40.html

A second challenge is a lack of data on the impacts of misinformation about science and the effectiveness of mitigation for underserved groups, a phenomenon recognized as data absenteeism (Lee & Viswanath, 2020; Viswanath et al., 2022c). The limited availability or lack of data on underserved groups has posed a significant hurdle in understanding the ways that spread and impact of misinformation about science may vary across different demographic groups (Southwell et al., 2023). Additionally, this kind of data challenge can manifest across methodological approaches (e.g., surveys, clinical trials, observational studies), and it can exist for a variety of reasons, such as low participant recruitment, mismatches between the general population and the user base of a given context of study, and the exclusion of the experiences of certain groups from consideration.

DIRECTIONS FOR FUTURE RESEARCH

Several gaps in the current understanding of misinformation about science emerged over the course of the committee's examination of the evidence base. These gaps spanned from being able to accurately estimate how widespread misinformation about science is to understanding when and how to effectively intervene to mitigate harms at different levels. Despite the challenging nature of conducting research on misinformation about science, researchers are still well positioned to advance the science and funders to support it. Areas of needed attention include expanding research to address more types of misinformation about science; improving and expanding methodological approaches; and expanding the measurement and evaluation of aggregate exposure, impacts, and effective mitigation of misinformation about science through intervention. Additionally, many of these areas of need are overlapping and interconnected.

Expanding the Types of Misinformation Studied

From the outset, we note that there is a critical need for an expansion of the types of topics related to misinformation about science that are studied. Topical coverage is currently narrow, with a lot of scholarly attention to issues on topics where there are political divisions, leaving other areas significantly understudied (e.g., misinformation in the area of women's health, environmental issues beyond climate change). There is also misalignment between the topics or scientific claims that people are more likely to be exposed to compared to those that attract scholarly attention. With the ability to track the incorrect scientific claims that people are exposed to on a daily basis, it may also be possible to better identify science information voids. Such a process could also serve as an indicator of alignment between research topics and questions that are studied vis-à-vis the misinformation about science that people are exposed to and is prospectively harmful.

Additionally, at the time of this report, the scholarship on the relationship between AI and misinformation about science was still in its infancy. Some of the preliminary research focuses on exploring ways for AI to be leveraged to address misinformation online through its capabilities to analyze patterns and language use, and detect falsehoods (e.g., Joshi et al., 2023; Ozbay et al., 2020). Other work has been more geared toward understanding the role of generative AI in the production and spread of misinformation and disinformation (e.g., Kreps et al., 2022; Zhou et al., 2023). Given these technologies are anticipated to become more integrated and in use across different sectors of society (e.g., science, medicine, education), the committee sees a critical need for more empirical research on the evolving role of AI.

It is also important to note that because misinformation research often touches upon topics of major societal importance, the study of misinformation about science can, at times, become controversial, with these controversies occasioning reputational risks for researchers. In some cases, these risks can translate to threats and harassment, potentially impinging on the free inquiry necessary to conduct rigorous scientific research on misinformation about science. The strengthening of institutional structures that continue to support the scholarship on this topic is therefore crucial.

Measuring Aggregate Exposure to Misinformation

Although there is some empirical evidence on how prevalent misinformation about science is within a given medium/channel (e.g., a social media platform), not much is known about aggregate exposure to misinformation over time and across media/channels. An outsized proportion of the current evidence base reflects studies of X (formerly Twitter), and this is primarily a result of the relatively broad access to Twitter data until early 2023. However, almost none of the research on X directly measured exposure, though some used indirect measures (e.g., by looking at who users followed on X; Grinberg et al., 2019). Here again, we note the difference between the abundance of misinformation within a given medium/channel and the degree of aggregate exposure to misinformation in a given population and on a given topic. It is quite possible for there to be large amounts of misinformation on a platform—as measured by unique pieces of information or by the number of times pieces of misinformation are shared—that is viewed by few people. This could occur either because the sharers of misinformation are substantially isolated from the more general population (e.g., see Grinberg et al., 2019) or because of content moderation policies that reduce the spread of misinformation on a platform (e.g., Vincent et al., 2022). The committee notes the importance of distinguishing between the effects of misinformation when a large number of people are occasionally exposed to misinformation, as compared to the effects when a small number of people are frequently exposed. The literature suggests that these are the two modal scenarios for misinformation exposure, and they may produce very different pathways to adverse effects. Both scenarios merit further research.

More generally, there is relatively very little research on real-world exposure to misinformation, at both the individual and aggregate levels—far too little, in the committee's opinion, given that the harms of misinformation will generally be mediated by exposure. Most of what is known about the effects of exposure to misinformation is based on data drawn from experimental and lab settings, which substantially limits generalizability. Additionally, while there are many studies that have documented the prevalence of misinformation on the internet, likely because of ease of measurement and data collection in this context, there are far fewer that capture exposure (Lazer, 2020). This is likely because the measurement-related affordances that internet platforms have provided have made it far easier to measure what is posted and not what is seen. There have been a few important exceptions, like browsing-based studies, that focus on what domains people have seen (Allcott & Gentzkow, 2017; Guess et al., 2018b). Furthermore, there have been some platform-provided data that included exposure and related data; for example, Meta- as well as some Facebook-provided data on exposure and engagement (e.g., Social Science One [Buntain et al., 2023a; King & Persily, 2020] and CrowdTangle [Edelson et al., 2021]). We note that CrowdTangle is now defunct, and that Social Science One is essentially moribund, not having been updated in years. A study conducted by Allen et al. (2020) is, perhaps, the most comprehensive effort to evaluate exposure to civic information and misinformation, using Comscore and Nielsen data from web browsing, television, and mobile use. Yet, even this impressive effort omits radio, interpersonal communication, intra-platform content (e.g., social media posts), and messaging apps, let alone news alerts on phones and information on Alexa devices, podcasts, and many other sources. Determining the scope of misinformation about science in these additional settings is an important area of need.

Finally, more data are needed from community and social contexts. To the limited extent that there has been research on exposure, very little of that research in turn contextualizes that individual exposure within communities; for example, how do norms, local culture, existing local informational resources, and social capital moderate the downstream effects of misinformation on beliefs and behavior? That is, the committee identified a need for more research on how individuals and groups in specific community contexts are exposed to specific types of misinformation about science and with what effects.

Validating Impacts of Misinformation About Science

Establishing a direct causal link between misinformation about science and a given outcome (i.e., individual-, community-, and societal-level harmful behaviors and/or actions) has been a challenging task, in large part because most consequential real-world outcomes are influenced by many factors outside of exposure to misinformation. Although it is assumed by many that misinformation has widespread and negative effects on individuals, groups, and society, such direct effects have not been well-documented or consistently demonstrated empirically. More research to substantiate causal impacts is a critical need, and equally critical is understanding how the impacts of misinformation about science may be different across social class, race, ethnicity, cultural ideologies, and geography, among other factors. There is also a need to determine how historical and contemporary discrimination, systemic racism, and social determinants of health may compound the impacts of misinformation about science on disparate communities. Understanding the role of such factors is essential to more accurately identify and document community-level impacts of misinformation about science and determine the most important and relevant outcomes for a given science topic, community type, or context. Moreover, as more types of misinformation about science are studied, it will be possible to identify and validate a wider range of impacts.

There are also aspects around the nature of the misinformation about science itself that are also important to understanding impacts, including how the form of the content might make it more or less impactful (e.g., a message delivered as a comment versus a video, an image, on TV, or via the radio), recognizing that a message interacts with the recipient, technology, and the social context to determine impact. Establishing criteria for harm (least harmful to most harmful) is another fundamental need. Such agreement around harms would help in determining the circumstances under which misinformation about science leads to harmful behaviors as well as in documenting accumulated harms (months to years) of misinformation about science on individuals, communities, and society.

Bolstering the Efficacy of Interventions Against Misinformation About Science

A great deal of attention has been directed toward identifying effective solutions to address misinformation about science, with a focus to mitigate the supply, demand, distribution, and/or uptake of misinformation. As noted earlier, a number of these approaches have demonstrated some efficacy in mitigating negative impacts of misinformation about science, but for a given class of interventions, the empirical evidence is uneven across models. Current understanding of effective misinformation interventions is limited by multiple factors including a lack of data access, the common use of artificial laboratory-based tasks, the disconnect between single-shot interventions and the persistent influence of misinformation, and the fact that many organizations currently intervening to combat misinformation about science lack the time and resources to evaluate their efforts. Additionally, there is not a robust evidence base for interventions that are being designed and implemented beyond the individual level or across multiple levels (e.g., institutional, policy, or combined approaches). More broadly, a theoretical accounting of why particular interventions are effective is needed for determining potential for generalizability across contexts and levels of analysis.

Beyond establishing the efficacy of existing approaches, the committee sees a more near-term need to specifically design, deploy, and evaluate interventions that are more tailored to populations and communities who may benefit the most: older adults who are more likely to share misinformation, those who are not exposed to common uptake-based interventions (e.g., fact-checks), and marginalized and underserved communities who lack access to high-quality information. The committee acknowledges that many interventions face implementation challenges including: limited access to data for evaluating effectiveness, and for identifying and addressing information voids; design features of platforms that may circumvent policy-related approaches to limit the spread of misinformation online; and limited scalability, durability, and reach, with respect to approaches that seek to reduce uptake. Nevertheless, there are still important areas of needs for bolstering existing efforts.

For some supply-based interventions, more research is needed to specifically understand and bolster the efficacy of removing and demoting content in search engine results or on social media platforms. In addition, there is need to evaluate specific approaches to reduce demand for misinformation about science carried out by CBOs to determine which are most effective across different populations (e.g., hardly-reached communities, groups that are hesitant to participate in scientist-led studies). Some distribution-based interventions leverage the distributed structures of online platforms (e.g., crowdsourced fact-checking), but whether such approaches can be adopted across all platforms, and especially those containing closed or private groups, is still an open area for inquiry. Additionally, interventions of this kind that pause and flag viral content for review before it can spread more widely have shown efficacy in environments where amplification is the main driver of exposure to misinformation, but it is unknown whether this approach would work in an environment where the primary audience is primed to be receptive to misinformation (e.g., in misinformation-focused groups on social media). Demonstrated efficacy of some uptake-based interventions is also limited, for example, for source labels that indicate the degree of credibility of a particular source and for warnings about common themes and narratives typically associated with misinformation about science. More generally, establishing the best way(s) to implement these kinds of intervention is still to be determined, given many people do not regularly attend to such signals (e.g., Fazio et al., 2023).

Improving and Expanding Methods for Studying Misinformation About Science

To address the areas of need that have been described above there is a need to overcome current methodological limitations in the field. As mentioned above, to date, there has been an overreliance on public social media data, particularly from X (formerly Twitter), in large part because of data availability; however, while digital media account for a substantial share of contemporary communication, other important media domains such as television, radio, podcasts, and private messaging apps, are understudied. Even less is known about the nature of misinformation about science in offline communication contexts, and the empirical record likely under-indexes modes of communication that are ephemeral in nature or cannot easily be converted to a digital format. The most obvious example of this is interpersonal communications, and the committee found little published evidence of how much misinformation about science people say or hear daily from others. Beyond speech, there are few rigorous methods for analyzing misinformation about science in transient media such as advertisements, billboards, bumper stickers, leaflets, and direct mail, and non-textual media (e.g., videos, photographs).

There is also a need for more mixed-methods studies (e.g., studies that combine quantitative and qualitative methods) and interdisciplinary research for gaining more comprehensive understandings of misinformation about science. Many community organizations are already engaged in research efforts that support community-based knowledge production. To this end, formal partnerships can be created between researchers and community members and CBOs to both inform and leverage such data to better understand the ways that misinformation about science moves across platforms, borders, languages, and cultures, and differentially impacts specific communities. Additionally, researchers can work more effectively across silos to establish more interdisciplinary collaborations that enable better integration of different theoretical frameworks and methodological approaches into the research on misinformation about science and a greater understanding across science topics. For example, more systematic research informed by insights from psychology (e.g., dual process theory, theory of planned behavior) and public policy (e.g., Advocacy Coalition Framework) could yield a clearer picture of the impacts of misinformation about environmental issues beyond the individual level. Overall, there is need for better incorporation of survey-based studies, interviews, ethnography (online and offline), focus groups, content analysis, discourse analysis, quasi-experiments, case studies, and longitudinal studies alongside the more widely employed randomized control trials, meta-analyses, and computational social science methods. Specifically, the committee sees the following types of studies as starting points:

- Field studies (offline and online) that can substantiate lab-setting findings about the causes, consequences, and effective solutions for misinformation about science.
- New models for studying the dynamics of misinformation in non-social media and non-textual media contexts (e.g., TV, radio, podcasts, videos, photographs).
- Mixed-methods studies to better accommodate populations that are not adequately represented in typical datasets (e.g., hardly reached communities, and groups who are hesitant to participate in scientific studies), including community-based participatory research and studies co-designed with communities.
- Studies that include complex experimental design as well as larger, diverse sample sizes to study and better understand the interactions between social, political, and technological factors within the contemporary information ecosystem and misinformation about science and how these interactions shape people's relationship to information and impact personal and policy decision making.

The current state of the science on misinformation about science beyond the individual level underscores the need for more qualitative insights into the social and contextual drivers of the negative impacts of misinformation about science experienced at larger scales. Such insights will also be essential for the design and/or selection of appropriate interventions. Qualitative work may also be a way to overcome some of the current challenges to studying misinformation outlined in Chapter 8 of this report. Indeed, as access to technology platforms' data becomes increasingly more restrictive, merging qualitative and quantitative insights into research on algorithmic insights needs much more investment and expansion. It is the belief of the committee that this larger suite of methodologies can especially support efforts to strengthen causal inferences, especially about contexts that may be harder to study using only quantitative methods such as closed/private interpersonal spaces. Overall, the methodological needs called for in this research agenda reflect a shift from the status quo in the field and will require sustained levels of adequate funding to make possible.

FINAL THOUGHTS

This report provides key conclusions drawn from disparate lines of evidence on the nature of misinformation about science; a conceptual understanding of the influences and mechanisms for the origins, spread, and impacts of misinformation about science at multiple levels; and actionable recommendations that are informed by perspectives and expertise from industry, academia, policy, and practice. In mapping the landscape, it became apparent that isolated, individual actions will be insufficient to make progress in this space given the confluence of forces known to shape the dynamics of misinformation about science. Lastly, the current state of knowledge about the scope and severity of misinformation about science is rapidly evolving, but still limited in many domains, and prioritized gaps in understanding have been identified to better orient future research directions in the field.

References

AAPIData, APIAVote, & Asian Americans Advancing Justice. (2020, September 15). *2020 Asian American voter survey*. https://www.advancingjustice-aajc.org/report/2020-asian-american-voter-survey

Abalakina-Paap, M., Stephan, W. G., Craig, T., & Gregory, W. L. (1999). Beliefs in conspiracies. *Political Psychology*, *20*(3), 637–647. https://doi.org/10.1111/0162-895X.00160

Abbott, R. (2007). Putting complex systems to work. *Complexity*, *13*(2), 30–49. https://doi.org/10.1002/cplx.20200

Abella, B. S., Jolkovsky, E. L., Biney, B. T., Uspal, J. E., Hyman, M. C., Frank, I., Hensley, S. E., Gill, S., Vogl, D. T., Maillard, I., Babushok, D. V., Huang, A. C., Nasta, S. D., Walsh, J. C., Wiletyo, E. P., Gimotty, P. A., Milone, M. C., & Amaravadi, R. K. (2021). Efficacy and safety of hydroxychloroquine vs placebo for pre-exposure SARS-CoV-2 prophylaxis among health care workers: A randomized clinical trial. *JAMA Internal Medicine*, *181*(2), 195–202. https://doi.org/10.1001/jamainternmed.2020.6319

Abernathy, P. M. (n.d.). Do you live in a news desert? *U.S. News Deserts*. UNC Hussman School of Journalism and Media, Knight Foundation. https://www.usnewsdeserts.com/

___. (2018). *The expanding news desert*. The Center for Innovation and Sustainability in Local Media, School of Media and Journalism, University of North Carolina at Chapel Hill. https://www.cislm.org/wp-content/uploads/2018/10/The-Expanding-News-Desert-10_14-Web.pdf

Abroms, L. C., Koban, D., Krishnan, N., Napolitano, M., Simmens, S., Caskey, B., Wu, T. C., & Broniatowski, D. A. (2024). Empathic engagement with the COVID-19 vaccine hesitant in private Facebook groups: A randomized trial. *Health Education & Behavior*, *51*(1), 10–20. https://doi.org/10.1177/10901981231188313

Abualsaud, M., & Smucker, M. D. (2019). Exposure and order effects of misinformation on health search decisions. In *Proceedings of the 42nd International ACM SIGIR Conference on Research and Development in Information Retrieval*. Association for Computing Machinery. https://rome2019.github.io/papers/Abualsaud_Smucker_ROME2019.pdf

Adams, R. C., Challenger, A., Bratton, L., Boivin, J., Bott, L., Powell, G., Williams, A., Chambers, C. C., & Sumner, P. (2019). Claims of causality in health news: A randomised trial. *BMC Medicine*, *17*(19), 1–11. https://doi.org/10.1186/s12916-019-1324-7

Adams, Z., Osman, M., Bechlivanidis, C., & Meder, B. (2023). (Why) is misinformation a problem? *Perspectives on Psychological Science*, *18*(6), 1436–1463. https://doi.org/10.1177/17456916221141344

Agley, J., Xiao, Y., Thompson, E. E., Chen, X., & Golzarri-Arroyo, L. (2021). Intervening on trust in science to reduce belief in COVID-19 misinformation and increase COVID-19 preventive behavioral intentions: Randomized controlled trial. *Journal of Medical Internet Research*, *23*(10), e32425. https://doi.org/10.2196/32425

Aikenhead, G. S. (2006). *Science education for everyday life: Evidence-based practice*. Teachers College Press.

Aikin, K. J., Betts, K. R., O'Donoghue, A. C., Rupert, D. J., Lee, P. K., Amoozegar, J. B., & Southwell, B. G. (2015). Correction of overstatement and omission in direct-to-consumer prescription drug advertising. *Journal of Communication*, *65*(4), 596–618. https://doi.org/10.1111/jcom.12167

Aikin, K. J., Southwell, B. G., Paquin, R. S., Rupert, D. J., O'Donoghue, A. C., Betts, K. R., & Lee, P. K. (2017). Correction of misleading information in prescription drug television advertising: The roles of advertisement similarity and time delay. *Research in Social and Administrative Pharmacy*, *13*(2), 378–388. https://doi.org/10.1016/j.sapharm.2016.04.004

Ajzen, I. (2020). The theory of planned behavior: Frequently asked questions. *Human Behavior and Emerging Technologies*, *2*(4), 314–324. https://doi.org/https://doi.org/10.1002/hbe2.195

Albertson, B., & Guiler, K. (2020). Conspiracy theories, election rigging, and support for democratic norms. *Research & Politics*, *7*(3). https://doi.org/10.1177/2053168020959859

Aldrich, D. P., & Meyer, M. A. (2015). Social capital and community resilience. *American Behavioral Scientist*, *59*(2), 254–269. https://doi.org/10.1177/0002764214550299

Ali, K., Li, C., Zain-ul-abdin, K., & Muqtadir, S. A. (2022). The effects of emotions, individual attitudes towards vaccination, and social endorsements on perceived fake news credibility and sharing motivations. *Computers in Human Behavior*, *134*, 107307. https://doi.org/10.1016/j.chb.2022.107307

Ali, S., Saeed, M. H., Aldreabi, E., Blackburn, J., De Cristofaro, E., Zannettou, S., & Stringhini, G. (2021, June). Understanding the effect of deplatforming on social networks. *13th ACM Web Science Conference 2021*, 187–195. https://doi.org/10.1145/3447535.3462637

Allcott, H., & Gentzkow, M. (2017). Social media and fake news in the 2016 election. *Journal of Economic Perspectives*, *31*(2), 211–236. https://doi.org/10.1257/jep.31.2.211

Allen J., Arechar, A. A., Pennycook, G., Rand, & D. G. (2021). Scaling up fact-checking using the wisdom of crowds. *Science Advances*, *7*(36), Article eabf4393.

Allen, J., Howland, B., Mobius, M., Rothschild, D., & Watts, D. J. (2020). Evaluating the fake news problem at the scale of the information ecosystem. *Science Advances*, *6*(14), eaay3539. https://doi.org/10.1126/sciadv.aay3539

Allen, J., Martel, C., & Rand, D. G. (2022, April 29–May 5). Birds of a feather don't fact-check each other: Partisanship and the evaluation of news in Twitter's Birdwatch crowd-sourced fact-checking program. *Proceedings of the 2022 CHI Conference on Human Factors in Computing Systems*. New Orleans, LA, US. ACM. https://doi.org/10.31234/osf.io/57e3q

Allen, J., Watts, D. J., & Rand, D. G. (2024). Quantifying the impact of misinformation and vaccine-skeptical content on Facebook. *Science*, *384*(6699), Article eadk3451. https://doi.org/10.1126/science.adk3451

Allport, G. W., & Postman, L. (1946). An analysis of rumor. *Public Opinion Quarterly*, *10*(4), 501–517.

Almodt, R. (2024). From criticism to conspiracies: The populist discourse of COVID-19 sceptics in Germany's Querdenken community on Telegram. *Discourse & Society*, *35*(1), 3–26. https://doi.org/10.1177/09579265231191971

Altay, S. (2022, May 30). How effective are interventions against misinformation? *PsyArXiv* https://doi.org/10.31234/osf.io/sm3vk

Altay, S., Berriche, M., Heuer, H., Farkas, J., & Rathje, S. (2023). A survey of expert views on misinformation: Definitions, determinants, solutions, and future of the field. *Harvard Kennedy School Misinformation Review*, *4*(4). https://doi.org/10.37016/mr-2020-119

Altay, S., Kleis Nielsen, R., & Fletcher, R. (2022). Quantifying the "infodemic": People turned to trustworthy news outlets during the 2020 coronavirus pandemic. *Journal of Quantitative Description: Digital Media*, *2*. https://doi.org/10.51685/jqd.2022.020

Altay, S., Majima, Y., & Mercier, H. (2020). It's my idea! Reputation management and idea appropriation. *Evolution and Human Behavior*, *41*(3), 235–243. https://doi.org/10.1016/j.evolhumbehav.2020.03.004

Alvarez, A., Caliskan, A., Crockett, M. J., Ho, S. S., Messeri, L., & West, J. (2024). Science communication with generative AI. *Nature Human Behaviour*, *8*(4), 625–627. https://doi.org/10.1038/s41562-024-01846-3

Amanullah, S., & Ramesh Shankar, R. (2020, October). The impact of COVID-19 on physician burnout globally: A review. *Healthcare*, *8*(4), 421. https://doi.org/10.3390/healthcare8040421

Amazeen, M. A. (2020). Journalistic interventions: The structural factors affecting the global emergence of fact-checking. *Journalism*, *21*(1), 95–111. https://doi.org/10.1177/1464884917730217

American Board of Obstetrics & Gynecology. (2021, September 27). *Statement regarding dissemination of COVID-19 misinformation*. https://www.abog.org/about-abog/news-announcements/2021/09/27/statement-regarding-dissemination-of-covid-19-misinformation

___. (2022, July 7). *Statement regarding misinformation and disinformation and medical professionalism*. https://www.abog.org/about-abog/news-announcements/2022/07/07/statement-regarding-misinformation-and-disinformation-and-medical-professionalism

Anderson, C. (2021). Propaganda, misinformation, and histories of media techniques. *Harvard Kennedy School Misinformation Review*, *2*(2). https://doi.org/10.37016/mr-2020-64

Anderson, S. J. (2011). Marketing of menthol cigarettes and consumer perceptions: a review of tobacco industry documents. *Tobacco Control*, *20* (Suppl 2), ii20–28. https://doi.org/10.1136/tc.2010.041939

Angel, M. P., & boyd, d. (2024). Techno-legal solutionism: Regulating children's online safety in the United States. In *Proceedings of the Symposium on Computer Science and Law*. https://doi.org/10.1145/3614407.3643705

Apollonio, D. E., & Malone, R. E. (2005). Marketing to the marginalised: Tobacco industry targeting of the homeless and mentally ill. *Tobacco Control*, *14*(6), 409–415. https://doi.org/10.1136/tc.2005.011890

Appel, M., & Malečkar, B. (2012). The influence of paratext on narrative persuasion: Fact, fiction, or fake? *Human Communication Research*, *38*(4), 459–484. https://doi.org/10.1111/j.1468-2958.2012.01432.x

Apuke, O. D., & Omar, B. (2021). User motivation in fake news sharing during the COVID-19 pandemic: An application of the uses and gratification theory. *Online Information Review*, *45*(1), 220–239. https://doi.org/10.1108/OIR-03-2020-0116

Ard, C. F., & Natowicz, M. R. (2001). A seat at the table: Membership in federal advisory committees evaluating public policy in genetics. *American Journal of Public Health*, *91*(5), 787. https://doi.org/10.2105/ajph.91.5.787

Ardèvol-Abreu, A., Delponti, P., & Rodríguez-Wangüemert, C. (2020). Intentional or inadvertent fake news sharing? Fact-checking warnings and users' interaction with social media content. *Profesional de la Información*, *29*(5). https://doi.org/10.3145/epi.2020.sep.07

Arguedas, A. R., Robertson, C. T., Fletcher, R., & Nielsen, R. K. (2022, January). *Echo chambers, filter bubbles, and polarisation: A literature review*. Reuters Institute. https://reutersinstitute.politics.ox.ac.uk/echo-chambers-filter-bubbles-and-polarisation-literature-review

Armstrong, D. (2019, November 19). Inside Purdue Pharma's media playbook: How it planted the opioid 'anti-story. *ProPublica*. https://www.propublica.org/article/inside-purdue-pharma-media-playbook-how-it-planted-the-opioid-anti-story

Armstrong, G. M., Gurol, M. N., & Russ, F. A. (1983). A Longitudinal evaluation of the Listerine corrective advertising campaign. *Journal of Public Policy & Marketing*, *2*(1), 16–28. https://doi.org/10.1177/074391568300200102

Aronczyk, M. (2022, Feb. 17). How PR firms captured the sustainability agenda. *Foreign Policy*. https://foreignpolicy.com/2022/02/17/climate-crisis-activism-edelman-pr-sustainability/

Aronczyk, M., & Espinoza, M. I. (2021). *A strategic nature: Public relations and the politics of American environmentalism*. Oxford University Press. https://doi.org/10.1093/oso/9780190055349.001.0001

Aronczyk, M., McCurdy, P., & Russill, C. (2024) Greenwashing, net-zero, and the oil sands in Canada: The case of Pathways Alliance. *Energy Research & Social Science*, *112*. https://doi.org/10.1016/j.erss.2024.103502

Arvin, M. (2019) *Possessing Polynesians: The science of settler colonial whiteness in Hawai'i and Oceania*. Duke University Press. https://doi.org/10.2307/j.ctv11312hc

Asch, S. E. (1951). Effects of group pressure upon the modification and distortion of judgments. In H. Guetzkow (Ed.), *Groups, leadership and men; research in human relations* (pp. 177–190). Carnegie Press.

Ash, E., Galletta, S., Hangartner, D., Margalit, Y., & Pinna, M. (2024). The effect of Fox News on health behavior during COVID-19. *Political Analysis*, *32*(2), 275–284. https://doi.org/10.1017/pan.2023.21

Asian American Disinformation Table. (2022). *Power, platforms, politics: Asian Americans and disinformation landscape report*. https://www.asianamdisinfo.org/wp-content/uploads/2022/08/AsianAmDisinformation_LandscapeReport2022.pdf

Aslett, K., Guess, A. M., Bonneau, R., Nagler, J., & Tucker, J. A. (2022). News credibility labels have limited average effects on news diet quality and fail to reduce misperceptions. *Science Advances*, *8*(18), Article eabl3844. https://doi.org/10.1126/sciadv.abl3844

Attari, S. Z., DeKay, M. L., Davidson, C. I., & Bruine de Bruin, W. (2010). Public perceptions of energy consumption and savings. *Proceedings of the National Academy of Sciences*, *107*(37), 16054–16059. https://doi.org/10.1073/pnas.1001509107

Aufderheide, P., Jaszi, P., & Chandra, M. (2009, September). *Honest truths: Documentary filmmakers on ethical challenges in their work*. Center for Media & Social Impact, American University. https://cmsimpact.org/resource/honest-truths-documentary-filmmakers-on-ethical-challenges-in-their-work/

Augenstein, I., Baldwin, T., Cha, M., Chakraborty, T., Ciampaglia, G. L., Corney, D., DiResta, R., Ferrara, E., Hale, S., Halevy, A., Hovy, E., Ji, H., Menczer, F., Miguez, R., Nakov, P., Scheufele, D., Sharma, S., & Zagni, G. (2024). Factuality challenges in the era of large language models and opportunities for fact-checking. *Nature Machine Intelligence*, *6*(8), 852–863. https://doi.org/10.1038/s42256-024-00881-z

Auxier, B., & Anderson, M. (2021, April 7). *Social media use in 2021*. Pew Research Center: Internet, Science & Tech. https://www.pewresearch.org/internet/2021/04/07/social-media-use-in-2021/

Avital, M., Baiyere, A., Dennis, A., Gibbs, J., & Te'eni, D. (2020). Fake news: What is it and why does it matter? *Academy of Management Proceedings*, *2020*(1), 20014. https://doi.org/10.5465/AMBPP.2020.20014symposium

Avraamidou, L. (2022). Identities in/out of physics and the politics of recognition. *Journal of Research in Science Teaching*, *59*(1), 58–94. https://doi.org/10.1002/tea.21721

Ayoob, K.-T., Duyff, R. L., & Quagliani, D. (2002). Position of the American Dietetic Association: Food and nutrition misinformation. *Journal of the American Dietetic Association*, *102*(2), 260–266. https://doi.org/10.1016/S0002-8223(02)90062-3

Bächtiger, A., Dryzek, J. S., Mansbridge, J., & Warren, M. E. (Eds.). (2018). *The Oxford handbook of deliberative democracy*. Oxford University Press. https://doi.org/10.1093/oxfordhb/9780198747369.001.0001

Baghdadi, J. D., Coffey, K. C., Belcher, R., Frisbie, J., Hassan, N., Sim, D., & Malik, R. D. (2023). #Coronavirus on TikTok: User engagement with misinformation as a potential threat to public health behavior. *JAMIA Open*, *6*(1). https://doi.org/10.1093/jamiaopen/ooad013

Bailey, D. H., Jung, A. J., Beltz, A. M., Eronen, M. I., Gische, C., Hamaker, E. L., Kording, K. P., Lebel, C., Lindquist, M. A., Moeller, J., Razi, A., Rohrer, J. M., Zhang, B., & Murayama, K. (2024). Causal inference on human behaviour. *Nature Human Behaviour*, *8*(8), 1448–1459. https://doi.org/10.1038/s41562-024-01939-z

Bailey, Z. (2024). Race, health, and equity: Integrating concepts of social justice into health behavior models. In K. Glanz, B. K. Rimer, & K. Viswanath (Eds.), *Health behavior: Theory, research, and practice* (6th ed., pp. 174–183). Jossey-Bass.

Bailey, Z. D., Krieger, N., Agénor, M., Graves, J., Linos, N., & Bassett, M. T. (2017). Structural racism and health inequities in the USA: Evidence and interventions. *Lancet*, *389*(10077), 1453–1463. https://doi.org/10.1016/S0140-6736(17)30569-X

Bailin, D., Goldman, G., & Phartiyal, P. (2014, May). *Sugar-coating science: How the food industry misleads consumers on sugar*. Center for Science and Democracy, Union of Concerned Scientists. https://www.ucsusa.org/sites/default/files/2019-09/sugar-coating-science.pdf

Bajaj, S. S., & Stanford, F. C. (2021). Beyond Tuskegee — Vaccine distrust and everyday racism. *The New England Journal of Medicine*, *384*(5), e12. https://doi.org/10.1056/NEJMpv2035827

Bak-Coleman, J. B., Kennedy, I., Wack, M., Beers, A., Schafer, J. S., Spiro, E. S., Starbird, K., & West, J. D. (2022). Combining interventions to reduce the spread of viral misinformation. *Nature Human Behaviour*, *6*(10), 1372–1380. https://doi.org/10.1038/s41562-022-01388-6

Baker, S., & Martinson, D. L. (2001). The TARES Test: Five principles for ethical persuasion. *Journal of Mass Media Ethics*, *16*(2–3), 148–175. https://doi.org/10.1080/08900523.2001.9679610

Baker, S. A. (2022). Alt. health influencers: How wellness culture and web culture have been weaponized to promote conspiracy theories and far-right extremism during the COVID-19 pandemic. *European Journal of Cultural Studies*, *25*(1), 3–24. https://doi.org/10.1177/13675494211062623

Baker, S. A., McLaughlin, E., & Rojek, C. (2024). Simple solutions to wicked problems: Cultivating true believers of anti-vaccine conspiracies during the COVID-19 pandemic. *European Journal of Cultural Studies*, *27*(4), 577–596. https://doi.org/10.1177/13675494231173536

Baker, S. A., & Rojek, C. (2020, February 20). The online wellness industry: Why it's so difficult to regulate. *The Conversation*. https://theconversation.com/the-online-wellness-industry-why-its-so-difficult-to-regulate-131847

Bakshy, E., Messing, S., & Adamic, L. A. (2015). Exposure to ideologically diverse news and opinion on Facebook. *Science, 348*(6239), 1130–1132. https://doi.org/10.1126/science.aaa1160

Baleta, A. (1999). South Africa's AIDS care thrown into confusion. *The Lancet, 354*(9191), 1711. https://doi.org/10.1016/S0140-6736(05)76703-9

Ballard, C., Goldstein, I., Mehta, P., Smothers, G., Take, K., Zhong, V., Greenstadt, R., Lauinger, T., & McCoy, D. (2022). Conspiracy brokers: Understanding the monetization of YouTube conspiracy theories. In *Proceedings of the ACM Web Conference 2022* (pp. 2707–2718). https://doi.org/10.1145/3485447.3512142

Banas, J. A., Palomares, N. A., Richards, A. S., Keating, D. M., Joyce, N., & Rains, S. A. (2022). When machine and bandwagon heuristics compete: Understanding users' response to conflicting AI and crowdsourced fact-checking. *Human Communication Research, 48*(3), 430–461. https://doi.org/10.1093/hcr/hqac010

Bandy, J. (2021). Problematic machine behavior: A systematic literature review of algorithm audits. *Proceedings of the ACM on Human-Computer Interaction, 5*, Article 74. https://doi.org/10.1145/3449148

Barnes, D. E., Hanauer, P., Slade, J., Bero, L. A., & Glantz, S. A. (1995). Environmental tobacco smoke. The Brown and Williamson documents. *JAMA, 274*(3), 248–253. https://doi.org/10.1001/jama.274.3.248

Barnidge, M., & Xenos, M.A. (2021). Social media news deserts: Digital inequalities and incidental news exposure on social media platforms. *New Media & Society, 26*(1), 368–388. https://doi.org/10.1177/14614448211059529

Baron, R. J. (2022, May 18). Standing up for the profession, protecting the public: Why ABIM is combatting medical misinformation. *American Board of Internal Medicine*. https://blog.abim.org/standing-up-for-the-profession-and-public-why-abim-is-combatting-medical-misinformation/

Baron, R. J., & Ejnes, Y. D. (2022). Physicians spreading misinformation on social media—Do right and wrong answers still exist in medicine? *The New England Journal of Medicine, 387*(1), 1–3. https://doi.org/10.1056/NEJMp2204813

Barthel, M., Mitchell, A., & Holcomb, J. (2016, December 15). *Many Americans believe fake news is sowing confusion*. Pew Research Center. https://www.pewresearch.org/journalism/2016/12/15/many-americans-believe-fake-news-is-sowing-confusion/

Bartholomew, R. E. (2014). Science for sale: the rise of predatory journals. *Journal of the Royal Society of Medicine, 107*(10), 384–385. https://doi.org/10.1177/0141076814548526

Barton, H. A. (1934). Science in the public press. *Review of Scientific Instruments, 5*(11), 386. https://doi.org/10.1063/1.1751756

Basch, C. H., Meleo-Erwin, Z., Fera, J., Jaime, C., & Basch, C. E. (2021). A global pandemic in the time of viral memes: COVID-19 vaccine misinformation and disinformation on TikTok. *Human Vaccines & Immunotherapeutics, 17*(8), 2373–2377. https://doi.org/10.1080/21645515.2021.1894896

Basol, M., Roozenbeek, J., & van der Linden, S. (2020). Good news about bad news: Gamified inoculation boosts confidence and cognitive immunity against fake news. *Journal of Cognition, 3*(1), 2. https://doi.org/10.5334/joc.91

Baum, L. M. (2012). It's not easy being green... or is it? A content analysis of environmental claims in magazine advertisements from the United States and United Kingdom. *Environmental Communication: A Journal of Nature and Culture, 6*(4), 423–440. https://doi.org/10.1080/17524032.2012.724022

Beard, M. (2022, November 23). Covid is no longer mainly a pandemic of the unvaccinated. Here's why. *The Washington Post*. https://www.washingtonpost.com/politics/2022/11/23/vaccinated-people-now-make-up-majority-covid-deaths/

Bebinger, M. (2021, April 27). Pandemic imperiled Non-English speakers more than others. *KFF Health News*. https://kffhealthnews.org/news/article/pandemic-imperiled-non-english-speakers-more-than-others/

Bedford, D. (2010). Agnotology as a teaching tool: Learning climate science by studying misinformation. *Journal of Geography*, *109*(4), 159–165. https://doi.org/10.1080/00221341.2010.498121

Béna, J., Rihet, M., Carreras, O., & Terrier, P. (2023). Repetition could increase the perceived truth of conspiracy theories. *Psychonomic Bulletin & Review*, *30*(6), 2397–2406. https://doi.org/10.3758/s13423-023-02276-4

Benestad, R. E., Nuccitelli, D., Lewandowsky, S., Hayhoe, K., Hygen, H. O., Van Dorland, R., & Cook, J. (2016). Learning from mistakes in climate research. *Theoretical and Applied Climatology*, *126*(3), 699–703.

Bennett, W. L. (1990). Toward a theory of press-state. *Journal of Communication*, *40*(2), 103–127. https://doi.org/10.1111/j.1460-2466.1990.tb02265.x

Bennett, W. L., & Livingston, S. (2018). The disinformation order: Disruptive communication and the decline of democratic institutions. *European Journal of Communication*, *33*(2), 122–139. https://doi.org/10.1177/0267323118760317

Bergner, D., & Vasconez, K. C. (2012). Expanding role of public works in emergency management. *Leadership and Management in Engineering*, *12*(3), 126–133. https://doi.org/10.1061/(ASCE)LM.1943-5630.0000174

Bergstrom, C. T., & West, J. D. (2023). How publishers can fight misinformation in and about science and medicine. *Nature Medicine*, *29*(9), 2174–2176. https://doi.org/10.1038/s41591-023-02411-7

Berinsky, A. J. (2023). *Political rumors: Why we accept misinformation and how to fight it*. Princeton University Press.

Berkman, N. D., Davis, T. C., & McCormack, L. (2010). Health literacy: What is it? *Journal of Health Communication*, *15*(S2), 9–19. https://doi.org/10.1080/10810730.2010.499985

Berkman, N. D., Sheridan, S. L., Donahue, K. E., Halpern, D. J., & Crotty, K. (2011). Low health literacy and health outcomes: an updated systematic review. *ANNALS of Internal Medicine*, *155*(2), 97–107.

Bernays, E. L. (1928). *Propoganda*. Liveright Publishing Corporation.

Beskow, L. M. (2016). Lessons from HeLa cells: The ethics and policy of biospecimens. *Annual Review of Genomics and Human Genetics*, *17*, 395–417. https://doi.org/10.1146/annurev-genom-083115-022536

Besley, J. C. (2018). The National Science Foundation's science and technology survey and support for science funding, 2006–2014. *Public Understanding of Science*, *27*(1), 94–109. https://doi.org/10.1177/0963662516649803

Besley, J. C., & Tanner, A. H. (2011). What science communication scholars think about training scientists to communicate. *Science Communication*, *33*(2), 239–263. https://doi.org/10.1177/1075547010386972

Beville, H. (1948). The challenge of the new media. In W. Schramm (Ed.), *Communications in modern society* (pp. 126–141). University of Illinois Press.

Bhargava, P., MacDonald, K., Newton, C., Lin, H., & Pennycook, G. (2023). How effective are TikTok misinformation debunking videos? *Harvard Kennedy School Misinformation Review*, *4*(2). https://doi.org/10.37016/mr-2020-114

Bing, C., & Schectman, J. (2024). Pentagon ran secret anti-vax campaign to undermine China during pandemic. *Reuters Institute*. https://www.reuters.com/investigates/special-report/usa-covid-propaganda/

Birchall, C., & Knight, P. (2022). Do your own research: Conspiracy theories and the internet. *Social Research: An International Quarterly*, *89*(3), 579–605. https://doi.org/10.1353/sor.2022.0049

Björnberg, K. E., Karlsson, M., Gilek, M., & Hansson, S. O. (2017). Climate and environmental science denial: A review of the scientific literature published in 1990–2015. *Journal of Cleaner Production*, *167*, 229–241. https://doi.org/10.1016/j.jclepro.2017.08.066

Blevins, J. L., Edgerton, E., Jason, D. P., & Lee, J. J. (2021). Shouting into the wind: Medical science versus "BS" in the Twitter maelstrom of politics and misinformation about hydroxychloroquine. *Social Media+ Society*, *7*(2). https://doi.org/10.1177/20563051211024977

Block, A. B. (2013, March 12). Updated: TV ratings: 'Dr. Phil' tops talkers during February sweep, 'Dr. Oz' sees steep declines. *The Hollywood Reporter*. https://www.hollywoodreporter.com/tv/tv-news/updated-tv-ratings-dr-phil-427733/

Bobkowski, P. S. (2015). Sharing the news: Effects of informational utility and opinion leadership on online news sharing. *Journalism & Mass Communication Quarterly*, *92*(2), 320–345. https://doi.org/10.1177/1077699015573194

Boness, C. L., Nelson, M., & Douaihy, A. B. (2022). Motivational interviewing strategies for addressing COVID-19 vaccine hesitancy. *Journal of the American Board of Family Medicine*, *35*(2), 420–426. https://doi.org/10.3122/jabfm.2022.02.210327

Bonilla-Silva, E. (1997). Rethinking racism: Toward a structural interpretation. *American Sociological Review*, *62*(3), 465–480. https://doi.org/10.2307/2657316

Bonnevie, E., Ricciulli, V., Fields, M., & O'Neill, R. (2023). Lessons learned from monitoring Spanish-language vaccine misinformation during the COVID-19 pandemic. *Public Health Reports*, *138*(4), 586–592. https://doi.org/10.1177/00333549231168452

Bowes, S. M., Costello, T. H., Ma, W., & Lilienfeld, S. O. (2021). Looking under the tinfoil hat: Clarifying the personological and psychopathological correlates of conspiracy beliefs. *Journal of Personality*, *89*(3), 422–436. https://doi.org/10.1111/jopy.12588

Bowles, J., Croke, K., Larreguy, H., Marshall, J., & Liu, S. (2023). *Sustaining exposure to fact-checks: Misinformation discernment, media consumption, and its political implications* (SSRN Scholarly Paper No. 4582703). SSRN. https://doi.org/10.2139/ssrn.4582703

boyd, d. (2017, January 5). Did media literacy backfire? *Medium, Data & Society: Points*. https://medium.com/datasociety-points/did-media-literacy-backfire-7418c084d88d

Boykoff, M. T. (2007). Flogging a dead norm? Newspaper coverage of anthropogenic climate change in the United States and United Kingdom from 2003 to 2006. *Area*, *39*(4), 470–481. http://www.jstor.org/stable/40346068

___. (2008). Lost in translation? United States television news coverage of anthropogenic climate change, 1995–2004. *Climatic Change*, *86*, 1–11. https://doi.org/10.1007/s10584-007-9299-3

Boykoff, M. T., & Boykoff, J. M. (2004). Balance as bias: Global warming and the US prestige press. *Global Environmental Change*, *14*(2), 125–136. https://doi.org/10.1016/j.gloenvcha.2003.10.001

Boynton, M. H., Portnoy, D. B., & Johnson, B. T. (2013). Exploring the ethics and psychological impact of deception in psychological research. *IRB: Ethics & Human Research*, *35*(2), 7–13.

Bozarth, L., & Budak, C. (2021). Market forces: Quantifying the role of top credible ad servers in the fake news ecosystem. In *Proceedings of the International AAAI Conference on Web and Social Media*, *15*(1), 83–94. https://doi.org/10.1609/icwsm.v15i1.18043

Bradshaw, A. S., Shelton, S. S., Fitzsimmons, A., & Treise, D. (2022). 'From cover-up to catastrophe:' How the anti-vaccine propaganda documentary 'Vaxxed' impacted student perceptions and intentions about MMR vaccination. *Journal of Communication in Healthcare*, *15*(3), 219–231. https://doi.org/10.1080/17538068.2022.2117527

Brady, H. E., & Kent, T. B. (2022). Fifty years of declining confidence & increasing polarization in trust in American institutions. *Daedalus*, *151*(4), 43–66. https://doi.org/10.1162/daed_a_01943

Brady, H. E., & Schlozman, K. L. (2022). Introduction. *Daedalus, the Journal of the American Academy of Arts and Sciences*, *151*(4), 6–22. https://doi.org/10.1162/daed_e_01941

Brandtzaeg, P. B., & Lüders, M. (2018). Time collapse in social media: Extending the context collapse. *Social Media + Society*, *4*(1). https://doi.org/10.1177/2056305118763349

Brannon, V. C., & Holmes, E. N. (2024, January 4). *Section 230: An overview* (CRS Report No. R46751). Congressional Research Service. https://crsreports.congress.gov/product/pdf/R/R46751

Brashier, N. M., Pennycook, G., Berinsky, A. J., & Rand, D. G. (2021). Timing matters when correcting fake news. *Proceedings of the National Academy of Sciences*, *118*(5), e2020043118. https://doi.org/10.1073/pnas.2020043118

Bratton, L., Adams, R. C., Challenger, A., Boivin, J., Bott, L., Chambers, C. D., & Sumner, P. (2019). The association between exaggeration in health-related science news and academic press releases: A replication study. *Wellcome Open Research*, *4*, 148. https://doi.org/10.12688/wellcomeopenres.15486.2

Braveman, P., & Gottlieb, L. (2014). The social determinants of health: It's time to consider the causes of the causes. *Public Health Reports*, *129*(1, Suppl 2), 19–31. https://doi.org/10.1177/00333549141291S206

Breakstone, J., Smith, M., Connors, P., Ortega, T., Kerr, D., & Wineburg, S. (2021). Lateral reading: College students learn to critically evaluate internet sources in an online course. *Harvard Kennedy School Misinformation Review*, *2*(1). https://doi.org/10.37016/mr-2020-56

Brechman, J. M., Lee, C. J., & Cappella, J. N. (2011). Distorting genetic research about cancer: From bench science to press release to published news. *Journal of Communication*, *61*(3), 496–513. https://doi.org/10.1111/j.1460-2466.2011.01550.x

Breckenridge, L. A., Burns, D., & Nye, C. (2022). The use of motivational interviewing to overcome COVID-19 vaccine hesitancy in primary care settings. *Public Health Nursing*, *39*(3), 618–623. https://doi.org/10.1111/phn.13003

Brennen, J. S., Simon, F. M., Howard, P. N., & Kleis Nielsen, R. (2020, April 7). *Types, sources, and claims of misinformation* [Fact Sheet]. Reuters Institute for the Study of Journalism. https://reutersinstitute.politics.ox.ac.uk/types-sources-and-claims-covid-19-misinformation

Brennen, J. S., Simon, F. M., & Nielsen, R. K. (2021). Beyond (mis)representation: Visuals in COVID-19 misinformation. *The International Journal of Press/Politics*, *26*(1), 277–299. https://doi.org/10.1177/1940161220964780

Brewer, S. E., Cataldi, J. R., Fisher, M., Glasgow, R. E., Garrett, K., & O'Leary, S. T. (2020). Motivational interviewing for maternal immunisation (MI4MI) study: A protocol for an implementation study of a clinician vaccine communication intervention for prenatal care settings. *BMJ Open*, *10*(11), e040226. https://doi.org/10.1136/bmjopen-2020-040226

Briand, S. C., Cinelli, M., Nguyen, T., Lewis, R., Prybylski, D., Valensise, C. M., Colizza, V., Tozzi, A. E., Perra, N., Baronchelli, A., Tizzoni, M., Zollo, F., Scala, A., Purnat, T., Czerniak, C., Kucharski, A. J., Tshangela, A., Zhou, L., & Quattrociocchi, W. (2021). Infodemics: A new challenge for public health. *Cell*, *184*(25), 6010–6014. https://doi.org/10.1016/j.cell.2021.10.031

Brierley, L. (2021). Lessons from the influx of preprints during the early COVID-19 pandemic. *The Lancet Planetary Health*, *5*(3), e115–e117. https://doi.org/10.1016/S2542-5196(21)00011-5

Bright, J. (2016). The social news gap: How news reading and news sharing diverge. *Journal of Communication*, *66*(3), 343–365. https://doi.org/10.1111/jcom.12232

BrightEdge. (2019). *Organic search improves ability to map to consumer intent: Organic channel share expands to 53.3% of traffic*. https://videos.brightedge.com/research-report/BrightEdge_ChannelReport2019_FINAL.pdf

Broda, E., & Strömbäck, J. (2024). Misinformation, disinformation, and fake news: Lessons from an interdisciplinary, systematic literature review. *Annals of the International Communication Association*, *48*(2), 139–166. https://doi.org/10.1080/23808985.2024.2323736

Broniatowski, D. A., Greene, K. T., Pisharody, N., Rogers, D. J., & Shapiro, J. N. (2023a). Measuring the monetization strategies of websites with application to pro- and anti-vaccine communities. *Scientific Reports*, *13*(1), 15964. https://doi.org/10.1038/s41598-023-43061-6

Broniatowski, D. A., Jamison, A. M., Johnson, N. F., Velasquez, N., Leahy, R., Restrepo, N. J., Dredze, M., & Quinn, S. C. (2020). Facebook pages, the "Disneyland" measles outbreak, and promotion of vaccine refusal as a civil right, 2009–2019. *American Journal of Public Health*, *110*(S3), S312–S318. https://doi.org/10.2105/ajph.2020.305869

Broniatowski, D. A., Jamison, A. M., Qi, S., AlKulaib, L., Chen, T., Benton, A., Quinn, S. C., & Dredze, M. (2018). Weaponized health communication: Twitter bots and Russian trolls amplify the vaccine debate. *American Journal of Public Health*, *108*(10), 1378–1384. https://doi.org/10.2105/ajph.2018.304567

Broniatowski, D. A., Kerchner, D., Farooq, F., Huang, X., Jamison, A. M., Dredze, M., Quinn, S. C., & Ayers, J. W. (2022). Twitter and Facebook posts about COVID-19 are less likely to spread misinformation compared to other health topics. *PLoS One*, *17*(1), e0261768. https://doi.org/10.1371/journal.pone.0261768

Broniatowski, D. A., Simons, J. R., Gu, J., Jamison, A. M., & Abroms, L. C. (2023b). The efficacy of Facebook's vaccine misinformation policies and architecture during the COVID-19 pandemic. *Science Advances*, *9*(37), eadh2132. https://doi.org/10.1126/sciadv.adh2132

Broockman, D. E., & Kalla, J. L. (2024). Selective exposure and echo chambers in partisan television consumption: Evidence from linked viewership, administrative, and survey data. *American Journal of Political Science*, 1–19. https://doi.org/10.1111/ajps.12886

Brossard D., & Lewenstein B. V. (2010). A critical appraisal of models of public understanding of science: Using practice to inform theory. In L. Kahlor & P. Stout (Eds.), *Communicating science: New agendas in communication* (pp. 11–39). Routledge.

Brossard, D., & Scheufele, D. A. (2013). Science, new media, and the public. *Science*, *339*(6115), 40–41. https://doi.org/10.1126/science.1232329

___. The chronic growing pains of communicating science online. *Science*, *375*(6581), 613–614. https://doi.org/10.1126/science.abo0668

Brown, B. A., Reveles, J. M., & Kelly, G. J. (2005). Scientific literacy and discursive identity: A theoretical framework for understanding science learning. *Science Education*, *89*(5), 779–802. https://doi.org/10.1002/sce.20069

Brown, L. A., Zhu, Y., Hamlett, G. E., Moore, T. M., DiDomenico, G. E., Visoki, E., Greenberg, D. M., Gur, R. C., Gur, R. E., & Barzilay, R. (2023). COVID-19 worries and insomnia: A follow-up study. *International Journal of Environmental Research and Public Health*, *20*(5), 4568. https://www.mdpi.com/1660-4601/20/5/4568

Brubaker, R. (2005). The 'diaspora' diaspora. *Ethnic and Racial Studies*, *28*(1), 1–19. https://doi.org/10.1080/0141987042000289997

Brulle, R. J., & Werthman, C. (2021). The role of public relations firms in climate change politics. *Climatic Change*, *169*(8). https://doi.org/10.1007/s10584-021-03244-4

Bryanov, K., Vasina, D., Pankova, Y., & Pakholkov, V. (2022). The other side of deplatforming: Right-wing Telegram in the wake of Trump's Twitter ouster. In D. A. Alexandrov, A. V. Boukhanovsky, A. V. Chugunov, Y. Kabanov, O. Koltsova, I. Musabirov, & S. Pashakhin (Eds.), *Digital transformation and global society* (Vol. 1503, pp. 417–428). Springer International Publishing. https://doi.org/10.1007/978-3-030-93715-7_30

Buckels, E. E., Trapnell, P. D., & Paulhus, D. L. (2014). Trolls just want to have fun. *Personality and Individual Differences*, *67*, 97–102. https://doi.org/10.1016/j.paid.2014.01.016

Buckingham, J., Beaman, R., & Wheldall, K. (2023). Why poor children are more likely to become poor readers: The early years. In J. Martin, M. Bowl, & G. Banks (Eds.), *Mapping the field* (pp. 185–203). Routledge.

Buckley, N., & Calo, R. (2023, unpublished). [The governance of science misinformation: A report to the National Academies]. Paper commissioned by the Committee on Understanding and Addressing Misinformation About Science, National Academies of Sciences, Engineering, and Medicine. Available on request in the National Academies' Public Access Files.

Budak, C., Goel, S., & Rao, J. M. (2016). Fair and balanced? Quantifying media bias through crowdsourced content analysis. *Public Opinion Quarterly*, *80*(S1), 250–271. https://doi.org/10.1093/poq/nfw007

Bui, K. X. (2021). Objects of warfare: Infrastructures of race and napalm in the Vietnam War. *Amerasia Journal*, *47*(2), 299–313. https://doi.org/10.1080/00447471.2021.2021775

Bull-Otterson, L., Gray, E. B., Budnitz, D. S., Strosnider, H. M., Schieber, L. Z., Courtney, J., García, M. C., Brooks, J. T., Mac Kenzie, W. R., & Gundlapalli, A. V. (2020). Hydroxychloroquine and chloroquine prescribing patterns by provider specialty following initial reports of potential benefit for COVID-19 treatment—United States, January–June 2020. *MMWR. Morbidity and Mortality Weekly Report*, *69*(35), 1210–1215. http://dx.doi.org/10.15585/mmwr.mm6935a4

Bullard, R. D. (2008). Differential vulnerabilities: Environmental and economic inequality and government response to unnatural disasters. *Social Research: An International Quarterly*, *75*(3), 753–784. https://dx.doi.org/10.1353/sor.2008.0035.

Buntain, C., Bonneau, R., Nagler, J., & Tucker, J. A. (2023a). Measuring the ideology of audiences for web links and domains using differentially private engagement data. *Proceedings of the International AAAI Conference on Web and Social Media*, *17*(1), 72–83. https://doi.org/10.1609/icwsm.v17i1.22127

Buntain, C., Innes, M., Mitts, T., & Shapiro, J. (2023b). Cross-platform reactions to the post-January 6 deplatforming. *Journal of Quantitative Description: Digital Media, 3*. https://doi.org/10.51685/jqd.2023.004

Burstin, H., Curry, S., Ranney, M. L., Arora, V., Wachler, B. B., Chou, W.-Y. S., Correa, R., Cryer, D., Dizon, D., Flores, E. J., Harmon, G., Jain, A., Johnson, K., Laine, C., Leininger, L., McMahon, G., Michaelis, L., Minhas, R., Mularski, R., Oldham, J., Padman, R., Pinnock, C., Rivera, J., Southwell, B., Villarruel, A., & Wallace, K. (2023). *Identifying credible sources of health information in social media: Phase 2–Considerations for non-accredited nonprofit organizations, for-profit entities, and individual sources* (Discussion Paper). National Academy of Medicine. https://doi.org/10.31478/202305b

Burton, A. G., & Koehorst, D. (2020). Research note: The spread of political misinformation on online subcultural platforms. *Harvard Kennedy School Misinformation Review*, *1*(6), https://doi.org/10.37016/mr-2020-40

Butler, A. C., Zaromb, F. M., Lyle, K. B., & Roediger III, H. L. (2009). Using popular films to enhance classroom learning: The good, the bad, and the interesting. *Psychological Science*, *20*(9), 1161–1168. https://doi.org/10.1111/j.1467-9280.2009.02410.x

Butler, L. D., Koopman, C., & Zimbardo, P. G. (1995). The psychological impact of viewing the film "JFK": Emotions, beliefs, and political behavioral intentions. *Political Psychology*, *16*(2), 237–257. https://doi.org/10.2307/3791831

Byrum, G., & Benjamin, R. (2022). *Disrupting the gospel of tech solutionism to build tech justice*. Stanford Social Innovation Review. https://doi.org/10.48558/9SEV-4D26

Cabrera, N., Alonso, A., Chen, Y., & Ghosh, R. (2022). *Latinx families' strengths and resilience contribute to their well-being*. National Research Center on Hispanic Children and Families. https://www.hispanicresearchcenter.org/research-resources/latinx-families-strengths-and-resilience-contribute-to-their-well-being/

Cacciatore M. A. (2021). Misinformation and public opinion of science and health: Approaches, findings, and future directions. *Proceedings of the National Academy of Sciences of the United States of America*, *118*(15), e1912437117. https://doi.org/10.1073/pnas.1912437117

Calo, R., Coward, C., Spiro, E. S., Starbird, K., & West, J. D. (2021). How do you solve a problem like misinformation? *Science Advances*, *7*(50), eabn0481. https://doi.org/doi:10.1126/sciadv.abn0481

Campeau, K. (2023). Who's a vaccine skeptic? Framing vaccine hesitancy in post-Covid news coverage. *Written Communication*, *40*(3), 976–1023. https://doi.org/10.1177/07410883231169622

Candidatu, L., & Ponzanesi, S. (2022). Digital diasporas: Staying with the trouble. *Communication, Culture and Critique*, *15*(2), 261–268. https://doi.org/10.1093/ccc/tcac010

Carey, J. M., Guess, A. M., Loewen, P. J., Merkley, E., Nyhan, B., Phillips, J. B., & Reifler, J. (2022). The ephemeral effects of fact-checks on COVID-19 misperceptions in the United States, Great Britain and Canada. *Nature Human Behaviour*, *6*, 236–243. https://doi.org/10.1038/s41562-021-01278-3

Carlone, H. B., Johnson, A., & Scott, C. M. (2015). Agency amidst formidable structures: How girls perform gender in science class. *Journal of Research in Science Teaching*, *52*(4), 474–488. https://doi.org/10.1002/tea.21224

Carrera, J. S., Key, K., Bailey, S., Hamm, J. A., Cuthbertson, C. A., Lewis, E. Y., Woolford, S. J., DeLoney, E. H., Greene-Moton, E., Wallace, K., Robinson, D. E., Byers, I., Piechowski, P., Evans, L., McKay, A., Vereen, D., Sparks, A., & Calhoun, K. (2019). Community science as a pathway for resilience in response to a public health crisis in Flint, Michigan. *Social Sciences*, *8*(3), 94. https://www.mdpi.com/2076-0760/8/3/94

Carrion, M. L. (2018). "You need to do your research": Vaccines, contestable science, and maternal epistemology. *Public Understanding of Science*, *27*(3), 310–324. https://doi.org/10.1177/0963662517728024

Castets-Renard, C. (2020). Algorithmic content moderation on social media in EU law: Illusion of perfect enforcement. *University of Illinois Journal of Law, Technology & Policy*, *2020*(2), 283–324. http://dx.doi.org/10.2139/ssrn.3535107

Cataldi, J. R. (2021). The many costs of measles outbreaks and undervaccination: Why we need to invest in public health. *Pediatrics*, *147*(4). https://doi.org/10.1542/peds.2020-035303

Caulfield, T. (2015). *Is Gwyneth Paltrow wrong about everything?: How the famous sell us elixirs of health, beauty & happiness*. Beacon Press.

___. (2018). Spinning the genome: Why science hype matters. *Perspectives in Biology and Medicine*, *61*(4), 560–571. https://doi.org/10.1353/pbm.2018.0065.

Caulfield, T., & Condit, C. (2012). Science and the sources of hype. *Public Health Genomics*, *15*(3-4), 209–217. https://doi.org/10.1159/000336533

Celadin, T., Capraro, V., Pennycook, G., & Rand, D. G. (2023). Displaying news source trustworthiness ratings reduces sharing intentions for false news posts. *Journal of Online Trust and Safety*, *1*(5). https://doi.org/10.54501/jots.v1i5.100

Centers for Disease Control and Prevention (CDC). (2021a) *Talking with patients about COVID-19 vaccination*. Centers for Disease Control and Prevention. https://www.cdc.gov/vaccines/covid-19/hcp/engaging-patients.html.

___. (2021b). *Social listening and monitoring tools: COVID-19 vaccine confidence: Rapid community assessment tool*. https://www.cdc.gov/vaccines/covid-19/vaccinate-with-confidence/rca-guide/downloads/cdc_rca_guide_2021_tools_appendixe_sociallistening-monitoring-tools-508.pdf

___. (2024). *How to conduct a rapid community assessment.* https://www.cdc.gov/vaccines/covid-19/vaccinate-with-confidence/rca-guide/index.html

Cerda, A. (2024, August 12). *Americans see many federal agencies favorably, but Republicans grow more critical of Justice Department.* Pew Research Center. https://www.pewresearch.org/short-reads/2024/08/12/americans-see-many-federal-agencies-favorably-but-republicans-grow-more-critical-of-justice-department/

Ceylan, G., Anderson, I. A., & Wood, W. (2023). Sharing of misinformation is habitual, not just lazy or biased. *Proceedings of the National Academy of Sciences, 120*(4), e2216614120. https://doi.org/10.1073/pnas.2216614120

Cha, M., Cha, C., Singh, K., Lima, G., Ahn, Y.-Y., Kulshrestha, J., & Varol, O. (2021). Prevalence of misinformation and factchecks on the COVID-19 pandemic in 35 countries: Observational infodemiology study. *JMIR Human Factors, 8*(1), e23279. https://doi.org/10.2196/23279

Chadwick, A. (2017). *The hybrid media system: Politics and power* (2nd ed.). Oxford University Press.

Chadwick, A., & Vaccari, C. (2019). *News sharing on UK social media: Misinformation, disinformation, and correction.* Loughborough University Online Civic Culture Centre. https://repository.lboro.ac.uk/articles/report/News_sharing_on_UK_social_media_misinformation_disinformation_and_correction/9471269

Chadwick, A., Vaccari, C., & Hall, N. A. (2023). What explains the spread of misinformation in online personal messaging networks? Exploring the role of conflict avoidance. *Digital Journalism, 12*(5), 574–593. https://doi.org/10.1080/21670811.2023.2206038

Chakrabarti, S., Rooney, C., & Kweon, M. (2018). *Verification, duty, credibility: Fake news and ordinary citizens in Kenya and Nigeria.* BBC. https://downloads.bbc.co.uk/mediacentre/bbc-fake-news-research-paper-nigeria-kenya.pdf

Chambers, D. (2013). Virtual communities and online social capital. In D. Chambers (Ed.), *Social media and personal relationships: Online intimacies and networked friendship* (pp. 142–161). Palgrave Macmillan UK. https://doi.org/10.1057/9781137314444_8

Chan, M. S., & Albarracín, D. (2023). A meta-analysis of correction effects in science-relevant misinformation. *Nature Human Behaviour, 7*(9), 1514–1525. https://doi.org/10.1038/s41562-023-01623-8

Chan, M. S., Jones, C. R., Hall Jamieson, K., & Albarracín, D. (2017). Debunking: A meta-analysis of the psychological efficacy of messages countering misinformation. *Psychological Science, 28*(11), 1531–1546. https://doi.org/10.1177/0956797617714579

Chandrasekharan, E., Pavalanathan, U., Srinivasan, A., Glynn, A., Eisenstein, J., & Gilbert, E. (2017). You can't stay here: The efficacy of Reddit's 2015 ban examined through hate speech. *Proceedings of the ACM on Human-Computer Interaction, 1*(CSCW), Article 31, 1–22. https://doi.org/10.1145/3134666

Chater, N., & Loewenstein, G. (2023). The i-frame and the s-frame: How focusing on individual-level solutions has led behavioral public policy astray. *Behavioral and Brain Sciences, 46*, e147. https://doi.org/10.1017/S0140525X22002023

Chatman, E. A. (1996). The impoverished life-world of outsiders. *Journal of the American Society for Information Science, 47*(3), 193–206. https://doi.org/10.1002/(SICI)1097-4571(199603)47:3<193::AID-ASI3>3.0.CO;2-T

Chen, C. (2003). On the shoulders of giants. In *Mapping scientific frontiers: The quest for knowledge visualization* (pp. 135–166). Springer. https://doi.org/10.1007/978-1-4471-0051-5_5

Chen, L., Zhang, Y., Young, R., Wu, X., & Zhu, G. (2021). Effects of vaccine-related conspiracy theories on Chinese young adults' perceptions of the HPV vaccine: An experimental study. *Health Communication, 36*(11), 1343–1353. https://doi.org/10.1080/10410236.2020.1751384

Chen, S., Xiao, L., & Kumar, A. (2023). Spread of misinformation on social media: What contributes to it and how to combat it. *Computers in Human Behavior*, *141*, 107643. https://doi.org/10.1016/j.chb.2022.107643

Chen, X., Sin, S.-C. J., Theng, Y.-L., & Lee, C. S. (2015). Why students share misinformation on social media: Motivation, gender, and study-level differences. *The Journal of Academic Librarianship*, *41*(5), 583–592. https://doi.org/10.1016/j.acalib.2015.07.003

Chien, A. A., Lin, L., Nguyen, H., Rao, V., Sharma, T., & Wijayawardana, R. (2023, August 2). Reducing the carbon impact of generative AI Inference (today and in 2035). *Proceedings of the 2nd Workshop on Sustainable Computer Systems*, Article 11. https://doi.org/10.1145/3604930.3605705

Chigwedere, P., Seage III, G. R., Gruskin, S., Lee, T. H., & Essex, M. (2008). Estimating the lost benefits of antiretroviral drug use in South Africa. *JAIDS Journal of Acquired Immune Deficiency Syndromes*, *49*(4), 410–415. https://doi.org/10.1097/QAI.0b013e31818a6cd5

Chinn, S., Hart, P. S., & Soroka, S. (2020). Politicization and polarization in climate change news content, 1985-2017. *Science Communication*, *42*(1), 112–129. https://doi.org/10.1177/1075547019900290

Chinn, S., & Hasell, A. (2023). Support for 'doing your own research' is associated with COVID-19 misperceptions and scientific mistrust. *Harvard Kennedy School Mis/information Review*, *4*(3), 1–15. https://doi.org/10.37016/mr-2020-117

Chiou, H., Voegeli, C., Wilhelm, E., Kolis, J., Brookmeyer, K., & Prybylski, D. (2022). The future of infodemic surveillance as public health surveillance. *Emerging Infectious Diseases*, *28*(Suppl 1), S121–S128. https://doi.org/10.3201/eid2813.220696

Chong, M., Froehlich, T. J., & Shu, K. (2021). Racial attacks during the COVID-19 pandemic: Politicizing an epidemic crisis on longstanding racism and misinformation, disinformation, and misconception. *Proceedings of the Association for Information Science and Technology*, *58*, 573–576. https://doi.org/10.1002/pra2.501

Chou, W.-Y. S., Gaysynsky, A., & Cappella, J. N. (2020). Where we go from here: Health misinformation on social media. *American Journal of Public Health*, *110*(S3), S273–S275. https://doi.org/10.2105/AJPH.2020.305905

Cialdini, R. B., & Goldstein, N. J. (2004). Social influence: Compliance and conformity. *Annual Review of Psychology*, *55*, 591–621. https://doi.org/10.1146/annurev.psych.55.090902.142015

Cinelli, M., De Francisci Morales, G., Galeazzi, A., Quattrociocchi, W., & Starnini, M. (2021). The echo chamber effect on social media. *Proceedings of the National Academy of Sciences*, *118*(9), e2023301118. https://doi.org/10.1073/pnas.2023301118

Clancy, K. A., & Clancy, B. (2016). Growing monstrous organisms: the construction of anti-GMO visual rhetoric through digital media. *Critical Studies in Media Communication*, *33*(3), 279–292. https://doi.org/10.1080/15295036.2016.1193670

Clarke, C. E. (2008). A question of balance: The autism-vaccine controversy in the British and American elite press. *Science Communication*, *30*(1), 77–107. https://doi.org/10.1177/107554700832026

Cogordan, C., Fressard, L., Ramalli, L., Rebaudet, S., Malfait, P., Dutrey-Kaiser, A., Attalah, Y., Roy, D., Berthiaume, P., Gagneur, A., & Verger, P. (2023). Motivational interview-based health mediator interventions increase intent to vaccinate among disadvantaged individuals. *Human Vaccines & Immunotherapeutics*, *19*(2). https://doi.org/10.1080/21645515.2023.2261687

Cohen, J. (2009, March 11). Reporters ask for direct access to federal scientists. *Science Insider*. https://www.science.org/content/article/reporters-ask-direct-access-federal-scientists

Colgrove, J., & Samuel, S. J. (2022). Freedom, rights, and vaccine refusal: The history of an idea. *American Journal of Public Health*, *112*(2), 234–241. https://doi.org/10.2105/AJPH.2021.306504

Collins, B., & Zadrozny, B. (2020, May 29). Troll farms from North Macedonia and the Philippines pushed coronavirus disinformation on Facebook. *NBC News*. https://www.nbcnews.com/tech/tech-news/troll-farms-macedonia-philippines-pushed-coronavirus-disinformation-facebook-n1218376

Collins-Dexter, B. (2020). *Canaries in the coal mine: COVID-19 misinformation and Black communities*. Shorenstein Center of Media, Politics, and Public Policy, Harvard Kennedy School. https://shorensteincenter.org/wp-content/uploads/2020/06/Canaries-in-the-Coal-Mine-Shorenstein-Center-June-2020.pdf

Conley, J. G. (2007). Conflict of interest and the EP's science advisory board. *Texas Law Review*, *86*, 165.

Cook, C. L., Patel, A., & Wohn, D. Y. (2021). Commercial versus volunteer: Comparing user perceptions of toxicity and transparency in content moderation across social media platforms. *Frontiers in Human Dynamics*, *3*, 626409. https://doi.org/10.3389/fhumd.2021.626409

Cook, J. (2020). Deconstructing climate science denial. In D. Holmes & L. M. Richardson (Eds.), *Edward Elgar research handbook in communicating climate change*. Edward Elgar. https://doi.org/10.4337/9781789900408.00014

Cook, J., Lewandowsky, S., & Ecker, U. K. H. (2017). Neutralizing misinformation through inoculation: Exposing misleading argumentation techniques reduces their influence. *PLoS One*, *12*(5), e0175799. https://doi.org/10.1371/journal.pone.0175799

Cooper, B. E., Lee, W. E., Goldacre, B. M., & Sanders, T. A. (2012). The quality of the evidence for dietary advice given in UK national newspapers. *Public Understanding of Science*, *21*(6), 664–673. https://doi.org/10.1177/0963662511401782

Cooper, K. E., & Nisbet, E. C. (2017). Documentary and edutainment portrayals of climate change and their societal impacts. *Oxford Research Encyclopedia of Climate Science*. https://doi.org/10.1093/acrefore/9780190228620.013.373

Cordonier, L., & Brest. A. (2021, March). *How do the French inform themselves on the internet? Analysis of online information and disinformation behaviors*. Fondation Descartes. https://hal.science/hal-03167734/document

Cox, K. (2024, June 15). Most Black Americans believe U.S. institutions were designed to hold Black people back. *Pew Research Center*. https://www.pewresearch.org/race-and-ethnicity/2024/06/15/most-black-americans-believe-u-s-institutions-were-designed-to-hold-black-people-back/

Crenshaw, K. W. (2017). *On intersectionality: Essential writings*. The New Press.

Criss, S., Nguyen, T. T., Norton, S., Virani, I., Titherington, E., Tillmanns, E. L., Kinnane, C., Maiolo, G., Kirby, A. B., & Gee, G. C. (2021). Advocacy, hesitancy, and equity: Exploring US race-related discussions of the COVID-19 vaccine on Twitter. *International Journal of Environmental Research and Public Health*, *18*(11), 5693. https://doi.org/10.3390/ijerph18115693

Crocker, J. (2011). The road to fraud starts with a single step. *Nature*, *479*(7372), 151. https://doi.org/10.1038/479151a

Curley, C., Siapera, E., & Carthy, J. (2022). Covid-19 protesters and the far right on telegram: Co-conspirators or accidental bedfellows? *Social Media + Society*, *8*(4). https://doi.org/10.1177/20563051221129187

Dabran-Zivan, S., Baram-Tsabari, A., Shapira, R., Yitshaki, M., Dvorzhitskaia, D., & Grinberg, N. (2023). "Is COVID-19 a hoax?": Auditing the quality of COVID-19 conspiracy-related information and misinformation in Google search results in four languages. *Internet Research*, *33*(5), 1774–1801. https://doi.org/10.1108/INTR-07-2022-0560

Dahlstrom, M. F. (2014). Using narratives and storytelling to communicate science with nonexpert audiences. *Proceedings of the National Academy of Sciences*, *111*(Suppl 4), 13614–13620. https://doi.org/10.1073/pnas.1320645111

___. (2021). The narrative truth about scientific misinformation. *Proceedings of the National Academy of Sciences*, *118*(15), e1914085117. https://doi.org/10.1073/pnas.1914085117

Davenport, T. H., & Beck, J. C. (2001). *The attention economy: Understanding the new currency of business*. Harvard Business School Press.

Davern, M., Bautista, R., Freese, J., Herd, P., & Morgan, S. L. (2024). *General social survey 1972-2024*. NORC at the University of Chicago. https://gssdataexplorer.norc.org

Davies, P., Chapman, S., & Leask, J. (2002). Antivaccination activists on the world wide web. *Archives of Disease in Childhood*, *87*(1), 22–25. https://doi.org/10.1136/adc.87.1.22

Davis, J. L., & Jurgenson, N. (2014). Context collapse: Theorizing context collusions and collisions. *Information, Communication & Society*, *17*(4), 476–485. https://doi.org/10.1080/1369118X.2014.888458

de Cock Buning, M. (2018, March). *A multi-dimensional approach to disinformation: Report of the independent high level group on fake news and online disinformation*. Publications Office of the European Union. https://op.europa.eu/en/publication-detail/-/publication/6ef4df8b-4cea-11e8-be1d-01aa75ed71a1/language-en

De Pryck, K., & Gemenne, F. (2017). The denier-in-chief: Climate change, science and the election of Donald J. Trump. *Law and Critique*, *28*, 119–126. https://doi.org/10.1007/s10978-017-9207-6

de Saint Laurent, C., Murphy, G., Hegarty, K., & Greene, C. M. (2022). Measuring the effects of misinformation exposure and beliefs on behavioural intentions: A COVID-19 vaccination study. *Cognitive Research*, *7*, 87. https://doi.org/10.1186/s41235-022-00437-y

Dechêne, A., Stahl, C., Hansen, J., & Wänke, M. (2010). The truth about the truth: A meta-analytic review of the truth effect. *Personality and Social Psychology Review*, *14*(2), 238–257. https://doi.org/10.1177/1088868309352251

Deinla, I., Mendoza, R. U., & Yap, J. (2021, December 1). Philippines: Diagnosing the infodemic. *Lowy Institute*. https://www.lowyinstitute.org/the-interpreter/philippines-diagnosing-infodemic

Del Vicario, M., Bessi, A., Zollo, F., Petroni, F., Scala, A., Caldarelli, G., Stanley, H. E., & Quattrociocchi, W. (2016). The spreading of misinformation online. *Proceedings of the National Academy of Sciences*, *113*(3), 554–559. https://doi.org/10.1073/pnas.1517441113

Delgado-López, P. D., & Corrales-García, E. M. (2018). Influence of internet and social media in the promotion of alternative oncology, cancer quackery, and the predatory publishing phenomenon. *Cureus*, *10*(5), e2617. https://doi.org/10.7759/cureus.2617

Denham, B. (2020). Magazine journalism in the golden age of muckraking: Patent-medicine exposures before and after the Pure Food and Drug Act of 1906. *Journalism & Communication Monographs*, *22*(2), 100–159. https://doi.org/10.1177/1522637920914979

Dewey, J. (1923). *The public and its problems*. Henry Holt.

Deyrup, A., & Graves Jr, J. L. (2022). Racial biology and medical misconceptions. *New England Journal of Medicine*, *386*(6), 501–503. https://doi.org/10.1056/NEJMp2116224

Diamond, L. L., Batan, H., Anderson, J., & Palen, L. (2022). The polyvocality of online COVID-19 vaccine narratives that invoke medical racism. In S. Barbosa, C. Lampe, C. Appert, D. A. Shamma, S. Drucker, J. Williamson, & K. Yatani (Eds.), *Proceedings of the 2022 CHI Conference on Human Factors in Computing Systems*, *145*. https://doi.org/10.1145/3491102.3501892

Dias, N., Pennycook, G., & Rand, D. G. (2020). Emphasizing publishers does not effectively reduce susceptibility to misinformation on social media. *Harvard Kennedy School Misinformation Review*, *1*(1). https://doi.org/10.37016/mr-2020-001

Diethelm, P., & McKee, M. (2009). Denialism: What is it and how should scientists respond? *European Journal of Public Health*, *19*(1), 2–4. https://doi.org/10.1093/eurpub/ckn139

Dietz T. (2013). Bringing values and deliberation to science communication. *Proceedings of the National Academy of Sciences*, *110*(Suppl 3), 14081–14087. https://doi.org/10.1073/pnas.1212740110

___. (2023). *Decisions for sustainability: Facts and values*. Cambridge University Press.

Dietz, T., Stern, P. C., & Rycroft, R. W. (1989). Definitions of conflict and the legitimation of resources: The case of environmental risk. *Sociological Forum*, *4*(1), 47–70. https://doi.org/10.1007/BF01112616

Dilenschneider, C. (2023). *More people trust museums now than before the pandemic (DATA)*. Impacts Experience. https://www.colleendilen.com/2023/03/01/more-people-trust-museums-now-than-before-the-pandemic-data/

DiResta, R. (2018, November 8). *Of virality and viruses: The anti-vaccine movement and social media*. Nautilus Institute for Security and Sustainability. https://nautilus.org/napsnet/napsnet-special-reports/of-virality-and-viruses-the-anti-vaccine-movement-and-social-media/

DiRusso, C., & Stansberry, K. (2022). Unvaxxed: A cultural study of the online anti-vaccination movement. *Qualitative Health Research*, *32*(2), 317–329. https://doi.org/10.1177/10497323211056050

Dorius, S. F., & Lawrence-Dill, C. J. (2018). Sowing the seeds of skepticism: Russian state news and anti-GMO sentiment. *GM Crops & Food*, *9*(2), 53–58. https://doi.org/10.1080/21645698.2018.1454192

Douglas, J., Bauer, E., Cain, G., Scott, D., & Mellman, T. A. (2023). Adapting motivational interviewing for vaccine hesitancy in underserved communities. *Journal of Clinical and Translational Science*, *7*(s1), 47–47. https://doi.org/10.1017/cts.2023.234

Douglas, K. M., Sutton, R. M., & Cichocka, A. (2017). The psychology of conspiracy theories. *Current Directions in Psychological Science*, *26*(6), 538–542. https://doi.org/10.1177/0963721417718261

Dowling, D., Johnson, P., & Ekdale, B. (2022). Hijacking journalism: Legitimacy and meta-journalistic discourse in right-wing podcasts. *Media and Communication*, *10*(3), 17–27. https://doi.org/10.17645/mac.v10i3.5260

Druckman, J. N. (2022). Threats to science: Politicization, misinformation, and inequalities. *The ANNALS of the American Academy of Political and Social Science*, *700*(1), 8–24. https://doi.org/10.1177/00027162221095431

Druckman, J. N., Klar, S., Krupnikov, Y., Levendusky, M., & Ryan, J. B. (2021). Affective polarization, local contexts and public opinion in America. *Nature Human Behaviour*, *5*(1), 28–38. https://doi.org/10.1038/s41562-020-01012-5

___. (2024a). *Partisan hostility and American democracy: Explaining political divisions and when they matter*. University of Chicago Press.

Druckman, J. N., & Levy, J. (2022). Affective polarization in the American public. In T. Rudolph (Ed.), *Handbook on politics and public opinion* (pp. 257–271). Edward Elgar Publishing.

Druckman, J. N., Schulman, J., Safarpout, A. C., Baum, M., Ognyanova, K., Trujillo, K. L., Mathé, A. Q., Qu, H., Uslu, A. A., Perlis, R. H., & Lazer, D. M. J. (2024b). Continuity and change in trust in scientists in the United States: Demographic stability and partisan polarization. *SSRN*. https://doi.org/10.2139/ssrn.4929030

Drummond, C., & Fischhoff, B. (2017a). Individuals with greater science literacy and education have more polarized beliefs on controversial science topics. *Proceedings of the National Academy of Sciences*, *114*(36), 9587–9592. https://doi.org/10.1073/pnas.1704882114

___. (2017b). Development and validation of the scientific reasoning scale. *Journal of Behavioral Decision Making*, *30*(1), 26–38. https://doi.org/https://doi.org/10.1002/bdm.1906

___. (2020). Predictors of public attitudes toward controversial science 1979–1990. *Journal of Risk Research*, *23*(10), 1318–1335. https://doi.org/10.1080/13669877.2019.1646313

Drummond, C., Gray, S. G., Raimi, K. T., Wilson, R., & Árvai, J. (2020). Public perceptions of federal science advisory boards depend on their composition. *Proceedings of the National Academy of Sciences*, *117*(37), 22668–22670.

Dubois, E., & Blank, G. (2018). The echo chamber is overstated: The moderating effect of political interest and diverse media. *Information, Communication & Society*, *21*(5), 729–745. https://doi.org/10.1080/1369118X.2018.1428656

Duffy, A., Tandoc, E., & Ling, R. (2020). Too good to be true, too good not to share: The social utility of fake news. *Information, Communication & Society*, *23*(13), 1965–1979. https://doi.org/10.1080/1369118X.2019.1623904

Dunlap, R. E., & Brulle, R. J. (2020). Sources and amplifiers of climate change denial. In D. C. Holmes & L. M. Richardson, L. M. (Eds.), *Research handbook on communicating climate change* (pp. 49–61). Edward Elgar Publishing.

Dunlap, R. E., & Jacques, P. J. (2013). Climate change denial books and conservative think tanks: Exploring the connection. *American Behavioral Scientist*, *57*(6), 699–731. https://doi.org/10.1177/0002764213477096

Dunlap, R. E., & McCright, A. M. (2011). Organized climate change denial. In J. S. Dryzek, R. B. Norgaard, & D. Schlosberg (Eds.), *The Oxford handbook of climate change and society* (pp. 144–160). Oxford University Press.

Dunn, A. G., Surian, D., Dalmazzo, J., Rezazadegan, D., Steffens, M., Dyda, A., Leask, J., Coiera, E., Dey, A., & Mandl, K. D. (2020). Limited role of bots in spreading vaccine-critical information among active Twitter users in the United States: 2017–2019. *American Journal of Public Health*, *110*(S3), S319–S325. https://doi.org/10.2105/AJPH.2020.305902

Dunna, A., Keith, K. A., Zuckerman, E., Vallina-Rodriguez, N., O'Connor, B., & Nithyanand, R. (2022). Paying attention to the algorithm behind the curtain: Bringing transparency to YouTube's demonetization algorithms. *Proceedings of the ACM on Human-Computer Interaction*, 6(CSCW2), Article 318, 1–31. https://doi.org/10.1145/3555209

Dunning, D. (2011). The Dunning–Kruger effect: On being ignorant of one's own ignorance. *Advances in Experimental Social Psychology*, *44*, 247–296. https://doi.org/10.1016/B978-0-12-385522-0.00005-6

Dunwoody, S. (2021). Science journalism: Prospects in the digital age. In M. Bucchi & B. Trench (Eds.), *Routledge handbook of public communication of science and technology* (3rd ed., pp. 14–32). Routledge.

Earl, J., James, R., Ramo, E., & Scovill, S. (2021). Protest, activism, and false information. In H. Tumber & S. Waisbord (Eds.), *The Routledge companion to media disinformation and populism* (pp. 290–301). Routledge.

Ecker, U. K. H., & Antonio, L. M. (2021). Can you believe it? An investigation into the impact of retraction source credibility on the continued influence effect. *Memory & Cognition*, *49*(4), 631–644. https://doi.org/10.3758/s13421-020-01129-y

Ecker, U. K. H., Hogan, J. L., & Lewandowsky, S. (2017). Reminders and repetition of misinformation: Helping or hindering its retraction? *Journal of Applied Research in Memory and Cognition*, 6(2), 185–192. https://doi.org/10.1016/j.jarmac.2017.01.014

Ecker, U. K. H., Lewandowsky, S., Cook, J., Schmid, P., Fazio, L. K., Brashier, N., Kendeou, P., Vraga, E. K., & Amazeen, M. A. (2022). The psychological drivers of misinformation belief and its resistance to correction. *Nature Reviews Psychology*, *1*, 13–29. https://doi.org/10.1038/s44159-021-00006-y

Ecker, U. K. H., O'Reilly, Z., Reid, J. S., & Chang, E. P. (2020). The effectiveness of short-format refutational fact-checks. *British Journal of Psychology*, *111*(1), 36–54. https://doi.org/10.1111/bjop.12383

Edelson, L., Nguyen, M. K., Goldstein, I., Goga, O., McCoy, D., & Lauinger, T. (2021, November). Understanding engagement with US (mis) information news sources on Facebook. In *Proceedings of the 21st ACM Internet Measurement Conference* (pp. 444–463).

Edgerly, S., Vraga, E. K., Bode, L., Thorson, K., & Thorson, E. (2018). New media, new relationship to participation? A closer look at youth news repertoires and political participation. *Journalism & Mass Communication Quarterly*, *95*(1), 192–212. https://doi.org/10.1177/1077699017706928

Edgerly, S., & Xu, Y. (2023). Local-level information-seeking in the COVID-19 pandemic: A repertoire approach. *The ANNALS of the American Academy of Political and Social Science*, *707*(1), 172–188.

Einstein, K. L., & Glick, D. M. (2015). Do I think BLS data are BS? The consequences of conspiracy theories. *Political Behavior*, *37*, 679–701. https://psycnet.apa.org/doi/10.1007/s11109-014-9287-z

El Mikati, I. K., Hoteit, R., Harb, T., El Zein, O., Piggott, T., Melki, J., Mustafa, R. A., & Akl, E. A. (2023). Defining misinformation and related terms in health-related literature: Scoping review. *Journal of Medical Internet Research*, *25*, e45731. https://doi.org/10.2196/45731

Ellery, S. (2023, March 28). Fake photos of Pope Francis in a puffer jacket go viral, highlighting the power and peril of AI. *CBS News*. https://www.cbsnews.com/news/pope-francis-puffer-jacket-fake-photos-deepfake-power-peril-of-ai/

Elliott, K. C. (2017). *A tapestry of values: An introduction to values in science*. Oxford University Press. https://doi.org/10.1093/acprof:oso/9780190260804.001.0001

Elsasser, S. W., & Dunlap, R. E. (2013). Leading voices in the denier choir: Conservative columnists' dismissal of global warming and denigration of climate science. *American Behavioral Scientist*, *57*(6), 754–776. https://doi.org/10.1177/0002764212469800

Epstein, Z., Sirlin, N., Arechar, A., Pennycook, G., & Rand, D. (2023). The social media context interferes with truth discernment. *Science Advances*, *9*(9), eabo6169. https://doi.org/10.1126/sciadv.abo6169

Equis Institute. (2022, January 1). *Latinos and a growing crisis of trust*. https://www.weareequis.us/research/disinfo-landscape-latinos

___. (2022, June 23). *Spanish-language recommendations and glossary*. https://weareequis.us/api/docs/11BmqnvEQ17jcqvoE6xqTm/bb0b351858e541f518255cb049f56ebd/Equis_Spanish-Language_Recommendations_and_Glossary.pdf

European Commission. (2015, April 22). *Fact sheet: Questions and answers on EU's policies on GMOs*. https://ec.europa.eu/commission/presscorner/detail/en/MEMO_15_4778

European Digital Rights. (2018, December 18). *The EU's attempt to regulate big tech: What it brings and what is missing*. https://edri.org/our-work/eu-attempt-to-regulate-big-tech/

European Parliament. (2022, January 20). *Digital Services Act: Regulating platforms for a safer online space for users* [Press Release]. https://www.europarl.europa.eu/news/en/press-room/20220114IPR21017/digital-services-act-regulating-platforms-for-a-safer-online-space-for-users

Evanega, S., Lynas, M., Adams, J., & Smolenyak, K. (2020). Coronavirus misinformation: Quantifying sources and themes in the COVID-19 'infodemic'. *JMIR Preprints*, *19*(10), 2020.

Fainaru-Wada, M., & Fainaru, S. (2014). *League of denial: The NFL, concussions, and the battle for truth*. Crown.

Fang, J. (2021, May 26) *Social media sites popular with Asian Americans have a big misinformation problem*. Prism. https://prismreports.org/2021/05/26/social-media-sites-often-used-by-asian-americans-have-a-big-problem-with-right-wing-misinformation/

Farrell, J. (2015). Corporate funding and ideological polarization about climate change. *Proceedings of the National Academy of Sciences, 113*(1), 92–97. https://doi.org/10.1073/pnas.1509433112

___. (2016). Network structure and influence of the climate change counter-movement. *Nature Climate Change*, 6(4), 370–374. https://doi.org/10.1038/nclimate2875

___. (2019). The growth of climate change misinformation in US philanthropy: Evidence from natural language processing. *Environmental Research Letters, 14*(3), 034013. http://dx.doi.org/10.1088/1748-9326/aaf939

Farrell, J., McConnell, K., & Brulle, R. (2019). Evidence-based strategies to combat scientific misinformation. *Nature Climate Change*, 9(3), 191–195. https://doi.org/10.1038/s41558-018-0368-6

Fazio, L. K. (2020a). Pausing to consider why a headline is true or false can help reduce the sharing of false news. *The Harvard Kennedy School Misinformation Review, 1*(2), 1–8. https://doi.org/10.37016/mr-2020-009

___. (2020b). Repetition increases perceived truth even for known falsehoods. *Collabra: Psychology*, 6(1), Article 38. https://doi.org/10.1525/collabra.347

Fazio, L. K., Barber, S. J., Rajaram, S., Ornstein, P. A., & Marsh, E. J. (2013). Creating illusions of knowledge: Learning errors that contradict prior knowledge. *Journal of Experimental Psychology: General, 142*(1), 1–5. https://doi.org/10.1037/a0028649

Fazio, L. K., Brashier, N. M., Payne, B. K., & Marsh, E. J. (2015). Knowledge does not protect against illusory truth. *Journal of Experimental Psychology: General, 144*(5), 993–1002. https://doi.org/10.1037/xge0000098

Fazio, L. K., Hong, M. K., & Pillai, R. M. (2023). Combatting rumors around the French election: the memorability and effectiveness of fact-checking articles. *Cognitive Research: Principles and Implications*, 8(1), 44. https://doi.org/10.1186/s41235-023-00500-2

Fazio, L. K., Pillai, R. M., & Patel, D. (2022). The effects of repetition on belief in naturalistic settings. *Journal of Experimental Psychology: General, 151*(10), 2604–2613. https://doi.org/10.1037/xge0001211

Fazio, L. K., Rand, D. G., & Pennycook, G. (2019). Repetition increases perceived truth equally for plausible and implausible statements. *Psychonomic Bulletin & Review, 26*, 1705–1710. https://doi.org/10.3758/s13423-019-01651-4

Federal Trade Commission (n.d.) *Truth in advertising*. https://www.ftc.gov/news-events/topics/truth-advertising

Federation of State Medical Boards. (2021, July 29). FSMB: Spreading COVID-19 vaccine misinformation may put medical license at risk. https://www.fsmb.org/advocacy/news-releases/fsmb-spreading-covid-19-vaccine-misinformation-may-put-medical-license-at-risk/

Feinstein, N. (2011). Salvaging science literacy. *Science Education, 95*(1), 168–185. https://doi.org/10.1002/sce.20414

Feinstein, N. W., Allen, S., & Jenkins, E. (2013). Outside the pipeline: Reimagining science education for nonscientists. *Science, 340*, 314–317. https://doi.org/10.1126/science.1230855

Feinstein, N. W., & Waddington, D. I. (2020). Individual truth judgments or purposeful, collective sensemaking? Rethinking science education's response to the post-truth era. *Educational Psychologist, 55*(3), 155–166. https://doi.org/10.1080/00461520.2020.1780130

Feldman, L., Maibach, E. W., Roser-Renouf, C., & Leiserowitz, A. (2012). Climate on cable: The nature and impact of global warming coverage on Fox News, CNN, and MSNBC. *The International Journal of Press/Politics, 17*(1), 3–31. https://doi.org/10.1177/1940161211425410

Feldman, L., Myers, T. A., Hmielowski, J. D., & Leiserowitz, A. (2014). The mutual reinforcement of media selectivity and effects: Testing the reinforcing spirals framework in the context of global warming. *Journal of Communication, 64*(4), 590–611. https://doi.org/10.1111/jcom.12108

Feldman, L., Wojcieszak, M., Stroud, N. J., & Bimber, B. (2018). Explaining media choice: The role of issue-specific engagement in predicting interest-based and partisan selectivity. *Journal of Broadcasting & Electronic Media*, *62*(1), 109–130. https://doi.org/10.1080/08838151.2017.1375502

Fernbach, P. M., Light, N., Scott, S. E., Inbar, Y., & Rozin, P. (2019). Extreme opponents of genetically modified foods know the least but think they know the most. *Nature Human Behaviour*, *3*(3), 251–256. https://doi.org/10.1038/s41562-018-0520-3

Ferrara, E., Cresci, S., & Luceri, L. (2020). Misinformation, manipulation, and abuse on social media in the era of COVID-19. *Journal of Computational Social Science*, *3*, 271–277. https://doi.org/10.1007/s42001-020-00094-5

Ferreira Caceres, M. M., Sosa, J. P., Lawrence, J. A., Sestacovschi, C., Tidd-Johnson, A., Rasool, M. H. U., Gadamidi, V. K., Ozair, S., Pandav, K., Cuevas-Lou, C., Parrish, M., Rodriguez, I., & Fernandez, J. P. (2022). The impact of misinformation on the COVID-19 pandemic. *AIMS Public Health*, *9*(2), 262–277. https://doi.org/10.3934/publichealth.2022018

Fischer, S. (2021, February 3). TikTok will prompt users when videos are flagged as misleading. *Axios*. https://www.axios.com/2021/02/03/tiktok-misleading-videos

Fiske, S. T., Cuddy, A. J. C., & Glick, P. (2007). Universal dimensions of social cognition: Warmth and competence. *Trends in Cognitive Sciences*, *11*(2), 77–83. https://doi.org/10.1016/j.tics.2006.11.005

Fleerackers, A., Riedlinger, M., Moorhead, L., Ahmed, R., & Alperin, J. P. (2022). Communicating scientific uncertainty in an age of COVID-19: An investigation into the use of preprints by digital media outlets. *Health Communication*, *37*(6), 726–738. https://doi.org/10.1080/10410236.2020.1864892

Flowers, C. C. (2020). *Waste: One woman's fight against America's dirty secret*. The New Press.

Fonseca, C., Pettitt, J., Woollard, A., Rutherford, A., Bickmore, W., Ferguson-Smith, A., & Hurst, L. D. (2023). People with more extreme attitudes towards science have self-confidence in their understanding of science, even if this is not justified. *PLoS Biology*, *21*(1), e3001915. https://doi.org/10.1371/journal.pbio.3001915

Food and Drug Administration. (n.d.a). *Rumor control*. https://www.fda.gov/news-events/rumor-control

___. (n.d.b). *News & events for human drugs*. https://www.fda.gov/drugs/news-events-human-drugs

___. (2024). *Addressing misinformation about medical devices and prescription drugs questions and answers guidance for industry* (Draft Guidance). https://www.fda.gov/media/179827/download

Forestal, J. (2021). *Designing for democracy: How to build community in digital environments*. Oxford University Press.

Frank, K. A., Chen, T., Brown, E., & Larsen, A. (2023). A network intervention for natural resource management in the context of climate change. *Social Networks*, *75*, 55–64. https://doi.org/10.1016/j.socnet.2022.03.003

Frank, L. B., Murphy, S. T., Chatterjee, J. S., Moran, M. B., & Baezconde-Garbanati, L. (2015). Telling stories, saving lives: Creating narrative health messages. *Health Communication*, *30*(2), 154–163. https://doi.org/10.1080/10410236.2014.974126

Frankfurt, H. G. (2005). *On bullshit*. Princeton University Press.

Fraser, N., Brierley, L., Dey, G., Polka, J. K., Pálfy, M., Nanni, F., & Coates, J. A. (2021). The evolving role of preprints in the dissemination of COVID-19 research and their impact on the science communication landscape. *PLoS Biology*, *19*(4), e3000959. https://doi.org/10.1371/journal.pbio.3000959

Freelon, D. (2023). The shared psychological roots of prejudice and conspiracy theory belief. *Current Opinion in Psychology*, 101773. https://doi.org/10.1016/j.copsyc.2023.101773

Freelon, D., & Wells, C. (2020). Disinformation as political communication. *Political Communication*, *37*(2), 145–156. https://doi.org/10.1080/10584609.2020.1723755

Freiling, I., Krause, N. M., & Scheufele, D. (2023). Science and ethics of "curing" misinformation. *AMA Journal of Ethics*, *25*(3), E228–E237. https://doi.org/10.1001/amajethics.2023.228

Freiling, I., Krause, N. M., Scheufele, D. A., & Brossard, D. (2023). Believing and sharing misinformation, fact-checks, and accurate information on social media: The role of anxiety during COVID-19. *New Media & Society*, *25*(1), 141–162. https://doi.org/10.1177/14614448211011451

Frenkel, S., Decker, B., & Alba, D. (2020, May 20). How the 'Plandemic' movie and its falsehoods spread widely online. *The New York Times*. https://www.nytimes.com/2020/05/20/technology/plandemic-movie-youtube-facebook-coronavirus.html

Friedman, A. (2023). *Mammography wars: Analyzing attention in cultural and medical disputes*. Rutgers University Press.

Funk, C. (2017). Mixed messages about public trust in science. *Issues in Science and Technology*, *34*(1), 86–88. https://issues.org/real-numbers-mixed-messages-about-public-trust-in-science/

Funk, C., Gottfried, J., & Mitchell, A. (2017, September 20). Science news and information today. *Pew Research Center*. https://www.pewresearch.org/journalism/2017/09/20/science-news-and-information-today/

Fürst, S. (2020). In the service of good journalism and audience interests? How audience metrics affect news quality. *Media and Communication*, *8*(3), 270–280. https://doi.org/10.17645/mac.v8i3.3228

Gabarda, A., & Butterworth, S. W. (2021). Using best practices to address COVID-19 vaccine hesitancy: The case for the motivational interviewing approach. *Health Promotion Practice*, *22*(5), 611–615. https://doi.org/10.1177/15248399211016463

Gagneur, A., Gosselin, V., & Dubé, È. (2018a). Motivational interviewing: A promising tool to address vaccine hesitancy. *Vaccine*, *36*(44), 6553–6555. https://doi.org/10.1016/j.vaccine.2017.10.049

Gagneur, A., Lemaître, T., Gosselin, V., Farrands, A., Carrier, N., Petit, G., Valiquette, L., & De Wals, P. (2018b). A postpartum vaccination promotion intervention using motivational interviewing techniques improves short-term vaccine coverage: PromoVac study. *BMC Public Health*, *18*(1), 811. https://doi.org/10.1186/s12889-018-5724-y

Gamble, V. N. (1997). Under the shadow of Tuskegee: African Americans and health care. *American Journal of Public Health*, *87*(11), 1773–1778. https://doi.org/10.2105/ajph.87.11.1773

Garcia, S. E. (2018, September 5). Goop agrees to pay $145,000 for 'unsubstantiated' claims about vaginal eggs. *The New York Times*. https://www.nytimes.com/2018/09/05/business/goop-vaginal-egg-settlement.html

Gauchat, G. (2012). Politicization of science in the public sphere: A study of public trust in the United States, 1974–2010. *American Sociological Review*, *77*(2) 167–187. https://doi.org/10.1177/0003122412438225

Geary, K. (2021). Section 230 of the Communications Decency Act, product liability, and a proposal for preventing dating-app harassment. *Penn State Law Review*, *125*(2), 4. https://elibrary.law.psu.edu/pslr/vol125/iss2/4

Gee, G. C., & Ford, C. L. (2011). Structural racism and health inequites: Old issues, new directions. *Du Bois Review: Social Science Research on Race*, *8*(1), 115–132. https://doi.org/10.1017/S1742058X11000130

Gentzkow, M., & Shapiro, J. M. (2011). Ideological segregation online and offline. *The Quarterly Journal of Economics*, *126*(4), 1799–1839. https://doi.org/10.1093/qje/qjr044

George, S., Duran, N., & Norris, K. (2014). A systematic review of barriers and facilitators to minority research participation among African Americans, Latinos, Asian Americans, and Pacific Islanders. *American Journal of Public Health*, *104*(2), e16–31. https://doi.org/10.2105/AJPH.2013.301706

Gerson, D., Chen, N. T. N., Wenzel, A., Ball-Rokeach, S., & Parks, M. (2020). From audience to reporter: Recruiting and training community members at a participatory news site serving a multiethnic city. In M. Wall (Ed.), *Mapping Citizen and Participatory Journalism in Newsrooms, Classrooms and Beyond* (pp. 203–221). Routledge.

Gerts, D., Shelley, C. D., Parikh, N., Pitts, T., Watson Ross, C., Fairchild, G., Chavez, N. Y. V., & Daughton, A. R. (2021). "Thought I'd share first" and other conspiracy theory tweets from the COVID-19 infodemic: Exploratory study. *JMIR Public Health and Surveillance*, *7*(4), e26527. https://doi.org/10.2196/26527

Gidengil, C., Goetz, M. B., Newberry, S., Maglione, M., Hall, O., Larkin, J., Motala, A., & Hempel, S. (2021). Safety of vaccines used for routine immunization in the United States: An updated systematic review and meta-analysis. *Vaccine*, *39*(28), 3696–3716. https://doi.org/10.1016/j.vaccine.2021.03.079

Gillespie, T. (2018). *Custodians of the internet: Platforms, content moderation, and the hidden decisions that shape social media.* Yale University Press.

Gillett, R., Gray, J. E., & Valdovinos Kaye, D. B. (2023). 'Just a little hack': Investigating cultures of content moderation circumvention by Facebook users. *New Media & Society*, *26*(11), 6183–6204. https://doi.org/10.1177/14614448221147661

Gisondi, M. A., Barber, R., Faust, J. S., Raja, A., Strehlow, M. C., Westafer, L. M., & Gottlieb, M. (2022). A deadly infodemic: Social media and the power of COVID-19 misinformation. *Journal of Medical Internet Research*, *24*(2), e35552. https://doi.org/10.2196/35552

Gitlin, T. (2007). *Media unlimited: How the torrent of images and sounds overwhelms our lives.* Henry Holt & Company.

Giusti, K., Hamermesh, R. G., & Krasnow, M. (2021, June 11). Addressing demographic disparities in clinical trials. *Harvard Business Review*. https://hbr.org/2021/06/addressing-demographic-disparities-in-clinical-trials

Givel, M. (2007). Consent and counter-mobilization: The case of the national smokers alliance. *Journal of Health Communication*, *12*(4), 339–357. https://doi.org/10.1080/10810730701326002

Givel, M. S., & Glantz, S. A. (2001). Tobacco lobby political influence on US state legislatures in the 1990s. *Tobacco Control*, *10*(2), 124–134. https://doi.org/10.1136/tc.10.2.124

Global Disinformation Index. (2019, September 1). *The quarter billion dollar question: How is disinformation gaming ad tech?* Global Disinformation Index. https://disinformationindex.org/wp-content/uploads/2019/09/GDI_Ad-tech_Report_Screen_AW16.pdf

Godel, W., Sanderson, Z., Aslett, K., Nagler, J., Bonneau, R., Persily, N., & Tucker, J. A. (2021). Moderating with the mob: Evaluating the efficacy of real-time crowdsourced fact-checking. *Journal of Online Trust and Safety*, *1*(1). https://doi.org/10.54501/jots.v1i1.15

Goel, P., Green, J., Lazer, D., & Resnik, P. (2023). Mainstream news articles co-shared with fake news buttress misinformation narratives. *arXiv*. http://arxiv.org/abs/2308.06459

Goldenberg, M. J. (2016). Public misunderstanding of science? Reframing the problem of vaccine hesitancy. *Perspectives on Science*, *24*(5), 552–581. https://doi.org/10.1162/POSC_a_00223

Goldman, A. I. (1999). *Knowledge in a social world.* Oxford University Press.

Goldman, E. (2021). Content moderation remedies. *Michigan Technical Law Review*, *28*, 1. http://dx.doi.org/10.2139/ssrn.3810580

Golebiewski, M., & boyd, d. (2019). *Data voids: Where missing data can easily be exploited.* Data & Society. https://datasociety.net/wp-content/uploads/2019/11/Data-Voids-2.0-Final.pdf

Gollust, S. E., Hull, S. C., & Wilfond, B. S. (2002). Limitations of direct-to-consumer advertising for clinical genetic testing. *JAMA*, *288*(14), 1762–1767. https://doi.org/10.1001/jama.288.14.1762

González-Bailón, S., Lazer, D., Barberá, P., Zhang, M., Allcott, H., Brown, T., Crespo-Tenorio, A., Freelon, D., Gentzkow, M., Guess, A. M., Iyengar, S., Kim, Y. M., Malhotra, N., Moehler, D., Nyhan, B., Pan, J., Rivera, C. V., Settle, J., Thorson, E., Tromble, R., Wilkins, A., Wojcieszak, M., de Jonge, C. K., Franco, A., Mason, W., Stroud., N. J., & Tucker, J. A. (2023). Asymmetric ideological segregation in exposure to political news on Facebook. *Science*, *381*(6656), 392–398. https://doi.org/10.1126/science.ade7138

González-Bailón, S., & Lelkes, Y. (2022) Do social media undermine social cohesion? A critical review. *Social Issues and Policy Review*, *17*(1), 155–180. https://doi.org/10.1111/sipr.12091

Goss, B. M. (2023). Introducing sham journalism: A case-study analysis of Newsmax' Discourse on Special Counsel John Durham in 2022. *Journalism Practice*, 1–19. https://doi.org/10.1080/17512786.2023.2202194

Goulbourne, T., & Yanovitzky, I. (2021). The communication infrastructure as a social determinant of health: Implications for health policymaking and practice. *The Milbank Quarterly*, *99*(1), 24–40. https://doi.org/10.1111/1468-0009.12496

Gould, S. J. (1996). *The mismeasure of man*. W. W. Norton & Company.

Grady, R. H., Ditto, P. H., & Loftus, E. F. (2021). Nevertheless partisanship persisted: Fake news warnings help briefly, but bias returns with time. *Cognitive Research: Principles and Implications*, *6*, 52. https://doi.org/10.1186/s41235-021-00315-z

Grant, R., & Mislán, C. 2020. "Improving the race": The discourse of science and eugenics in local news coverage, 1905-1922. *American Journalism*, *37*(4), 476–499. https://doi.org/10.1080/08821127.2020.1830627

Granter, S. R., & Papke Jr., D. J. (2018). Opinion: Medical misinformation in the era of Google: Computational approaches to a pervasive problem. *Proceedings of the National Academy of Sciences, 115*(25), 6318–6321. https://doi.org/10.1073/pnas.1808264115

Green, J., Druckman, J. N., Baum, M. A., Lazer, D., Ognyanova, K., Simonson, M. D., Lin, J., Santillana, M., & Perlis, R. H. (2023a). Using general messages to persuade on a politicized scientific issue. *British Journal of Political Science*, *53*(2), 698–706. https://doi.org/10.1017/S0007123422000424

Green, M. C., & Brock, T. C. (2000). The role of transportation in the persuasiveness of public narratives. *Journal of Personality and Social Psychology*, *79*(5), 701–721. https://doi.org/10.1037/0022-3514.79.5.701

Green, M. C., Garst, J., & Brock, T. C. (2003). The power of fiction: Determinants and boundaries. In L. J. Shrum (Ed.), *The psychology of entertainment media: Blurring the lines between entertainment and persuasion* (pp. 169–184). Erlbaum Psych Press.

Green, Y., Gully, A., Roth, Y., Roy, A., Tucker, J. A., & Wanless, A. (2023b, January). *Evidence-based misinformation interventions: Challenges and opportunities for measurement and collaboration*. Carnegie Endowment for International Peace. https://carnegieendowment.org/2023/01/09/evidence-based-misinformation-interventions-challenges-and-opportunities-for-measurement-and-collaboration-pub-88661

Greenhalgh, T. (2020). Will COVID-19 be evidence-based medicine's nemesis? *PLoS Medicine*, *17*(6), e1003266. https://doi.org/10.1371/journal.pmed.1003266

Greenhalgh, T., Fisman, D., Cane, D. J., Oliver, M., & Macintyre, C. R. (2022). Adapt or die: How the pandemic made the shift from EBM to EBM+ more urgent. *BMJ Evidence-Based Medicine*, *27*(5), 253–260. Advance online publication. https://doi.org/10.1136/bmjebm-2022-111952

Greiner, A., Smith, K. C., & Guallar, E. (2010). Something fishy? News media presentation of complex health issues related to fish consumption guidelines. *Public Health Nutrition*, *13*(11), 1786–1794. https://doi.org/10.1017/S1368980010000923

Grimmelmann, J. (2015). The virtues of moderation. *Yale Journal of Law and Technology*, *17*(42), 42–109.

Grinberg, N., Joseph, K., Friedland, L., Swire-Thompson, B., & Lazer, D. (2019). Fake news on Twitter during the 2016 U.S. presidential election. *Science*, *363*(6425), 374–378. https://doi.org/10.1126/science.aau2706

Gruzd, A., Abul-Fottouh, D., Song, M. Y., & Saiphoo, A. (2023). From Facebook to YouTube: The potential exposure to COVID-19 anti-vaccine videos on social media. *Social Media+ Society*, *9*(1). https://doi.org/10.1177/20563051221150403

Grzesiak-Feldman, M. (2013). The effect of high-anxiety situations on conspiracy thinking. *Current Psychology*, *32*, 100–118. https://doi.org/10.1007/s12144-013-9165-6

Gu, J., Dor, A., Li, K., Broniatowski, D. A., Hatheway, M., Fritz, L., & Abroms, L. C. (2022). The impact of Facebook's vaccine misinformation policy on user endorsements of vaccine content: An interrupted time series analysis. *Vaccine*, *40*(14), 2209–2214. https://doi.org/10.1016/j.vaccine.2022.02.062

Guenther, L. (2019). Science journalism. In H. Örnebring (Ed.), *The Oxford encyclopedia of journalism studies*. Oxford University Press. https://doi.org/10.1093/acrefore/9780190228613.013.901.

Guess, A., Aslett, K., Tucker, J., Bonneau, R., & Nagler, J. (2021). Cracking open the news feed: Exploring what us Facebook users see and share with large-scale platform data. *Journal of Quantitative Description: Digital Media*, *1*. https://doi.org/10.51685/jqd.2021.006

Guess, A., Nagler, J., & Tucker, J. (2019). Less than you think: Prevalence and predictors of fake news dissemination on Facebook. *Science Advances*, *5*(1), eaau4586. https://doi.org/10.1126/sciadv.aau4586

Guess, A., Nyhan, B., Lyons, B., & Reifler, J. (2018a). *Avoiding the echo chamber about echo chambers: Why selective exposure to like-minded political news is less prevalent than you think*. Knight Foundation. https://kf-site-production.s3.amazonaws.com/media_elements/files/000/000/133/original/Topos_KF_White-Paper_Nyhan_V1.pdf

Guess, A., Nyhan, B., & Reifler, J. (2018b). *Selective exposure to misinformation: Evidence from the consumption of fake news during the 2016 US presidential campaign*. European Research Council. https://about.fb.com/wp-content/uploads/2018/01/fake-news-2016.pdf

Guess, A. M. (2021). (Almost) everything in moderation: New evidence on Americans' online media diets. *American Journal of Political Science*, *65*(4), 1007–1022. https://doi.org/10.1111/ajps.12589

Guess, A. M., Lerner, M., Lyons, B., Montgomery, J. M., Nyhan, B., Reifler, J., & Sircar, N. (2020). A digital media literacy intervention increases discernment between mainstream and false news in the United States and India. *Proceedings of the National Academy of Sciences*, *117*(27), 15536–15545 https://doi.org/10.1073/pnas.1920498117

Guess, A. M., & Lyons, B. A. (2020). Misinformation, disinformation, and online propaganda. In N. Persily & J. A. Tucker (Eds.), *Social media and democracy: The state of the field and prospects for reform*. Cambridge University Press

Guidry, J. P. D., Vraga, E. K., Laestadius, L. I., Miller, C. A., Occa, A., Nan, X., Ming, H. M., Qin, Y., Fuemmeler, B. F., & Carlyle, K. E. (2020). HPV vaccine searches on Pinterest: Before and after Pinterest's actions to moderate content. *American Journal of Public Health*, *110*(S3), S305–S311. https://doi.org/10.2105/AJPH.2020.305827

Habermas, J. (1970). *Towards a rational society*. Beacon Press.

Habgood-Coote, J. (2019). Stop talking about fake news! *Inquiry*, *62*(9–10), 1033–1065. https://doi.org/10.1080/0020174X.2018.1508363

Hadland, S. E., Rivera-Aguirre, A., Marshall, B. D., & Cerdá, M. (2019). Association of pharmaceutical industry marketing of opioid products with mortality from opioid-related overdoses. *JAMA Network Open*, *2*(1), e186007–e186007. https://doi.org/10.1001/jamanetworkopen.2018.6007

Hagar, N., & Diakopoulos, N. (2019). Optimizing content with A/B headline testing: Changing newsroom practices. *Media and Communication*, *7*(1), 117–127. https://doi.org/10.17645/mac.v7i1.1801

Haglin, K. (2017). The limitations of the backfire effect. *Research & Politics*, *4*(3). https://doi.org/10.1177/2053168017716547

Hall, V., Banerjee, E., Kenyon, C., Strain, A., Griffith, J., Como-Sabetti, K., Heath, J., Bahta, L., Martin, K., McMahon, M., Johnson, D., Roddy, M., Dunn, D., & Ehresmann, K. (2017). Measles outbreak—Minnesota April–May 2017. *Morbidity and Mortality Weekly Report*, *66*(27), 713–717. https://doi.org/10.15585/mmwr.mm6627a1

Hameleers, M. (2023). The (un)intended consequences of emphasizing the threats of mis- and disinformation. *Media and Communication*, *11*(2). https://doi.org/10.17645/mac.v11i2.6301

Hameleers, M., & van der Meer, T. G. L. A. (2020). Misinformation and polarization in a high-choice media environment: How effective are political fact-checkers? *Communication Research*, *47*(2), 227–250. https://doi.org/10.1177/0093650218819671

Hamilton, L. C., & Safford, T. G. (2021). Elite cues and the rapid decline in trust in science agencies on COVID-19. *Sociological Perspectives*, *64*(5), 988–1011. https://doi.org/10.1177/07311214211022391

Hampton, K. N., Shin, I., & Lu, W. (2017). Social media and political discussion: When online presence silences offline conversation. *Information, Communication & Society*, *20*(7), 1090–1107. https://doi.org/10.1080/1369118X.2016.1218526

Han, C., Kumar, D., & Durumeric, Z. (2022, May). On the infrastructure providers that support misinformation websites. In C. Budak, M. Cha, & D. Quercia (Eds.), *Proceedings of the International AAAI Conference on Web and Social Media*, *16*(1), 287–298. https://doi.org/10.1609/icwsm.v16i1.19292

Han, R. (2015). Manufacturing consent in cyberspace: China's "fifty-cent army". *Journal of Current Chinese Affairs*, *44*(2), 105–134. https://doi.org/10.1177/186810261504400020

Hansson, S. O. (2017). Science denial as a form of pseudoscience. *Studies in History and Philosophy of Science Part A*, *63*, 39–47. https://doi.org/10.1016/j.shpsa.2017.05.002

Harris, Y., Gorelick, P. B., Samuels, P., & Bempong, I. (1996). Why African Americans may not be participating in clinical trials. *Journal of the National Medical Association*, *88*(10), 630–634.

Hart, P. S., Chinn, S., & Soroka, S. (2020). Politicization and polarization in COVID-19 News coverage. *Science Communication*, *42*(5), 679–697. https://doi.org/10.1177/1075547020950735

Hasebrink, U., & Popp, J. 2006. Media repertoires as a result of selective media use. A conceptual approach to the analysis of patterns of exposure. *Communications* *31*(3), 369–387. https://doi.org/10.1515/COMMUN.2006.023

Hassan, A. I., Raman, A., Castro, I., Zia, H. B., De Cristofaro, E., Sastry, N., & Tyson, G. (2021, December). Exploring content moderation in the decentralised web: The pleroma case. In *Proceedings of the 17th International Conference on Emerging Networking EXperiments and Technologies* (pp. 328–335). https://doi.org/10.1145/3485983.3494838

Haughey, M. M., Povolo, M., & Starbird, K. (2022). Bridging contextual and methodological gaps on the "misinformation beat": Insights from journalist-researcher collaborations at speed. In *Proceedings of the 2022 CHI Conference on Human Factors in Computing Systems*, Article 244. https://doi.org/10.1145/3491102.3517503

Hawkins, S. A., & Hoch, S. J. (1992). Low-involvement learning: Memory without evaluation. *Journal of Consumer Research*, *19*(2), 212–225. https://doi.org/10.1086/209297

Hayes, D., & Lawless, J. L. (2021). *News hole: The demise of local journalism and political engagement*. Cambridge University Press.

Head, M. L., Holman, L., Lanfear, R., Kahn, A. T., & Jennions, M. D. (2015). The extent and consequences of p-hacking in science. *PLoS Biology*, *13*(3), e1002106. https://doi.org/10.1371/journal.pbio.1002106

Heaven, W. D. (2022, November 18). Why Meta's latest large language model survived only three days online. *MIT Technology Review*. https://www.technologyreview.com/2022/11/18/1063487/meta-large-language-model-ai-only-survived-three-days-gpt-3-science/

Heller, J. (2015). Rumors and realities: Making sense of HIV/AIDS conspiracy narratives and contemporary legends. *American Journal of Public Health*, *105*(1), e43–e50. https://doi.org/10.2105/AJPH.2014.302284

Helm, R. K., & Nasu, H. (2021). Regulatory responses to 'fake news' and freedom of expression: Normative and empirical evaluation. *Human Rights Law Review*, *21*(2), 302–328. https://doi.org/10.1093/hrlr/ngaa060

Henderson, E. L., Westwood, S. J., & Simons, D. J. (2022). A reproducible systematic map of research on the illusory truth effect. *Psychonomic Bulletin & Review*, *29*(3), 1065–1088. https://doi.org/10.3758/s13423-021-01995-w

Hendrix, J. (2022). What's next for the digital services act. *Tech Policy Press*. https://www.techpolicy.press/whats-next-for-the-digital-services-act/

Hennekens, C. H., Rane, M., Solano, J., Alter, S., Johnson, H., Krishnaswamy, S., Shih, R., Maki, D., & DeMets, D. L. (2022). Updates on hydroxychloroquine in prevention and treatment of COVID-19. *The American Journal of Medicine*, *135*(1), 7–9. https://doi.org/10.1016/j.amjmed.2021.07.035

Henrich, J., Heine, S. J., & Norenzayan, A. (2010). Most people are not WEIRD. *Nature*, *466*(7302), 29. https://doi.org/10.1038/466029a

Henry, A. D. (2017). *Network segregation and policy learning*. In J. N. Victor, A. H. Montgomery, & M. Lubell (Eds.), *The Oxford handbook of political networks* (pp. 559–588). Oxford University Press.

Henry, A. D., Dietz, T., & Sweeney, R. L. (2021). Coevolution of networks and beliefs in US environmental risk policy. *Policy Studies Journal*, *49*(3), 675–702. https://doi.org/10.1111/psj.12407

Herasimenka, A., Au, Y., George, A., Joynes-Burgess, K., Knuutila, A., Bright, J., & Howard, P. N. (2023). The political economy of digital profiteering: Communication resource mobilization by anti-vaccination actors. *Journal of Communication*, *73*(2), 126–137. https://doi.org/10.1093/joc/jqac043

Herbst, R. S., Hatsukami, D., Acton, D., Giuliani, M., Moushey, A., Phillips, J., Sherwood, S., Toll, B. A., Viswanath, K., Warren, N. J. H., Warren, G. W., & Alberg, A. J. (2022). Electronic nicotine delivery systems: An updated policy statement from the American Association for Cancer Research and the American Society of Clinical Oncology. *Clinical Cancer Research*, *28*(22), 4861–4870. https://doi.org/10.1158/1078-0432.CCR-22-2429

Hern, A. (2020, June 11). Twitter aims to limit people sharing articles they have not read. *The Guardian*. https://www.theguardian.com/technology/2020/jun/11/twitter-aims-to-limit-people-sharing-articles-they-have-not-read

Hevner, A. R., March, S. T., Park, J., & Ram, S. (2004). Design science in information systems research. *MIS Quarterly*, *28*(1), 75–105. https://doi.org/10.5555/2017212.2017217

Himelboim, I. (2017). Social network analysis (social media). In J. Matthes (Ed.), *The international encyclopedia of communication research methods*. John Wiley & Sons, Inc.

Hindman, M. (2010). *The myth of digital democracy*. Princeton University Press.

Hinojosa, L., Riedy, R., Polman, J., Swanson, R., Nuessle, T., & Garneau, N. (2021). Expanding public participation in science practices beyond data collection. *Citizen Science: Theory & Practice*, *6*(1), 1–15. https://doi. org/10.5334/cstp.292

Hlubocky, F. J., McFarland, D. F., Spears, P. A., Smith, L., Patten, B., Peppercorn, J., & Holcombe, R. (2020). Direct-to-consumer advertising for cancer centers and institutes: Ethical dilemmas and practical implications. *American Society of Clinical Oncology Educational Book*, *40*, 1–11. https://doi.org/10.1200/EDBK_279963

Hocevar, K. P., Metzger, M., & Flanagin, A. J. (2017). Source credibility, expertise, and trust in health and risk messaging. *Oxford Research Encyclopedia of Communication*. https://doi.org/10.1093/acrefore/9780190228613.013.287

Hoes, E., Aitken, B., Zhang, J., Gackowski, T., & Wojcieszak, M. (2024). Prominent misinformation interventions reduce misperceptions but increase scepticism. *Nature Human Behaviour*, *8*(8), 1545–1553. https://doi.org/10.1038/s41562-024-01884-x

Hoffman, B. L., Felter, E. M., Chu, K. H., Shensa, A., Hermann, C., Wolynn, T., Williams, D., & Primack, B. A. (2019). It's not all about autism: The emerging landscape of anti-vaccination sentiment on Facebook. *Vaccine*, *37*(16), 2216–2223. https://doi.org/10.1016/j.vaccine.2019.03.003

Hoffman, B. L., Hoffman, R., VonVille, H. M., Sidani, J. E., Manganello, J. A., Chu, K.-H., Felter, E M., Miller, E., & Burke, J. G. (2023). Characterizing the influence of television health entertainment narratives in lay populations: A scoping review. *American Journal of Health Promotion*, *37*(5), 685–697. https://doi.org/10.1177/08901171221141080

Hoffman, K. M., Trawalter, S., Axt, J. R., & Oliver, M. N. (2016). Racial bias in pain assessment and treatment recommendations, and false beliefs about biological differences between blacks and whites. *Proceedings of the National Academy of Sciences*, *113*(16), 4296–4301. https://doi.org/10.1073/pnas.1516047113

Hofstadter, R. (1964, November). The paranoid style in American politics. *Harper's Magazine*. https://harpers.org/archive/1964/11/the-paranoid-style-in-american-politics/

Hofstetter, C. R., Barker, D., Smith, J. T., Zari, G. M., & Ingrassia, T. A. (1999). Information, misinformation, and political talk radio. *Political Research Quarterly*, *52*(2), 353–369. https://doi.org/10.2307/449222

Holder, F., Mirza, S., Namson-Ngo-Lee, Carbone, J., & McKie, R. E. 2023. Climate obstruction and Facebook advertising: How a sample of climate obstruction organizations use social media to disseminate discourses of delay. *Climatic Change*, *176*, 16. https://doi.org/10.1007/s10584-023-03494-4

Hollon, M. F. (1999). Direct-to-consumer marketing of prescription drugs: Creating consumer demand. *JAMA*, *281*(4), 382–384. https://doi.org/10-1001/pubs.JAMA-ISSN-0098-7484-281-4-jcv80002

Holman, E. A., Garfin, D. R., & Silver, R. C. (2024). It matters what you see: Graphic media images of war and terror may amplify distress. *Proceedings of the National Academy of Sciences*, *121*(29), e2318465121. https://doi.org/10.1073/pnas.2318465121

Holmes, E. N. (2023, October 12). *Liability for algorithmic recommendations* (Report No. R47753). Congressional Research Service. https://crsreports.congress.gov/product/pdf/R/R47753

Holt, L. F., Kjærvik, S. L., & Bushman, B. J. (2022). Harming and shaming through naming: Examining why calling the Coronavirus the "COVID-19 Virus," not the "Chinese Virus," matters. *Media Psychology*, *25*(5), 639–652. https://doi.org/10.1080/15213269.2022.2034021

Hornik, R., Woko, C., Siegel, L., KIm, K., Kikut, A., Jesch, E., & Clark, D. (2020). What beliefs are associated with COVID vaccination intentions? Implications for campaign planning. *PsyArXiv Preprints*. https://doi.org/10.31234/osf.io/t3kyx

Houn, F., Bober, M. A., Huerta, E. E., Hursting, S. D., Lemon, S., & Weed, D. L. (1995). The association between alcohol and breast cancer: Popular press coverage of research. *American Journal of Public Health*, *85*(8, pt. 1), 1082–1086. https://doi.org/10.2105/ajph.85.8_pt_1.1082

Hua, Y., Horta Ribeiro, M., Ristenpart, T., West, R., & Naaman, M. (2022). Characterizing alternative monetization strategies on YouTube. In *Proceedings of the ACM on Human-Computer Interaction*, *6*(CSCW2). https://doi.org/10.48550/arXiv.2203.10143

Hughes, B., Miller-Idriss, C., Piltch-Loeb, R., Goldberg, B., White, K., Criezis, M., & Savoia, E. (2021). Development of a codebook of online anti-vaccination rhetoric to manage COVID-19 vaccine misinformation. *International Journal of Environmental Research and Public Health*, *18*(14), 7556. https://doi.org/10.3390/ijerph18147556

Hughes, H. C., & Waismel-Manor, I. (2021). The Macedonian fake news industry and the 2016 US election. *Political Science & Politics*, *54*(1), 19–23. https://doi.org/10.1017/S1049096520000992

Hyland, K., & Jiang, F. (2021). 'Our striking results demonstrate ...': Persuasion and the growth of academic hype. *Journal of Pragmatics*, *182*, 189–202. https://doi.org/10.1016/j.pragma.2021.06.018

Imhoff, R., & Lamberty, P. K. (2017). Too special to be duped: Need for uniqueness motivates conspiracy beliefs. *European Journal of Social Psychology*, *47*(6), 724–734. https://doi.org/10.1002/ejsp.2265

Institute of Medicine. (2003). *Unequal treatment: Confronting racial and ethnic disparities in health care*. The National Academies Press. https://doi.org/10.17226/12875

___. (2004). *Immunization safety review: Vaccines and autism*. National Academies Press. https://doi.org/10.17226/10997

Interactive Advertising Bureau. (2020, December). *Understanding brand safety & brand suitability in a contemporary media landscape*. https://www.iab.com/wp-content/uploads/2020/12/IAB_Brand_Safety_and_Suitability_Guide_2020-12.pdf

Ioannidis, J. P., Stuart, M. E., Brownlee, S., & Strite, S. A. (2017). How to survive the medical misinformation mess. *European Journal of Clinical Investigation*, *47*(11), 795–802. https://doi.org/10.1111/eci.12834

Iqbal, H. (2021, February 1). How the CIA's fake Hepatitis B vaccine program in Pakistan helped fuel vaccine distrust. *Vox*. https://www.vox.com/first-person/22256595/vaccine-covid-pakistan-cia-program

Irfan A., Bieniek-Tobasco A., & Golembeski C. (2021). Pandemic of racism: Public health implications of political misinformation. *Harvard Public Health Review*, *26*. https://doi.org/10.54111/0001/Z6

Iskiev, M. (2023). The way people search the web is changing: 4 stats marketers & SEOs should know. *HubSpot Data*. https://blog.hubspot.com/marketing/how-search-behaviors-are-changing

Iyengar, S., Lelkes, Y., Levendusky, M., Malhotra, N., & Westwood, S. J. (2019). The origins and consequences of affective polarization in the United States. *Annual Review of Political Science*, *22*, 129–146. https://doi.org/10.1146/annurev-polisci-051117-073034

Jaafar, M., Vafamansouri, R., Tareen, M., Kamel, D., Ayroso, V. C., Tareen, F., & Spielman, A. I. (2021). Elixirs of the past: Quackery, claims and cures - snake oil and Indian liniment. *Journal of the History of Dentistry*, *69*(3), 205–215.

Jacques, P. J., Dunlap, R. E., & Freeman, M. (2008). The organisation of denial: Conservative think tanks and environmental scepticism. *Environmental Politics*, *17*(3), 349–385. https://doi.org/10.1080/09644010802055576

Jain, A., Marshall, J., Buikema, A., Bancroft, T., Kelly, J. P., & Newschaffer, C. J. (2015). Autism occurrence by MMR vaccine status among US children with older siblings with and without autism. *JAMA*, *313*(15), 1534–1540. https://doi.org/10.1001/jama.2015.3077

Jaiswal, J., LoSchiavo, C., & Perlman, D. C. (2020). Disinformation, misinformation and inequality-driven mistrust in the time of COVID-19: Lessons unlearned from AIDS denialism. *AIDS and Behavior*, *24*, 2776–2780. https://doi.org/10.1007/s10461-020-02925-y

Jamison, A. M., Broniatowski, D. A., Dredze, M., Wood-Doughty, Z., Khan, D., & Quinn, S. C. (2019a). Vaccine-related advertising in the Facebook Ad Archive. *Vaccine*, *38*(3), 512–520. https://doi.org/10.1016/j.vaccine.2019.10.066

Jamison, A. M., Quinn, S. C., & Freimuth, V. S. (2019b). "You don't trust a government vaccine": Narratives of institutional trust and influenza vaccination among African American and white adults. *Social Science & Medicine*, *221*, 87–94. https://doi.org/https://doi.org/10.1016/j.socscimed.2018.12.020

Jang, S. M. (2014). Seeking congruency or incongruency online? Examining selective exposure to four controversial science issues. *Science Communication*, *36*(2), 143–167. https://doi.org/10.1177/107554701350273

Jenke, L. (2023). Affective polarization and misinformation belief. *Political Behavior*, *46*, 825–884. https://doi.org/10.1007/s11109-022-09851-w

Jhaver, S., Boylston, C., Yang, D., & Bruckman, A. (2021). Evaluating the effectiveness of deplatforming as a moderation strategy on Twitter. In *Proceedings of the ACM on Human-Computer Interaction*, *5*(CSCW2), Article 381. https://doi.org/10.1145/3479525

Joelving, F. (2023, October 6). Signs of undeclared ChatGPT use in papers mounting. *Retraction Watch*. https://retractionwatch.com/2023/10/06/signs-of-undeclared-chatgpt-use-in-papers-mounting/

Johansen, N., Marjanovic, S. V., Kjaer, C. V., Baglini, R. B., & Adler-Nissen, R. (2022). Ridiculing the "tinfoil hats:" Citizen responses to COVID-19 misinformation in the Danish facemask debate on Twitter. *Harvard Misinformation Review*, *3*(2). https://doi.org/10.37016/mr-2020-93

Johnson, C., & Marcellino, W. (2021). *Bad actors in news reporting: tracking news manipulation by state actors*. RAND Corporation. https://www.rand.org/pubs/research_reports/RRA112-21.html

Johnson, M. K., Hashtroudi, S., & Lindsay, D. S. (1993). Source monitoring. *Psychological Bulletin*, *114*(1), 3–28. https://doi.org/10.1037/0033-2909.114.1.3

Johnson, N. F., Leahy, R., Restrepo, N. J., Velasquez, N., Zheng, M., Manrique, P., Devkota, P., & Wuchty, S. (2019). Hidden resilience and adaptive dynamics of the global online hate ecology. *Nature*, *573*, 261–265. https://doi.org/10.1038/s41586-019-1494-7

Johnson, N. F., Velásquez, N., Restrepo, N. J., Leahy, R., Gabriel, N., El Oud, S., Zheng, M., Manrique, P., Wuchty, S., & Lupu, Y. (2020). The online competition between pro- and anti-vaccination views. *Nature*, *582*(7811), 230–233. https://doi.org/10.1038/s41586-020-2281-1

Johnson, S. (1773). Misinformation, n.s. In *A dictionary of the English language*. https://johnsonsdictionaryonline.com/1773/misinformation_ns

Johnson, S. B., Park, H. S., Gross, C. P., & Yu, J. B. (2018). Use of alternative medicine for cancer and its impact on survival. *Journal of the National Cancer Institute*, *110*(1), 121–124. https://doi.org/10.1093/jnci/djx145

Johnson, S. B., Parsons, M., Dorff, T., Moran, M. S., Ward, J. H., Cohen, S. A., Akerley, W., Bauman, J., Hubbard, J., Spratt, D. E., Bylund, C. L., Swire-Thompson, B., Onega, T., Scherer, L. D., Tward, J., & Fagerlin, A. (2022). Cancer misinformation and harmful information on Facebook and other social media: A brief report. *Journal of the National Cancer Institute*, *114*(7), 1036–1039. https://doi.org/10.1093/jnci/djab141

Johnson, T. (2023). Cable news ratings 2023: Fox News dominates, but MSNBC is only major network with year-over-year audience growth. *Deadline*. https://deadline.com/2023/12/cable-news-ratings-2023-1235682966/

Johnston, K. L. (2021, April 21). Vietnamese Americans say their parents are falling for videos pushing COVID misinformation. *BuzzFeed News*. https://www.buzzfeednews.com/article/katejohnston2/vietnamese-american-youtube-misinformation-covid-vaccine

Jolley, D., & Douglas, K. M. (2014). The effects of anti-vaccine conspiracy theories on vaccination intentions. *PLoS One*, *9*(2), e89177. https://doi.org/10.1371/journal.pone.0089177

___. (2017). Prevention is better than cure: Addressing anti-vaccine conspiracy theories. *Journal of Applied Social Psychology*, *47*(8), 459–469. https://doi.org/10.1111/jasp.12453

Jolley, D., & Paterson, J. L. (2020). Pylons ablaze: Examining the role of 5G COVID-19 conspiracy beliefs and support for violence. *British Journal of Social Psychology*, *59*(3), 628–640. https://doi.org/10.1111/bjso.12394

Jones, D. (2024, February 12). How journals are fighting back against a wave of questionable images. *Nature News Explainer*. https://doi.org/10.1038/d41586-024-00372-6

Joshi, G., Srivastava, A., Yagnik, B., Hasan, M., Saiyed, Z., Gabralla, L. A., Abraham, A., Walambe, R., & Kotecha, K. (2023). Explainable misinformation detection across multiple social media platforms. *IEEE Access*, *11*, 23634–23646. https://doi.org/10.1109/ACCESS.2023.3251892

Jost, J. T., Baldassarri, D. S., & Druckman, J. N. (2022). Cognitive–motivational mechanisms of political polarization in social-communicative contexts. *Nature Reviews Psychology*, *1*(10), 560–576. https://doi.org/10.1038/s44159-022-00093-5

Judge, M., Kashima, Y., Steg, L., & Dietz, T. (2023). Environmental decision-making in times of polarization. *Annual Review of Environment and Resources*, *48*(1), 477–503. https://doi.org/https://doi.org/10.1146/annurev-environ-112321-115339

Jurecic, Q. (2023, March 23). The professional price of falsehoods. *Knight First Amendment Institute at Columbia University*. https://knightcolumbia.org/content/the-professional-price-of-falsehoods

Kahan, D. M., Peters, E., Wittlin, M., Slovic, P., Ouellette, L. L., Braman, D., & Mandel, G. (2012). The polarizing impact of science literacy and numeracy on perceived climate change risks. *Nature Climate Change*, *2*, 732–735. https://doi.org/10.1038/nclimate1547

Kalichman, S. C., Eaton, L. A., Earnshaw, V. A., & Brousseau, N. (2022). Faster than warp speed: Early attention to COVD-19 by anti-vaccine groups on Facebook. *Journal of Public Health*, *44*(1), e96–e105. https://doi.org/10.1093/pubmed/fdab093

Kata, A. (2010). A postmodern Pandora's box: Anti-vaccination misinformation on the Internet. *Vaccine*, *28*(7), 1709–1716. https://doi.org/10.1016/j.vaccine.2009.12.022

___. (2012). Anti-vaccine activists, Web 2.0, and the postmodern paradigm–An overview of tactics and tropes used online by the anti-vaccination movement. *Vaccine*, *30*(25), 3778–3789. https://doi.org/10.1016/j.vaccine.2011.11.112

Katz, A. J. (2023, January 3). These are the top-rated cable news shows of 2022. *TVNewser*. https://www.adweek.com/tvnewser/these-are-the-top-rated-cable-news-shows-of-2022/521247/#

Kauanui, J. K. (2008). *Hawaiian blood: Colonialism and the politics of sovereignty and indigeneity*. Duke University Press. https://doi.org/10.2307/j.ctv120qr70

Kavanagh, J., & Rich, M. D. (2018, January). *Truth decay: An initial exploration of the diminishing role of facts and analysis in American public life*. RAND Corporation. https://doi.org/10.7249/RR2314

Kearns, C. E., Schmidt, L. A., & Glantz, S. A. (2016). Sugar industry and coronary heart disease research: A historical analysis of internal industry documents. *JAMA Internal Medicine*, *176*(11), 1680–1685. https://doi.org/10.1001/jamainternmed.2016.5394

Keene Woods, N., Ali, U., Medina, M., Reyes, J., & Chesser, A. K. (2023). Health literacy, health outcomes and equity: A trend analysis based on a population survey. *Journal of Primary Care & Community Health*, *14*. https://doi.org/10.1177/21501319231156132

Kemp, E., Trigg, J., Beatty, L., Christensen, C., Dhillon, H. M., Maeder, A., Williams, P. A. H., & Koczwara, B. (2021). Health literacy, digital health literacy and the implementation of digital health technologies in cancer care: The need for a strategic approach. *Health Promotion Journal of Australia*, *32*(S1), 104–114. https://doi.org/https://doi.org/10.1002/hpja.387

Kendeou, P., Butterfuss, R., Kim, J., & Van Boekel, M. (2019). Knowledge revision through the lenses of the three-pronged approach. *Memory & Cognition*, *47*, 33–46. https://doi.org/10.3758/s13421-018-0848-y

Kendeou, P., Smith, E. R., & O'Brien, E. J. (2013). Updating during reading comprehension: Why causality matters. *Journal of Experimental Psychology: Learning, Memory, and Cognition*, *39*(3), 854–865. https://doi.org/10.1037/a0029468

Khan, Y. H., Mallhi, T. H., Alotaibi, N. H., Alzarea, A. I., Alanazi, A. S., Tanveer, N., & Hashmi, F. K. (2020). Threat of COVID-19 vaccine hesitancy in Pakistan: The need for measures to neutralize misleading narratives. *The American Journal of Tropical Medicine and Hygiene*, *103*(2), 603–604. https://doi.org/10.4269/ajtmh.20-0654

Kharazian, Z., Jalbert, M., Dash, S., Memon, S. A., Starbird, K., Spiro, E. S., & West, J. D. (2024, January 24). Our field was built on decades-old bodies of research across a range of disciplines. It wasn't invented by a 'class of misinformation experts' in 2016. *University of Washington Center for an Informed Public*. https://www.cip.uw.edu/2024/01/24/misinformation-field-research/

Kim, E., Shepherd, M. E., & Clinton, J. D. (2020a). The effect of big-city news on rural America during the COVID-19 pandemic. *Proceedings of the National Academy of Sciences*, *117*(36), 22009–22014. https://doi.org/ 10.1073/pnas.2009384117

Kim, J. J., Um, R. S., Lee, J. W., & Ajilore, O. (2024). Generative AI can fabricate advanced scientific visualizations: ethical implications and strategic mitigation framework. *AI and Ethics*, 1–13. https://doi.org/10.1007/s43681-024-00439-0

Kim, J. W., & Kim, E. (2019). Identifying the effect of political rumor diffusion using variations in survey timing. *Quarterly Journal of Political Science*, *14*(3), 293–311. http://dx.doi.org/10.2139/ssrn.3133334

Kim, J. Y., & Kesari, A. (2021). Misinformation and hate speech: The case of anti-Asian hate speech during the COVID-19 pandemic. *Journal of Online Trust and Safety*, *1*(1). https://doi.org/10.54501/jots.v1i1.13

Kim, S., Yalcin, O. F., Bestvater, S. E., Munger, K., Monroe, B. L., & Desmarais, B. A. (2020b, May). The effects of an informational intervention on attention to anti-vaccination content on YouTube. In *Proceedings of the International AAAI Conference on Web and Social Media*, *14*(1), 949–953. https://doi.org/10.1609/icwsm.v14i1.7364

Kim, S. A. (2017). Social media algorithms: Why you see what you see. *Georgetown Law Technology Review*, *2*(1), 147–154. https://perma.cc/J3LD-DX2

Kim, S. J. (2016). A repertoire approach to cross-platform media use behavior. *New Media & Society*, *18*(3), 353–372. https://doi.org/10.1177/1461444814543162

King, G., & Persily, N. (2020). A new model for industry–academic partnerships. *Political Science & Politics*, *53*(4), 703–709. https://doi.org/10.1017/S1049096519001021

Kington, R. S., Arnesen, S., Chou, W.-Y. S., Curry, S. J., Lazer, D., & Villarruel, A. M. (2021). Identifying credible sources of health information in social media: Principles and attributes (Discussion Paper). *NAM Perspectives*. National Academy of Medicine. https://doi.org/10.31478/202107a

Kirby, D. A. (2013). Forensic fictions: Science, television production, and modern storytelling. *Studies in History and Philosophy of Science Part C: Studies in History and Philosophy of Biological and Biomedical Sciences*, *44*(1), 92–102. https://doi.org/10.1016/j.shpsc.2012.09.007

___. (2017). The changing popular images of science. In K. H. Jamieson, D. Kahan, & D. A. Scheufele (Eds.), *The Oxford handbook of the science of science communication* (pp. 291–300). Oxford University Press.

Klinenberg, D. (2024). Does deplatforming work? *Journal of Conflict Resolution*, *68*(6), 1199–1225. https://doi.org/10.1177/00220027231188909

Klitzman, R. (2022). Needs to address clinicians' moral distress in treating unvaccinated COVID-19 patients. *BMC Medical Ethics*, *23*, 110. https://doi.org/10.1186/s12910-022-00859-9

Knudsen, J., Perlman-Gabel, M., Uccelli, I. G., Jeavons, J., & Chokshi, D. A. (2023). Combating misinformation as a core function of public health. *NEJM Catalyst*, *4*(2), CAT.22.0198. https://doi.org/doi:10.1056/CAT.22.0198

Koehler, D. J. (2016). Can journalistic "false balance" distort public perception of consensus in expert opinion? *Journal of Experimental Psychology: Applied, 22*(1), 24–38. https://doi.org/10.1037/xap0000073

Kolis, J., Brookmeyer, K., Chuvileva, Y., Voegeli, C., Juma, S., Ishizumi, A., Renfro, K., Wilhelm, E., Tice, H., Fogarty, H., Kocer, I., Helms, J., & Verma, A. (2024). Infodemics and vaccine confidence: protocol for social listening and insight generation to inform action. *JMIR Public Health and Surveillance, 10,* e51909. https://doi.org/10.2196/51909

Kopans, D. B. (2024). More than a half century of misinformation about breast cancer screening. *Radiologic Clinics of North America*, *62*(6), 993–1002. https://doi.org/10.1016/j.rcl.2024.04.001

Korin, M. R., Araya, F., Idris, M. Y., Brown, H., & Claudio, L. (2022). Community-based organizations as effective partners in the battle against misinformation. *Frontiers in Public Health*, *10*, 853736. https://doi.org/10.3389/fpubh.2022.853736

Korownyk, C., Kolber, M. R., McCormack, J., Lam, V., Overbo, K., Cotton, C., Finley, C., Turgeon, R. D., Garrison, S., Lindblad, A. J., Banh, H. L., Campbell-Scherer, D., Vandermeer, B., & Allan, G. M. (2014). Televised medical talk shows—What they recommend and the evidence to support their recommendations: A prospective observational study. *British Medical Journal*, *349*, g7346. https://doi.org/10.1136/bmj.g7346

Kowalski, P., & Taylor, A. K. (2017). Reducing students' misconceptions with refutational teaching: For long-term retention, comprehension matters. *Scholarship of Teaching and Learning in Psychology*, *3*(2), 90–100. https://doi.org/10.1037/stl0000082

Kozyreva, A., Lorenz-Spreen, P., Herzog, S. M., Ecker, U. K. H., Lewandowsky, S., Hertwig, R., Ali, A., Bak-Coleman, J., Barzilai, S., Basol, M., Berinsky, A. J., Betsch, C., Cook, J., Fazio, L. K., Geers, M., Guess, A. M., Huang, H., Larreguy, H., Maertens, R., Panizza, F., ... Wineburg, S. (2024). Toolbox of individual-level interventions against online misinformation. *Nature Human Behaviour*, *8*(6), 1044–1052. https://doi.org/10.1038/s41562-024-01881-0

Krafft, P., & Donovan, J. M. (2020). Disinformation by design: The use of evidence collages and platform filtering in a media manipulation campaign. *Political Communication*, *37*(2), 194–214. https://doi.org/10.1080/10584609.2019.1686094

Krause, N. M., Brossard, D., Scheufele, D. A., Xenos, M. A., & Franke, K. (2019). Trends: Americans' trust in science and scientists. *Public Opinion Quarterly*, *83*(4), 817–836. https://doi.org/10.1093/poq/nfz041

Krause, N. M., Freiling, I., Beets, B., & Brossard, D. (2020). Fact-checking as risk communication: The multi-layered risk of misinformation in times of COVID-19. *Journal of Risk Research*, *23*(7–8), 1052–1059. https://doi.org/10.1080/13669877.2020.1756385

Krause, N. M., Freiling, I., & Scheufele, D. A. (2022). The "infodemic" infodemic: Toward a more nuanced understanding of truth-claims and the need for (not) combatting misinformation. *The ANNALS of the American Academy of Political and Social Science*, *700*(1), 112–123. https://doi.org/10.1177/00027162221086263

Kreps, S., McCain, R. M., & Brundage, M. (2022). All the news that's fit to fabricate: AI-generated text as a tool of media misinformation. *Journal of Experimental Political Science*, *9*(1), 104–117. https://doi.org/10.1017/XPS.2020.37

Kriebel, D., Tickner, J., Epstein, P., Lemons, J., Levins, R., Loechler, E. L., Quinn, M., Rudel, R., Schettler, T., & Stoto, M. (2001). The precautionary principle in environmental science. *Environmental Health Perspectives*, *109*(9), 871–876. https://doi.org/10.1289/ehp.01109871

Kümpel, A. S. (2020). The Matthew Effect in social media news use: Assessing inequalities in news exposure and news engagement on social network sites (SNS). *Journalism*, *21*(8), 1083–1098. https://doi.org/10.1177/1464884920915374

Kunda, Z. (1990). The case for motivated reasoning. *Psychological Bulletin*, *108*(3), 480–498. https://doi.org/10.1037/0033-2909.108.3.480

Kuo, R., & Marwick, A. (2021). Critical disinformation studies: History, power, and politics. *Harvard Kennedy School Misinformation Review*, 2(4), 1–11. https://doi.org/10.37016/mr-2020-76

Kwon, J., Pelletiers, W., Galloway Peña, J., van Duin, D., Ledbetter, L., Baum, K., Ruffin, F., Knisely, J. M., Bizzell, E., Fowler Jr., V. G., Chambers, H. F., & Pettigrew, M. M. (2024). Participant diversity in United States randomized controlled trials of antibacterials for Staphylococcus aureus infections, 2000-2021. *Clinical Infectious Disease: An Official Publication of The Infectious Diseases Society of America*, *79*(1), 141–147. https://doi.org/10.1093/cid/ciae049

Lai, K., Xiong, X., Jiang, X., Sun, M., & He, L. (2020). Who falls for rumor? Influence of personality traits on false rumor belief. *Personality and Individual Differences*, *152*, 109520. https://doi.org/10.1016/j.paid.2019.109520

Lai, W. Y. Y., & Lane, T. (2009). Characteristics of medical research news reported on front pages of newspapers. *PLoS One*, *4*(7), e6103. https://doi.org/10.1371/journal.pone.0006103

Landrum, A. R., Olshansky, A., & Richards, O. (2021). Differential susceptibility to misleading flat Earth arguments on YouTube. *Media Psychology*, *24*(1), 136–165. https://doi.org/10.1080/15213269.2019.1669461

Lantian, A., Muller, D., Nurra, C., & Douglas, K. M. (2017). "I know things they don't know!": The role of need for uniqueness in belief in conspiracy theories. *Social Psychology*, *48*(3), 160–173. https://doi.org/10.1027/1864-9335/a000306

Larson, H. J., & Broniatowski, D. A. (2021). Why debunking misinformation is not enough to change people's minds about vaccines. *American Journal of Public Health*, *111*(6), 1058–1060. https://doi.org/10.2105/AJPH.2021.306293

Larson, H. J., Cooper, L. Z., Eskola, J., Katz, S. L., & Ratzan, S. (2011). Addressing the vaccine confidence gap. *The Lancet*, *378*(9790), 526–535. https://doi.org/10.1016/S0140-6736(11)60678-8

Latapí Agudelo, M. A., Jóhannsdóttir, L., & Davídsdóttir, B. (2019). A literature review of the history and evolution of corporate social responsibility. *International Journal of Corporate Social Responsibility*, *4*(1), 1–23. https://doi.org/10.1186/s40991-018-0039-y

Latkin, C. A., Dayton, L., Strickland, J. C., Colon, B., Rimal, R., & Boodram, B. (2020). An assessment of the rapid decline of trust in US sources of public information about COVID-19. *Journal of Health Communication*, *25*(10), 764–773. https://doi.org/10.1080/10810730.2020.1865487

Lazer, D. (2020). Studying human attention on the Internet. *Proceedings of the National Academy of Sciences*, *117*(1), 21–22. https://doi.org/10.1073/pnas.1919348117

Lazer, D., Baum, M. A., Benkler, Y., Berinsky, A. J., Greenhill, K. M., Menczer, F., Metzger, M. J., Nyhan, B., Pennycook, G., Rothschild, D., Schudson, M., Sloman, S. A., Sunstein, C. R., Thorson, E. A., Watts, D. J., & Zittrain, J. L. (2018). The science of fake news. *Science*, *359*(6380), 1094–1096. https://doi.org/10.1126/science.aao2998

Lazer, D., Ruck, D. J., Quintana, A., Shugars, S., Joseph, K., Grinberg, N., Gallagher, R. J., Horan, L., Gitomer, A., Bajak, A., Baum, M. A., Ognyanova, K., Qu, H., Hobbs, W. R., McCabe, S., & Green, J. (2020, October). *COVID-19 fake news on Twitter. The state of the nation: A 5-state COVID-19 survey* (Report No. 18). The COVID States Project. https://www.covidstates.org/reports/covid-19-fake-news-on-twitter

Leder, J., Schellinger, L., Maertens, R., Chryst, B., Linden, S., & Roozenbeek, J. (2023, September 24). Feedback exercises boost discernment and longevity for gamified misinformation interventions. *Journal of Experimental Psychology: General*, *153*(8), 2068–2087. https://doi.org/10.1037/xge0001603

Ledford, H. (2023). Researchers scramble as Twitter plans to end free data access. *Nature*, *614*, 602–603. https://doi.org/10.1038/d41586-023-00460-z

Lee, A. Y., Moore, R. C., & Hancock, J. T. (2023, February 7). Designing misinformation interventions for all: Perspectives from AAPI, Black, Latino, and Native American community leaders on misinformation educational efforts. *Harvard Kennedy School Misinformation Review*, *4*(1), 1–16. https://doi.org/10.37016/mr-2020-111

Lee, C., Yang, T., Inchoco, G. D., Jones, G. M., & Satyanarayan, A. (2021). Viral visualizations: How Coronavirus skeptics use orthodox data practices to promote unorthodox science online. In *Proceedings of the 2021 CHI Conference on Human Factors in Computing Systems*, Article 607. https://doi.org/10.1145/3411764.3445211

Lee, D. (2019, July 8). Instagram now asks bullies: "Are you sure?" *BBC*. https://www.bbc.com/news/technology-48916828

Lee, E. W. J., & Viswanath, K. (2020). Big data in context: Addressing the twin perils of data absenteeism and chauvinism in the context of health disparities research. *Journal of Medical Internet Research*, *22*(1), e16377. https://doi.org/10.2196/16377

Legg, T., Hatchard, J., & Gilmore, A. B. (2021). The science for profit model—how and why corporations influence science and the use of science in policy and practice. *PLoS One*, *16*(6), e0253272. https://doi.org/10.1371/journal.pone.0253272

Lemaitre, T., Carrier, N., Farrands, A., Gosselin, V., Petit, G., & Gagneur, A. (2019). Impact of a vaccination promotion intervention using motivational interview techniques on long-term vaccine coverage: The PromoVac strategy. *Human Vaccines & Immunotherapeutics*, *15*(3), 732–739. https://doi.org/10.1080/21645515.2018.1549451

Leo, C. G., Sabina, S., Tumolo, M. R., Bodini, A., Ponzini, G., Sabato, E., & Mincarone, P. (2021). Burnout among healthcare workers in the COVID 19 era: A review of the existing literature. *Frontiers in Public Health*, *9*, 750529. https://doi.org/10.3389/fpubh.2021.750529

Levendusky, M. (2013). *How partisan media polarize America*. University of Chicago Press.

Levinson-Waldman, R. (2011). *Academic freedom and the public's right to know: How to counter the chilling effect of FOIA requests on scholarship* [Issue Brief]. American Constitution Society for Law and Policy. https://www.acslaw.org/wp-content/uploads/2018/04/Levinson_-_ACS_FOIA_First_Amdmt_Issue_Brief_1.pdf

Levy, J., Bayes, R., Bolsen, T., & Druckman, J. N. (2021). Science and the politics of misinformation. In H. Tumber & S. Waisbord (Eds.), *The Routledge companion to media disinformation and populism* (pp. 231–241). Routledge. https://doi.org/10.4324/9781003004431

Lewandowsky, S. (2021a). Climate change disinformation and how to combat it. *Annual Review of Public Health*, *42*, 1–21. https://doi.org/https://doi.org/10.1146/annurev-publhealth-090419-102409

___. (2021b). Liberty and the pursuit of science denial. *Current Opinion in Behavioral Sciences*, *42*, 65–69. https://doi.org/10.1016/j.cobeha.2021.02.024

___. (2022). Fake news and participatory propaganda. In R. Pohl (Ed.), *Cognitive illusions* (pp. 324–340). Routledge. https://doi.org/10.4324/9781003154730-23

Lewandowsky, S., Cook, J., Ecker, U., Albarracín, D., Kendeou, P., Newman, E., Pennycook, G., Porter, E., Rand, D., Rapp, D., Reifler, J., Roozenbeek, J., Schmid, P., Seifert, C., Sinatra, G., Swire-Thompson, B., van der Linden, S., Wood, T., & Zaragoza, M. (2020). *The debunking handbook 2020*. Skeptical Science. https://skepticalscience.com/docs/DebunkingHandbook2020.pdf

Lewandowsky, S., Ecker, U. K. H., & Cook, J. (2017). Beyond misinformation: Understanding and coping with the "post-truth" era. *Journal of Applied Research in Memory and Cognition*, *6*(4), 353–369. https://doi.org/10.1016/j.jarmac.2017.07.008

Lewandowsky, S., Ecker, U. K. H., Cook, J., van der Linden, S., Roozenbeek, J., & Oreskes, N. (2023). Misinformation and the epistemic integrity of democracy. *Current Opinion in Psychology*, *54*, 101711. https://doi.org/10.1016/j.copsyc.2023.101711

Lewandowsky, S., Ecker, U. K., Seifert, C. M., Schwarz, N., & Cook, J. (2012). Misinformation and its correction: Continued influence and successful debiasing. *Psychological Science in the Public Interest*, *13*(3), 106–131. http://www.jstor.org/stable/23484653

Lewandowsky, S., & Oberauer, K. (2016). Motivated rejection of science. *Current Directions in Psychological Science*, *25*(4), 217–222. https://doi.org/10.1177/0963721416654436

Lewandowsky, S., Oreskes, N., Risbey, J. S., Newell, B. R., & Smithson, M. (2015). Seepage: Climate change denial and its effect on the scientific community. *Global Environmental Change*, *33*, 1–13. https://doi.org/10.1016/j.gloenvcha.2015.02.013

Lewandowsky, S., & van der Linden, S. (2021). Countering misinformation and fake news through inoculation and prebunking. *European Review of Social Psychology*, *32*(2), 348–384. https://doi.org/10.1080/10463283.2021.1876983

Lewandowsky, S., & Whitmarsh, L. (2018). Climate communication for biologists: When a picture can tell a thousand words. *PLoS Biology*, *16*(10), e2006004. https://doi.org/10.1371/journal.pbio.2006004

Li, A., Deyrup, A. T., Graves, J. L., & Ross, L. F. (2022a). Race in the reading: A study of problematic uses of race and ethnicity in a prominent pediatrics textbook. *Academic Medicine, 97,* 1521–1527.

Li, H.O-Y., Bailey, A., Huynh, D., & Chan, J. (2020). YouTube as a source of information on COVID-19: A pandemic of misinformation? *BMJ Global Health*, *5*(5), e002604. https://doi.org/10.1136/bmjgh-2020-002604

Li, H.O-Y., Pastukhova, E., Brandts-Longtin, O., Tan, M. G., & Kirchhof, M. G. (2022b). YouTube as a source of misinformation on COVID-19 vaccination: A systematic analysis. *BMJ Global Health*, *7*(3), e008334. https://doi.org/10.1136/bmjgh-2021-008334

Liang, W., Zhang, Y., Wu, Z., Lepp, H., Ji, W., Zhao, X.,Cho, H., Liiu, S., He, S., Huang, Z., Yang, D., Potts, C., Manning, C. D., & Zou, J. Y. (2024). Mapping the increasing use of LLMs in scientific papers. *arXiv*. https://doi.org/10.48550/arXiv.2404.01268

Liedke, J., & Gottfried, J. (2022). U.S. adults under 30 now trust information from social media almost as much as from national news outlets. *Pew Research Center*. https://www.pewresearch.org/short-reads/2022/10/27/u-s-adults-under-30-now-trust-information-from-social-media-almost-as-much-as-from-national-news-outlets/

Light, N., Fernbach, P. M., Rabb, N., Geana, M. V., & Sloman, S. A. (2022). Knowledge overconfidence is associated with anti-consensus views on controversial scientific issues. *Science Advances*, *8*(29), eabo0038. https://doi.org/10.1126/sciadv.abo0038

Lim, G., & Donovan, J. (2020). Detect, document, and debunk: Studying media manipulation and disinformation. In D. A. Rohlinger & S. Sobieraj (Eds.), *The Oxford handbook of digital media sociology*. Oxford University Press. https://doi.org/10.1093/oxfordhb/9780197510636.013.44

Livingstone, S. (2011). Media literacy for all? On the intellectual and political challenges of implementing media literacy policy. In S. Livingstone (Ed.), *Media literacy: Ambitions, policies and measures* (pp. 31–35). European Commission in Science and Technology. http://eprints.lse.ac.uk/id/eprint/56879

Lloyd, D. R., Medina, D. J., Hawk, L. W., Fosco, W. D., & Richards, J. B. (2014). Habituation of reinforcer effectiveness. *Frontiers in Integrative Neuroscience*, 7, Article 107. https://doi.org/10.3389/fnint.2013.00107

Loomba, S., de Figueiredo, A., Piatek, S. J., de Graaf, K., & Larson, H. J. (2021). Measuring the impact of COVID-19 vaccine misinformation on vaccination intent in the UK and USA. *Nature Human Behaviour*, *5*, 337–348. https://doi.org/10.1038/s41562-021-01056-1

Lopez, L. K. (2021). *Micro media industries: Hmong American media innovation in the diaspora*. Rutgers University Press.

Lord, C. G., Ross, L., & Lepper, M. R. (1979). Biased assimilation and attitude polarization: The effects of prior theories on subsequently considered evidence. *Journal of Personality and Social Psychology*, *37*(11), 2098–2109. https://doi.org/10.1037/0022-3514.37.11.2098

Lorenz-Spreen, P., Lewandowsky, S., Sunstein, C. R., & Hertwig, R. (2020). How behavioural sciences can promote truth, autonomy and democratic discourse online. *Nature Human Behaviour*, *4*(11), 1102–1109.

Lorenz-Spreen, P., Mønsted, B. M., Hövel, P., & Lehmann, S. (2019). Accelerating dynamics of collective attention. *Nature Communications*, *10*, 1759. https://doi.org/10.1038/s41467-019-09311-w

Love, B., Himelboim, I., Holton, A., & Stewart, K. (2013). Twitter as a source of vaccination information: Content drivers and what they are saying. *American Journal of Infection Control*, *41*(6), 568–570. https://doi.org/10.1016/j.ajic.2012.10.016

Lu, C., Hu, B., Li, Q., Bi, C., & Ju, X. D. (2023). Psychological inoculation for credibility assessment, sharing intention, and discernment of misinformation: Systematic review and meta-analysis. *Journal of Medical Internet Research*, *25*, e49255. https://doi.org/10.2196/49255

Luhmann, N. (1979). *Trust and power*. John Wiley and Sons.

Lundahl, B., Moleni, T., Burke, B. L., Butters, R., Tollefson, D., Butler, C., & Rollnick, S. (2013). Motivational interviewing in medical care settings: A systematic review and meta-analysis of randomized controlled trials. *Patient Education and Counseling*, *93*(2), 157–168. https://doi.org/https://doi.org/10.1016/j.pec.2013.07.012

Luo, B., Lau, R. Y. K., Li, C., & Si, Y.-W. (2022). A critical review of state-of-the-art chatbot designs and applications. *Wiley Interdisciplinary Reviews: Data Mining and Knowledge Discovery*, *12*(1), e1434. https://doi.org/10.1002/widm.1434

Lupia, A. (2013). Communicating science in politicized environments. *Proceedings of the National Academy of Sciences*, *110*(Suppl 3), 14048–14054. https://doi.org/10.1073/pnas.1212726110

___. (2021). Practical and ethical reasons for pursuing a more open science. *Political Science & Politics*, *54*(2), 301–304. https://doi.org/10.1017/S1049096520000979

Lupia, A., Allison, D. B., Jamieson, K. H., Heimberg, J., Skipper, M., & Wolf, S. M. (2024). Trends in US public confidence in science and opportunities for progress. *Proceedings of the National Academy of Sciences*, *121*(11), e2319488121. https://doi.org/10.1073/pnas.2319488121

Luscombe, A., Dick, K., & Walby, K. (2022). Algorithmic thinking in the public interest: Navigating technical, legal, and ethical hurdles to web scraping in the social sciences. *Quality & Quantity*, *56*(3), 1023–1044. https://doi.org/10.1007/s11135-021-01164-0

Lynas, M., Adams, J., & Conrow, J. (2022). Misinformation in the media: Global coverage of GMOs 2019-2021. *GM Crops & Food*, 1–10. https://doi.org/10.1080/21645698.2022.2140568

Lyon, T. P., & Montgomery, A. W. (2015). The means and end of greenwash. *Organization & Environment*, *28*(2), 223–249. https://doi.org/10.1177/1086026615575332

Lyotard, J. F. (1984). *The postmodern condition: A report on knowledge*. University of Minnesota Press.

Maani, N., van Schalkwyk, M. C., Petticrew, M., & Buse, K. (2022). The pollution of health discourse and the need for effective counter-framing. *BMJ*, *377*, o1128. https://doi.org/10.1136/bmj.o1128

MacGregor, K. (2000, September 3). Conspiracy theories fuel row over AIDS crisis in South Africa. *Irish Independent*. https://www.independent.ie/world-news/conspiracy-theories-fuel-row-over-aids-crisis-in-south-africa-26108323.html

Mach, K. J., Salas Reyes, R., Pentz, B., Taylor, J., Costa, C. A., Cruz, S. G., Thomas, K. E., Arnott, J. C., Donald, R., Jagannathan, K., Kirchhoff, C. J., Rosella, L. C., & Klenk, N. (2021). News media coverage of COVID-19 public health and policy information. *Humanities and Social Sciences Communications*, *8*, 220. https://doi.org/10.1057/s41599-021-00900-z

Madiega, T. (2024, May 20). *Proposal for a regulation of the European Parliament and of the Council on a single market for digital services (Digital Services Act) and amending Directive 2000/31/EC*. Legislative Train Schedule, European Parliament. https://www.europarl.europa.eu/legislative-train/theme-a-europe-fit-for-the-digital-age/file-digital-services-act

Madrid-Morales, D., Wasserman, H., Gondwe, G., Ndlovu, K., Sikanku, E., Tully, M., Umejei, E., & Uzuegbunam, C. (2021). Motivations for sharing misinformation: A comparative study in six Sub-Saharan African countries. *International Journal of Communication*, *15*, 1200–1219. https://ijoc.org/index.php/ijoc/article/view/14801

Madsen, K. M., Hviid, A., Vestergaard, M., Schendel, D., Wohlfahrt, J., Thorsen, P., Olsen, J., & Melbye, M. (2002). A population-based study of measles, mumps, and rubella vaccination and autism. *New England Journal of Medicine*, *347*(19), 1477–1482. https://doi.org/10.1056/NEJMoa021134

Maertens, R., Anseel, F., & van der Linden, S. (2020). Combatting climate change misinformation: Evidence for longevity of inoculation and consensus messaging effects. *Journal of Environmental Psychology*, *70*, Article 101455. https://doi.org/10.1016/j.jenvp.2020.101455

Maertens, R., Roozenbeek, J., Basol, M., & van der Linden, S. (2021). Long-term effectiveness of inoculation against misinformation: Three longitudinal experiments. *Journal of Experimental Psychology: Applied*, *27*(1), 1–16. https://doi.org/10.1037/xap0000315

Májovský, M., Černý, M., Kasal, M., Komarc, M., & Netuka, D. (2023). Artificial intelligence can generate fraudulent but authentic-looking scientific medical articles: Pandora's box has been opened. *Journal of Medical Internet Research*, *25*, e46924. https://doi.org/10.2196/46924

Malhotra, P. (2023) Misinformation in WhatsApp family groups: Generational perceptions and correction considerations in a meso-news space, *Digital Journalism*, *12*(5), 594–612. https://doi.org/10.1080/21670811.2023.2213731

Malhotra, P., & Pearce, K. (2022). Facing falsehoods: Strategies for polite misinformation correction. *International Journal of Communication*, *16*(22), 2303–2324. https://ijoc.org/index.php/ijoc/article/view/18361

Malhotra P., Zhong, R., Kuan V., Panatula G., Weng M., Bras A., Sehat M. C., Roesner F., & Zhang, X. A. (2023). User experiences and needs when responding to misinformation on social media. *Harvard Kennedy School Misinformation Review*, *4*(6). https://doi.org/10.37016/mr-2020-129

Manheim, J. (2011). *Strategy in information and influence campaigns*. Routledge.

Marcon, A. R., Murdoch, B., & Caulfield, T. (2017). Fake news portrayals of stem cells and stem cell research. *Regenerative Medicine*, *12*(7), 765–775. https://doi.org/10.2217/rme-2017-0060

Maréchal, N., & Biddle, E. R. (2020). *It's not just the content, it's the business model: Democracy's online speech challenge*. New America Foundation. https://www.newamerica.org/oti/reports/its-not-just-content-its-business-model/

Maréchal, N., MacKinnon, R., Dheere, J. (2020). *Getting to the source of infodemics: It's the business model*. New America Foundation. https://www.newamerica.org/oti/reports/getting-to-the-source-of-infodemics-its-the-business-model/

Markel, H., & Stern, A. M. (2002). The foreignness of germs: The persistent association of immigrants and disease in American society. *The Milbank Quarterly*, *80*(4), 757–788. https://doi.org/10.1111/1468-0009.00030

Martel, C., Allen, J., Pennycook, G., & Rand, D. G. (2024). Crowds can effectively identify misinformation at scale. *Perspectives on Psychological Science*, *19*(2), 477–488. https://doi.org/10.1177/17456916231190388

Martinez-Bravo, M., & Stegmann, A. (2022). In vaccines we trust? The effects of the CIA's vaccine ruse on immunization in Pakistan. *Journal of the European Economic Association*, *20*(1), 150–186. https://doi.org/10.1093/jeea/jvab018

Marwick, A. E. (2018). Why do people share fake news? A sociotechnical model of media effects. *Georgetown Law Technology Review*, *2*, 474–512. https://georgetownlawtechreview.org/why-do-people-share-fake-news-a-sociotechnical-model-of-media-effects/GLTR-07-2018/

Marwick, A. E., & boyd, d. (2011). I tweet honestly, I tweet passionately: Twitter users, context collapse, and the imagined audience. *New Media & Society*, *13*(1), 114–133. https://doi.org/10.1177/1461444810365313

Marwick, A., & Lewis, R. (2017, May). *Media manipulation and disinformation online*. Data & Society. https://datasociety.net/library/media-manipulation-and-disinfo-online/

Mascaro, O., & Sperber, D. (2009). The moral, epistemic, and mindreading components of children's vigilance towards deception. *Cognition*, *112*(3), 367–380. https://doi.org/10.1016/j.cognition.2009.05.012

Masip, P., Suau, J., Ruiz-Caballero, C., Capilla, P., & Zilles, K. (2021). News engagement on closed platforms. Human factors and technological affordances influencing exposure to news on WhatsApp. *Digital Journalism*, *9*(8), 1062–1084. https://doi.org/10.1080/21670811.2021.1927778

Matsaganis, M. D., Katz, V. S., & Ball-Rokeach, S. J. (2011). *Understanding ethnic media: Producers, consumers, and societies*. SAGE Publications, Inc.

Mazzeo, V., Rapisarda, A., & Giuffrida, G. (2021). Detection of fake news on COVID-19 on web search engines. *Frontiers in Physics*, *9*, 685730. https://doi.org/10.3389/fphy.2021.685730

McAllister, L., Daly, M., Chandler, P., McNatt, M., Benham, A., & Boykoff, M. (2021). Balance as bias, resolute on the retreat? Updates & analyses of newspaper coverage in the United States, United Kingdom, New Zealand, Australia and Canada over the past 15 years. *Environmental Research Letters*, *16*(9), 094008. https://doi.org/10.1088/1748-9326/ac14eb

McCall, L. (2005). The complexity of intersectionality. *Signs: Journal of Women in Culture and Society*, *30*(3), 1771–1800. https://doi.org/10.1086/426800

McChesney, R. W. (2015). *Rich media, poor democracy: Communication politics in dubious times*. The New Press.

McClaran, N., & Rhodes, N. (2021). Portrayals of vaccination in entertainment television: A content analysis. *Health Communication*, *36*(10), 1242–1251. https://doi.org/10.1080/10410236.2020.1749356

McCright, A. M., Dentzman, K., Charters, M., & Dietz, T. (2013). The influence of political ideology on trust in science. *Environmental Research Letters*, *8*(4), 044029. https://doi.org/10.1088/1748-9326/8/4/044029

McCright, A. M., & Dunlap, R. E. (2000). Challenging global warming as a social problem: An analysis of the conservative movement's counter-claims. *Social Problems*, *47*(4), 499–522. https://doi.org/10.2307/3097132

___. (2003). Defeating Kyoto: The conservative movement's impact on US climate change policy. *Social Problems*, *50*(3), 348–373. https://doi.org/10.1525/sp.2003.50.3.348

McCulloch, J., & Tweedale, G. (2008). *Defending the indefensible: The global asbestos industry and its fight for survival*. Oxford University Press. https://doi.org/10.1093/oso/9780199534852.001.0001

McFadden, B. R., & Lusk, J. L. (2018). Effects of the national bioengineered food disclosure standard: Willingness to pay for labels that communicate the presence or absence of genetic modification. *Applied Economic Perspectives and Policy*, *40*(2), 259–275. https://doi.org/10.1093/aepp/ppx040

McGrew, S. (2020). Learning to evaluate: An intervention in civic online reasoning. *Computers & Education*, *145*, Article 103711. https://doi.org/10.1016/j.compedu.2019.103711

___. (2024). Teaching lateral reading: Interventions to help people read like fact checkers. *Current Opinion in Psychology*, *55*, 101737. https://doi.org/10.1016/j.copsyc.2023.101737

McGrew, S., Breakstone, J., Ortega, T., Smith, M., & Wineburg, S. (2018). Can students evaluate online sources? Learning from assessments of civic online reasoning. *Theory & Research in Social Education*, *48*(2), 165–193. https://doi.org/10.1080/00933104.2017.1416320

McKnight, D. (2010). A change in the climate? The journalism of opinion at News Corporation. *Journalism*, *11*(6), 693–706. https://doi.org/10.1177/1464884910379704

Meier, B. (2018). *Pain killer: An empire of deceit and the origin of America's opioid epidemic*. Random House.

Mejova, Y., & Kalimeri, K. (2020, June). COVID-19 on Facebook ads: Competing agendas around a public health crisis. In *Proceedings of the 3rd ACM SIGCAS Conference on Computing and Sustainable Societies* (pp. 22–31). Association for Computing Machinery. https://doi.org/10.1145/3378393.3402241

Mellor, F. (2009). The politics of accuracy in judging global warming films. *Environmental Communication*, *3*(2), 134–150. https://doi.org/10.1080/17524030902916574

Memmi, D. (2008). The nature of virtual communities. In S. Gill (Ed.), *Cognition, communication and interaction: Transdisciplinary perspectives on interactive technology* (pp. 70–82). Springer London. https://doi.org/10.1007/978-1-84628-927-9_5

Memon, S., & West, J. (2024, February 18). Search engines post-ChatGPT: How generative artificial intelligence could make search less reliable. *University of Washington Center for an Informed Public*. https://www.cip.uw.edu/2024/02/18/search-engines-chatgpt-generative-artificial-intelligence-less-reliable/

Mendoza, R. U., Dayrit, M. M., Alfonso, C. R., & Ong, M. M. A. (2021). Public trust and the COVID-19 vaccination campaign: Lessons from the Philippines as it emerges from the Dengvaxia controversy. *The International Journal of Health Planning and Management*, *36*(6), 2048–2055. https://doi.org/10.1002/hpm.3297

Merkley, E. (2020). Are experts (news) worthy? Balance, conflict, and mass media coverage of expert consensus. *Political Communication, 37*(4), 530–549. https://doi.org/10.1080/10584609.2020.1713269

Metz, R. (2021, August 6). How a deepfake Tom Cruise on TikTok turned into a very real AI company. *CNN Business*. https://www.cnn.com/2021/08/06/tech/tom-cruise-deepfake-tiktok-company/index.html.

Metzger, M. J., Flanagin, A. J., Mena, P., Jiang, S., & Wilson, C. (2021). From dark to light: The many shades of sharing misinformation online. *Media and Communication, 9*(1), 134–143. https://doi.org/10.17645/mac.v9i1.3409

Metzl, J. M., & Hansen, H. (2014). Structural competency: Theorizing a new medical engagement with stigma and inequality. *Social Science & Medicine, 103*, 126–133. https://doi.org/10.1016/j.socscimed.2013.06.032

Michaels, D. (2006). Manufactured uncertainty: Protecting public health in the age of contested science and product defense. *Annals of the New York Academy of Sciences, 1076*, 149–162.

___. (2008). *Doubt is their product: How industry's assault on science threatens your health*. Oxford University Press.

___. (2020). *The triumph of doubt: Dark money and the science of deception*. Oxford University Press.

Michaels, D., & Monforton, C. (2005). Manufacturing uncertainty: Contested science and the protection of the public's health and environment. *American Journal of Public Health, 95*(S1), S39–S48. https://doi.org/10.2105/AJPH.2004.043059

Millar, N., Batalo, B., & Budgell, B. (2022). Trends in the use of promotional language (hype) in abstracts of successful National Institutes of Health grant applications, 1985-2020. *JAMA Network Open, 5*(8), e2228676–e2228676. https://doi.org/10.1001/jamanetworkopen.2022.28676

Millar, N., Budgell, B., & Salager-Meyer, F. (2020). Hype in reports of clinical research: The authors' perspectives. *English for Specific Purposes, 60*, 53–64. https://doi.org/10.1016/j.esp.2020.07.001

Millar, N., Salager-Meyer, F., & Budgell, B. (2019). "It is important to reinforce the importance of…": 'Hype' in reports of randomized controlled trials. *English for Specific Purposes, 54*, 139–151. https://doi.org/10.1016/j.esp.2019.02.004

Miller, J. M. (2020). Psychological, political, and situational factors combine to boost COVID-19 conspiracy theory beliefs. *Canadian Journal of Political Science, 53*(2), 327–334. https://doi.org/10.1017/S000842392000058X

Miller, S., & Fahy, D. (2009). Can science communication workshops train scientists for reflexive public engagement?: The ESConet experience. *Science Communication, 31*(1), 116–126. https://doi.org/10.1177/1075547009339048

Miller, W. R., & Rollnick, S. (2023). *Motivational interviewing: Helping people change and grow* (4th ed.). Guilford Press.

Minnesota Department of Health. (2017). *Measles, 2017*. https://www.health.state.mn.us/diseases/reportable/dcn/sum17/measles.html

Minow, M. (2021). *Saving the news: Why the constitution calls for government action to preserve freedom of speech*. Oxford University Press.

Mitts, T., Pisharody, N., & Shapiro, J. (2022, June). Removal of anti-vaccine content impacts social media discourse. In *Proceedings of the 14th ACM Web Science Conference 2022* (pp. 319–326). https://doi.org/10.1145/3501247.3531548

Mnookin, S. (2012). *The panic virus: The true story behind the vaccine-autism controversy*. Simon and Schuster.

Modirrousta-Galian, A., & Higham, P. A. (2023). Gamified inoculation interventions do not improve discrimination between true and fake news: Reanalyzing existing research with receiver operating characteristic analysis. *Journal of Experimental Psychology: General, 152*(9), 2411–2437. https://doi.org/10.1037/xge0001395

Molteni, M. (2017, May 7). Anti-vaxxers brought their war to Minnesota—Then came measles. *Wired.* https://www.wired.com/2017/05/anti-vaxxers-brought-war-minnesota-came-measles/

Moore, R. C., & Hancock, J. T. (2022). A digital media literacy intervention for older adults improves resilience to fake news. *Scientific Reports, 12*(1), 6008. https://doi.org/10.1038/s41598-022-08437-0.

Moran, M. B., Lucas, M., Everhart, K., Morgan, A., & Prickett, E. (2016). What makes anti-vaccine websites persuasive? A content analysis of techniques used by anti-vaccine websites to engender anti-vaccine sentiment. *Journal of Communication in Healthcare, 9*(3), 151–163. https://doi.org/10.1080/17538068.2016.1235531

Moran, R. E., & Prochaska, S. (2023). Misinformation or activism?: Analyzing networked moral panic through an exploration of #SaveTheChildren. *Information, Communication & Society, 26*(16), 3197–3217. https://doi.org/10.1080/1369118X.2022.2146986

Moran, R. E., Swan, A. L., & Agajanian, T. (2024). Vaccine misinformation for profit: Conspiratorial wellness influencers and the monetization of alternative health. *International Journal of Communication, 18*, 1202–1224. https://ijoc.org/index.php/ijoc/article/view/21128/4494

Morosoli, S., Van Aelst, P., Humprecht, E., Staender, A., & Esser, F. (2022a). Identifying the drivers behind the dissemination of online misinformation: A study on political attitudes and individual characteristics in the context of engaging with misinformation on social media. *American Behavioral Scientist.* https://doi.org/10.1177/00027642221118300

Morosoli, S., Van Aelst, P., & Van Erkel, P. (2022b). To convince, to provoke or to entertain? A study on individual motivations behind engaging with conspiracy theories online. *Convergence, 28*(4), 1030–1059. https://doi.org/10.1177/13548565221105797

Morozov, E. (2013). *To save everything, click here: The folly of technological solutionism.* PublicAffairs.

Morrison, S. (2021, January 20). Facebook and Twitter made special world leader rules for Trump. What happens now? *Vox.* https://www.vox.com/recode/22233450/trump-twitter-facebook-ban-world-leader-rules-exception

Morrow, G., Swire-Thompson, B., Polny, J. M., Kopec, M., & Wihbey, J. P. (2022). The emerging science of content labeling: Contextualizing social media content moderation. *Journal of the Association for Information Science and Technology, 73*(10), 1365–1386. https://dx.doi.org/10.2139/ssrn.3742120

Motta, M. (2019). Explaining science funding attitudes in the United States: The case for science interest. *Public Understanding of Science, 28*(2), 161–176. https://doi.org/10.1177/0963662518795397

Motta, M., Callaghan, T., & Sylvester, S. (2018). Knowing less but presuming more: Dunning-Kruger effects and the endorsement of anti-vaccine policy attitudes. *Social Science & Medicine, 211*, 274–281. https://doi.org/10.1016/j.socscimed.2018.06.032

Motta, M., Hwang, J., & Stecula, D. (2023). What goes down must come up? Pandemic-related misinformation search behavior during an unplanned Facebook outage. *Health Communication, 39*(10), 2041–2052. https://doi.org/10.1080/10410236.2023.2254583

Motta, M., Stecula, D., & Farhart, C. (2020). How right-leaning media coverage of COVID-19 facilitated the spread of misinformation in the early stages of the pandemic in the US. *Canadian Journal of Political Science, 53*(2), 335–342. https://doi.org/10.1017/S0008423920000396

Muddiman, A., Budak, C., Murray, C., Kim, Y., & Stroud, N. J. (2022). Indexing theory during an emerging health crisis: How US TV news indexed elite perspectives and amplified COVID-19 misinformation. *Annals of the International Communication Association*, *46*(3), 174–204. https://doi.org/10.1080/23808985.2022.2120521

Muise, D., Hosseinmardi, H., Howland, B., Mobius, M., Rothschild, D., & Watts, D. J. (2022). Quantifying partisan news diets in Web and TV audiences. *Science Advances*, *8*(28), eabn0083. https://doi.org/10.1126/sciadv.abn0083

Mummolo, J. (2016). News from the other side: How topic relevance limits the prevalence of partisan selective exposure. *The Journal of Politics*, *78*(3), 763–773. https://doi.org/10.1086/685584

Munger, K. (2019). The limited value of non-replicable field experiments in contexts with low temporal validity. *Social Media + Society*, *5*(3). https://doi.org/10.1177/2056305119859294

Murdoch, B., Zarzeczny, A., & Caulfield, T. (2018). Exploiting science? A systematic analysis of complementary and alternative medicine clinic websites' marketing of stem cell therapies. *BMJ Open*, *8*, e019414. https://doi.org/10.1136/bmjopen-2017-019414

Murphy, G., de Saint Laurent, C., Reynolds, M., Aftab, O., Hegarty, K. Sun, Y. & Greene, C. M. (2023). What do we study when we study misinformation? A scoping review of experimental research (2016-2022). *Harvard Kennedy School Misinformation Review*, *4*(6). https://doi.org/10.37016/mr-2020-130

Murphy, G., & Greene, C. M. (2023). Conducting ethical misinformation research: Deception, dialogue, and debriefing. *Current Opinion in Psychology, 54*, Article 101713. https://doi.org/10.1016/j.copsyc.2023.101713

Murtfeldt, R., Alterman, N., Kahveci, I., & West, J. D. (2024). RIP Twitter API: A eulogy to its vast research contributions. *arXiv*. https://doi.org/10.48550/arXiv.2404.07340

Muvuka, B., Combs, R. M., Ayangeakaa, S. D., Ali, N. M., Wendel, M. L., & Jackson, T. (2020). Health literacy in African-American communities: Barriers and strategies. H*ealth Literacy Research and Practice*, *4*(3), e138–e143. https://doi.org/10.3928/24748307-20200617-01

Nagler, R. H., Fowler, E. F., & Gollust, S. E. (2015). Covering controversy: What are the implications for women's health? *Women's Health Issues*, *25*(4), 318–321. http://dx.doi.org/10.1016/j.whi.2015.04.011

Nagler, R. H., Gollust, S. E., Yzer, M. C., Vogel, R. I., & Rothman, A. J. (2023). Sustaining positive perceptions of science in the face of conflicting health information: An experimental test of messages about the process of scientific discovery. *Social Science & Medicine*, *334*, 116194. https://doi.org/10.1016/j.socscimed.2023.116194

Nagler, R. H., Ramanadhan, S., Minsky, S., & Viswanath, K. (2013). Recruitment and retention for community-based eHealth interventions with populations of low socioeconomic position: Strategies and challenges. *Journal of Communication*, *63*(1), 201–220. https://doi.org/10.1111/jcom.12008

Nam, H. H., & Sawyer, K. (2024). Scientific supremacy: How do genetic narratives relate to racism? *Politics and the Life Sciences*, *43*(1), 99–131. https://doi.org/10.1017/pls.2023.15

Nan, X., Wang, Y., & Thier, K. (2022). Why do people believe health misinformation and who is at risk? A systematic review of individual differences in susceptibility to health misinformation. *Social Science & Medicine*, *314*, 115398. https://doi.org/10.1016/j.socscimed.2022.115398

Napoli P. M. (2019). *Social media and the public interest: Media regulation in the disinformation age*. Columbia University Press.

Nasir, N. I. S., & Vakil, S. (2017). STEM-focused academies in urban schools: Tensions and possibilities. *Journal of the Learning Sciences*, *26*(3), 376–406. https://doi.org/10.1080/10508406.2017.1314215

Nasol, K., & Francisco-Menchavez, V. (2021). Filipino home care workers: Invisible frontline workers in the COVID-19 crisis in the United States. *American Behavioral Scientist, 65*(10), 1365–1383. https://doi.org/10.1177/00027642211000410

Nasser, R. (2017, April 27). *Techniques for the processing of the Arabic language on modern computers: Recorded at Interrupt 4 at Brown University, Providence, RI* [Video]. Vimeo. https://vimeo.com/225567483

National Academies of Sciences, Engineering, and Medicine (National Academies). (2016a). *Genetically engineered crops: Experiences and prospects.* The National Academies Press. https://doi.org/10.17226/23395

___. (2016b). *Science literacy: Concepts, contexts, and consequences.* The National Academies Press. https://doi.org/10.17226/23595

___. (2017). *Communicating science effectively: A research agenda.* The National Academies Press. https://doi.org/10.17226/23674

___. (2019a). *Reproducibility and replicability in science.* The National Academies Press. https://doi.org/10.17226/25303

___. (2019b). *Taking action against clinician burnout: A systems approach to professional well-being.* The National Academies Press. https://doi.org/10.17226/25521

___. (2021). *Section 230 protections: Can legal revisions or novel technologies limit online misinformation and abuse?: Proceedings of a workshop–in brief.* The National Academies Press. https://doi.org/10.17226/26280

National Association of Science Writers (n.d.). NASW survey finds that many journalists continue to face hurdles when reporting on federal agencies and seeking access to government scientists and experts. https://www.nasw.org/article/nasw-survey-finds-many-journalists-continue-face-hurdles-when-reporting-federal-agencies

National Commission for the Protection of Human Subjects of Biomedical and Behavioral Research. (1979). *The Belmont report: Ethical principles and guidelines for the protection of human subjects of research.* U.S. Department of Health and Human Services. https://www.hhs.gov/ohrp/regulations-and-policy/belmont-report/read-the-belmont-report/index.html

National Council of State Boards of Nursing. (2021). *Policy statement: Dissemination of non-scientific and misleading COVID-19 information by nurses.* https://www.ncsbn.org/public-files/PolicyBriefDisseminationofCOVID19Info.pdf

National Institute of Standards and Technology. (2024). *NIST trustworthy and responsible AI NIST AI 600-1: Artificial intelligence risk management framework: Generative artificial intelligence profile.* U.S. Department of Commerce. https://nvlpubs.nist.gov/nistpubs/ai/NIST.AI.600-1.pdf

National Institutes of Health Community Engagement Alliance. (2023, June 13). *Barbers in Jacksonville serve as information hubs during pandemic.* https://nihceal.org/news/barbers-jacksonville-serve-information-hubs-during-pandemic

National Research Council (NRC). (1996). *Understanding risk: Informing decisions in a democratic society.* National Academy Press. https://doi.org/10.17226/5138

___. (2002). *Scientific research in education.* The National Academies Press. https://doi.org/10.17226/10236

___. (2008). *Public participation in environmental assessment and decision making.* National Academy Press. https://doi.org/10.17226/12434

___. (2012a). *A framework for K-12 science education: Practices, crosscutting concepts, and core ideas.* The National Academies Press. https://doi.org/10.17226/13165

___. (2012b). *Using science as evidence in public policy.* The National Academies Press. https://doi.org/10.17226/13460

___. (2013). *Next generation science standards: For states, by states.* The National Academies Press. https://doi.org/10.17226/18290

National Science Board, National Science Foundation. (2022). *Science and technology: Public perceptions, awareness, and information sources* (Publication No. NSB-2022-7). Science and Engineering Indicators 2022. https://ncses.nsf.gov/pubs/nsb20227.

___. (2024, February). *Science and technology: Public perceptions, awareness, and information sources* (Publication No. NSB-2024-4). Science and Engineering Indicators 2024. https://ncses.nsf.gov/pubs/nsb20244

National Science & Technology Council. (2022, December). *Roadmap for researchers on priorities related to information integrity research and development.* United States Office of Science and Technology Policy. https://www.whitehouse.gov/wp-content/uploads/2022/12/Roadmap-Information-Integrity-RD-2022.pdf

Neff, T., & Pickard, V. (2021). Funding democracy: Public media and democratic health in 33 countries. *The International Journal of Press/Politics*, *29*(3), 601–627. https://doi.org/10.1177/19401612211060255

Nelson, J. L., & Taneja, H. (2018). The small, disloyal fake news audience: The role of audience availability in fake news consumption. *New Media & Society*, *20*(10), 3720–3737. https://doi.org/10.1177/1461444818758715

Newell, E., Jurgens, D., Saleem, H., Vala, H., Sassine, J., Armstrong, C., & Ruths, D. (2021). User migration in online social networks: A case study on Reddit during a period of community unrest. *Proceedings of the International AAAI Conference on Web and Social Media*, *10*(1), 279–288. https://doi.org/10.1609/icwsm.v10i1.14750

Newman, E., & Reynolds, K. (2021, August 19). Is it actually false, or do you just disagree? Why Twitter's user-driven experiment to tackle misinformation is complicated. *The Conversation.* http://theconversation.com/is-it-actually-false-or-do-you-just-disagree-why-twitters-user-driven-experiment-to-tackle-misinformation-is-complicated-166335

Ng, L. H. X., & Loke, J. Y. (2021). Analyzing public opinion and misinformation in a COVID-19 telegram group chat. *IEEE Internet Computing, 25*(2), 84–91. https://doi.org/10.1109/MIC.2020.3040516

Ngai, M. M. (2004). *Impossible subjects: Illegal aliens and the making of modern America.* Princeton University Press

___. (2014). Undocumented migration to the United States: A history. In L. A. Lorentzen (Ed.), *Hidden lives and human rights in the United States.* Praeger.

Nguyen, C. T. (2020). Echo chambers and epistemic bubbles. *Episteme*, *17*(2), 141–161. https://doi.org/10.1017/epi.2018.32

Nguyen, H., & Nguyen, A. (2020). COVID-19 misinformation and the social (media) amplification of risk: A Vietnamese perspective. *Media and Communication*, *8*(2), 444–447. https://doi.org/10.17645/mac.v8i2.3227

Nguyễn, S., & Kuo, R. (2023, unpublished). [Misinformation in non-English language information networks]. Paper commission by the Committee on Understanding and Addressing Misinformation About Science, National Academies of Sciences, Engineering, and Medicine. Available on request in the National Academies' Public Access Files.

Nguyễn, S., Kuo, R., Reddi, M., Li, L., & Moran, R. E. (2022). Studying mis-and disinformation in Asian diasporic communities: The need for critical transnational research beyond Anglocentrism (Commentary). *Harvard Kennedy School Misinformation Review*, *3*(2). https://doi.org/10.37016/mr-2020-95

Nicholas, G., & Bhatia, A. (2023, May 23). Lost in translation: Large language models in non-English content analysis. *Center for Democracy and Technology*. https://cdt.org/insights/lost-in-translation-large-language-models-in-non-english-content-analysis/

Nichols, T. (2017). *The death of expertise: The campaign against established knowledge and why it matters* (1st ed.). Oxford University Press.

Nickerson, R. S. (1998). Confirmation bias: A ubiquitous phenomenon in many guises. *Review of General Psychology*, 2(2), 175–220. https://doi.org/10.1037/1089-2680.2.2.175

Nogara, G., Vishnuprasad, P. S., Cardoso, F., Ayoub, O., Giordano, S., & Luceri, L. (2022). The disinformation dozen: An exploratory analysis of COVID-19 disinformation proliferation on Twitter. In *Proceedings of the 14th ACM Web Science Conference 2022*, 348–358. https://doi.org/10.1145/3501247.3531573

Nordon, C., Karcher, H., Groenwold, R. H., Ankarfeldt, M. Z., Pichler, F., Chevrou-Severac, H., Rossignol, M., Abbe, A., & Abenhaim, L. (2016). The "efficacy-effectiveness gap": Historical background and current conceptualization. *Value in Health*, *19*(1), 75–81. https://doi.org/10.1016/j.jval.2015.09.2938

Nuriddin, A., Mooney, G., & White, A. I. R. (2020). Reckoning with histories of medical racism and violence in the USA. *The Lancet*, *396*(10256), 949–951. https://doi.org/10.1016/S0140-6736(20)32032-8

Nutbeam, D. (2000). Health literacy as a public health goal: A challenge for contemporary health education and communication strategies into the 21st century. *Health Promotion International*, *15*(3), 259–267. https://doi.org/10.1093/heapro/15.3.259

Nutbeam, D., & Lloyd, J. E. (2021). Understanding and responding to health literacy as a social determinant of health. *Annual Review of Public Health*, *42*, 159–173. https://doi.org/10.1146/annurev-publhealth-090419-102529

Nyhan, B. (2020). Facts and myths about misperceptions. *Journal of Economic Perspectives*, *34*(3), 220–236. https://doi.org/10.1257/jep.34.3.220

Nyhan, B., Porter, E., Reifler, J., & Wood, T. J. (2019). Taking fact-checks literally but not seriously? The effects of journalistic fact-checking on factual beliefs and candidate favorability. *Political Behavior*, 1–22. http://dx.doi.org/10.2139/ssrn.2995128

Nyhan, B., & Reifler, J. (2010). When corrections fail: The persistence of political misperceptions. *Political Behavior*, *32*(2), 303–330. https://doi.org/10.1007/s11109-010-9112-2

___. (2015). Does correcting myths about the flu vaccine work? An experimental evaluation of the effects of corrective information. *Vaccine*, *33*(3), 459–464. https://doi.org/10.1016/j.vaccine.2014.11.017

Nyhan, B., Settle, J., Thorson, E., Wojcieszak, M., Barberá, P., Chen, A. Y., Allcott, H., Brown, T., Crespo-Tenorio, A., Dimmery, D., Freelon, D., Gentzkow, M., González-Bailón, S., Guess, A. M., Kennedy, E., Kim, Y. M., Lazer, D., Malhotra, N., Moehler, D., Pan, J., Thomas, D. R.. Tromble, R., Rivera, C. V., Wilkins, A., Ziong, B., de Jong, C. K., Franco, A., Mason, W., Stroud, N. J., and Tucker, J. A. (2023). Like-minded sources on Facebook are prevalent but not polarizing. *Nature*, *620*(7972), 137–144. https://doi.org/10.1038/s41586-023-06297-w

O'Brien, T. C., Palmer, R., & Albarracin, D. (2021). Misplaced trust: When trust in science fosters belief in pseudoscience and the benefits of critical evaluation. *Journal of Experimental Social Psychology*, *96*, 104184. https://doi.org/10.1016/j.jesp.2021.104184

O'Connor, C., & Weatherall, J. O. (2019, September 1). How misinformation spreads—and why we trust it. *Scientific American*. https://www.scientificamerican.com/article/how-misinformation-spreads-and-why-we-trust-it/

O'Donoghue, A. C., Boudewyns, V., Aikin, K. J., Geisen, E., Betts, K. R., & Southwell, B. G. (2015). Awareness of FDA's Bad Ad program and education regarding pharmaceutical advertising: A national survey of prescribers in ambulatory care settings. *Journal of Health Communication*, *20*(11), 1330–1336. https://doi.org/10.1080/10810730.2015.1018649

O'Keeffe, M., Nickel, B., Dakin, T., Maher, C. G., Albarqouni, L., McCaffery, K., Barratt, A., & Moynihan, R. (2021). Journalists' views on media coverage of medical tests and overdiagnosis: A qualitative study. *BMJ Open*, *11*, e043991. https://doi.org/10.1136/bmjopen-2020-043991

Occeñola, P. (2019, September 10). Exclusive: PH was Cambridge Analytica's 'petri dish'—Whistle-blower Christian Wylie. *Rappler*. https://rappler.com/technology/social-media/cambridge-analytica-philippines-online-propaganda-christopher-wylie

Office of the Surgeon General. (2022). Addressing health worker burnout: The U.S. Surgeon General's advisory on building a thriving health workforce. https://www.hhs.gov/surgeongeneral/priorities/health-worker-burnout/index.html

Ognyanova, K., Lazer, D., Robertson, R. E., & Wilson, C. (2020, June 2). Misinformation in action: Fake news exposure is linked to lower trust in media, higher trust in government when your side is in power. *Harvard Kennedy School Misinformation Review*, *1*(4). https://doi.org/10.37016/mr-2020-024

Olshansky, A., Peaslee, R. M., & Landrum, A. R. (2020). Flat-smacked! Converting to flat Eartherism. *Journal of Media & Religion*, *19*(2), 46–59. https://doi.org/10.1080/15348423.2020.1774257

Ong, J. C., & Cabañes, J. V. (2019). When disinformation studies meets production studies: Social identities and moral justifications in the political trolling industry. *International Journal of Communication*, *13*, 20. https://ijoc.org/index.php/ijoc/article/view/11417

Oransky, I., & Marcus, A. (2020, February 3). Quick retraction of a faulty coronavirus paper was a good moment for science. *Stat News*. https://www.statnews.com/2020/02/03/retraction-faulty-coronavirus-paper-good-moment-for-science/

Oreskes, N., & Conway, E. M. (2010a). Defeating the merchants of doubt. *Nature*, *465*(7299), 686–687. https://doi.org/10.1038/465686a

———. (2010b). *Merchants of doubt: How a handful of scientists obscured the truth on issues from tobacco smoke to global warming*. Bloomsbury Publishing.

Ornstein, C., & Weber, T. (2011, December 23). The champion of painkillers. *ProPublica*. https://www.propublica.org/article/the-champion-of-painkillers

Osborne, J., & Pimentel, D. (2022). Science, misinformation, and the role of education. *Science*, *378*(6617), 246–248. https://doi.org/10.1126/science.abq8093

Osmundsen, M., Bor, A., Vahlstrup, P. B., Bechmann, A., & Petersen, M. B. (2021). Partisan polarization is the primary psychological motivation behind political fake news sharing on Twitter. *American Political Science Review*, *115*(3), 999–1015. https://doi.org/10.1017/S0003055421000290

Otero, J. (2021, August 10). *The art of meeting people where they are: A community partnership approach for COVID equity*. Center for Primary Care, Harvard Medical School. https://info.primarycare.hms.harvard.edu/review/art-of-meeting-people

Ousey, G. C., & Kubrin, C. E. (2018). Immigration and crime: Assessing a contentious issue. *Annual Review of Criminology*, *1*, 63–84. https://doi.org/10.1146/annurev-criminol-032317-092026

Owen, L. H. (2021, February 12). The dark side of translation: The Epoch Times reportedly spreads disinformation through new brands. *Nieman Lab*. https://www.niemanlab.org/2021/02/the-dark-side-of-translation-the-epoch-times-is-now-spreading-disinformation-through-new-brands/

Ozbay, F. A., & Alatas, B. (2020). Fake news detection within online social media using supervised artificial intelligence algorithms. *Physica A: Statistical Mechanics and its Applications*, *540*, 123174. https://doi.org/10.1016/j.physa.2019.123174

Paik, A. N. (2013). Carceral quarantine at Guantánamo: Legacies of US imprisonment of Haitian refugees, 1991–1994. *Radical History Review*, *2013*(115), 142–168. https://doi.org/10.1215/01636545-1724751

Palacio, A., Garay, D., Langer, B., Taylor, J., Wood, B. A., & Tamariz, L. (2016). Motivational Interviewing improves medication adherence: A systematic review and meta-analysis. *Journal of General Internal Medicine*, *31*(8), 929–940. https://doi.org/10.1007/s11606-016-3685-3

Paletz, S. B. F., Johns, M. A., Murauskaite, E. E., Golonka, E. M., Pandža, N. B., Rytting, C. A., Butain, A., & Ellis, D. (2023). Emotional content and sharing on Facebook: A theory cage match. *Science Advances*, *9*(39), eade9231. https://doi.org/10.1126/sciadv.ade9231

Pamuk, Z. (2021). *Politics and expertise: How to use science in a democratic society.* Princeton University Press.

Papadogiannakis, E., Papadopoulos, P., Markatos, E. P., & Kourtellis, N. (2023, April). Who funds misinformation? A systematic analysis of the ad-related profit routines of fake news sites. In *Proceedings of the ACM Web Conference 2023* (pp. 2765–2776). https://doi.org/10.1145/3543507.3583443

Paquin, R. S., Boudewyns, V., Betts, K. R., Johnson, M., O'Donoghue, A. C., & Southwell, B. G. (2022). An empirical procedure to evaluate misinformation rejection and deception in mediated communication contexts. *Communication Theory*, *32*(1), 25–47. https://doi.org/10.1093/ct/qtab011

Parrella, J. A., Koswatta, T. J., Leggette, H. R., Ramasubramanian, S., & Rutherford, T. (2022). Teaching scientists to communicate: Developing science communication training based on scientists' knowledge and self-reflectiveness. *International Journal of Science Education, Part B*, *12*(3), 235–253. https://doi.org/10.1080/21548455.2022.2068809

Pasquetto, I. V., Jahani, E., Atreja, S., & Baum, M. (2022). Social debunking of misinformation on WhatsApp: The case for strong and in-group ties. In *Proceedings of the ACM on Human-Computer Interaction*, 6(CSCW1), Article 117. https://doi.org/10.1145/3512964

Pearson, G. (2021). Sources on social media: Information context collapse and volume of content as predictors of source blindness. *New Media & Society*, *23*(5), 1181–1199. https://doi.org/10.1177/1461444820910505

Pechar, E., Bernauer, T., & Mayer, F. (2018). Beyond political ideology: The impact of attitudes towards government and corporations on trust in science. *Science Communication*, *40*(3), 291–313. https://doi.org/10.1177/1075547018763970

Pedersen, M. A., Albris, K., & Seaver, N. (2021). The political economy of attention. *Annual Review of Anthropology*, *50*(1), 309–325. https://doi.org/10.1146/annurev-anthro-101819-110356

Peña D. G. (1997). *The terror of the machine*. University of Texas Press.

Peña, J. M., Schwartz, M. R., Hernandez-Vallant, A., & Sanchez, G. R. (2023). Social and structural determinants of COVID-19 vaccine uptake among racial and ethnic groups. *Journal of Behavioral Medicine*, *46*(1-2), 129–139. https://doi.org/10.1007/s10865-023-00393-y

Pennycook, G., Bear, A., Collins, E. T., & Rand, D. G. (2020). The implied truth effect: Attaching warnings to a subset of fake news headlines increases perceived accuracy of headlines without warnings. *Management Science*, *66*(11), 4944–4957. https://doi.org/10.1287/mnsc.2019.3478

Pennycook, G., Cannon, T. D., & Rand, D. G. (2018). Prior exposure increases perceived accuracy of fake news. *Journal of Experimental Psychology: General*, *147*(12), 1865–1880. https://doi.org/10.1037/xge0000465

Pennycook, G., Epstein, Z., Mosleh, M., Arechar, A. A., Eckles, D., & Rand, D. G. (2021). Shifting attention to accuracy can reduce misinformation online. *Nature*, *592*, 590–595. https://doi.org/10.1038/s41586-021-03344-2

Pennycook, G., & Rand, D. G. (2019). Lazy, not biased: Susceptibility to partisan fake news is better explained by lack of reasoning than by motivated reasoning. *Cognition*, *188*, 39–50. https://doi.org/10.1016/j.cognition.2018.06.011

___. (2021). The psychology of fake news. *Trends in Cognitive Sciences*, *25*(5), 388–402. https://doi.org/10.1016/j.tics.2021.02.007

___. (2022a). Accuracy prompts are a replicable and generalizable approach for reducing the spread of misinformation. *Nature Communications*, *13*, Article 1. https://doi.org/10.1038/s41467-022-30073-5

___. (2022b). Nudging social media toward accuracy. *The ANNALS of the American Academy of Political and Social Science*, *700*(1), 152–164. https://doi.org/10.1177/00027162221092342

Pequeño IV, A. (2023, June 13). Reddit stands by controversial API change as Subreddit protest continues. *Forbes*. https://www.forbes.com/sites/antoniopequenoiv/2023/06/13/reddit-stands-by-controversial-api-changes-as-subreddit-protest-continues/

Perach, R., Joyner, L., Husbands, D., & Buchanan, T. (2023). Why do people share political information and misinformation online? Developing a bottom-up descriptive framework. *Social Media+ Society*, *9*(3). https://doi.org/10.1177/20563051231192032

Pereira, A., Harris, E., & Van Bavel, J. J. (2023). Identity concerns drive belief: The impact of partisan identity on the belief and dissemination of true and false news. *Group Processes & Intergroup Relations*, *26*(1), 24–47. https://doi.org/10.1177/1368430221103000

Percy, C., & Murray S. (2010). The role of an online peer-to-peer health community in addressing psychosocial concerns and social support in polycystic ovary syndrome. *International Journal of Web Based Communities*, *6*(4), 349–361. https://doi.org/10.1504/IJWBC.2010.035838

Perera, P., Selvanathan, S., Bandaralage, J., & Su, J.-J. (2023). The impact of digital inequality in achieving sustainable development: A systematic literature review. *Equality, Diversity and Inclusion*, *42*(6), 805–825. https://doi.org/10.1108/EDI-08-2022-0224

Perlis, R. H., Lunz Trujillo, K., Green, J., Safarpour, A., Druckman, J. N., Santillana, M., Ognyanova, K., & Lazer, D. (2023). Misinformation, trust, and use of ivermectin and hydroxychloroquine for COVID-19. *JAMA Health Forum*, *4*(9), e233257–e233257. https://doi.org/10.1001/jamahealthforum.2023.3257

Perlis, R. H., Ognyanova, K., Santillana, M., Lin, J., Druckman, J., Lazer, D., Green, J., Simonson, M., Baum, M. A., & Della Volpe, J. (2022). Association of major depressive symptoms with endorsement of COVID-19 vaccine misinformation among US adults. *JAMA Network Open*, *5*(1), e2145697. https://doi.org/10.1001/jamanetworkopen.2021.45697

Perry, B. (2003). *Hate and bias crime: A reader*. Routledge.

Peters, E., Tompkins, M. K., Knoll, M. A. Z., Ardoin, S. P., Shoots-Reinhard, B., & Meara, A. S. (2019). Despite high objective numeracy, lower numeric confidence relates to worse financial and medical outcomes. *Proceedings of the National Academy of Sciences*, *116*(39), 19386–19391. https://doi.org/10.1073/pnas.1903126116

Peters, H. P., Brossard, D., de Cheveigné, S., Dunwoody, S., Kallfass, M., Miller, S., & Tsuchida, S. (2008). Science-media interface: It's time to reconsider. *Science Communication*, *30*(2), 266–276. https://doi.org/10.1177/1075547008324809

Petersen, M. B., Osmundsen, M., & Arceneaux, K. (2023). The "need for chaos" and motivations to share hostile political rumors. *American Political Science Review*, *117*(4), 1486–1505. https://doi.org/10.1017/S0003055422001447

Peterson, E., & Iyengar, S. (2021). Partisan gaps in political information and information-seeking behavior: Motivated reasoning or cheerleading? *American Journal of Political Science*, *65*(1), 133–147. https://doi.org/10.1111/ajps.12535

Peterson, J. S., Swire-Thompson, B., & Johnson, S. B. (2020). What's the alternative? Responding strategically to cancer misinformation, *Future Oncology*, *25*, 1883–1888. https://doi.org/10.2217/fon-2020-0440

Petty, R. E., & Cacioppo, J. T. (1986). The elaboration likelihood model of persuasion. In L. Berkowitz (Ed.), *Advances in experimental social psychology* (Vol. 19, pp. 123–205). Academic Press. https://doi.org/10.1016/S0065-2601(08)60214-2

Pew Research Center. (2019a, August 2). *Findings at a glance: Medical doctors*. https://www.pewresearch.org/science/2019/08/02/findings-at-a-glance-medical-doctors/

___. (2019b). *Trusting the news media in the Trump era*. https://www.pewresearch.org/journalism/wp-content/uploads/sites/8/2019/12/PJ_2019.12.12_Trust-In-Media_FINAL.pdf

___. (2019c, November 15). *Americans have positive views about religion's role in society, but want it out of politics*. https://www.pewresearch.org/religion/2019/11/15/most-congregants-trust-clergy-to-give-advice-about-religious-issues-fewer-trust-clergy-on-personal-matters/

___. (2022, April). *Black Americans' views of and engagement with science*. https://www.pewresearch.org/science/2022/04/07/black-americans-views-of-and-engagement-with-science/

___. (2023a, November). Americans' trust in scientists, positive views of science continue to decline. https://www.pewresearch.org/science/2023/11/14/americans-trust-in-scientists-positive-views-of-science-continue-to-decline/

___. (2023b, September 14). Local TV news fact sheet. https://www.pewresearch.org/journalism/fact-sheet/local-tv-news/

___. (2024a, January). *Americans' social media use*. https://www.pewresearch.org/internet/2024/01/31/americans-social-media-use/

___. (2024b, March). *How Hispanic Americans get their news*. https://www.pewresearch.org/race-and-ethnicity/2024/03/19/how-hispanic-americans-get-their-news/

___. (2024c). News platform fact sheet. https://www.pewresearch.org/journalism/fact-sheet/news-platform-fact-sheet/

Pham, T.-N. (2021). You don't say he was kidnapped! Vietnamese diasporic media's coverage of Trinh Xuan Thanh issue. *Journalism Studies*, *22*(4), 496–515. https://doi.org/10.1080/1461670X.2021.1882878

Phillips, C. V., Wang, C., & Guenzel, B. (2005). You might as well smoke; the misleading and harmful public message about smokeless tobacco. *BMC Public Health*, *5*, Article 31. https://doi.org/10.1186/1471-2458-5-31

Phillips, T., & Elledge, J. (2022). *Conspiracy: A history of boll*cks theories, and how not to fall for them*. Wildfire.

Pickard, V. (2019). *Democracy without journalism?: Confronting the misinformation society*. Oxford University Press.

Pierri, F., DeVerna, M. R., Yang, K.-C., Axelrod, D., Bryden, J., & Menczer, F. (2023). One year of COVID-19 Vaccine misinformation on Twitter: Longitudinal study. *Journal of Medical Internet Research*, *25*, e42227. https://doi.org/10.2196/42227

Pierri, F., Perry, B. L., DeVerna, M. R., Yang, K.-C., Flammini, A., Menczer, F., & Bryden, J. (2022). Online misinformation is linked to early COVID-19 vaccination hesitancy and refusal. *Scientific Reports*, *12*, Article 5966. https://doi.org/10.1038/s41598-022-10070-w

Pietrantonj, C. D., Rivetti, A., Marchione, P., Debalini, M. G., & Demicheli, V. (2021). Vaccines for measles, mumps, rubella, and varicella in children. *Cochrane Database of Systematic Reviews*, *11*, Article CD004407. https://doi.org/10.1002/14651858.CD004407.pub5

Pike, J., Melnick, A., Gastañaduy, P. A., Kay, M., Harbison, J., Leidner, A. J., Rice, S., Asato, K., Schwartz, L., & DeBolt, C. (2021). Societal costs of a measles outbreak. *Pediatrics*, *147*(4), e2020027037. https://doi.org/10.1542/peds.2020-027037

Pillai, R. M., & Fazio, L. K. (2023). Explaining why headlines are true or false reduces intentions to share false information. *Collabra: Psychology*, *9*(1), 87617. https://doi.org/10.1525/collabra.87617

___. (2024). Repeated by many versus repeated by one: Examining the role of social consensus in the relationship between repetition and belief. *Journal of Applied Research in Memory and Cognition*. https://doi.org/10.1037/mac0000166

Pillai, R. M., Fazio, L. K., & Effron, D. (2023). Repeatedly encountered descriptions of wrongdoing seem more true but less unethical: Evidence in a naturalistic setting. *Psychological Science*, *34*(8), 863–874. https://doi.org/10.1177/09567976231180578

Pimentel, D. R. (2024). Learning to evaluate sources of science (mis)information on the internet: Assessing students' scientific online reasoning. *Journal of Research in Science Teaching*, 1–37. https://doi.org/10.1002/tea.21974

Pinna, M., Picard, L., & Goessmann, C. (2022). Cable news and COVID-19 vaccine uptake. *Scientific Reports*, *12*(1), 16804. https://doi.org/10.1038/s41598-022-20350-0

Pluta, A., Mazurek, J., Wojciechowski, J., Wolak, T., Soral, W., & Bilewicz, M. (2023). Exposure to hate speech deteriorates neurocognitive mechanisms of the ability to understand others' pain. *Scientific Reports*, *13*(1), 4127. https://doi.org/10.1038/s41598-023-31146-1

Podlas, K. (2005). "The CSI effect": Exposing the media myth. *Fordham Intellectual Property Media & Entertainment Law Journal*, 16(2), 429–465. https://ir.lawnet.fordham.edu/iplj/vol16/iss2/2

Polleri, M. (2022). Towards an anthropology of misinformation. *Anthropology Today*, 38(5), 17–20. https://doi.org/10.1111/1467-8322.12754

Polman, J. L. (2023, unpublished). [Science learning for navigating a complex informational landscape]. Paper commissioned by the Committee on Understanding and Addressing Misinformation about Science, National Academies of Sciences, Engineering, and Medicine. Available on request in the National Academies' Public Access Files.

Polman, J. L., & Miller, D. (2010). Changing stories: Trajectories of identification among African American youth in a science outreach apprenticeship. *American Educational Research Journal*, 47(4), 879–918. https://doi.org/10.3102/000283121036751

Polman, J. L., Newman, A., Saul, E. W., & Farrar, C. (2014). Adapting practices of science journalism to foster science literacy. *Science Education*, *98*(5), 766–791. https://doi.org/10.1002/sce.21114

Polny, J. M., & Wihbey, J. P. (2021, June 3). *The evolution of social media content labeling: An online archive*. The Ethics Institute at Northeastern University. https://cssh.northeastern.edu/ethics/the-evolution-of-social-media-content-labeling-an-online-archive/

Popiel, P., & Pickard, V. (2022). Digital redlining and the endless divide: Philadelphia's COVID-19 digital inclusion efforts. *International Journal of Communication*, *16*, 3329–3353. https://ijoc.org/index.php/ijoc/article/view/18305

Porter, E., & Wood, T. J. (2021). The global effectiveness of fact-checking: Evidence from simultaneous experiments in Argentina, Nigeria, South Africa, and the United Kingdom. *Proceedings of the National Academy of Sciences*, 118(37), e2104235118.

Porter, E., Velez, Y., & Wood, T. J. (2022). Factual corrections eliminate false beliefs about COVID-19 vaccines. *Public Opinion Quarterly*, *86*(3), 762–773.

___. (2023). Correcting COVID-19 vaccine misinformation in 10 countries. *Royal Society Open Science*, *10*(3), 221097.

Porterfield, C. (2021, September 13). Facebook reportedly allowed powerful users to break platform rules. *Forbes*. https://www.forbes.com/sites/carlieporterfield/2021/09/13/facebook-reportedly-allowed-powerful-users-to-break-platform-rules/

Prasad, V. K., & Cifu, A. S. (2015). *Ending medical reversal: Improving outcomes, saving lives*. Johns Hopkins University Press.

Prike, T., Butler, L., & Ecker, U. K. H. (2023, April 1). Source-credibility information and social norms improve truth discernment and reduce engagement with misinformation online. *PsyArXiv Preprints*. https://doi.org/10.31234/osf.io/dhx6f

Prike, T., & Ecker, U. K. H. (2023). Effective correction of misinformation. *Current Opinion in Psychology*, *54*, 101721. https://doi.org/10.1016/j.copsyc.2023.101712

Prior, M. (2007). *Post-broadcast democracy: How media choice increases inequality in political involvement and polarizes elections*. Cambridge University Press.

___. (2013). Media and political polarization. *Annual Review of Political Science*, *16*, 101–127. https://doi.org/10.1146/annurev-polisci-100711-135242

Proctor, R. N., & Schiebinger, L. (2008). *Agnotology: The making and unmaking of ignorance*. Stanford University Press.

Prue, C. E., Williams, P. N., Joseph, H. A., Johnson, M., Wojno, A. E., Zulkiewicz, B. A., Macom, J., Alexander, J. P., Ray, S. E., & Southwell, B. G. (2019). Factors that mattered in helping travelers from countries with Ebola outbreaks participate in post-arrival monitoring during the 2014-2016 Ebola epidemic. *INQUIRY: The Journal of Health Care Organization, Provision, and Financing*, *56*. https://doi.org/10.1177/0046958019894795

Pummerer, L., Böhm, R., Lilleholt, L., Winter, K., Zettler, I., & Sassenberg, K. (2022). Conspiracy theories and their societal effects during the COVID-19 pandemic. *Social Psychological and Personality Science*, *13*(1), 49–59. https://doi.org/10.1177/19485506211000217

Puri, N., Coomes, E. A., Haghbayan, H., & Gunaratne, K. (2020). Social media and vaccine hesitancy: New updates for the era of COVID-19 and globalized infectious diseases. *Human Vaccines & Immunotherapeutics*, *16*(11), 2586–2593. https://doi.org/10.1080/21645515.2020.1780846

Purnat, T. D., Vacca, P., Czerniak, C., Ball, S., Burzo, S., Zecchin, T., Wright, A., Bezbaruah, S., Tanggol, F., Dubé, È., Labbé, F., Dionne, M., Lamichhane, J., Mahajan, A., Briand, S., & Nguyen, T. (2021). Infodemic signal detection during the COVID-19 pandemic: Development of a methodology for identifying potential information voids in online conversations. *JMIR Infodemiology*, *1*(1), e30971. https://doi.org/10.2196/30971

Putnam, R. D. (1993). The prosperous community: Social capital and public life. *The American Prospect*, *4*(13), 35–42.

___. (2000). *Bowling alone: The collapse and revival of American community*. Simon & Schuster.

Pyne, J. M., Seal, K. H., Manuel, J. K., DeRonne, B., Oliver, K. A., Bertenthal, D., Esserman, D., Purcell, N., Petrakis, B. A., & Elwy, A. R. (2023). Developing and testing a COVID-19 vaccination acceptance intervention: A pragmatic trial comparing vaccine acceptance intervention vs usual care – Rationale, methods, and implementation. *Contemporary Clinical Trials*, *133*, 107325. https://doi.org/https://doi.org/10.1016/j.cct.2023.107325

Quinn, R. (2023, December 4). Misinformation research plows ahead—but so do political detractors. *Inside Higher Ed*. https://www.insidehighered.com/news/faculty-issues/academic-freedom/2023/12/04/misinformation-research-plows-ahead-so-do

Rachul, C., & Caulfield, T. (2015). Gordie Howe's stem cell 'miracle': A qualitative analysis of news coverage and readers' comments in newspapers and sports websites. *Stem Cell Reviews and Reports*, *11*, 667–675. https://doi.org/10.1007/s12015-015-9606-8

Rachul, C., Marcon, A. R., Collins, B., & Caulfield, T. (2020). COVID-19 and 'immune boosting' on the internet: A content analysis of Google search results. *BMJ Open*, *10*, e040989. https://doi.org/10.1136/bmjopen-2020-040989

Radinsky, J., & Tabak, I. (2022). Data practices during COVID: Everyday sensemaking in a high-stakes information ecology. *British Journal of Educational Technology*, *53*(5), 1221–1243. https://doi.org/10.1111/bjet.13252

Radrizzani, S., Fonseca, C., Woollard, A., Pettitt, J., & Hurst, L. D. (2023). Both trust in, and polarization of trust in, relevant sciences have increased through the COVID-19 pandemic. *PLoS One*, *18*(3), e0278169. https://doi.org/10.1371/journal.pone.0278169

Rajagopalan, K. (2021). Asian media on the front lines: How community media have served Asian Americans during the pandemic. *Center for Community Media, Asian Media Initiative*. https://asianmediafrontlines.journalism.cuny.edu/

The RECOVERY Collaborative Group. (2020). Effect of hydroxychloroquine in hospitalized patients with Covid-19. *New England Journal of Medicine*, *383*(21), 2030–2040. https://doi.org/10.1056/NEJMoa2022926

Reed, G., Hendlin, Y., Desikan, A., MacKinney, T., Berman, E., & Goldman, G. T. (2021). The disinformation playbook: How industry manipulates the science-policy process—and how to restore scientific integrity. *Journal of Public Health Policy*, *42*(4), 622–634. https://doi.org/10.1057/s41271-021-00318-6

Reinhart, R. J. (2020). Fewer in U.S. continue to see vaccines as important (2019 Survey Results). *Gallup*. https://news.gallup.com/poll/276929/fewer-continue-vaccines-important.aspx

Ren, Z., Dimant, E., & Schweitzer, M. (2023). Beyond belief: How social engagement motives influence the spread of conspiracy theories. *Journal of Experimental Social Psychology*, *104*, 104421. https://doi.org/10.1016/j.jesp.2022.104421

Reno, J. E., O'Leary, S., Garrett, K., Pyrzanowski, J., Lockhart, S., Campagna, E., Barnard, J., & Dempsey, A. F. (2018). Improving provider communication about HPV vaccines for vaccine-hesitant parents through the use of motivational interviewing. *Journal of Health Communication*, *23*(4), 313–320. https://doi.org/10.1080/10810730.2018.1442530

Reno, J. E., Thomas, J., Pyrzanowski, J., Lockhart, S., O'Leary, S. T., Campagna, E. J., & Dempsey, A. F. (2019). Examining strategies for improving healthcare providers' communication about adolescent HPV vaccination: Evaluation of secondary outcomes in a randomized controlled trial. *Human Vaccines & Immunotherapeutics*, *15*(7–8), 1592–1598. https://doi.org/10.1080/21645515.2018.1547607

Reo, N. J., Whyte, K., Ranco, D., Brandt, J., Blackmer, E., & Elliott, B. (2017). Invasive species, indigenous stewards, and vulnerability discourse. *The American Indian Quarterly*, *41*(3), 201–223. https://dx.doi.org/10.5250/amerindiquar.41.3.0201.

Reyna V. F. (2021). A scientific theory of gist communication and misinformation resistance, with implications for health, education, and policy. *Proceedings of the National Academy of Sciences*, *118*(15), e1912441117. https://doi.org/10.1073/pnas.1912441117

Reyna, V. F., Broniatowski, D. A., & Edelson, S. M. (2021). Viruses, vaccines, and COVID-19: explaining and improving risky decision-making. *Journal of Applied Research in Memory and Cognition*, *10*(4), 491–509. https://doi.org/10.1016/j.jarmac.2021.08.004

Ribeiro, M., Jhaver, S., Martinell, J., Reignier-Tayar, M., & West, R. (2024). Deplatforming norm-violating influencers on social media reduces overall online attention toward them. *arXiv*. https://doi.org/10.48550/arXiv.2401.01253

Ricard, J., & Medeiros, J. (2020). Using misinformation as a political weapon: COVID-19 and Bolsonaro in Brazil. *Harvard Kennedy School Misinformation Review*, *1*(2). https://doi.org/10.37016/mr-2020-013

Rive, N., Jackson, B., & Rado, D. (2007, June 11). *Complaint to Ofcom regarding "The great global warming swindle"*. Ofcom Swindle Complaint. http://www.ofcomswindlecomplaint.net/FullComplaint.pdf

Roberts, D. A. (2007). Scientific literacy/science literacy. In S. Abell & N. Lederman (Eds.), *Handbook of research on science education* (pp. 729–780). Lawrence Erlbaum Associates.

___. (2011). Competing visions of scientific literacy: Influence of a science curriculum policy image. In C. Linder, L. Östman, D. A. Roberts, P.-O. Wickman, G. Erickson, & A. MacKinnon (Eds.), *Exploring the landscape of scientific literacy* (pp. 11–27). Routledge/Taylor and Francis Group.

Robertson, R. E., Green, J., Ruck, D. J., Ognyanova, K., Wilson, C., & Lazer, D. (2023). Users choose to engage with more partisan news than they are exposed to on Google Search. *Nature*, *618*(7964), 342–348. https://doi.org/10.1038/s41586-023-06078-5

Robertson, R. E., Jiang, S., Joseph, K., Friedland, L., Lazer, D., & Wilson, C. (2018). Auditing partisan audience bias within Google Search. In *Proceedings of the ACM on Human-Computer Interaction*, *2*(CSCW), 1–22. https://doi.org/10.1145/3274417

Roller, M. R. (2022). The unique attributes of qualitative research: A collection of 16 articles. *Research Design Review.* https://researchdesignreview.com/2022/10/28/unique-attributes-qualitative-research-collection-16-articles/

Roose, K. (2020, October 24). How The Epoch Times created a giant influence machine. *The New York Times.* https://www.nytimes.com/2020/10/24/technology/epoch-times-influence-falun-gong.html

Roozenbeek, J., Schneider, C. R., Dryhurst, S., Kerr, J., Freeman, A. L. J., Recchia, G., van der Bles, A. M., & van der Linden, S. (2020). Susceptibility to misinformation about COVID-19 around the world. *Royal Society Open Science*, 7(10), 201199. https://doi.org/10.1098/rsos.201199

Roozenbeek, J., van der Linden, S., Goldberg, B., Rathje, S., & Lewandowsky, S. (2022). Psychological inoculation improves resilience against misinformation on social media. *Science Advances*, *8*(34), Article eabo6254. https://doi.org/10.1126/sciadv.abo6254

Rosenfeld, S. (2018). *Democracy and truth: A short history*. University of Pennsylvania Press.

Rummans, T. A., Burton, M. C., & Dawson, N. L. (2018, March). How good intentions contributed to bad outcomes: the opioid crisis. *Mayo Clinic Proceedings,* 93(3), 344–350. https://doi.org/10.1016/j.mayocp.2017.12.020

Russell, C. (2006, January 1). *Covering controversial science: Improving reporting on science and public policy* (Publication No. 2006-4). Joan Shorenstein Center on the Press, Politics, and Public Policy. https://shorensteincenter.org/covering-controversial-science-improving-reporting-on-science-and-public-policy/

Rutjens, B. T., van der Linden, S., & van der Lee, R. (2021). Science skepticism in times of COVID-19. *Group Processes & Intergroup Relations*, *24*(2), 276–283. https://doi.org/10.1177/1368430220981415

Rutjens, B. T., & Većkalov, B. (2022). Conspiracy beliefs and science rejection. *Current Opinion in Psychology*, *46*, 101392. https://doi.org/10.1016/j.copsyc.2022.101392

Ryan, C. D., Schaul, A. J., Butner, R., & Swarthout, J. T. (2020). Monetizing disinformation in the attention economy: The case of genetically modified organisms (GMOs). *European Management Journal*, *38*(1), 7–18. https://doi.org/10.1016/j.emj.2019.11.002

Ryan-Mosley, T. (2021, May 4). The internet is excluding Asian-Americans who don't speak English. *MIT Technology Review*. https://www.technologyreview.com/2021/05/04/1024507/asian-american-language-justice-online-hmong/

Sakellari, M. (2015). Cinematic climate change, a promising perspective on climate change communication. *Public Understanding of Science*, *24*(7), 827–841. https://doi.org/10.1177/0963662514537028

Saks, E., & Tyson, A. (2022, November 10). Americans report more engagement with science news than in 2017. *Pew Research Center*. https://www.pewresearch.org/short-reads/2022/11/10/americans-report-more-engagement-with-science-news-than-in-2017/

Saleem, H. M., & Ruths, D. (2018). The aftermath of disbanding an online hateful community. *arXiv*. http://arxiv.org/abs/1804.07354

Samudzi, Z. (2017, July 17). *We need to talk about anti-vaxxing in black communities*. Afropunk. https://afropunk.com/2017/07/need-talk-anti-vaxxing-black-communities/

Sanchez, G. R., & Bennett, C. (2022, Nov. 4). Why Spanish language mis- and disinformation is a huge issue in 2022. *Brookings*. https://www.brookings.edu/articles/why-spanish-language-mis-and-disinformation-is-a-huge-issue-in-2022/

Santos, H. C., Varnum, M. E. W., & Grossmann, I. (2017). Global increases in individualism. *Psychological Science*, *28*(9), 1228–1239. https://doi.org/10.1177/0956797617700622

Sassan, C., Mahat, P., Aronczyk, M., & Brulle, R. J. (2023). Energy citizens "just like you"? Public relations campaigning by the climate change counter-movement. *Environmental Communication*, *17*(7), 794–810. https://doi.org/10.1080/17524032.2023.2255388

Satcher, L. A. (2022). Multiply-deserted areas: Environmental racism and food, pharmacy, and greenspace access in the urban south. *Environmental Sociology*, *8*(3), 279–291. https://doi.org/10.1080/23251042.2022.2031513

Scales, D., Gorman, J. M., DiCaprio, P., Hurth, L., Radhakrishnan, M., Windham, S., Akunne, A., Florman, J., Leininger, L., & Starks, T. J. (2023). Community-oriented Motivational Interviewing (MI): A novel framework extending MI to address COVID-19 vaccine misinformation in online social media platforms. *Computers in Human Behavior*, *141*, 107609. https://doi.org/https://doi.org/10.1016/j.chb.2022.107609

Scales, D., Hurth, L., Xi, W., Gorman, S., Radhakrishnan, M., Windham, S., Akunne, A., Florman, J., Leininger, L., & Gorman, J. (2023). Addressing antivaccine sentiment on public social media forums through web-based conversations based on motivational interviewing techniques: Observational study. *JMIR Infodemiology*, *3*, Article e50138. https://doi.org/10.2196/50138

Schellewald, A. (2021). Communicative forms on TikTok: Perspectives from digital ethnography. *International Journal of Communication*, *15*(2021), 1437–1457. https://ijoc.org/index.php/ijoc/article/view/16414

Scheufele, D. A., Krause, N. M., & Freiling, I. (2021). Misinformed about the "infodemic?" Science's ongoing struggle with misinformation. *Journal of Applied Research in Memory and Cognition*, *10*(4), 522–526. https://doi.org/10.1016/j.jarmac.2021.10.009

Schilke, O., Reimann, M., & Cook, K. S. (2021). Trust in social relations. *Annual Review of Sociology*, *47*(1), 239–259. https://doi.org/10.1146/annurev-soc-082120-082850

Schmid, P., Altay, S., & Scherer, L. D. (2023). The psychological impacts and message features of health misinformation: A systematic review of randomized controlled trials. *European Psychologist*, *28*(3), 162–172. https://doi.org/10.1027/1016-9040/a000494

Schmidt, K., & Ernst, E. (2004). Assessing websites on complementary and alternative medicine for cancer. *Annals of Oncology*, *15*(5), 733–742. https://doi.org/10.1093/annonc/mdh174

Schwartz, J. L. (2012). New media, old messages: Themes in the history of vaccine hesitancy and refusal. *Virtual Mentor*, *14*(1), 50–55. https://doi.org/10.1001/virtualmentor.2012.14.1.mhst1-1201

Schwenker, R., Dietrich, C. E., Hirpa, S., Nothacker, M., Smedslund, G., Frese, T., & Unverzagt, S. (2023). Motivational interviewing for substance use reduction. *The Cochrane Database of Systematic Reviews*, *12*(12), Article CD008063. https://doi.org/10.1002/14651858.CD008063.pub3

Seah, S., & Weimann, G. (2020). What influences the willingness of Chinese WeChat users to forward food-safety rumors? *International Journal of Communication*, *14*, 22. https://ijoc.org/index.php/ijoc/article/view/11869

Seale, H., Harris-Roxas, B., Heywood, A., Abdi, I., Mahimbo, A., Chauhan, A., & Woodland, L. (2022). The role of community leaders and other information intermediaries during the COVID-19 pandemic: Insights from the multicultural sector in Australia. *Humanities and Social Sciences Communications*, *9*, 174. https://doi.org/10.1057/s41599-022-01196-3

Seifert, C. M. (2002). The continued influence of misinformation in memory: What makes a correction effective? *Psychology of Learning and Motivation*, *41*(2022), 265–292. https://doi.org/10.1016/S0079-7421(02)80009-3

Selvaraj, S., Borkar, D. S., & Prasad, V. (2014). Media coverage of medical journals: Do the best articles make the news?. *PLoS ONE*, *9*(1), e85355. https://doi.org/10.1371/journal.pone.0085355

Senft, T. (2021). *COVID-19 Vaccination Rapid Community Assessment teen investigators report*. CDC Vaccine Confidence and Demand Team. http://dx.doi.org/10.13140/RG.2.2.28648.34560

Sengupta-Irving, T. (2021). Positioning and positioned apart: Mathematics learning as becoming undesirable. *Anthropology & Education Quarterly*, *52*(2), 187–208. https://doi.org/10.1111/aeq.12378

Serazio, M. (2021). The other 'fake' news: Professional ideals and objectivity ambitions in brand journalism. *Journalism*, *22*(6), 1340–1356. https://doi.org/10.1177/1464884919829923

Sesin, C. (2020, December 20). Mistrust, disinformation among Latinos on Covid vaccine has to be tackled, warn Hispanic doctors. *NBC News*. https://www.nbcnews.com/news/latino/mistrust-disinformation-among-latinos-covid-vaccine-worries-hispanic-doctors-n1251636

Seth, P., Rudd, R. A., Noonan, R. K., & Haegerich, T. M. (2018). Quantifying the epidemic of prescription opioid overdose deaths. *American Journal of Public Health*, *108*(4), 500–502. https://doi.org/10.2105/AJPH.2017.304265

Seymour, B., Getman, R., Saraf, A., Zhang, L. H., & Kalenderian, E. (2015). When advocacy obscures accuracy online: Digital pandemics of public health misinformation through an antifluoride case study. *American Journal of Public Health*, *105*(3), 517–523. https://doi.org/10.2105/AJPH.2014.302437

Shafto, P., Eaves, B., Navarro, D. J., & Perfors, A. (2012). Epistemic trust: Modeling children's reasoning about others' knowledge and intent. *Developmental Science*, *15*(3), 436–447. https://doi.org/10.1111/j.1467-7687.2012.01135.x

Shah, N. (2001). *Contagious divides: Epidemics and race in San Francisco's Chinatown*. University of California Press.

Shams, T. (2020). *Here, there, and elsewhere: The making of immigrant identities in a globalized world*. Stanford University Press.

Shao, C., Ciampaglia, G. L., Flammini, A., & Menczer, F. (2016). Hoaxy: A Platform for tracking online misinformation. In *Proceedings of the 25th International Conference Companion on World Wide Web* (pp. 745–750). https://doi.org/10.1145/2872518.2890098

Sharifi, M., Asadi-Pooya, A. A., & Mousavi-Roknabadi, R. S. (2020). Burnout among healthcare providers of COVID-19: A systematic review of epidemiology and recommendations. *Archives of Academic Emergency Medicine*, *9*(1), e7. https://doi.org/10.22037/aaem.v9i1.1004

Sheets, L., Johnson, J., Todd, T., Perkins, T., Gu, C., & Rau, M. (2011). Unsupported labeling of race as a risk factor for certain diseases in a widely used medical textbook. *Academic Medicine*, *86*(10), 1300–1303. https://doi.org/10.1097/ACM.0b013e31822bbdb5

Shelton, D. E., Kim, Y. S., & Barak, G. (2006). A study of juror expectations and demands concerning scientific evidence: Does the CSI effect exist. *Vanderbilt Journal of Entertainment & Technology Law*, *9*(2), 331–368. https://scholarship.law.vanderbilt.edu/jetlaw/vol9/iss2/3/

Shi, Z., Liu, X., & Srinivasan, K. (2022). Hype news diffusion and risk of misinformation: the Oz effect in health care. *Journal of Marketing Research*, *59*(2), 327–352. https://doi.org/10.1177/00222437211044447

Shibutani, T. (1966). *Improvised news: A sociological study of rumor*. The Bobbs-Merrill Company, Inc.

Shin, J., & Valente, T. (2020). Algorithms and health misinformation: A case study of vaccine books on Amazon. *Journal of Health Communication*, *25*(5), 394–401. https://doi.org/10.1080/10810730.2020.1776423

Shirk, J. L., Ballard, H. L., Wilderman, C. C., Phillips, T., Wiggins, A., Jordan, R., McCallie, E., Minarchek, M., Lewenstein, B. V., Krasney, M. E., & Bonney, R. (2012). Public participation in scientific research: A framework for deliberate design. *Ecology and Society*, *17*(2). https://www.jstor.org/stable/26269051

Shu, K., Silva, A, Wang, S., Tang, J., & Liu, H. (2017). Fake news detection on social media: A data mining perspective. *ACM SIGKDD Explorations Newsletter*, *19*(1), 22–36. https://doi.org/10.48550/arXiv.1708.01967

Shuman, E. L. (1894). *Steps into journalism; helps and hints for young writers*. Correspondence School of Journalism.

Siegrist, M., Gutscher, H., & Earle, T. C. (2005). Perception of risk: The influence of general trust, and general confidence. *Journal of Risk Research*, *8*(2), 145–156. https://doi.org/10.1080/1366987032000105315

SignalFire. (2020, November 29). *SignalFire's creator economy market map*. https://www.signalfire.com/blog/creator-economy

Silverman, C., & Alexander, L. (2016). How teens in the Balkans are duping Trump supporters with fake news. *Buzzfeed News*. https://www.buzzfeednews.com/article/craigsilverman/how-macedonia-became-a-global-hub-for-pro-trump-misinfo

Simon, H. A. (1988). The science of design: Creating the artificial. *Design Issues*, *4*(1/2), 67–82. https://www.jstor.org/stable/1511391

Simonov, A., Sacher, S., Dubé, J. P., & Biswas, S. (2022). Frontiers: the persuasive effect of Fox News: Noncompliance with social distancing during the COVID-19 pandemic. *Marketing Science*, *41*(2), 230–242. https://doi.org/10.1287/mksc.2021.1328

Simpson, E., & Conner, A. (2020, August 18). Fighting Coronavirus misinformation and disinformation. *Center for American Progress*. https://www.americanprogress.org/article/fighting-coronavirus-misinformation-disinformation/

Singh, K., Lima, G., Cha, M., Cha, C., Kulshrestha, J., Ahn, Y.-Y., & Varol, O. (2022). Misinformation, believability, and vaccine acceptance over 40 countries: Takeaways from the initial phase of the COVID-19 infodemic. *PLoS One*, *17*(2), e0263381. https://doi.org/10.1371/journal.pone.0263381

Sirlin, N., Epstein, Z., Arechar, A. A., & Rand, D. G. (2021). Digital literacy is associated with more discerning accuracy judgments but not sharing intentions. *Harvard Kennedy School Misinformation R*eview, *2*(6). https://doi.org/10.37016/mr-2020-83

Slater, M. D. (2007). Reinforcing spirals: The mutual influence of media selectivity and media effects and their impact on individual behavior and social identity. *Communication Theory*, *17*(3), 281–303. https://doi.org/10.1111/j.1468-2885.2007.00296.x

Smedley, B. D. (2012). The lived experience of race and its health consequences. *American Journal of Public Health*, *102*(5), 933–935. https://doi.org/10.2105/AJPH.2011.300643

Smith, H., Markowitz, D. M., & Gilbert, C. (2022). Science training for political reporters: Understanding impact with a mixed methods approach. *Journalism Practice*, *18*(4), 938–953. https://doi.org/10.1080/17512786.2022.2065337

Smith, J. E. H. (2023). "I believe because it is absurd"; or, pseudoscience. In A. Finger & M. Wagner (Eds.), *Bias, belief, and conviction in an age of fake facts* (pp. 59–85). Routledge.

Smith, L. T. (1999). *Decolonizing methodologies: Research and Indigenous peoples*. Zed Books Ltd.

Smith, N., & Graham, T. (2019). Mapping the anti-vaccination movement on Facebook. *Information, Communication & Society*, *22*(9), 1310–1327. https://doi.org/10.1080/1369118X.2017.1418406

Smith, N., & Rock, J. (2014). Documentary as a statement: Defining old genre in a new age. *Journal of Media Practice*, *15*(1), 58–62. https://doi.org/10.1080/14682753.2014.892698

Smith-Roberts, A. (2018). Facebook, fake news, and the first amendment. *Denver Law Review Forum*, *95*, Article 21, 118–126. https://digitalcommons.du.edu/dlrforum/vol95/iss1/21

Sobieraj, S., & Berry, J. M. (2011). From incivility to outrage: Political discourse in blogs, talk radio, and cable news. *Political Communication*, *28*(1), 19–41. https://doi.org/10.1080/10584609.2010.542360

Søe, S. O. (2021). A unified account of information, misinformation, and disinformation. *Synthese*, *198*(6), 5929–5949. https://doi.org/10.1007/s11229-019-02444-x

Somerville, R. C. J., & Hassol, J. (2011). Communicating the science of climate change. *Physics Today*, *64*(10), 48–53. https://doi.org/10.1063/PT.3.1296

Sørensen, K., Pelikan, J. M., Röthlin, F., Ganahl, K., Slonska, Z., Doyle, G., Fullam, J., Kondilis, B., Agrafiotis, D., Uiters, E., Falcon, M., Mensing, M., Tchamov, K., Broucke, S. van den, & Brand, H. (2015). Health literacy in Europe: Comparative results of the European health literacy survey (HLS-EU). *European Journal of Public Health*, *25*(6), 1053–1058. https://doi.org/10.1093/eurpub/ckv043

Soto-Vásquez, A. D. (2023). *A review of academic literature on U.S. Latinos and disinformation.* Digital Democracy Institute of the Americas. https://ddia.org/en/review-of-literature-on-us-latinos-and-disinformation

Soto-Vásquez, A. D., Gonzalez, A. A., Shi, W., Garcia, N., & Hernandez, J. (2020). COVID-19: Contextualizing misinformation flows in a US Latinx border community (media and communication during COVID-19). *Howard Journal of Communications*, *32*(5), 421–439. https://doi.org/10.1080/10646175.2020.1860839

Southwell, B. G. (2005). Between messages and people: A multilevel model of memory for television content. *Communication Research*, *32*(1), 112–140. https://doi.org/10.1177/0093650204271401

Southwell, B. G., Brennen, J. S. B., Paquin, R., Boudewyns, V., & Zeng, J. (2022). Defining and measuring scientific misinformation. *The ANNALS of the American Academy of Political and Social Science*, *700*(1), 98–111. https://doi.org/10.1177/00027162221084709

Southwell, B., Corin, D., Eck, M., Hessenius, A., Li, L., Magnuson, A., Parkman, J., Sauer, R., Turner, C., & Stansbury, S. (2021). Dimensions of trust and information seeking on natural disasters, hazards, and extreme weather in North Carolina (USA). *European Meteorological Society Annual Meeting Abstracts*, *18*, Article EMS2021-25. https://doi.org/10.5194/ems2021-25

Southwell, B. G., Niederdeppe, J., Cappella, J. N., Gaysynsky, A., Kelley, D. E., Oh, A., Peterson, E. B., & Chou, W. S. (2019). Misinformation as a misunderstood challenge to public health. *American Journal of Preventive Medicine*, *57*(2), 282–285. https://doi.org/10.1016/j.amepre.2019.03.009

Southwell, B. G., Otero Machuca, J., Cherry, S. T., Burnside, M., & Barrett, N. J. (2023). Health misinformation exposure and health disparities: Observations and opportunities. *Annual Review of Public Health*, *44*, 113–130. https://doi.org/10.1146/annurev-publhealth-071321-031118

Southwell, B. G., & Thorson, E. A. (2015). The prevalence, consequence, and remedy of misinformation in mass media systems. *Journal of Communication*, *65*(4), 589–595. https://doi.org/10.1111/jcom.12168

Southwell, B. G., Thorson, E. A., & Sheble, L. (Eds.). (2018). *Misinformation and mass audiences.* University of Texas Press.

Spampatti, T., Hahnel, U. J. J., Trutnevyte, E., & Brosch, T. (2024). Psychological inoculation strategies to fight climate disinformation across 12 countries. *Nature Human Behaviour*, *8*, 380–398. https://doi.org/10.1038/s41562-023-01736-0

Stanovich, K. E., & West, R. F. (2000). Advancing the rationality debate. *Behavioral and Brain Sciences*, *23*(5), 701–717. https://doi.org/10.1017/S0140525X00623439

Starbird, K. (2023, September 18). *A battle for better information.* The Lawfare Institute. https://www.lawfaremedia.org/article/a-battle-for-better-information

Stecula, D. A., Motta, M., Kuru, O., & Jamieson, K. H. (2022). The great and powerful Dr. Oz? Alternative health media consumption and vaccine views in the United States. *Journal of Communication*, *72*(3), 374–400. https://doi.org/10.1093/joc/jqac011

Steelman, T. A., McCaffrey, S. M., Velez, A.-L. K., & Briefel, J. A. (2015). What information do people use, trust, and find useful during a disaster? Evidence from five large wildfires. *Natural Hazards*, *76*(1), 615–634. https://doi.org/10.1007/s11069-014-1512-x

Stefanik-Sidener, K. (2013). Nature, nurture, or that fast food hamburger: Media framing of diabetes in the New York Times from 2000 to 2010. *Health Communication*, *28*(4), 351–358. https://doi.org/10.1080/10410236.2012.688187

Steg, L. (2016). Values, norms, and intrinsic motivation to act proenvironmentally. *Annual Review of Environment and Resources, 41*, 277–292.

___. (2023). Psychology of climate change. *Annual Review of Psychology*, *74*, 391–421. https://doi.org/10.1146/annurev-psych-032720-042905

Steiger, M., Bharucha, T. J., Venkatagiri, S., Riedl, M. J., & Lease, M. (2021, May). The psychological well-being of content moderators: The emotional labor of commercial moderation and avenues for improving support. *Proceedings of the 2021 CHI Conference on Human Factors in Computing Systems*, Article 341. https://doi.org/10.1145/3411764.3445092

Steinke, J., Gilbert, C., Opat, K., & Landrum, A. R. (2024). Fostering inclusive science media: Insights from examining the relationship between women's identities and their anticipated engagement with Deep Look YouTube science videos. *PLoS One*, *19*(8), e0308558. https://doi.org/10.1371/journal.pone.0308558

Stevens, G. A., Bennett, J. E., Hennocq, Q., Lu, Y., De-Regil, L. M., Rogers, L., Danaei, G., Li, G., White, R. A., Flaxman, S. R., Oehrle, S.-P., Finucane, M. M., Guerrero, R., Bhutta, Z. A., Then-Paulino, A., Fawzi, W., Black, R. E., & Ezzati, M. (2015). Trends and mortality effects of vitamin A deficiency in children in 138 low-income and middle-income countries between 1991 and 2013: A pooled analysis of population-based surveys. *The Lancet Global Health*, *3*(9), e528–e536. https://doi.org/10.1016/S2214-109X(15)00039-X

Stone, W. (2021). An anti-vaccine film targeted to Black Americans spreads false information. *KFF Health News*. https://kffhealthnews.org/news/article/an-anti-vaccine-film-targeted-to-black-americans-spreads-false-information/

Stormacq, C., Van den Broucke, S., & Wosinski, J. (2019). Does health literacy mediate the relationship between socioeconomic status and health disparities? Integrative review. *Health Promotion International*, *34*(5), e1–e17. https://doi.org/10.1093/heapro/day062

Strange, J. J., & Leung, C. C. (1999). How anecdotal accounts in news and in fiction can influence judgments of a social problem's urgency, causes, and cures. *Personality and Social Psychology Bulletin*, *25*(4), 436–449. https://doi.org/10.1177/0146167299025004004

Stroud, N. J. (2008). Media use and political predispositions: Revisiting the concept of selective exposure. *Political Behavior, 30*(3), 341–366. https://doi.org/10.1007/s11109-007-9050-9

___. (2010). Polarization and partisan selective exposure. *Journal of Communication*, *60*(3), 556-576. https://doi.org/10.1111/j.1460-2466.2010.01497.x

___. (2011). *Niche news: The politics of news choice*. Oxford University Press.

Stroupe, D. (2014). Examining classroom science practice communities: How teachers and students negotiate epistemic agency and learn science-as-practice. *Science Education*, *98*(3), 487–516. https://doi.org/10.1002/sce.21112

Stryker, C., & Kavlakoglu, E. (2024). *What is AI?* IBM. https://www.ibm.com/topics/artificial-intelligence

Su, S. (2022). Updating politicized beliefs: How motivated reasoning contributes to polarization. *Journal of Behavioral and Experimental Economics*, *96*, 101799. https://doi.org/10.1016/j.socec.2021.101799

Suarez-Lledo, V., & Alvarez-Galvez, J. (2021). Prevalence of health misinformation on social media: Systematic review. *Journal of Medical Internet Research*, *23*(1), p.e17187. https://doi.org/10.2196/17187

Sugihara, G., May, R., Ye, H., Hsieh, C. H., Deyle, E., Fogarty, M., & Munch, S. (2012). Detecting causality in complex ecosystems. *Science, 338*(6106), 496–500. https://doi.org/10.1126/science.1227079

Suldovsky, B. (2016). In science communication, why does the idea of the public deficit always return? Exploring key influences. *Public Understanding of Science*, *25*(4), 415–426. https://doi.org/10.1177/0963662516629750

Sumner, P., Vivian-Griffiths, S., Boivin, J., Williams, A., Venetis, C. A., Davies, A., Ogden, J., Whelan, L., Hughes, B., Dalton, B., Boy, F., & Chambers, C. C. (2014). The association between exaggeration in health related science news and academic press releases: retrospective observational study. *BMJ*, *349*, g7015. https://doi.org/10.1136/bmj.g7015

Supran, G., & Oreskes, N. (2017). Assessing ExxonMobil's climate change communications (1977–2014). *Environmental Research Letters* 12(8), 084019. https://doi.org/10.1088/1748-9326/aa815f

___. (2021). Rhetoric and frame analysis of ExxonMobil's climate change communications. *One Earth*, *4*(5), 696–719. https://doi.org/10.1016/j.oneear.2021.04.014

Susmann, M. W., & Wegener, D. T. (2023). How attitudes impact the continued influence effect of misinformation: The mediating role of discomfort. *Personality and Social Psychology Bulletin*, *49*(5), 744–757. https://doi.org/10.1177/01461672221077519

Swire-Thompson, B., Cook, J., Butler, L. H., Sanderson, J. A., Lewandowsky, S., & Ecker, U. K. H. (2021). Correction format has a limited role when debunking misinformation. *Cognitive Research: Principles and Implications*, 6, 83. https://doi.org/10.1186/s41235-021-00346-6

Swire-Thompson, B., DeGutis, J., & Lazer, D. (2020). Searching for the backfire effect: Measurement and design considerations. *Journal of Applied Research in Memory and Cognition*, *9*(3), 286–299. https://doi.org/10.1016/j.jarmac.2020.06.006

Swire-Thompson, B., Dobbs, M., Thomas, A., & DeGutis, J. (2023). Memory failure predicts belief regression after the correction of misinformation. *Cognition*, *230*, 105276. https://doi.org/10.1016/j.cognition.2022.105276

Swire-Thompson, B., & Lazer, D. (2020). Public health and online misinformation: Challenges and recommendations. *Annual Review of Public Health*, *41*, 433–451. https://doi.org/10.1146/annurev-publhealth-040119-094127

___. (2022). Reducing health misinformation in science: A call to arms. *The ANNALS of the American Academy of Political and Social Science*, *700*(1), 124–135. https://doi.org/10.1177/00027162221087686

Taber, C. S., & Lodge, M. (2006). Motivated skepticism in the evaluation of political beliefs. *American Journal of Political Science*, *50*(3), 755–769. https://doi.org/10.1111/j.1540-5907.2006.00214.x

Taddeo, M. (2009). Defining trust and e-trust: From old theories to new problems. *International Journal of Technology and Human Interaction*, *5*(2), 23–35. https://doi.org/10.4018/jthi.2009040102

Tanner, A. H. (2004). Agenda building, source selection, and health news at local television stations: A nationwide survey of local television health reporters. *Science Communication*, *25*(4), 350–363. https://doi.org/10.1177/1075547004265127

Tay, L. Q., Lewandowsky, S., Hurlstone, M. J., Kurz, T., & Ecker, U. K. H. (2023). A focus shift in the evaluation of misinformation interventions. *Harvard Kennedy School Misinformation Review*, *4*(5). https://doi.org/10.37016/mr-2020-124

Taylor, L. E., Swerdfeger, A. L., & Eslick, G. D. (2014). Vaccines are not associated with autism: An evidence-based meta-analysis of case-control and cohort studies. *Vaccine*, *32*(29), 3623–3629. https://doi.org/10.1016/j.vaccine.2014.04.085

Teaiwa, T. K. (1994). Bikinis and other s/pacific n/oceans. *The Contemporary Pacific*, *6*(1), 87–109. https://www.jstor.org/stable/23701591

Tenhundfeld, N. L., de Visser, E. J., Ries, A. J., Finomore, V. S., & Tossell, C. C. (2020). Trust and distrust of automated parking in a Tesla Model X. *Human Factors*, *62*(2). 194–210. https://doi.org/10.1177/0018720819865412

Teplinsky, E., Ponce, S. B., Drake, E. K., Garcia, A. M., Loeb, S., van Londen, G. J., Teoh, D., Thompson, M., & Schapira, L. (2022). Online medical misinformation in cancer: Distinguishing fact from fiction. *JCO Oncology Practice*, *18*(8), 584–589. https://doi.org/10.1200/OP.21.00764

Terren, L., & Borge, R. (2021). Echo chambers on social media: A systematic review of the literature. *Review of Communication Research*, *9*, 99–118. https://doi.org/10.12840/ISSN.2255-4165.028

Tessler, H., Choi, M., & Kao, G. (2020). The anxiety of being Asian American: Hate crimes and negative biases during the COVID-19 pandemic. *American Journal of Criminal Justice*, *45*, 636–646. https://doi.org/10.1007/s12103-020-09541-5

Thacker, P. D. (2022). Stealing from the tobacco playbook, fossil fuel companies pour money into elite American universities. *BMJ*, *378*, o2095. https://doi.org/10.1136/bmj.o2095

Thomas, D. R., & Wahedi, L. A. (2023). Disrupting hate: The effect of deplatforming hate organizations on their online audience. *Proceedings of the National Academy of Sciences*, *120*(24), e2214080120. https://doi.org/10.1073/pnas.2214080120

Tichenor, P., Donohue, G., & Olien, C. (1980). *Community conflict and the press*. Sage Publications.

Tomes, N., & Parry, M. S. (2022). *What are the historical roots of the COVID-19 infodemic? Lessons From the past* (WHO Health Evidence Network Synthesis Report No. 77). World Health Organization Regional Office for Europe. https://www.ncbi.nlm.nih.gov/books/NBK585501/

Torres, A., Pina, G., Southwell, B., & Garcia-Baza, I. (2023). Can local TV news affect parents' perceptions of parenting and child development research? Evidence from the Positive Parenting Newsfeed Project. *Psychology, Public Policy, and Law*, *29*(1), 106–124. https://doi.org/10.1037/law0000369

Traberg, C. S., Roozenbeek, J., & van der Linden, S. (2022). Psychological inoculation against misinformation: Current evidence and future directions. *The ANNALS of the American Academy of Political and Social Science*, *700*(1), 136–151. https://doi.org/10.1177/00027162221087936

Trauthig, I. K., & Woolley, S. C. (2023). "On WhatsApp I say what I want": Messaging apps, diaspora communities, and networked counterpublics in the United States. *New Media & Society*, *0*(0). https://doi.org/10.1177/14614448231203695

Trezza D. (2023). To scrape or not to scrape, this is dilemma. The post-API scenario and implications on digital research. *Frontiers in Sociology*, *8*, 1145038. https://doi.org/10.3389/fsoc.2023.1145038.

Tripodi, F. B. (2022). *The propagandists' playbook: How conservative elites manipulate search and threaten democracy*. Yale University Press.

Tripodi, F. B., & Dave, A. (2023). Abortion near me? The implications of semantic media on accessing health information. *Social Media + Society*, *9*(3). https://doi.org/10.1177/20563051231195548

Tripodi, F. B., Garcia, L. C., & Marwick, A. E. (2024). 'Do your own research': Affordance activation and disinformation spread. *Information, Communication & Society*, *27*(6), 1212–1228. https://doi.org/10.1080/1369118X.2023.2245869

Tromble, R. (2021). Where have all the data gone? A critical reflection on academic digital research in the post-API age. *Social Media+ Society*, *7*(1). https://doi.org/10.1177/2056305121988929

Tsfati, Y., Boomgaarden, H. G., Strömbäck, J., Vliegenthart, R., Damstra, A., & Lindgren, E. (2020). Causes and consequences of mainstream media dissemination of fake news: Literature review and synthesis. *ANNALS of the International Communication Association*, *44*(2), 157–173. https://doi.org/10.1080/23808985.2020.1759443

Tucker, J. A., Guess, A., Barbera, P., Vaccari, C, Siegel, A, Sanovich, S., Stukal, D, & Nyhan, B. (2018, March 19). *Social media, political polarization, and political disinformation: A review of the scientific literature.* Social Science Research Network. https://dx.doi.org/10.2139/ssrn.3144139

Tversky, A., & Kahneman, D. (1974). Judgment under uncertainty: Heuristics and biases. *Science, 185*(4157), 1124–1131. https://doi.org/10.1126/science.185.4157.1124

Union of Concerned Scientists. (2019, April 9). Purdue Pharma's use of hospital, academic ties helped fuel opioid crisis. https://www.ucsusa.org/resources/disinformation-playbook-purdue-pharma

University of Maryland School of Public Health, (n.d.). *The Health Advocates In-Reach and Research Campaign (HAIR): Maryland Center for Health Equity.* https://sph.umd.edu/hair

Unkelbach, C., Koch, A., Silva, R. R., & Garcia-Marques, T. (2019). Truth by repetition: Explanations and implications. *Current Directions in Psychological Science, 28*(3), 247–253. https://doi.org/10.1177/0963721419827854

U.S. Food and Drug Administration. (2022, June 2). *FDA 101: Dietary supplements.* https://www.fda.gov/consumers/consumer-updates/fda-101-dietary-supplements

U.S. National Cancer Institute. (2017). A *socioecological approach to addressing tobacco-related health disparities* (NIH Publication No. 17-CA-8035A). National Cancer Institute Tobacco Control Monograph 22. U.S. Department of Health and Human Services, National Institutes of Health. https://cancercontrol.cancer.gov/brp/tcrb/monographs/monograph-22#chapters

U.S. Preventive Services Task Force (2024, April 30). *Breast cancer: Screening.* https://www.uspreventiveservicestaskforce.org/uspstf/recommendation/breast-cancer-screening#bcei-recommendation-title-area

Valkenburg, P. M., & Peter, J. (2013). The differential susceptibility to media effects model. *Journal of Communication, 63*(2), 221–243. https://doi.org/10.1111/jcom.12024

Van Aelst, P., Toth, F., Castro, L., Štětka, V., Vreese, C. D., Aalberg, T., Cardenal, A. S., Corbu, N., Esser, F., Hopman, D. N., Koc-Michalska, K., Matthes, J., Schemer, C., Sheafer, T., Splendore, S., Stanyer, J., Stępińska, A., Strömbäck, J., & Theocharis, Y. (2021). Does a crisis change news habits? A comparative study of the effects of COVID-19 on news media use in 17 European countries. *Digital Journalism, 9*(9), 1208–1238. https://doi.org/10.1080/21670811.2021.1943481

Van Bavel, J. J., Harris, E. A., Pärnamets, P., Rathje, S., Doell, K. C., & Tucker, J. A. (2021). Political psychology in the digital (mis)information age: A model of news belief and sharing. *Social Issues and Policy Review, 15*(1), 84–113. https://doi.org/10.1111/sipr.12077

van den Besselaar, P., & Heimeriks, G. (2001). Disciplinary, multidisciplinary, interdisciplinary - Concepts and indicators. In M. Davis & C. S. Wilson (Eds.), *8th international conference on scientometrics and informetrics* (pp. 705–716).

van der Linden, S. (2015). The conspiracy-effect: Exposure to conspiracy theories (about global warming) decreases pro-social behavior and science acceptance. *Personality and Individual Differences, 87*, 171–173. https://doi.org/10.1016/j.paid.2015.07.045

van der Linden, S., Albarracín, D., Fazio, L., Freelon, D., Roozenbeek, J., Swire-Thompson, B., & Van Bavel, J. (2023, November). *Using psychological science to understand and fight health misinformation.* American Psychological Association. https://www.apa.org/pubs/reports/misinformation-consensus-statement.pdf

van der Linden, S., Panagopoulos, C., & Roozenbeek, J. (2020). You are fake news: Political bias in perceptions of fake news. *Media, Culture & Society, 42*(3), 460–470. https://doi.org/10.1177/0163443720906992

van der Vlist, F. N., Helmond, A., Burkhardt, M., & Seitz, T. (2022). API governance: the case of Facebook's evolution. *Social Media+ Society*, *8*(2). https://doi.org/10.1177/20563051221086228

Van Duyn, E., & Collier, J. (2019). Priming and fake news: The effects of elite discourse on evaluations of news media. *Mass Communication and Society*, *22*(1), 29–48. https://doi.org/10.1080/15205436.2018.1511807

van Kampen, K., Laski, J., Herman, G., & Chan, T. M. (2022). Investigating COVID-19 vaccine communication and misinformation on TikTok: Cross-sectional study. *JMIR Infodemiology*, *2*(2), e38316. https://doi.org/10.2196/38316

van Prooijen, J. W., & Acker, M. (2015). The influence of control on belief in conspiracy theories: Conceptual and applied extensions. *Applied Cognitive Psychology*, *29*(5), 753–761. https://doi.org/10.1002/acp.3161

van Prooijen, J. W., & Böhm, N. (2023). Do conspiracy theories shape or rationalize vaccination hesitancy over time? *Social Psychological and Personality Science*, *15*(4), 421–429. https://doi.org/10.1177/19485506231181659

van Prooijen, J. W., Ligthart, J., Rosema, S., & Xu, Y. (2022a). The entertainment value of conspiracy theories. *British Journal of Psychology*, *113*(1), 25–48. https://doi.org/10.1111/bjop.12522

van Prooijen, J. W., Spadaro, G., & Wang, H. (2022b). Suspicion of institutions: How distrust and conspiracy theories deteriorate social relationships. *Current Opinion in Psychology*, *43*, 65–69. https://doi.org/10.1016/j.copsyc.2021.06.013

van Schalkwyk, F., & Dudek, J. (2022). Reporting preprints in the media during the COVID-19 pandemic. *Public Understanding of Science*, *31*(5), 608–616. https://doi.org/10.1177/09636625221077392

Vandenbergh, M., & Gilligan, J. M. (2017). *Beyond politics: The private governance response to climate change*. Cambridge University Press.

Vandenbergh, M., Light, S. E., & Salzman, J. (2024). *Private environmental governance*. West Academic.

Vaportzis, E., Clausen, M. G., & Gow, A. J. (2017). Older adults perceptions of technology and barriers to interacting with tablet computers: A focus group study. *Frontiers in Psychology*, *8*, Article 1687. https://doi.org/10.3389/fpsyg.2017.01687

Vargo, C. J., Guo, L., & Amazeen, M. A. (2018). The agenda-setting power of fake news: A big data analysis of the online media landscape from 2014 to 2016. *New Media & Society*, *20*(5), 2028–2049. https://doi.org/10.1177/1461444817712086

Varkey B. (2021). Principles of clinical ethics and their application to practice. *Medical Principles and Practice*, *30*(1), 17–28. https://doi.org/10.1159/000509119

Vassilakopoulou, P., & Hustad, E. (2021). Bridging digital divides: A literature review and research agenda for information systems research. *Information Systems Frontiers, 25*, 955–969. https://doi.org/10.1007/s10796-020-10096-3

Vegetti, F., & Mancosu, M. (2020). The impact of political sophistication and motivated reasoning on misinformation. *Political Communication*, *37*(5), 678–695. https://doi.org/10.1080/10584609.2020.1744778

Velásquez, N., Leahy, R., Restrepo, N. J., Lupu, Y., Sear, R., Gabriel, N., Jha, O. K., Goldberg, B., & Johnson, N. F. (2021). Online hate network spreads malicious COVID-19 content outside the control of individual social media platforms. *Scientific Reports*, *11*, 11549. https://doi.org/10.1038/s41598-021-89467-y

Vespa, J., Medina, L., & Armstrong, D. M. (2020, February). *Demographic turning points for the United States: Population projections for 2020 to 2060* (Current Populations Report No. P25-1144). U.S. Census Bureau. https://www.census.gov/content/dam/Census/library/publications/2020/demo/p25-1144.pdf

Vincent, E. M., Théro, H., & Shabayek, S. (2022). Measuring the effect of Facebook's downranking interventions against groups and websites that repeatedly share misinformation. *Harvard Kennedy School Misinformation Review, 3*(3). https://doi.org/10.37016/mr-2020-100

Vinck, P., Pham, P. N., Bindu, K. K., Bedford, J., & Nilles, E. J. (2019). Institutional trust and misinformation in the response to the 2018–19 Ebola outbreak in North Kivu, DR Congo: A population-based survey. *The Lancet Infectious Diseases, 19*(5), 529–536. https://doi.org/10.1016/S1473-3099(19)30063-5

The Virality Project. (2022, February). *Memes, magnets and microchips: Narrative dynamics around COVID-19 vaccines.* Stanford Digital Repository. https://doi.org/10.25740/mx395xj8490

Visperas, C. M. (2022). *Skin theory: Visual culture and the postwar prison laboratory.* New York University Press.

Viswanath, K. (2006). Public communications and its role in reducing and eliminating health disparities. In G. E. Thompson, F. Mitchell, & M. B. Williams (Eds.), *Examining the health disparities research plan of the National Institutes of Health: Unfinished business.* The National Academies Press. https://doi.org/10.17226/11602

Viswanath, K., Bekalu, M., Dhawan, D., Pinnamaneni, R., Lang, J., & McLoud, R. (2021). Individual and social determinants of COVID-19 vaccine uptake. *BMC Public Health, 21*(1), 818. https://doi.org/10.1186/s12889-021-10862-1

Viswanath, K., & Finnegan, J. R. (1996). The knowledge gap hypothesis: Twenty-five years later. *Annals of the International Communication Association, 19*(1), 187–228. https://doi.org/10.1080/23808985.1996.11678931

Viswanath, K., Kosicki, G. M., Fredin, E. S., & Park, E. (2000). Local community ties, community-boundedness, and local public affairs knowledge gaps. *Communication Research, 27*(1), 27–50. https://doi.org/10.1177/009365000027001002

Viswanath, K., Lee, E. J., & Dryer, E. (2024). Communication inequalities and incomplete data hinder understanding of how social media affect vaccine uptake. *BMJ, 385*, e076478. https://doi.org/10.1136/bmj-2023-076478

Viswanath K., Lee E. W., & Pinnamaneni R. (2020). We need the lens of equity in COVID-19 communication. *Health Communication, 35*(14), 1743–1746. https://doi.org/10.1080/10410236.2020.1837445

Viswanath, K., McCloud, R. F., & Bekalu, M. A. (2022a). Communication, health, and equity: Structural influences. In T. L. Thompson & N. G. Harrington (Eds.), *The Routledge handbook of health communication* (3rd ed., pp. 426–440). Routledge/Taylor & Francis Group.

___. (2022b). Communication, health, and equity: Structural influences. In T. L. Thompson & N. G. Harrington (Eds.), *The Routledge handbook of health communication* (3rd ed., pp. 426–440). Routledge/Taylor & Francis Group.

Viswanath, K., McCloud, R. F., Lee, E. W. J., & Bekalu, M. A. (2022c). Measuring what matters: Data absenteeism, science communication, and the perpetuation of inequities. *The ANNALS of the American Academy of Political and Social Science, 700*(1), 208–219. https://doi.org/10.1177/00027162221093268

Viswanath, K., Nagler, R. H., Bigman-Galimore, C. A., McCauley, M. P., Jung, M., & Ramanadhan, S. (2012). The communications revolution and health inequalities in the 21st century: Implications for cancer control. *Cancer Epidemiology, Biomarkers & Prevention, 21*(10), 1701–1708. https://doi.org/10.1158/1055-9965.EPI-12-0852

Voss, M. (2002). Checking the pulse: Midwestern reporters' opinions on their ability to report health care news. *American Journal of Public Health, 92*(7), 1158–1160. https://doi.org/10.2105/AJPH.92.7.1158

Vraga, E. K., & Bode, L. (2020). Defining misinformation and understanding its bounded nature: Using expertise and evidence for describing misinformation. *Political Communication, 37*(1), 136–144. https://doi.org/10.1080/10584609.2020.1716500

Waddell, K., & Bergmann, A. (2020, August 13). On social media, only some lies are against the rules. *Consumer Reports.* https://www.consumerreports.org/social-media/social-media-misinformation-policies/

Waddell, M. (2023, May 17). The science on GMOs isn't settled – here's why. *Non-GMO Project.* https://www.nongmoproject.org/blog/the-science-on-gmos-isnt-settled-heres-why/

Wagner, D. N., Marcon, A. R., & Caulfield, T. (2020). "Immune Boosting" in the time of COVID: Selling immunity on Instagram. *Allergy, Asthma & Clinical Immunology, 16*(76), 1–5. https://doi.org/10.1186/s13223-020-00474-6

Wagoner, K. G., Lazard, A. J., Romero-Sandoval, E. A., & Reboussin, B. A. (2021). Health claims about cannabidiol products: A retrospective analysis of U.S. Food and Drug Administration warning letters from 2015 to 2019. *Cannabis and Cannabinoid Research, 6*(6), 559–563. https://doi.org/10.1089/can.2020.0166

Wailoo, K. (2021). *Pushing cool: Big tobacco, racial marketing, and the untold story of the menthol cigarette.* University of Chicago Press.

Wakefield, A. J., Murch, S. H., Anthony, A., Linnell, J., Casson, D. M., Malik, M., Berelowitz, M., Dhillon, A. P., Thomson, M. A., Harvey, P., Valentine, A., Davies, S. E., & Walker-Smith, J. A. (1998). Ileal-lymphoid-nodular hyperplasia, non-specific colitis, and pervasive developmental disorder in children. *Lancet, 351*(9103), 637–641. https://doi.org/10.1016/s0140-6736(97)11096-0

Wall, L. L. (2006). The medical ethics of Dr J Marion Sims: A fresh look at the historical record. *Journal of Medical Ethics, 32*(6), 346–350. https://doi.org/10.1136/jme.2005.012559

Walsh, E. M., & Tsurusaki, B. K. (2018). "Thank you for being epublican": Negotiating science and political identities in climate change learning. *Journal of the Learning Sciences, 27*(1), 8–48. https://doi.org/10.1080/10508406.2017.1362563

Walsh-Childers, K., Braddock, J., Rabaza, C., & Schwitzer, G. (2018). One step forward, one step back: Changes in news coverage of medical interventions. *Health Communication, 33*(2), 174–187. https://doi.org/10.1080/10410236.2016.1250706

Walters, W. H., & Wilder, E. I. (2023). Fabrication and errors in the bibliographic citations generated by ChatGPT. *Scientific Reports, 13*(1), 14045. https://doi.org/10.1038/s41598-023-41032-5

Wang, L., Yue, M., & Wang, G. (2023). Too real to be questioned: Analysis of the factors influencing the spread of online scientific rumors in China. *Sage Open, 13*(4). https://doi.org/10.1177/21582440231215586

Wang, R., He, Y., Xu, J., & Zhang, H. (2020). Fake news or bad news? Toward an emotion-driven cognitive dissonance model of misinformation diffusion. *Asian Journal of Communication, 30*(5), 317–342. https://doi.org/10.1080/01292986.2020.1811737

Wanless, A., & Berk, M. (2019). The audience is the amplifier: Participatory propaganda. In P. Baines, N. O'Shaughnessy, & N. Snow (Eds.), *The Sage handbook of propaganda* (pp. 85–104). Sage.

___. (2021). The changing nature of propaganda: Coming to terms with influence in conflict. In T. Clack & R. Johnson (Eds.), *The world information war: Western resilience, campaigning, and cognitive effects* (pp. 63–80). Routledge. https://doi.org/10.4324/9781003046905-7

Ward, S. J. A. (2010). Inventing objectivity: New philosophical foundations. In C. Meyers (Ed.), *Journalism ethics: A philosophical approach* (pp. 137–152). Oxford University Press.

Wardle, C. (2023). Misunderstanding misinformation. *Issues in Science and Technology, 39*(3), 38–40. https://doi.org/10.58875/ZAUD1691

Wardle, C., & Derakhshan, H. (2017, September). *Information disorder: Toward an interdisciplinary framework for research and policy making* (Council of Europe Report No. DGI(2017)09). Council of Europe. https://edoc.coe.int/en/media/7495-information-disorder-toward-an-interdisciplinary-framework-for-research-and-policy-making.html

Waruwu, B. K., Tandoc Jr., E. C., Duffy, A., Kim, N., & Ling, R. (2021). Telling lies together? Sharing news as a form of social authentication. *New Media & Society*, *23*(9), 2516–2533. https://doi.org/10.1177/1461444820931017

Watts, D. J., Rothschild, D. M., & Mobius, M. (2021). Measuring the news and its impact on democracy. *Proceedings of the National Academy of Sciences of the United States of America*, *118*(15), e1912443118. https://doi.org/10.1073/pnas.1912443118

Wayback Machine. (n.d.). HealthNewsReview.Org: Improving your critical thinking about health care. https://web.archive.org/web/20220803193934/https://www.healthnewsreview.org/

Webster, J., & Phalen, P. F. (1996). *The mass audience: Rediscovering the dominant model*. Routledge.

Weeks, B., & Southwell, B. (2010). The symbiosis of news coverage and aggregate online search behavior: Obama, rumors, and presidential politics. *Mass Communication and Society*, *13*(4), 341–360. https://doi.org/10.1080/15205430903470532

Wehrman, A. M. (2022). *The contagion of liberty*. John Hopkins University Press.

___. (1972). Science and trans-science. *Science*, *177*(4045), 211. https://doi.org/10.1126/science.177.4045.211

Weingart, P. (2017). Is there a hype problem in science? If so, how is it addressed. In K. H. Jamieson, D. Kahan, & D. Scheufele (Eds.), *The Oxford handbook of the science of science communication* (pp. 111–118). Oxford University Press.

West, J. D. (2023, March 31). The chatbot era: Better or worse off? *The Seattle Times*. https://www.seattletimes.com/opinion/the-chatbot-era-better-or-worse-off/

West, J. D., & Bergstrom, C. T. (2021). Misinformation in and about science. *Proceedings of the National Academy of Sciences*, *118*(15), e1912444117. https://doi.org/10.1073/pnas.1912444117

Whitacre, B., Strover, S., & Gallardo, R. (2015). How much does broadband infrastructure matter? Decomposing the metro–non-metro adoption gap with the help of the National Broadband Map. *Government Information Quarterly*, *32*(3), 261–269. https://doi.org/10.1016/j.giq.2015.03.002

Whyte, K. P., Brewer, J. P., & Johnson, J. T. (2016). Weaving Indigenous science, protocols and sustainability science. *Sustainability Science*, *11*(1), 25–32. https://doi.org/10.1007/s11625-015-0296-6

Wilhelm, E. (2023). *Community stories guide – Understanding community information needs through stories*. Information Futures Lab. https://communitystoriesguide.org/

Wilkie, W. L., McNeill, D. L., & Mazis, M. B. (1984). Marketing's "Scarlet Letter": The theory and practice of corrective advertising. *Journal of Marketing*, *48*(2), 11–31. https://doi.org/10.2307/1251211

Williams, D. (2024, January 10). Misinformation researchers are wrong: There can't be a science of misleading content. *Conspicuous Cognition*. https://www.conspicuouscognition.com/p/misinformation-researchers-are-wrong

Williams, E. L., Bartone, S. A., Swanson, E. K., & Stokes, L. C. (2022). The American electric utility industry's role in promoting climate denial, doubt, and delay. *Environmental Research Letters*, *17*(9), 094026. https://doi.org/10.1088/1748-9326/ac8ab3

Wilson, S. L., & Wiysonge, C. (2020). Social media and vaccine hesitancy. *BMJ Global Health*, *5*(10), e004206. https://doi.org/10.1136/bmjgh-2020-004206

Wineburg, S., Breakstone, J., McGrew, S., Smith, M. D., & Ortega, T. (2022). Lateral reading on the open Internet: A district-wide field study in high school government classes. *Journal of Educational Psychology*, *114*(5), 893–909. https://doi.org/10.1037/edu0000740

Wineburg, S., & McGrew, S. (2019). Lateral reading and the nature of expertise: Reading less and learning more when evaluating digital information. *Teachers College Record*, *121*(11), 1–40. https://doi.org/10.1177/016146811912101102

Wojcieszak, M. (2021). What predicts selective exposure online: Testing political attitudes, credibility, and social identity. *Communication Research*, *48*(5), 687–716. https://doi.org/10.1177/0093650219844868

Wolfe, S. M. (2002). Direct-to-consumer advertising—education or emotion promotion? *New England Journal of Medicine*, *346*(7), 524–526. https://doi.org/10.1056/NEJM200202143460713

Wolkoff, K. N. (1996). The problem of holocaust denial literature in libraries. *Library Trends*, *45*(1), 87–96. https://hdl.handle.net/2142/8070

Woloshin, S., & Schwartz, L. M. (2006). Giving legs to restless legs: A case study of how the media helps make people sick. *PLoS Medicine*, *3*(4), e170. https://doi.org/10.1371/journal.pmed.0030170

Woloshin, S., Schwartz, L. M., Casella, S. L., Kennedy, A. T., & Larson, R. J. (2009a). Press releases by academic medical centers: Not so academic? *Annals of Internal Medicine*, *150*(9), 613–618. https://doi.org/10.7326/0003-4819-150-9-200905050-00007

Woloshin, S., Schwartz, L. M., & Kramer, B. S. (2009b). Promoting healthy skepticism in the news: Helping journalists get it right. *Journal of the National Cancer Institute*, *101*(23), 1596–1599. https://doi.org/10.1093/jnci/djp409

Wood, T., & Porter, E. (2019). The elusive backfire effect: Mass attitudes' steadfast factual adherence. *Political Behavior*, *41*, 135–163. https://doi.org/10.1007/s11109-018-9443-y

Woolf, S. H., & Harris, R. (2012). The harms of screening: New attention to an old concern. *JAMA*, *307*(6), 565–566. https://doi.org/10.1001/jama.2012.100

Woolston, C. (2018, October 4). University tenure decisions still gloss over scientists' public outreach. *Nature News*. https://www.nature.com/articles/d41586-018-06906-z

World Health Organization (WHO). (n.d.) *Infodemic*. https://www.who.int/health-topics/infodemic

___. (2014, May 1). *Food, genetically modified*. https://www.who.int/news-room/questions-and-answers/item/food-genetically-modified

World Health Organization (WHO) & UNICEF. (2023). *How to build an infodemic insights report in six steps*. https://iris.who.int/bitstream/handle/10665/370317/9789240075658-eng.pdf?sequence=1

Wu, F., Wesseler, J., Zilberman, D., Russell, R. M., Chen, C., & Dubock, A. C. (2021). Allow Golden Rice to save lives. *Proceedings of the National Academy of Sciences*, *118*(51), Article e2120901118. https://doi.org/10.1073/pnas.2120901118

Wu, S., Zhang, J., & Du, L. (2024). "I do not trust health information shared by my parents": Credibility judgement of health (mis)information on social media in China. *Health Communication*, *39*(1), 96–106. https://doi.org/10.1080/10410236.2022.2159143

Xu, W., & Sasahara, K. (2022). Characterizing the roles of bots on Twitter during the COVID-19 infodemic. *Journal of Computational Social Science*, *5*, 591–609. https://doi.org/10.1007/s42001-021-00139-3

Yang, F., & Horning, M. (2020). Reluctant to share: How third person perceptions of fake news discourage news readers from sharing "real news" on social media. *Social Media+ Society*, *6*(3). https://doi.org/10.1177/2056305120955173

Yang, K. C., Pierri, F., Hui, P.-M., Axelrod, D., Torres-Lugo, C., Bryden, J., & Menczer, F. (2021). The COVID-19 infodemic: Twitter versus Facebook. *Big Data & Society*, *8*(1), http://dx.doi.org/10.1177/20539517211013861

Yang, Y., Davis, T., & Hindman, M. (2023). Visual misinformation on Facebook. *Journal of Communication*, *73*(4), 316–328. https://doi.org/10.1093/joc/jqac051

Yavchitz, A., Boutron, I., Bafeta, A., Marroun, I., Charles, P., Mantz, J., & Ravaud, P. (2012). Misrepresentation of randomized controlled trials in press releases and news coverage: A cohort study. *PLoS Medicine*, *9*(9), Article e1001308. https://doi.org/10.1371/journal.pmed.1001308

Yeh, D. A., Gomez, M. I., & Kaiser, H. M. (2019). Signaling impacts of GMO labeling on fruit and vegetable demand. *PLoS One*, *14*(10), e0223910. https://doi.org/10.1371/journal.pone.0223910

Yeo, S. K., & Silberg, J. N. (2021). Environmental documentaries in a digital age should be ethical, not just captivating. *One Earth*, *4*(6), 780–782. https://doi.org/10.1016/j.oneear.2021.05.016

Yeo, S. K., Xenos, M. A., Brossard, D., & Scheufele, D. A. (2015). Selecting our own science: How communication contexts and individual traits shape information seeking. *The ANNALS of the American Academy of Political and Social Science*, *658*(1), 172–191. https://doi.org/10.1177/0002716214557782

Yip, J., Roldan, W., Gonzalez, C., Pina, L. R., Ruiz, M., & Vanegas, P. (2022). Youth invisible work: The sociocultural and collaborative processes of online search and brokering between adolescents and English-language learning families. *Information and Learning Science*, *123*(7/8), 330–350. https://doi.org/10.1108/ILS-01-2022-0004

Young, D. G. (2023a). *Wrong: How media, politics and identity drive our appetite for misinformation.* Johns Hopkins University Press.

Young, D. G., Jamieson, K. H., Poulsen, S., & Goldring, A. (2018). Fact-checking effectiveness as a function of format and tone: Evaluating FactCheck.org and FlackCheck.org. *Journalism & Mass Communication Quarterly*, *95*(1), 49–75. fhttps://doi.org/10.1177/1077699017710453

Young, D. G., & Miller, J. M. (2023c). Political communication. In L. Huddy, D. Sears, J. Levy, & J. Jerit (Eds.), *The Oxford handbook of political psychology* (3rd ed., pp. 555–600). Oxford University Press. https://doi.org/10.1093/oxfordhb/9780197541302.013.15

Young, J. (2023b, April 19). Misinformation in rural and indigenous communities [PowerPoint Slides]. University of Washington. Available on request in the National Academies' Public Access Files.

Young, J. C., Boyd, B., Yefimova, K., Wedlake, S., Coward, C., & Hapel, R. (2021). The role of libraries in misinformation programming: A research agenda. *Journal of Librarianship and Information Science*, *53*(4), 539–550. https://doi.org/10.1177/0961000620966650

Yu, W., Payton, B., Sun, M., Jia, W., & Huang, G. (2022). Toward an integrated framework for misinformation and correction sharing: A systematic review across domains. *New Media & Society*, *25*(8), 2241–2267. https://doi.org/10.1177/14614448221116569

Yuan, X., Schuchard, R. J., & Crooks, A. T. (2019). Examining emergent communities and social bots within the polarized online vaccination debate in Twitter. *Social Media+ Society*, *5*(3). https://doi.org/10.1177/2056305119865465

Zeng, E., Kohno, T., Roesner, F., & Allen, P. G. (2020). *Bad news: Clickbait and deceptive ads on news and misinformation websites.* Workshop on Technology and Consumer Protection (ConPro '20). https://badads.cs.washington.edu/files/Zeng-ConPro2020-BadNews.pdf

Zenone, M. A., Snyder, J., & Crooks, V. (2021). Selling cannabidiol products in Canada: A framing analysis of advertising claims by online retailers. *BMC Public Health*, *21*, Article 1285, 1–10. https://doi.org/10.1186/s12889-021-11282-x

Zhang, C. (2018, April). *WeChatting American politics: Misinformation, polarization, and immigrant Chinese media.* Columbia Journalism Review. https://www.cjr.org/tow_center_reports/wechatting-american-politics-misinformation-polarization-and-immigrant-chinese-media.php

Zhang, J., Featherstone, J. D., Calabrese, C., & Wojcieszak, M. (2021). Effects of fact-checking social media vaccine misinformation on attitudes toward vaccines. *Preventive Medicine*, *145*, 106408. https://doi.org/10.1016/j.ypmed.2020.106408

Zhang, Y., Chen, F., & Lukito, J. (2023). Network amplification of politicized information and misinformation about COVID-19 by conservative media and partisan influencers on Twitter. *Political Communication*, *40*(1), 24–47. https://doi.org/10.1080/10584609.2022.2113844

Zhao, S., Hu, S., Zhou, X., Song, S., Wang, Q., Zheng, H., Zhang, Y., & Hou, Z. (2023). The prevalence, features, influencing factors, and solutions for COVID-19 vaccine misinformation: Systematic review. *JMIR Public Health and Surveillance*, *9*(1), e40201. https://doi.org/10.2196/40201

Zhong, M., Kshirsagar, M., Johnston, R., Dodhia, R., Glazer, T., Kim, A., Michael, D., Nair-Desai, S., Tsai, T. C., Friedhoff, S., & Ferres, J. M. L. (2022). Estimating vaccine-preventable COVID-19 deaths under counterfactual vaccination scenarios in the United States. *medRxiv*. https://doi.org/10.1101/2022.05.19.22275310

Zhong, W., Bailard, C., Broniatowski, D., & Tromble, R. (2024). Proud Boys on telegram. *Journal of Quantitative Description: Digital Media*, *4*, 1–47. https://doi.org/10.51685/jqd.2024.003

Zhou, J., Zhang, Y., Luo, Q., Parker, A. G., & De Choudhury, M. (2023). Synthetic lies: Understanding AI-generated misinformation and evaluating algorithmic and human solutions. In *Proceedings of the 2023 CHI Conference on Human Factors in Computing Systems* (p. 436). https://doi.org/10.1145/3544548.3581318

Zhou, T. (2020). Understanding users' participation in online health communities: A social capital perspective. *Information Development*, *36*(3), 403–413. https://doi.org/10.1177/0266666919864620

Zhou, Y., & Shen, L. (2022). Confirmation bias and the persistence of misinformation on climate change. *Communication Research*, *49*(4), 500–523. https://doi.org/10.1177/00936502211028049

Zhu, Y., Qian, P., Su, F., & Xu, J. (2022). WeChat users' debunking strategies in response to COVID-19 conspiracy theories: A mixed-methods study. *Convergence*, *28*(4), 1060–1082. https://doi.org/10.1177/13548565221102594

Zimmermann, F., & Kohring, M. (2020). Mistrust, disinforming news, and vote choice: A panel survey on the origins and consequences of believing disinformation in the 2017 German Parliamentary Election. *Political Communication, 37*(2), 215–237. https://doi.org/10.1080/10584609.2019.1686095

Zollo, F., Bessi, A., Vicario, M. D., Scala, A., Caldarelli, G., Shekhtman, L., Havlin, S., & Quattrociocchi, W. (2017). Debunking in a world of tribes. *PLoS One*, *12*(7), e0181821. https://doi.org/10.1371/journal.pone.0181821

Zuckerman, D. (2003). Hype in health reporting: "Checkbook science" buys distortion of medical news. *International Journal of Health Services*, *33*(2), 383–389. https://doi.org/10.2190/pmm9-dput-hn3y-lmjq

Appendix A

Public Meeting Agendas

Committee on Understanding and Addressing Misinformation About Science

Division of Behavioral and Social Sciences and Education (DBASSE)
Board on Science Education (BOSE)

Public Information Gathering Session #1
December 14, 2022

ALL TIMES ARE EASTERN TIME

12:45 pm **Arrival of Speakers**

1:00 pm **Welcome and Overview of the Study**
Heidi Schweingruber, Director, BOSE
Vish Viswanath, Study Chair
Tiffany E. Taylor, Study Director

1:15 pm **Discussion of the Study Charge with the Sponsor**
Moderator: *Vish Viswanath*, Study Chair
Robert O'Connor, *Program Director, Decision, Risk and Management Sciences, National Science Foundation*

2:00 pm **Break**

2:10 pm **Understanding the Science Information Landscape: Composition, Scope, and Impact**
Moderator: *Lauren Feldman,* Committee Member
Cary Funk, *Pew Research Center*
Tina Purnat, *World Health Organization*

3:10 pm **Break**

3:20 pm **Frameworks and Considerations for Defining Mis- and Disinformation**
Moderator: *Vish Viswanath,* Study Chair

Claire Wardle, *Brown University*
Alice Marwick, *University of North Carolina-Chapel Hill*
Dietram Scheufele, *University of Wisconsin-Madison and Study Co-Chair, Addressing Inaccurate and Misleading Information About Biological Threats*

4:45 pm **Adjourn**

Committee on Understanding and Addressing Misinformation About Science

DBASSE
BOSE

Public Information Gathering Session #2
February 22, 2023

ALL TIMES ARE EASTERN TIME

2:00 pm **Arrival of Speakers**

2:15 pm **Welcome and Overview of the Session**
Vish Viswanath, Study Chair

2:20 pm **Interventions for Addressing Mis and Disinformation: An Overview**
Moderator: *Lisa Fazio,* Committee Member
Sacha Altay, *University of Oxford*
Kelly Born, *Packard Foundation*

3:05 pm **Q&A and Discussion**

3:45 pm **Adjourn**

Understanding and Addressing Misinformation About Science:
A Public Workshop

National Academy of Sciences Building
Fred Kavli Auditorium
2101 Constitution Ave, NW
Washington, DC and virtual

April 19, 2023

ALL TIMES ARE EASTERN TIME

Workshop Goals:

- To understand the nature and complexity of misinformation about science
- To understand the differential impacts of misinformation and identify existing gaps in our knowledge
- To examine select interventions for addressing misinformation and explore ways to bolster effectiveness

10:00 am **Welcome and Introduction**
Heidi Schweingruber, Director, BOSE
Vish Viswanath, Committee Chair
Tiffany E. Taylor, Study Director

10:15 am **Science Misinformation Across Select Domains**
Moderator: *David Scales,* Committee Member

Melissa Aronczyk, Rutgers University
Heidi Larson, London School for Hygiene and Tropical Medicine *(virtual)*
Mark Lynas, Alliance for Science
Briony Swire-Thompson, Northeastern University

10:55 am **Moderated Discussion**

11:10 am **Q&A with Audience**

11:30 am **Break**

11:45 am **Differential Impacts of Science Misinformation**
Moderator: *Nadine Barrett,* Committee Member
Cabral Bigman-Galimore, University of Illinois at Urbana-Champaign *(virtual)*
Roberta Braga, Equis Labs
Leezel Tanglao & Mark Calaguas, Filipino Young Leaders Program
Jason Young, University of Washington *(virtual)*

12:30 pm **Moderated Discussion**

12:40 pm **Q&A with Audience**

1:00 pm **Lunch Available in the Great Hall**

2:00 pm **Individual-Level Interventions to Address Misinformation**
Moderator: *Asheley Landrum,* Committee Member
Joel Breakstone, Stanford University
Ethan Porter, George Washington University
Emily Vraga, University of Minnesota

2:30 pm **Moderated Discussion**

2:45 pm **Q&A with Audience**

3:00 pm **Break**

3:15 pm **Institutional/Organizational/Community-Level Interventions to Address Misinformation**
Moderator: *Brian Southwell,* Committee Member
Victor Pickard, University of Pennsylvania *(virtual)*
Kavitha Rajagopalan, Asian Media Initiative, CUNY *(virtual)*
Abhishek Roy, Google

3:45 pm **Moderated Discussion**

4:00 pm **Q&A with Audience**

4:15 pm **Discussion across Interventions**
Moderator: *Vish Viswanath,* Committee Chair

4:55 pm **Closing Remarks**
Vish Viswanath, Committee Chair

5:00 pm **Reception in the Great Hall**

6:00 pm **Adjourn Workshop**

Committee on Understanding and Addressing Misinformation About Science

DBASSE
BOSE

Public Information Gathering Session #4
July 11, 2023

ALL TIMES ARE EASTERN TIME

1:50 pm **Arrival of Speakers**

2:00 pm **Welcome and Overview of the Session**
Vish Viswanath, Study Chair

2:05 pm **Understanding Science Misinformation in the Context of the History and Nature of Science**
Moderator: *Jevin West*, Committee Member
Michael Strevens, *New York University*

2:30 pm **Q&A and Discussion**

2:45 pm **Break**

2:50 pm **Advancements in Information Technology and Implications for Addressing Misinformation**
Moderator: *Afua Bruce*, Committee Member
Sarah Kreps, *Cornell University*
Jenn Wortman Vaughan, *Microsoft Research*

3:40 pm **Q&A and Discussion**

4:00 pm **Adjourn**

Appendix B

Committee and Staff Biographies

KASISOMAYAJULA "VISH" VISWANATH (*Chair*) is Lee Kum Kee Professor of Health Communication at the Harvard T. H. Chan School of Public Health and Professor of Population Sciences at the Dana-Farber Cancer Institute (DFCI). He is also the faculty director of the Health Communication Core of the Dana-Farber/Harvard Cancer Center. Other additional administrative and scientific leadership positions held by Viswanath include director of the Center for Translational Communication Science, DFCI; director, Harvard Chan India Research Center; and Director, Lee Kum Sheung Center for Health and Happiness, Harvard Chan. The central goal of the program of research in his lab is to influence public health policy and practice through knowledge translation and communication. His work draws from literatures in communication science, social epidemiology, dissemination and implementation, and social and health behavior sciences. Viswanath's work is driven by two fundamental concerns: (a) how to center equity in drawing on translational communication science to promote health and well-being for ALL population groups and (b) to involve community-based organizations and all stakeholders through participatory research in promoting social change. His work so far has documented the relationship between communication inequalities, poverty and health disparities, and knowledge translation to address health disparities. He has written more than 325 journal articles and book chapters and is a co-editor or co-author of five books. He has served and continues to serve on several national committees including for the U.S. Department of Health and Human Services, the Centers for Disease Control and Prevention, and the National Academies of Sciences, Engineering, and Medicine.

NICK ALLUM is professor of research methodology at the University of Essex. His research encompasses survey methodology, research integrity, public understanding of science, and social and political trust. Allum teaches statistical methods and research methodology at Essex. He served as general secretary of the European Survey Research Association from 2012 to 2016. Allum served on the National Academies of Sciences, Engineering, and Medicine's Committee on Science Literacy and Public Perception of Science in 2016. Previously he was also a member of the National Science Foundation's expert panel on Science Literacy Indicators, which contributed to the National Science Board chapters on public attitudes and knowledge about science and technology. Allum received his B.A. in political economy from the University of East London, his M.Sc. in social research methods from the London School of Economics, and his Ph.D. in social psychology at the London School of Economics.

NADINE J. BARRETT is the senior associate dean of equity in research and community engagement at the Wake Forest School of Medicine. She previously served as an assistant professor in the Department of Family Medicine and Community Health at Duke University, and as co-director of the Duke Clinical and Translational Science Institute (CTSI), inaugural and founding director of the Duke CTSI Center for Equity in Research, and associate director of Equity and Stakeholder Strategy for the Duke Cancer Institute (DCI). Barrett is a health disparities researcher, expert equity strategist, and a nationally-recognized leader in facilitating community and academic partnerships to advance health equity. She develops multi-level interventions to address structural and systemic racism and implicit biases that limit access to quality health information, health care, and research among historically marginalized populations. Barrett created Just ASK, a national program designed to enhance diverse participation and representation in clinical research and trials. She successfully develops and implements community-based interventions to increase research participation of underrepresented race and ethnic groups in biomedical, clinical, and translational research. Barrett contributes to national guidelines and reports including the 2022 ASCO and ACCC joint guidelines and recommendations to increase diverse representation in clinical trials, and the *2020 AACR Health Disparities Report*. She is the 2017 recipient of the ACCC National Innovator Award as the inaugural director of the DCI's Office of Health Equity. Barrett completed a master's of arts in sociology and social inequities at the University of Central Florida, a joint master of science in community health sciences, a Ph.D. in medical sociology and race and ethnic relations from Texas Woman's University, and a National Institutes of Health postdoctoral fellowship at the University of North Carolina at Chapel Hill.

DAVID A. BRONIATOWSKI is professor of engineering management and systems engineering in the George Washington (GW) University's School of Engineering and Applied Science, where he directs the Decision-Making and Systems Architecture Laboratory. He conducts research in decision making under risk, the design and analysis of complex systems, and the relationships between online and offline behavior. This research program draws upon a wide range of techniques including formal mathematical modeling, experimental design, automated text analysis and natural language processing, social and technical network analysis, and big data. He also served as associate director of the GW Institute for Data, Democracy, and Politics. His work on systematic distortions of public opinion about vaccines by state-sponsored social media users has been widely reported in the academic and popular press. Prior to joining GW, Broniatowski completed a postdoctoral fellowship in the Johns Hopkins Department of Emergency Medicine's Center for Advanced Modeling in the Behavioral and Health Sciences. He earned a Ph.D. in engineering systems, an S.M. in technology and policy, and an S.M. and S.B. in aerospace engineering, all from the Massachusetts Institute of Technology.

AFUA A. N. BRUCE is a leading public interest technologist who has spent her career working at the intersection of technology, policy, and society. She has worked in and across the government, non-profit, private, and academic sectors as well as held senior science and technology positions at DataKind, New America, the White House, the FBI, and IBM. With Bruce's background in software engineering, data science, and artificial intelligence, combined with experience developing and deploying technology in and with communities, she incorporates an equity-based framework into her engagements. Bruce is currently an adjunct professor of the Heinz College of Information Sciences at Carnegie Mellon University, a Visiting Practitioner for Cornell Tech's Public Interest Tech program, an affiliate of the Berkman Klein Center for Internet & Society at Harvard University, and an affiliate of The Tayarisha African Centre of Excellence in Digital Governance at the University of Witwatersrand-Johannesburg. Her newest book, *The Tech That Comes Next: How Changemakers, Technologists, and Philanthropists Can Build an Equitable World*, describes how technology can advance equity. Bruce has a bachelor's degree in computer engineering from Purdue University and a master's degree in business administration from the University of Michigan.

LISA K. FAZIO is associate professor of psychology at Vanderbilt University. Her research focuses on how children and adults learn true and false information from the world around them, and on how to correct errors in people's knowledge. Her work spans multiple disciplines including cognitive, developmental, educational, and social psychology and informs basic theories about psychological processes, while also having clear applications for practitioners, such as journalists and teachers. She received the Early Career Impact Award from the Federation of Associations in Behavioral & Brain Sciences and the Frank Research Prize in Public Interest Communications. Her research is currently supported by major grants from both the National Science Foundation and the Mercury Project. Fazio is a fellow of the Association for Psychological Science and the Psychonomic Society. She earned her doctorate from Duke University and graduated summa cum laude from Washington University in St. Louis.

LAUREN FELDMAN is a professor in the School of Communication & Information at Rutgers University. She was previously on the faculty at American University. Her current research emphasizes three intersecting areas of interest: climate change communication, partisan media and misinformation, and comedy and social change. Feldman's research has been widely published in peer-reviewed journals and edited volumes, and she is co-author of the book, *A Comedian and an Activist Walk into a Bar: The Serious Role of Comedy in Social Justice* (University of California Press, 2020). Her work has been recognized with various academic awards, including article of the year awards from Mass Communication & Society and from the political communication division of the International Communication Association. Feldman serves on the editorial boards of the *Journal of Communication*, *Communication Research*, and *Environmental Communication*, and she is an affiliate of the Rutgers Climate Institute and the George Mason University Center for Climate Change Communication. Feldman earned a B.A. in English from Duke University and an M.A. and Ph.D. from the Annenberg School for Communication at the University of Pennsylvania.

DEEN FREELON is presidential professor, Annenberg School for Communication at the Annenberg School for Communication at the University of Pennsylvania. His theoretical interests address how ordinary citizens use social media and other digital communication technologies for political purposes, paying particular attention to the diffusion and mitigation of misinformation and disinformation. Methodologically, he is interested in how computational research techniques can be used to answer some of the most fundamental questions of communication science. His scholarship has been financially supported by grantmakers including the U.S. Institute of Peace, the Spencer Foundation, the Knight Foundation, and the Hewlett Foundation, and he has published in top-tier journals including *Nature*, *Science*, and the *Proceedings of the National Academy of Sciences*. Freelon earned his Ph.D. from the University of Washington in 2012 and formerly taught at American University in Washington, DC.

ASHELEY R. LANDRUM is an associate professor in the Walter Cronkite School for journalism and mass communication at Arizona State University. Prior to this, she served as an associate professor in the College of Media & Communication at Texas Tech University, and was a Howard Deshong Postdoctoral Fellow in the Science of Science Communication at the Annenberg Public Policy Center of the University of Pennsylvania and a life sciences fellow at the Wissenschaftskolleg zu Berlin. Landrum's research investigates how values and worldviews influence people's selection and processing of science (mis)information. Her work on the Flat Earth YouTube phenomenon, specifically, won her Texas Tech's Chancellor's Council Distinguished Research Award and the Billy I. and Avis M. Ross Achievement Award. Landrum's research (in collaboration with KQED Science) has been funded by the National Science Foundation, the Templeton Religion Trust, and the Templeton World Charity Foundation. She holds a Ph.D. in psychological sciences, an M.S. in cognitive science from the University of Texas at Dallas, and a B.A. in philosophy from the University of Texas at Austin.

DAVID M. J. LAZER is university distinguished professor of political science and computer sciences, Northeastern University, and visiting fellow at the Institute for Quantitative Social Science at Harvard University. He has published prominent work on misinformation, democratic deliberation, collective intelligence, computational social science, and algorithmic auditing, across a wide range of prominent journals. His research has received extensive coverage in the media, including *The New York Times,* NPR, *The Washington Post*, *The Wall Street Journal*, and CBS Evening News. He is a co-leader of the COVID States Project, one of the leading efforts to understand the social and political dimensions of the pandemic in the United States. He is a fellow in the National Academy of Public Administration and is a member of the Standing Committee on Advancing Science Communication Research and Practice for the National Academies of Sciences, Engineering, and Medicine. He has a Ph.D. from the University of Michigan in political science.

EZRA M. MARKOWITZ is professor of environmental decision-making in the Department of Environmental Conservation at the University of Massachusetts; he is also a fellow with the FrameWorks Institute. Formerly, he was a postdoctoral research associate at Princeton University and an Earth Institute postdoctoral fellow at Columbia University. His research, teaching, and outreach focus on the intersection of decision making, persuasive communication, public engagement with science, and environmental sustainability. He is particularly interested in the practical application of behavioral science to improve individuals' and communities' environmental decision making; he also has deep expertise in the field of climate change communication and public engagement. He is the author of over five dozen peer-reviewed research papers, book chapters, and reports, including the 2015 Connecting on Climate guide to climate change communication. He is a fellow of the American Psychological Association and an author on the 5th National Climate Assessment for the USGCRP; he was awarded the Early Career Achievement award by the Society for Environmental, Population and Conservation Psychology. He received his Ph.D. in environmental sciences, studies and policy and his M.S. in psychology from the University of Oregon; he completed his B.A. in psychology at Vassar College.

PAMELA C. RONALD is a distinguished professor in the Department of Plant Pathology and the Genome Center at the University of California (UC), Davis. Her research focuses on the use of genetic techniques to understand the plant response to infection and tolerance to environmental stress. With her collaborators, she received the U.S. Department of Agriculture's National Research Initiative Discovery Award and the Tech Award for the innovative use of technology to benefit humanity. The Scientific American named her one of the 100 most influential people in biotechnology. Ronald's book, *Tomorrow's Table: Organic Farming, Genetics and the Future of Food* was selected as one of a 25 most influential books with the power to inspire college readers to change the world. Her TED talk has been viewed by more than 2 million people and translated into 26 languages. She also received the American Society of Plant Biologists Leadership Award and an honorary doctorate from the Swedish Agricultural University. She was named a World Agricultural Prize Laureate by the Global Confederation of Higher Education Associations for Agricultural and Life Sciences. In 2022 she was awarded the Wolf Prize in Agriculture. Ronald is an elected member of the U.S. National Academy of Sciences and the American Academy of Arts and Sciences. She completed her Ph.D. at UC Berkeley, earned a B.S. from the Reed College, an M.S. from Stanford University, and an M.S. from the University of Uppsala, Sweden.

DAVID SCALES is an internal medicine hospitalist and assistant professor of medicine at Weill Cornell Medicine and Chief Medical Officer at Critica, a non-governmental organization focused on building scientific literacy. His research focuses on medical communication in clinical and online settings, including understanding how structural factors affect our information environments to allow misinformation to propagate and misconceptions to persist. Scales' work leverages qualitative and quantitative methods to address the problem of health-related misinformation, training "infodemiologists" to build COVID-19 vaccine confidence in online communities with community-oriented motivational interviewing. Scales received his M.D. and Ph.D. from Yale University, where his sociology dissertation examined how the World Health Organization seeks to control the spread of diseases across international borders. He completed a primary care internal medicine residency at Cambridge Health Alliance in Cambridge, Massachusetts. Scales holds a certificate of medical interpretation in Levantine Colloquial Arabic from the University of Massachusetts Amherst and has worked with refugees in the United States and throughout the Levant.

BRIAN G. SOUTHWELL is lead scientist for public understanding of science at RTI International. He also is adjunct professor of internal medicine at Duke University and adjunct associate professor in health behavior at the University of North Carolina at Chapel Hill. In addition, Southwell hosts a public radio show called The Measure of Everyday Life. He co-founded the Duke Program on Medical Misinformation to improve patient-provider conversations; has published a relevant book, *Misinformation and Mass Audiences*; and has been featured in outlets such as JAMA. He has consulted with the National Academies of Science, Engineering, and Medicine and the National Institutes of Health on misinformation mitigation and served on the Advisory Committee for the Council of Medical Specialty Societies-National Academy of Medicine-World Health Organization Collaboration on Identifying Credible Sources of Health Information in Social Media. Southwell has organized summits on trust in science and misinformation with support from the Rita Allen Foundation and the Aspen Institute. He also has won awards for scholarship from the International Communication Association and the National Communication Association and teaching recognition at the University of Minnesota. Southwell holds a Ph.D. and M.A. from the University of Pennsylvania and a B.A. from the University of Virginia.

JEVIN WEST is a professor in the Information School at the University of Washington (UW). He is the co-founder of the new Center for an Informed Public at UW aimed at resisting strategic misinformation, promoting an informed society and strengthening democratic discourse. He is also the co-founder of the DataLab at UW, a data science fellow at the eScience Institute, and affiliate faculty for the Center for Statistics & Social Sciences. His research and teaching focus on the impact of data and technology on science and society, with a focus on slowing the spread of misinformation. He is the co-author of the new book, *Calling Bullshit: The Art of Skepticism in a Data-Driven World*, which helps non-experts question numbers, data, and statistics without an advanced degree in data science. He earned his B.S. and M.S. at Utah State University, holds a Ph.D. from the University of Washington Department of Biology, and completed a postdoc in physics at Umea University in Sweden.

STAFF

TIFFANY E. TAYLOR (*study director*) is a senior program officer for the Board on Science Education at the National Academies of Sciences, Engineering, and Medicine. She is currently the study director for the consensus study on Understanding and Addressing Misinformation about Science, and also provides leadership, management, and support for several ongoing projects including the Standing Committee on Advancing Science Communication, the Expert Meeting Series to Support Effective Federal Health Communications, the Expert Meeting on Implications for Science Education of Increasing AI and Robotics Capabilities, and the Convocation on Informal Science and Engineering Education. She came to the National Academies as a Christine Mirzayan Science and Technology Policy Fellow, where she also worked with the Board on Science Education. She holds a B.S. in biology from Howard University and a Ph.D. in biomedical sciences from the University of California, San Diego.

LETICIA GARCILAZO GREEN is an associate program officer for the Board on Science Education at the National Academies of Sciences, Engineering, and Medicine. As a member of the board staff, she has supported studies focusing on criminal justice, science education, science communication, and climate change. She has a B.S. in psychology and a B.A. in sociology with a concentration in criminology from Louisiana State University and an M.A. in forensic psychology from The George Washington University.

HOLLY G. RHODES is a senior program officer at the National Academies of Sciences, Engineering, and Medicine in the Division of Behavioral and Social Sciences and Education. She is study director of the Standing Committee on Advancing Science Communication, study director for Effective Health Communication in the Current Information Environment and the Role of the Federal Government: A Workshop, and a co-lead of the Climate Communications Initiative. Rhodes directed the Roundtable on the Communication and Use of Social and Behavioral Sciences and contributed to Communicating Science Effectively: A Research Agenda. Previously, she was a deputy project director at RTI International. She holds master's and doctorate degrees in education from the University of North Carolina at Chapel Hill.

LAUREN RYAN is a senior program assistant for the Board on Science Education at the National Academies of Sciences, Engineering, and Medicine. In her work at the National Academies, she has supported projects related to K–12 science standards, data science education, undergraduate STEM education, and science communication. Ryan received her B.S. in biomedical engineering from the University of Maine and is currently pursuing an M.S. in educational psychology from George Mason University.

HEIDI SCHWEINGRUBER is the director of the Board on Science Education at the National Academies of Sciences, Engineering, and Medicine. She oversees a portfolio of work that includes K–12 science education, informal science education, and higher education. Schweingruber joined the staff of the board as a senior program officer. In this role, she directed or co-directed several projects including the study that resulted in the report *A Framework for K-12 Science Education*, the blueprint for the Next Generation Science Standards. Schweingruber is a nationally recognized leader in leveraging research findings to catalyze improvements in science and STEM education policy and practice. She holds a Ph.D. in psychology (developmental) and anthropology from the University of Michigan.

NATIONAL ACADEMY OF MEDICINE FELLOW

PAULE JOSEPH is Lasker Clinical Research Scholar Tenure Track Clinical Investigator and chief of the Section of Sensory Science and Metabolism in the Division of Intramural Clinical and Biological Research at the National Institute of Alcohol Abuse and Alcoholism with a joint appointment at the National Institute of Nursing Research (NINR). She is the inaugural American Academy of Nursing fellow. Joseph leads a multidimensional translational research program combining research and clinical practice focused on chemosensation (taste and smell), obesity, and substance abuse. Joseph is a leader of national and global non-profit organizations dedicated to decreasing health disparities and increasing minority health promotion and access. When individuals reported taste and smell loss during the COVID-19 pandemic, Joseph and her team began investigating the effects of the SARS-CoV-2 virus on the chemical senses. Joseph received an associate degree in applied sciences in nursing at Hostos Community College, a B.S.N. from the College of New Rochelle, an M.B.A. from Quantic School of Business & Technology, and an M.S. with a specialty as a Family Nurse Practitioner from Pace University. She completed a Ph.D. in nursing with a focus in genomics at the University of Pennsylvania and conducted her Ph.D. work at the Monell Chemical Senses Center. She then completed a Clinical and Translational Postdoctoral Fellowship focused on genomics, nutrition, and gastrointestinal diseases at the NINR, which was supported by the Office of Workforce Diversity. Joseph is a certified nurse practitioner with clinical privileges at the National Institutes of Health (NIH) Clinical Center and outside NIH.